A POLITICAL ECONOMY OF JUSTICE

A Political Economy of Justice

+ + + + + + + + + + + + + + + + + + + +

EDITED BY
DANIELLE ALLEN,
YOCHAI BENKLER,
LEAH DOWNEY,
REBECCA HENDERSON,
JOSH SIMONS

THE UNIVERSITY OF CHICAGO PRESS
CHICAGO AND LONDON

The University of Chicago Press, Chicago 60637
The University of Chicago Press, Ltd., London
© 2022 by The University of Chicago
Published 2022
Printed in the United States of America

31 30 29 28 27 26 25 24 23 22   1 2 3 4 5

ISBN-13: 978-0-226-81842-9 (cloth)
ISBN-13: 978-0-226-81844-3 (paper)
ISBN-13: 978-0-226-81843-6 (e-book)
DOI: https://doi.org/10.7208/chicago/9780226818436.001.0001

Library of Congress Cataloging-in-Publication Data
Names: Allen, Danielle S., 1971– editor.
Title: A political economy of justice / edited by Danielle Allen
     [and four others]
Description: First edition. | Chicago : University of Chicago
     Press, 2022. | Includes bibliographical references and index.
Identifiers: LCCN 2021047902 | ISBN 9780226818429 (cloth) |
     ISBN 9780226818443 (paperback) | ISBN 9780226818436
     (ebook)
Subjects: LCSH: Social justice—Economic aspects—United
     States. | Capitalism—United States.
Classification: LCC HN90.S6 P65 2022 | DDC 305.50973—dc23
LC record available at https://lccn.loc.gov/2021047902

♾ This paper meets the requirements of ANSI/NISO
Z39.48-1992 (Permanence of Paper).

Contents

Introduction

D. ALLEN, Y. BENKLER, L. DOWNEY, R. HENDERSON, J. SIMONS

The Grand Challenge

Democratic market societies are in crisis. Broad-based economic insecurity, rising inequality, and a resurgent nationalism expressed as anti-immigrant sentiment and ever-more frank racism are underwriting a new illiberal populism in the United States and throughout the European Union. Mainstream media, scientific expertise, and judicial competence are challenged across these diverse countries. The 2020 pandemic has only brought these challenges into starker relief.

The elite consensus that emerged after the fall of the Soviet Union—a view that embraced the free movement of goods, finance, and people; deregulation and privatization of government companies and some public functions; and a robust commitment to pluralism and liberal rights—is coming under sustained attack. In the middle of the second decade of the twenty-first century, parties representing this consensus lost major elections. Donald Trump's election was a rejection of both the Republican and Democratic elites. Brexit was opposed by both the Conservative and Labour parties. The second round of the 2017 French elections pitted against one another two candidates who rejected the historical major parties of the left and the right, with Emmanuel Macron's victory representing a victory for the mainstream but only under a new brand. By 2020, the Covid-19 pandemic laid bare deep divisions as a prolonged lockdown created economic and political pressures. Political identity came to dominate even basic beliefs about science, and the legitimacy of the US election came under attack in a way not seen since the defeat of Reconstruction. The 2020s seem poised for a conflict between parties dedicated to nationalist atavistic populism and those dedicated to a pluralist democratic project, but how that pluralistic side of the conflict will integrate economic policy and politics into its basic democratic commitment remains highly uncertain.

In the face of these deep challenges, academics have been reviving the concept of "political economy" across diverse disciplines in an effort to develop a new understanding of how the economy interacts with the polity, and how decisions about political economy intersect with understandings of justice, legitimacy, human flourishing, ethics, and moral commitments. Can we find a way forward to a just economy that neither doubles down on the elite-consensus neoliberal political economy of the past four decades, nor reflects nostalgia for a golden age of capitalism, a "glorious thirty," a progressivism that could survive only by ignoring racial and gender hierarchies?

Capitalism is not a "single-level system" consisting merely of property rights and markets but a "multilevel" system of economic governance involving economic markets that (1) are embedded in institutions created and governed by political authority, (2) reflect economic, political, and cultural power, (3) rest on social norms, and (4) instantiate specific values. Neoliberalism ignored these levels and insisted on a "one right path" packet, for many years called "the Washington Consensus," built on the assumption that a single, universal rationality applied to all people as people; that all economic activity was best understood as rational pursuit of self-interest by self-interested rational actors; and that government functioned best when it receded, to the extent possible, from the economic sphere, limiting its role to defining and protecting clear property rights, providing impartial rule of law to enforce contracts around those rights, and reducing the ambition of the pursuit of collective goals through public action. The result was a transfer of power to companies, and these too were reconceived as best run by self-interested managers and owners whose behavior would best be governed by well-designed incentive pay systems rather than by any normative commitments. The result was an unusual degree of power in the hands of public firms, hierarchical organizations whose decision rights reflect a commitment to wealth maximization and to survival in capital and product markets dominated by conventional performance metrics. The result was not stable, broadly shared growth and prosperity but repeated cycles of financial crises, dramatic increases in inequality, and the rise of illiberal, nationalist populism. And these results demand answers to the question of whether principles of legitimacy and justice—of rights, liberties, and a just distribution of resources—can best be served through these kinds of institutions or whether progress requires a fundamental rethinking of the basic rules that govern economic production and exchange, the nature of firms, and the institutions by which they are constrained.

Merely recognizing these facts does not answer the questions of how to define justice and legitimacy in relation to economic and political questions in a world with high degrees of social heterogeneity in individual polities. There is a need to return to first principles—to explore the question of how political economy functions and what it is for in the first place. Only with direct attention to basic questions of the social values orienting the development of political economy can we revisit the building blocks of economic thought. Tackling questions of political economy from the root requires a sustained, hard-hitting, multidisciplinary conversation that bridges the normative and the positive. Such conversation is necessary, now more than ever, as the coronavirus crisis has thrown societies and economies into a state of uncertainty and anxiety—including about what the overarching purposes of governance should be.

This multidisciplinary volume offers a new framework for thinking about political economy and human well-being. We look squarely at how normative and positive questions about political economy interact with each other. From that beginning, we aspire to chart a way forward toward a just economy.

The chapters take up issues of human flourishing, ethics, and moral commitments; of democracy, system governance, and legitimacy; of corporate governance and legitimacy; of alienation and consumerism; of labor and quality of life; of social, political, and economic equality and opportunity; of the role of power and the social relations of production in shaping markets and their outcomes; of inclusion and sustainability; of globalization, cosmopolitanism, and tribalism.

Our collective work has come to consolidate around some shared themes, as well as ongoing points of debate. The shared themes include (1) a need to rethink the relationship between politics and the economy, with attention to democratic accountability and governance regimes; (2) a need to broaden the focus of justice from purely questions of distribution to encompassing the organization of production; (3) recognition of the value of markets coupled with diverse perspectives on how capitalism can be reformed or transformed; (4) emphasis on integrating and explicitly addressing the role of race, gender, and other dimensions of status-subordination in the political economy of market societies; and (5) a need to focus on broader definitions of human purpose and to build metrics for the economy around those broader definitions—for instance, around the capacity of an economy to produce "good jobs." The central points of debate concern capital and growth. What is the place of each in a just economy in the twenty-first century generally, and after the coronavirus crisis specifically?

Our Vision

The coronavirus crisis has thrown societies and economies around the world into a state of unplanned and unexpected transition. No society entered into the crisis with an eye to establishing a just economy; nevertheless, an economic transition of some sort has already begun. In the US, the failure of society to protect all portions of the population consistently and equally cast into painful relief the fundamentally broken nature of the existing social order and has already yielded new efforts to define the content of a social compact that would deliver the foundations of health and economic security for all.

The contributors to this volume come from diverse backgrounds and disciplines, and we did not seek to converge, nor do we think it possible to converge, on a single, ideal end state before taking action. Yet we all shared a core set of commitments: avoiding domination, ensuring broad-based economic security and social and ecological sustainability, and preserving dynamism in the face of uncertainty and continuous change. Because of our shared commitment to recognizing uncertainty and fallibility of institutions as a basic condition, our method has been fundamentally pragmatist in its orientation, translated into the shared assumption that *a transition toward a more just economy involves a dynamic process that is guided by principles and that expects and requires iterations.* The transition would begin without preconceptions about the details of the solutions, but with a belief that solutions are embedded in knowledge that emerges from learning in society, and is best discoverable through a process of iteration—learning, doing, adapting, and learning once more. Taking as given the conditions of extreme uncertainty in which we live, it would be dangerous, contentious, and counterproductive to try and identify an end state. What we need to begin transitioning to a just economy is a commitment to collaborative investigation, subject to a set of guiding principles.

What guiding principles might put us on our way toward a more just economy? Consistent with a pluralist and pragmatist commitment, we do not propose a comprehensive list or single overarching principle. One that we are confident should not be left off the list is non-domination, where domination is defined as having arbitrary reserve control over others.[1] A just economy is one that is not constructed on foundations of, nor permits, domination. Promoting non-domination will involve developing social relations of production that are attentive to power in markets and redress power by providing the resources for building counterpower for those presently operating under domination. It will involve developing economic models that, if adopted at a sufficient scale, offer distinctive opportunities to satisfy basic needs and desires and engage in the economy, without being subject to systematically imbalanced economic power, and that support sources of political power necessary for more egalitarian politics.

What should we seek? Economic policy, and often social policy associated with it, has in the past been focused on maximizing economic performance, usually measured as gross domestic product (GDP) per capita, on the assumption that once "the pie" is as large as it can be, social policy can be pursued around distribution. Our shared understanding that political economy involves values and conflicts in production, not only in distribution, and that a stark distinction between the political and economic cannot be sustained, requires a different set of goals and a different set of measurements. If we seek an economy and society committed to non-domination, broad-based economic security, and social and economic sustainability while preserving and encouraging social, cultural, and economic dynamism, we cannot continue to rely on economic growth as a single aggregate goal or metric. In part, the goal is to move past poorly calibrated, aggregate measures and proxies for well-being like GDP. Instead, we would like to push toward metrics that will both help people steer toward the goal of a just economy and help others to gauge whether they are steering effectively.

But the primary goal is to explore institutions and processes that would lead to a political economy that avoids domination, ensures broad-based economic security and sustainability, and preserves dynamism. Such a goal cannot be pursued through a predetermined path, say, a proper "mix" of the economy in terms of public and private ownership. Instead, we imagine this to be a *dynamic process that expects and requires iterations.* Our shared view is that advanced economies are in pressing need of institutional experimentation to include exploring new forms of corporate governance, public-private partnerships, and redesigned structures and goals for the administrative state. These models and their performance must be continuously developed through experimentation and iteration, judged by the extent to which they deliver on the core social, economic, and political needs, and then further advanced and refined over time.

Our Analytic Framework and Working Method

The articulation of the grand challenge and vision laid out above emerged from working conversations among a multidisciplinary group of economists, philosophers, political scientists, political theorists, business experts, sociologists, and legal scholars. Atypically for such processes, we achieved significant convergence. Here it is worth saying something about our working method.

The contributors to this volume all began work together with a shared conviction that political economy is a mode of intellectual analysis that distinctively aspires to unite normative commitments to empirical and positive assessments of human behavior, at both the micro and macro level, with a view to supporting the efforts of policymakers to steer a society in desirable directions. The twentieth century has offered several different frames for political economy—among them, Keynesianism and neoliberalism.

As Wendy Carlin and Sam Bowles put it,[2] any given policy paradigm for political economy rests on normative foundations, attaches to those foundations an economic model, proffers some emblematic policies, and provides a vernacular vocabulary to capture them.

Our working method was similarly designed to forge linkages among normative foundations, economic models, prescriptions, and vernaculars. The goal of our conversation was to lay out what we saw as the grand challenges of political economy and justice in the twenty-first century. As we pursued that overarching question, we sought to disentangle where we were invoking values, where we were proffering empirical diagnoses, where we were beginning to identify prescriptions, and where we were pointing to institutional transformations, political pathways, or vernacular framings that would be necessary to move in the direction of the prescriptions that flowed from the conjunction of our values commitments and empirical diagnoses. As shown in Figure I.1, we used a basic visualization to track our early conversations.

Intentional use of this circle to track discussions helps make explicit all the interconnected questions in any given policy domain and provides a tool for helping a group develop answers across the different themes of *values,*

Figure I-1. The Safra Seminar Process Circle, a framework for values-based iterative policy-making.

diagnosis, prescriptions, and *action strategies* that align with one another. The next section of the introduction summarizes the fruits of our conversation across all four of these dimensions.

VALUES

Seven core values are especially prominent in this volume: non-domination, political equality, freedom, universal economic security, egalitarian plural-ism, community, and sustainability. One of these values is negative: it picks out a feature of the social and political world we wish to avoid. The other six have both negative and positive elements: they also seek to identify pre-scriptive goals to guide the arguments we advance, or the institutional ar-rangements we propose, as we continue this project of redefining political economy.

Non-Domination

Running through the volume are several important distinctions. First, what are the possible sources of domination? We need to think of *structures—* including those not intentionally constructed or maintained by any indi-vidual or set of actors—as possible sources of domination. These might be exclusionary patterns or access to or ownership of social infrastructure; hi-erarchical organizations within the marketplace, such as firms; relations of power in markets; or forms of private property relations (to name only a few). Second, what is the relation between different forms of domination? For in-stance, how should we think about the relationship between monopolistic practices in markets and forms of political domination? Several contributors take the view that one inexorably produces the other and that a key prin-ciple for pursuing a just economy is an anti-monopoly principle. Nonethe-less, simple anti-monopoly cannot be an absolute value once one recognizes that markets are pervaded by power even in the absence of monopoly. Regu-lated monopolies or public utilities, for example, may be less susceptible to domination or exploitation than "competitive" unregulated markets; indeed, because they are monopolies they can enjoy economies of scale while pub-lic political power counteracts their market power. Also, there is a sense in which the ownership of property is intrinsically monopolistic, leading, for instance, to the inefficient allocation and use of property.

Third, how high is the bar we are setting up when we seek to build our political economy on non-domination? Difference is an irreducible and even desirable feature of any society. The hard question is when and how difference *becomes* domination. In particular—a question for all of us to reflect on, related to the prescriptive aspect of our work—how do we design institutions that detect when difference becomes domination? And what kinds of institutions can correct for domination?[3]

Fourth, how should we understand the relationship between politics and economics and how does that bear on the value of non-domination (and other values)? The volume generally challenges the neoliberal commitment to the principle of "the government that governs least, governs best," but recognizes that public shaping of the economy is itself fraught with risks of capture and leveraging of opportunities for domination. What sort of approach, then, must we take to secure the primacy of the political over the economic while yielding a just economy?

Finally, there was broad agreement that to understand domination, we should look to structures and patterns of resistance. There are a wide range of movements and groups that are themselves articulating objections to domination. They are theorizing in 'real time' what domination means and how it can best be overcome. We might learn much about a political economy of non-domination by understanding the arguments and demands of these movements. Several chapters in this volume tap into these insights.

Political Equality

Political equality and domination are closely related. Political equality is a means for ensuring non-domination, and non-domination is also a necessary condition for a regime of political equality. Two ideas of political equality emerged in our discussion. The first was the familiar and straightforward sense of equal participation in the political processes (e.g., voting rights, party political funding). The second was somewhat subtler: equal *standing* in the political process or sphere. This means more than simply the effective capacity to vote. It means the ability to equally understand and leverage the political process, to have the possibility of shaping the process itself through collective action. With these two different pictures of political equality in view—one relating to formal civil and political rights, the other to a capabilities conception (cf. the work of Amartya Sen and Martha Nussbaum), we sought to address the question of what pursuit of political equality implies for political economy. Throughout the volume, contributors turn to democratic mechanisms of decision-making, including for economic decisions, as a way to ensure that a political economy reinforces rather than undermines political equality.

Freedom

Of course, freedom is closely connected both to non-domination and to political equality. Three concepts of freedom were relevant to our work: the straightforward political freedom to vote, a necessary condition for any electoral democracy; the freedom from the arbitrary power of the majority, most notably the protection of minorities, a necessary condition of a liberal democracy; and then positive freedom, which is the freedom to participate on equal terms, or "real" liberty as one participant put it. Perhaps unsurprisingly, most discussion focused on what positive freedom was and what the conditions for its effective exercise were.

While positive freedom is another way of describing political equality, the connection of the concept of freedom to markets and property brings an additional question to the fore. What are the conditions for the exercise of effective freedom and how does this bear on political economy? For instance, what is the relationship between the ownership of property and effective freedom? Do those who own property have an unavoidable power over the freedom of those who do not? Another way of putting this might be: Is domination intrinsic to private property? What does a property regime that avoids structures of domination look like? This was a question we did not resolve and was the component of our debate on which there was the most disagreement. Nonetheless, it feeds into the next value we consider to be central to a just economy.

Universal Economic Security

We do not adopt here any particular theory of justice or any particular distribution of wealth as our lodestar. But we recognize that fear of destitution—unemployment, hunger, loss of housing, illness, the loss of freedom and social standing associated with having a job and being able to sustain oneself and one's family—is among the most repressive conditions millions of people suffer at the end of the neoliberal era. Different contributors to this volume would adopt different positions on how generous this universal commitment should be, or what elements might go into a basket of the basic capabilities or needs to which there ought to be a public commitment. But regardless of the specification of the elements of economic security, discussions among the contributors evinced a shared recognition that broad-based economic insecurity is not only physically and emotionally damaging to millions but also presents a critical pathway for domination over those whose lives are precarious, reinforces tribalism that conflicts with the goal of egalitarian pluralism and community, and feeds the populism that threatens political equality. For all these reasons, public commitment to and pursuit of broad-based economic security, well beyond a minimal means-tested safety net, is a necessary ingredient of a just economy and an egalitarian polity.

Egalitarian Pluralism

The ideal of egalitarian pluralism aims to ensure that people have control over their own lives, relationships, and communities. It recognizes that people value community in different ways and that they have distinct hopes and ambitions for life.

Part of the value of egalitarian pluralism is that it makes us think harder about *how* to pursue a just political economy. That is, it draws our attention to those who are subject to patterns of domination or injustice, to listen to their conception of community and justice, rather than impose our own. It does not assume that every well-intention proposal for action in pursuit of justice is necessarily justified by its purpose.

This implies, for instance, that we have to reevaluate other values when weighing up proposals for action—such as diversity or efficiency. We have to think about the *relation* between our values as we seek to enact them in the world: How should we pursue an "infrastructure of inclusion"? How should we build institutions to detect and correct for relations of domination? Egalitarian pluralism reminds us that these are not simply straightforward second-order questions whose answers follow from identifying our first-order values.

Community

The concept of community appears throughout the volume and at a number of levels: from neighborhoods, to cities, to regions, nations, and even a global community. The assumption was that each of these communities has value.

The hard question, which we say more about below, was this: At what *level* of community should we seek to explore and build a just political economy? On the whole, the contributors to this volume agree that the nation remains a unit of political action that was unlikely to be supplanted by others, even if it is also perfectly consistent to think about political economy at other levels of community—from the city (housing) to the globe (climate change).

But *why* does the nation seem an irreplaceable unit of political action to so many, including within our group? Is it simply a fact-about-the-world we ought to reflect in our theorizing? Or is the nation a political value we hold? This is an important and unresolved question since it will guide many of the diagnostic and prescriptive aspects of the project going forward.

In particular, the hard question is: How should we think about the relationship between democracy and nationhood? In the era of modern states, does one depend on the other? This, of course, leads to further questions about borders. What are the boundaries of communities? Who gets to define them? How should *we* define them?

Sustainability

The climate challenge may well become the single most important challenge to human society and economy in the coming decades. No political economy developed in the early twenty-first century can be relevant if it does not commit to sustainability as a core value. While different contributors in the volume may take different perspectives regarding what sustainability requires—whether it requires or permits abandonment of growth, for instance, or requires some form of "green growth," with or without integration into a universal jobs commitment—all these views are critically important details about which many can and do disagree. But if the past decades have taught us anything it is that the material and social environment have a carrying capacity, and no policy or politics that does not integrate a recognition and intentional pursuit of sustainability within the carrying capacity of the natural world and the social environment will lead to collapse and defeat any efforts to pursue a just economy. Note, however, that we mention not only ecological but also social sustainability and democratic sustainability, because we do not see the present crisis of democratic society as separate and distinct from decades of neoliberal policies that may have increased the wealth of various nations as a whole, but rather as a crisis of the social and democratic environment analogous to the crisis we face in the natural environment.

The seven values that defined the normative foundations of this volume do not resolve into a neat, systematic moral and political philosophy. Instead, they capture core elements of an account of well-being. Well-being, anchored in positive freedom, will depend on political equality, non-domination, and anti-monopoly efforts while sustainably delivering broad-based economic security and an experience of community in societies that simultaneously embrace pluralism and egalitarianism. Each of the chapters in this volume either lays out one of these values (the normative chapters), explores emblematic policies or institutional forms that make those values concrete (the positive chapters), or makes a transit from normative to positive, linking normative foundations either to an economic model or to emblematic policies and vernacular formulations.

DIAGNOSES

If these are the values that should guide us, what are the diagnoses that we are responding to? What's gone wrong and why? In considering diagnoses, five different approaches appear in this work. Some contributors focus on macro regimes, some on dualities in domestic political economy, some on concentrations of power, some on the state, and some on uncertainty.

Macro Regimes

Following Mark Blyth, several chapters identify a shift in domestic regimes of political economy around the early to mid-1970s. The regime that emerged after the 1970s was aimed at price stability and involved impatient capital, a declining share of income to labor, and financialization. Whether our current political economy is best thought of as continuous with this regime, or whether we are, for instance, in some way in a new regime of "platform" political economy continues to be a matter of debate.

Dualities in Domestic Political Economy

A different line of attack for evaluating our current political economy focused on dualities or pairs roles that are, in some sense, in conflict with each other. These were *manager versus labor, manager versus investor,* and *investor versus owner.* All of these dualities were, in various ways, considered to be a challenge for constructing a just political economy.

These dualities prompted a number of discussion points. What kinds of dualities should we welcome as part of a just political economy? What kind of dualities should we guard against? By what criteria should we judge a particular dualism to be a threat to freedom, non-domination, or political equality? Is it simply about a *balance* of power, or are some dualisms of power inherently problematic?

The idea of dualisms within elites was also raised in several contexts. There was a sense that the way elites choose to divide themselves, and subsequently to highlight or attempt to make salient divisions within the broader populace, had significant consequences for political economy.

Concentrations of Power

Also captured by the dualisms laid out above is the issue of the relative power of different parties or sectors within the economy and how that balance has changed over time. Another way to analyze where we find ourselves in our current political economic moment is to focus on how labor's power has declined relative to capital and relative to managers over the last half century. The decline of power for labor has resulted in a concentration of power "in the hands of a few." This concentration of power is at the center of our analysis.

The State

The role of the state also features prominently in this volume. Cuts to public services, the retreat of the state from various dimensions of activity, and privatization in other areas characterize our current regime of political economy. On the other hand, there are also many features of the current regime that would not be possible without a *strong* state—the diminishment of the power of labor, for instance. As we contemplated what the role of the state *ought* to be, we agreed that there should be sufficient state capacity for effective governance, but different contributors place the appropriate boundaries of state power in different places.

Uncertainty

Uncertainty is a theme that runs throughout the volume. Our diagnosis of the present conditions of political economy focused on the complexity of the problems now facing human societies—climate change, pandemics, how to organize production and protect labor in a globalized economy. The complexity of the world's economy increases the uncertainty attached to any particular process of decision-making. Consequently, we came to realize that pursuing a just political economy under present conditions must necessarily be about fair processes for managing through uncertainty and making decisions in conditions of uncertainty. The kinds of institutions required to respond to uncertainty and to enact political equality or accountability in a *particular* economic sphere—both may imply a certain kind of institution characterized by pragmatism. By pragmatism, here we mean an "orient-do-learn-reorient-do" cycle. One orients toward values, then chooses an action path, learning from experimentation and then taking the time to reorient before adjusting the action path.

The values we elevated to guide our work—universal well-being and economic security, positive freedom, political equality, non-domination, egalitarian pluralism, community, and sustainability—do not constitute the components of an ideal end state. Instead, they are principles to manage toward in conditions of uncertainty, and the goal of institutional design is to develop organizational forms that can steer toward these principles, iteratively over time with experimentation.

PRESCRIPTIONS

But where should time and attention be spent first in developing a forward policy path for pursuit of these values with this pragmatist methodology? This volume offers a diversity of prescriptions to respond to our diagnosis about the problems stemming from concentrations of power. The authors of the different chapters have focused their own contribution to prescription in four areas: revised approaches to production; identity work; institutional design; and mechanisms of democracy.

Focus on Production

One set of prescriptions is to focus on the modes of production and interventions at that stage. Most policy interventions are focused preproduction, such as education or health care provision, or postproduction mostly in the form of economic redistribution of gains. However, we need to consider how to develop a productivist economic policy agenda that directly targets production-stage interventions. Specifically, what is produced, how is it produced, and ultimately who will be rewarded and how? Then in this vein, how does one design industrial policies that are productive and transformative socially, economically, and politically? What does the concept of political equality have to say about these production-focused policies?

Identity Work

Another approach focuses on how people's identities shape their engagement with political economy. Here the argument is that political movements and coalitions can reshape what matters to people and, in so doing, establish new goals for political economy. The argument is that if we are to succeed at installing well-being rather than growth at the center of political economy, it will require people to develop more clarity about how economic structures are shaping the lives available to them to lead.

Institutional Design and Mechanisms of Democracy

A clear prescription is a redesign of current institutions. Social infrastructure should ensure flourishing lives and allow individuals to have power over their destiny in a way currently unavailable. Some contributors have focused on the redesign of the firm, others on the redesign of democratic economic decision-making from regulation to macroeconomic policy or even on how democracies determine the boundaries of membership and therefore the parameters of labor policy. What sorts of institutions should we cultivate, what are their characteristics, and how would they be implemented? Furthermore, how would we ensure that these institutions do not reproduce the same adverse outcomes for large swaths of the population while keeping the elites permanently entrenched? There is a diversity of possible institutional forms that could be adopted as a result. How does this institutional design reflect the identity work and coalition building that appear to be critical?

ACTION/STRATEGY/IMPLEMENTATION

The volume's contributors bring a diversity of action strategies to the table, to make the pivot from normative foundations and economic models to emblematic policies and a vernacular. While the full picture is not captured in this volume, some are connecting their arguments directly to policymaking, some to education and to efforts to transform the orientation of business elites, and some to social movement engagement.

Taken together, however, the pieces in the volume collectively offer a theory of change by identifying the set of blockages that stand in the way of successful iteration and experimentation guided by new principles. Conventional metrics of GDP and quarterly earnings routinely reproduce an economy steering in one direction only. Politics organized around siloed identities (race, class, party, geography, etc.) rather than intersectional identities traps people in forms of the economy as we know it. The structure of the labor market is badly entangled in global politics around migration. Bureaucratic and technocratic autopilot blocks creative institutional design and policy development. And a failure of policymakers to revisit first principles leads to continued use of old policy paradigms that no longer fit contemporary realities. The coronavirus pandemic has knocked many of these blockages out of the way. In that regard, it is an opportune moment for energetic forward movement in the direction of a more just political economy.

Book Overview: Economy, Organizations, and the Role of Government

The themes of a just economy, organizations, and government structure the three sections of the book. They are also themes that weave throughout. This structure recognizes that the economy is structured by organizations and institutions. If one seeks new goals for political economy, one must also reenvision the shape of the firm and modes of governance. Conversely, if one seeks to help firms, democratic political institutions, and civil society of associations in offering greater support for a just economy, one needs clarity about which economic questions to prioritize. An overarching political economy can help answer that question.

Yochai Benkler opens the volume by introducing the theme of production and productivity, linking it to power. He offers a revival of "political economy" as a frame for understanding the relationship between productivity and justice in market societies. In his framework, political economy reintegrates power and the social and material context—institutions, ideology, and technology—into our analysis of social relations of production, or how we make and distribute what we need and want to have. Organizations and individuals, alone and in networks, struggle over how much of a society's production happens in a market sphere, how much happens in nonmarket relations, and how embedded those aspects that do occur in markets are in social relations of mutual obligation and solidarism. These struggles, at the micro, meso, and macro levels, involve efforts to shape institutions, ideology, and technology in ways that produce trade-offs in productivity and power, both in the short and long term, including through the production and exploitation of atavistic status-hierarchies, primarily race, gender, and immigration. The outcome of this struggle shapes the divergent paths that diverse market societies take, from oligarchic to egalitarian, and their stability as pluralistic democracies.

Dani Rodrik and Charles Sabel also ask us to turn our attention to production. They view the shortfall in "good jobs" not just a source of inequality and economic exclusion, but as a massive market failure—a kind of gross economic malfunction, caused by the gap between the private returns to investing in good jobs and the public benefits of doing so. They argue that standard regulatory responses to this externality, such as Pigovian subsidies, fail in this case. Pervasive uncertainty, dependence on differentiated local conditions, and the evolving nature of the goals call for a high-dimensional policy space and an iterative model of highly contextualized or place-based problem solving grounded in strategic collaboration between private actors and the state. They illustrate the governance principles and organizational framework they have in mind first by examples from two analogous policy domains, where they are already established: fostering of advanced technologies in the context of US Departments of Defense and Energy (DARPA and ARPA-E) and regulation of diffuse sources of water pollution (in Ireland). They then show how these ideas are contributing to successful reform of workforce development in US community colleges—a core area of an eventual good jobs strategy—where traditional approaches have failed.

Glen Weyl then proposes a way to move beyond the standard tension between markets and democracy. As he sees it, this tension stands in the way of building a political economy commensurate to the challenges technology poses to the twenty-first century. Democracy flexible and responsive enough to provide the public goods we require today must harness market mechanisms, he argues. Markets capable of coping with a world pervaded by networks must rely on democratic governance throughout. Weyl's argument is not only theoretical. He is one of the contributors connecting his ideas to a social movement. The RadicalxChange movement seeks to build a new political economy based on these principles, as part of a broader process of social innovation commensurate to technological change.

Deva Woodly, too, is also closely engaged with social movements, in her case as a scholar of the Movement for Black Lives. Like the Movement, Woodly takes the view that people's lived experience can help us find the path to justice. She critiques philosophical liberals and modern conservatives who have long used Aristotle's thoughts on *eudaemonia* or, flourishing, as a justification for a limited state and the primacy of negative liberty because they read the Nicomachean Ethics (Aristotle 1893) as a treatise on the possibilities of individual moral development. On this version of an Aristotelian account, people are best able to achieve their highest good without the interference of the state. Woodly argues, however, that if we take Aristotle seriously and respect his methodological edict, we must begin philosophical inquiry with "what is known to us," then we must acknowledge that in assessing the flourishing of a polis, we cannot look at the isolated individual but must instead observe the individual-in-context. Through a discussion of the concepts of flourishing and well-being in philosophy, psychology, and economics and a look at the empirical indicators of what increases well-being in a polity and how we can measure it, Woodly proposes a political economy that prioritizes people and their lived experience over graphs recording the infinite increase of the gross national product.

Like Woodly, Julie Rose too seeks to displace a focus on gross national or domestic product and to anchor a new political economy in a different human aspiration. As she sees it, economic growth is almost universally treated as a central policy aim and measure of societal success, yet challenges to the growth paradigm are increasingly prominent. These challenges have spurred searches for alternative indicators of social progress and raised fundamental normative questions about the values and aims that ought to guide a society. Though these questions are foundational to current discussions of whether and how to move "beyond GDP," or indeed, beyond the perpetual pursuit of economic growth itself, contemporary theories of justice have given these questions little sustained attention. To the extent that they do, they suggest either that a society must aim to make people indefinitely better off and even wealthy societies must continue to pursue economic growth, or that whether and on what dimensions a wealthy society pursues further gains is a matter of societal discretion. In her chapter, Rose examines John Stuart Mill's, John Maynard Keynes's, and John Rawls's challenges to the perpetual pursuit of economic growth and argues that they suggest an alternative approach. Reconstructing and extending their accounts more broadly within the contours of liberal principles of justice, she argues, supports a *just agrowth* position. This position maintains that a society ought to aim to make people indefinitely better off, but denies that this entails that a society must indefinitely pursue economic growth.

Having laid out a wide-ranging set of reconsiderations of the basic goals of political economy, the second section of the volume then turns to the question of how particular institutional building blocks of the economy might be reconceived, ranging from the prison to the firm to the platform.

Tommie Shelby tackles the question of whether the conventional association of neoliberalism with privatization can suffice to answer the question of when functions should be controlled by the state and when by private actors. To tackle this question, he takes up the theme of prison abolition. One of the core objections of prison abolitionists and radical prison reformers to incarceration in the United States is that it is an immoral alliance of ineffective crime control measures, the privatization of public functions, and the maximization of corporate profit. Abolitionists, such as the philosopher and activist Angela Y. Davis, seek to abolish prisons partly because they view them as components of a vast and destructive "prison-industrial complex." This designation is meant to draw attention to the fact that prison construction, prison administration, and inmate labor attract large amounts of private capital and that commercial profit from imprisonment is a driver of prison growth and mass incarceration. Shelby highlights the power but also the limits of this line of argument and suggests one way in which prison privatization could promote justice.

Rebecca Henderson also argues that the private sector could be an important ally in addressing the great problems of our time. As she sees it, the private sector has a strong collective interest in containing the threat of climate change, in addressing inequality, and in strengthening the institutions that keep markets free and fair and provide the public goods on which every firm depends. Acting on this interest presents significant challenges since it requires overcoming the free-riding problems inherent in any form of collective action, but these challenges can be overcome. Authentically purpose-driven firms—firms that have committed themselves to prosocial goals beyond simple profit maximization—have the potential to trigger a reinforcing process of change that could lead to the rewiring of finance and to a significant fraction of firms actively advocating for strengthening government and rebuilding democracy. Catalyzing this process will require keeping a careful balance between supporting those firms that are authentically committed to change and ensuring that progress against these commitments is measured, audited, and ultimately enforced.

Malcolm Salter also sees potential in the private sector, but only with a dramatically different approach to corporate purpose. Like Woodly, he draws on Aristotle. As Salter sees it, the canonization of shareholder value maximization as the only legitimate expression of corporate purpose has contributed to a widening gulf between what markets value and what people value. Narrowing this gulf in a post-Covid world requires a very different conception of corporate purpose based on moral and economic principles that challenge the theory underlying shareholder value maximization. To this end, he first explains what the theoretical underpinnings of shareholder value maximization are, how this conception of corporate purpose has become so deeply ingrained in our capitalist system, and what practical and conceptual problems this widely accepted doctrine presents. He then proposes an alternative guideline for corporate purpose that that blends Aristotle's theory of reciprocal justice with considerations of corporate purpose, along with Chester Barnard's compatible theory of business organizations as cooperative systems. Aristotle stresses the ethicality of cooperation in transactional settings; Barnard stresses the efficiencies and adaptive benefits flowing from cooperation. Both see utility in truly reciprocal, cooperative relationships, which is not a priority in a shareholder value maximization regime. This alternative approach—referred to as ethical reciprocity—not only provides the basis for a rebuttal of the shareholder-primacy doctrine based on principles of justice and economic efficiency, but more importantly offers a practical guideline for balancing the interests of shareholders and other corporate constituencies in the conduct of everyday business affair. He ends by turning to two practical questions related to the adoption of ethical reciprocity as a substitute guideline for corporate purpose: (a) how "reciprocity practition-ers" can survive in a world dominated by shareholder value maximizers, and (b) what those with the most power to foster change in corporate purpose and governance—namely, large asset holders and asset managers—can do, and increasingly are doing, to encourage public corporations to retreat from their paramount focus on shareholder value maximization.

Christopher Eaglin follows Henderson and Salter with a cautionary note, warning about the risks of capture that flow from corporate efforts to partici-pate in political processes or addressing social problems. He proposes that such engagement by firms would need to be accompanied by more demo-cratic governance within firms. A large literature posits that firms can en-gage in political processes to improve their financial performance. However, the question of whether they should do so and under what circumstances remains critically underdeveloped. In his chapter, Eaglin argues that if we wish to mitigate the risk of corporate capture we ought to consider either meaningfully introducing the voices of external stakeholders to decisions about political actions that firms might undertake or democratizing the shareholder structure of the firm itself. He proposes that if we find a close relationship between firms and political processes advantageous to them, then new theoretical and practical tools should be developed to guide firm behavior.

Finally, Juliet Schor and Samantha Eddy take us into an exploration of the possibilities and limits of the platform economy. The sharing economy emerged with enthusiasm about its ability to provide economic opportunity, fairness, and autonomy for earners. Yet, after a decade, its results have been decidedly mixed, with many earners suffering from low wages and a lack of self-determination. Their findings suggest that while the sharing economy is operating reasonably well for casual earners, the experience of dependent workers is much less positive. At the same time, nonprofit sharing initiatives have failed to scale. For this reason, there has been growing interest in plat-form cooperatives that are owned and governed by earners. Schor and Eddy report on the first academic study of a platform cooperative, Stocksy United, a stock photography company. They find it has been able to offer better earn-ings for platform workers, robust governance, and satisfied members and therefore argue that platform cooperatives can be an important component of a just and democratic political economy.

With intensifying climate change, widening inequalities, and in the af-termath of Covid-19, everything is up for grabs in political economy in a way that we have not seen for generations. The second section of this volume provides a powerful sense of how much flux and dynamism there is in the private sector presently, offering visionary pictures of an alternate landscape of firms that might populate our economy. It then turns to politics, and to the question of how political decision-making ultimately provides the frame for the real economy.

Marc Stears leads off by directly asking a question about change and action strategy. As he points out, even before the virus broke, an increasing number of thinkers and activists were calling for a whole new economic system, and they were being taken seriously when doing so. But if we are going to shape a new economic system, what kind of democratic politics are called for in its construction? What kinds of constraints should structure its campaigning style? How should activists consider themselves, and how should they think about their opponents in these bleak and often highly partisan times? His chapter addresses those questions in three parts. First, it looks in detail at the ways in which contemporary system change thinkers and activists themselves understand their democratic position. Second, it then considers whether those desiring system change might better be advised to focus on creating real, lived experiments that are immediately accessible and address the practical concerns of the every day. Third, it asks whether such apparently "small scale" solutions can ever be expected to rise to the enormous challenges that we currently face.

Sabeel Rahman takes us from the small to the structural. As he puts it, one of the foundations for the pursuit of justice is the construction of state institutions that are capable of tackling and dismantling root causes of injustice. Because of how critical state action and state capacity is to the pursuit of justice, battles over the scope and operation of governmental authority represent one of the most important battlegrounds for justice. Often, projects for hoarding economic wealth and inequities of power have been advanced through proxy fights over the scope and nature of state authority; by dismantling state capacity, interest groups are able to perpetuate structural injustices. Conversely, building new state institutions is central to the project of advancing structural justice.

Leah Downey, in a sense, combines the positions of Stears and Rahman. She highlights an ordinary, everyday decision taken by members of Congress not to revisit their powers of delegation to the Federal Reserve. She explores a recapacitation of democratic politics and the democratic state that would flow from teaching legislators to know and show their own power. The Federal Reserve is an independent agency with the power to govern the US money supply. Congress delegated these powers to the Federal Reserve System in 1913. Downey argues in favor of regularly rechartering the Federal Reserve. In the absence of regular rechartering, we are more likely to see an ossification of who wins and who loses from monetary policy. This is in direct contradiction with the democratic principle that the people hold ultimate political power. She also argues in favor of transitioning the regional Federal Reserve Banks to regional state investment banks—a provocative proposal to demonstrate the sort of creative thinking that rechartering could engender. Finally, she concludes by considering how this reawakening of democratic power and control over monetary policy could help address climate change.

Lastly, Danielle Allen takes up the thorny politics of immigration. Recognizing that the membership and migration policies of the world's states in fact set the terms of the global labor market, Allen drives home the point that politics steers the economy and establishes the parameters of political economy. She tackles the job of articulating an approach to membership policies that could align with the values articulated in the volume of non-domination, anti-monopoly, political equality, freedom, egalitarian pluralism, and community.

Conclusion

This is not a conventional edited volume—the product, for instance, of a single conference at which participants arrived with completed papers and then edited them modestly for publication. This project emerged, first, out of the identification of a grand challenge too big for any single scholar or discipline to address and, second, from the constitution of a team of scholars, with diverse expertise, to address it. From chapter to chapter, you will note different citational styles. Some chapters use in-text author-date references; this is the style of the sciences and social sciences where research findings change rapidly and citations are used to track the development of lines of analysis. Other chapters use footnotes; these are the chapters from humanistic disciplines where the original text of the cited material matters and where enabling readers to find the cited passages is critical. These diverse citation styles reflect the varying intellectual tools that we believe are necessary for tackling any grand challenge—intellectual tools that permit us to achieve positive descriptions of our contemporary social world and intellectual tools that permit us to trace the architecture of normative and jurisprudential arguments over time, and to modify those for present purposes.

Contributors met three times over the course of eighteen months for extended conversations running through multiple days. We began, at our first meeting, by formulating questions together. We used our second meeting to present drafts of papers developed in response to our initial conversations and to reflect directly on the three themes that had emerged from our initial conversation. We reconsidered our essays and revised. We used our third meeting, then, for synthetic discussion—to trace the points of convergence and dissonance within our essays and to come to a clearer understanding of their theoretical implications. And we continued our conversations in cyberspace.

In its merger of the empirical and the interpretive, of the positive and the normative, this volume exemplifies a working method that we think is important for the future of the social sciences generally. As empirical scholars develop their descriptive accounts, they inevitably do so with reference at the very least to implicit ideals. The questions of what "works" or of "how" something "works" cannot escape reference to our aspirations. Good work in the social sciences, then, will be self-conscious about the role of ideals in directing the critical gaze of the empirical scholar. Good work will make implicit aspirations and ideals explicit. But then scholars must also be self-conscious about the source of those ideals and critical with regard to their caliber. These ideals are most valuable when they develop closely bound to direct analysis of their consequences for lived human relations and material social relations. The work of building and assessing ideals itself requires delving into social realities. Then, the conversion of work on values and diagnoses into changes in our world requires a focus on both prescriptions and action strategies. In this volume we have, in short, employed a four-step analytic method, which we recommend as a way forward for other hard questions in the social sciences. Importantly, this four-step analytic method is perhaps best practiced as a collective endeavor. Such teamwork is what we have sought to achieve.

While we have been ambitious in this volume—seeking to link normative foundations of political economy to economic models, emblematic policies, and new vernaculars—we have by no means tackled all the questions that are on the table for all those interested in a new political economy. More might be said about the debate about what should be the province of the state versus civil society. We left largely unaddressed the question of when it is possible to rely on moral motivations and when we need to design mechanisms to structure incentives. We largely skirted around the all-important debate about the relation between labor and property. We conducted our analyses mainly with reference to a nation-state frame, even as the structure of the global economy was also always very present to us. Finally, we only glancingly engaged with questions of temporality, short-term versus long-term interests, and climate change. Clearly, those are topics that merit a frontal look.

We hope that others might perhaps follow the method used here to address the subjects we failed to come to grips with.

Notes

1.   Philip Pettit, *Just Freedom: A Moral Compass for A Complex World* (New York: W. W. Norton, 2014); Philip Pettit, *Republicanism: A Theory of Freedom and Government* (New York: Oxford University Press, 1997); Melvin Rogers, "Race, Domination, and Republicanism," in *Difference without Domination: Pursuing Justice in Diverse Democracies*, edited by D. Allen and R. Somanathan (University of Chicago Press, 2020), 59–89.

2.   Samuel Bowles and Wendy Carlin, "Shrinking Capitalism," *AEA Papers and Proceedings* 110 (2020): 372–77, DOI: 10.1257/pandp.20201001.

3.   Cf. D. Allen and R. Somanathan, eds., *Difference without Domination: Pursuing Justice in Diverse Democracies* (University of Chicago Press, 2020).

Part 1

NEW GOALS FOR A JUST ECONOMY

1 Power and Productivity: Institutions, Ideology, and Technology in Political Economy

YOCHAI BENKLER

Introduction

Neoliberalism was an ideology and institutional transformation program that aimed to shrink the role of the state in the economy and "liberate" market actors to pursue their profits in response to market signals. It was a reaction to the post–Great Depression ascendance of high modernism in economic policy (Keynesianism and dirigisme): the idea that expertise and scientific management by the state and managerial elites could provide a stable, growing economy liberated from the boom-bust cycles that bedeviled capitalism in the long nineteenth century.[1] Neoliberal epistemology was Hayekian: markets offer better information about the complexity of human need, desire, and ability than a state administration ever could. Its political morality was libertarian: efforts by the state to get the clear signals it requires to manage the economy necessarily result in oppression. The neoliberal policy packet therefore aimed to shrink the state and expand the market through deregulation, privatization, low taxes, and free trade. It promised economic dynamism in exchange for publicly governed economic security and enhanced consumer sovereignty and entrepreneurial freedom in exchange for social solidarity. Together, these promised to increase productivity and sustain growth that would raise all boats.

The reality of the past four decades has been the inverse of the promise. Instead of broadly shared wealth driven by newly dynamic markets, the United States saw less dynamic markets coupled with dramatic rent extraction by a small oligarchic elite. Productivity growth since 1973 has been slower than in the preceding century, excepting the 1995–2004 interlude.[2] Business dynamism and entrepreneurship, measured by firm entry and share of employment in young firms, declined.[3] Industry concentration rose[4] and markups increased.[5] Real median income stagnated[6] while the share of income going to the 1 percent and the 0.1 percent skyrocketed.[7] Economic insecurity became widespread. Forty percent of American households report that they cannot cover a $400 emergency.[8] Americans are the only population in the developed world that saw declining life expectancy in the past 30 years.[9] Economic insecurity appears to be a driver of the rise of populism.[10]

Understanding neoliberalism as reactionary—an effort to revive laissez-faire against then-dominant progressive and social-democratic alternatives—helps us focus on the critical theoretical and methodological elements that distinguished it as an intellectual and political movement. Postwar social-democratic institutions were built on both sides of the Atlantic by harnessing the solidarity and collective efficacy developed through two World Wars and the Great Depression. The core tasks of neoliberalism were to replace that solidarity with individualism and undermine the sense of collective efficacy. The "social" was reinterpreted purely as the aggregation of individuals. Social welfare was framed as simple aggregation of individual preference-satisfaction; democracy, as simple aggregation of voter preferences. Preferences, in turn, were exogenous, interpreted as something with which individuals come into markets and elections, and so they are pre-political and reflect the individual's authentic exercise of freedom. The behavior of these individuals could be formalized by rendering them transhistorical rational, self-interested actors operating in perfect markets with perfect information and no power, except in well-defined exceptional circumstances. These same agents came to a state in which gaining and leveraging power were the primary objective, and so these rational, self-interested individuals made well-functioning government impossible. From here, the workhorses of neoliberalism flowed from the abstract to the concrete: rational actor theory; regulatory capture; efficient markets; agency theory; shareholder value; Friedman's monetarism; Lucas's microfoundationalism; Buchanan and Stigler's assaults on the possibility of public governance; Becker's rationale for increased criminal punishment—all were based on these core epistemological and methodological foundations.

The revival of "political economy" as a frame for work on the relationship between productivity and justice in market societies encourages us to reintegrate history, power, and the social and material context—institutions, ideology, and technology—into our analysis of the economy. The economy, in turn, is understood not as "markets," which are but one crucial part of the economy, but as social relations of production: how we make and distribute what we need and want to have. The "political" in "political economy" stands for two distinct but interrelated ideas. First, power is pervasive *within* economic relations: production and distribution in market societies follow

historically path-dependent patterns of conflict, coordination, and cooperation, rather than a single ahistorical pattern of coordination around prices
among self-referential agents. Second, the deployment of the polity proper—
the legitimate threat of violent coercion—is an integral part of economic relations. The political and economic structure each other and are the arena
of conflict and cooperation about both. The implication of these two simple
points is that there is no single, natural, and efficient equilibrium to which
market societies move if regulation is minimized to remove known, neutral,
and ahistorical sources of market imperfection. Instead, market societies at
the same productivity frontier develop along diverse historical trajectories,
resulting in large differences in the productivity and justice of social relations of production, sustained over significant periods. Understanding why
Denmark and Mississippi, small market societies integrated into larger im-
perfect political and economic unions at the cutting edge of global technology and productivity, have diverged in justice and human development is the
core analytic task of political economy. Harnessing that understanding to
pursuing justice is the core programmatic role of the new political economy.

Various chapters in this volume focus on different aspects of the rejection
of the neoliberal frame. Woodly takes aim at the ahistorical, unsituated self
as a preference-bearer as the proper basis for determining society's goals, replacing it with "the individual-in-context" who "has their own perceptions,
dreams, desires, and agency, but they are nevertheless born into a world that
is given and that givenness includes power asymmetries rooted in and reproduced by unjust inequality." Shelby's proposal for a public-private nonprofit
prison management system is expressly anchored in the specific historical
context: focusing on how for-profit systems interact with government "under the current unjust background . . . conditions," rather than in individual
rights or abstract principles of criminal justice. It is under these conditions,
where "social conditions are grossly unjust and the state lacks legitimacy in
the eyes of the most disadvantaged," that Shelby seeks to justify specifically
nonprofit private institutions, leveraging diverse human motivations and
social arrangements to underwrite production by neither market nor state.
Henderson's intervention leans heavily on understanding corporate leaders
not as they are in agency theory—self-interested actors who must be managed by precisely calibrated compensation mechanisms—but as socialized
individuals who can be persuaded to pursue prosocial goals and shift the behaviors of firms. Salter focuses on the ethical and practical value of reciprocity to argue that more cooperative enterprises will in fact do better, but must
be released of the institutions and ideology embodied in shareholder value
theory. Schor and Eddy examine the effectiveness, advantages, and limita-

tions of a new approach to embedding economic production: platform cooperatives. Eaglin takes as his starting premise the observation that firms invest in building and deploying political power. Rahman takes head-on the central programmatic thrust of neoliberalism—shrinking the state—and advocates for a committed strategy to construct public capacity. Downey engages in institutional innovation aimed at making the Federal Reserve democratically accountable. Rodrik and Sabel challenge the core epistemic claim of neoliberalism—that public administration operates in the dark—designing a good jobs policy that sees the government as not only directly responsible for training and job placement opportunities, but also best able to identify these opportunities through iterative, cooperative models of information exchange, experimentation, and learning that already function across a range of mission-critical public administration fields.

Theoretical Antecedents

The new political economy challenges three core theoretical moves that anchored neoliberalism. First, it replaces transhistorical assumptions about human nature with historically grounded explanations of social relations. Second, it replaces self-interested rational actors with socialized or embedded individuals, while avoiding the fallacy of purely structural explanations. Third, it replaces models that treat power as the exception in markets and insists on understanding conflict and power as central determinants of economic relations, interacting with coordination and cooperation.

Historical versus Transhistorical Explanations of the Human Condition. From Smith to Marshall and neoclassical economics, markets are conceived as the natural outgrowth of human nature left to its own devices. Individuals interact freely according to their nature, pursuing their rational self-interest and coordinating their desires and abilities through the price system toward ever-more productive arrangements to satisfy their needs and desires. The explanation flows from human nature rather than from any particular historical set of facts that could have been otherwise. It explains larger structures (the division of labor in society; production and allocation of resources) as the aggregation of microfoundational choices of these individual agents.

Marx is the fountainhead of understanding economic relations as historically specific results of earlier struggles, but the twentieth century saw a sustained flow of economic history that explained the emergence and divergence of market societies as products of struggles along dimensions of class, race, and gender. As Stuart Hall put it, "Appeals to 'human nature' are not explanations, they are an alibi."[11] Other works—Webb's *History of Trade Unionism* in 1894; Weber's *Protestant Work Ethic* in 1905; the Hammonds trilogy and Beard's *Economic Interpretation of the Constitution of the United States* in the 1910s; Du Bois's *Black Reconstruction* and Pinchbeck's *Women Workers and the Industrial Revolution* in the 1930s; and Polanyi's *Great Transformation* in 1944—offered sustained analyses of the development and shaping of social relations through struggle over institutions and ideology in the emergence of capitalism. Historical analysis continued to provide a counternarrative to neoliberalism in the 1970s through 1990s. Horwtiz's *Transformation of American Law*, Wertheimer's *We Were There*, Davis's *Women, Race, and Class*, Fields's *Slavery, Race, and Ideology*, or Berg's *Age of Manufactures* all offered sustained historical analysis of market societies alongside, and rarely in conversation with, work that continued specifically within the Marxian tradition but developed a more institutional and political version, most prominently Brenner's *Agricultural Class Structure* and Meiksins-Wood's *The Origin of Capitalism*. All this work was distinct and opposed to cliometrics, the effort to understand history through the prism of neoclassical economic assumptions, typified by the early work of Douglass North (though less so by North's later work). Its insistence on historical specificity is also different from new institutional economics, most prominently North's *Institutions, Institutional Change, and Economic Performance* and its most sophisticated present-day version in the work of Acemoglu and Robinson in *Why Nations Fail* and the associated formal papers it builds on. That line of work suggests a cleaner, more consistent alignment of optimal (inclusive) and suboptimal (extractive) institutions across all societies and time, rather than focusing on understanding capitalism as a distinctive system or on divergences among contemporary market societies. Indeed, Acemoglu, Robinson, and Verdier go as far as to describe Nordic social democracies as "cuddly" capitalism that free-rides on innovation from more "cutthroat" capitalist economies that are the primary driver of innovation and growth.[12] Countering this line of "false necessity" of a single path to opulence, as Unger called it, is most often found in comparative politics and the new institutionalism in political science, as Pierson's *Politics in Time* epitomizes and work by Hacker, Pierson, and Thelen theorizes.[13] Esping-Andersen's *Three Worlds of Welfare Capitalism* and Thelen's synthesis between that work and the "varieties of capitalism" literature in *Varieties of Liberalization* are central to understanding the divergence among market societies along the dimension of justice without sacrificing productivity.

Agency versus Structure. Perhaps the thorniest problem in social science is teasing out the roles of individual agency and social structure in shaping human behavior and patterns of social relations. Neoliberalism was committed to explaining patterns of economic and social behavior in purely microfoundational terms: the aggregation of individual choices driven by exogenously given preferences. The intellectual roots of refuting this position are deep and broad. Rejecting the determinism of both early Marx materialism and Durkheim's social facts, the twentieth century saw a flow of efforts, across disciplines, to reconcile the lived experience of individual choice with the obvious force of social structure. In economics, the clearest articulation was Veblen's.[14] But his insistence that beliefs and preferences were always structured by the same institutions that structured markets and were therefore endogenous to market actors' preference-shaping investments destabilized the entire project of welfare economics and so was ignored. Contemporary behavioral economics has only flourished by bracketing preference formation and focusing on well-behaved "deviations from rationality" and "misperceptions," ignoring the fact that preference shifting is the object of massive investments by firms (Google and Facebook's business model depends on selling preference-shaping services to advertisers). Sociology has struggled with this question since its inception. Some will emphasize a line from Goffman's frame analysis to the new institutionalism in sociology.[15] Others will point to Foucault's governmentality or Bourdieu's *habitus* and *fields* as the clear genealogy of understanding individuals as both made by their context and retaining their individuality within it. And of course there is the line of critical theory from Adorno and Horkheimer's "culture industry," through Althusser's interpellation and ideology, to Gramsci's ideology and hegemony.

Understanding the self as socially embedded and always grounded in a specific historical moment allows us to identify individuals as neither inherently selfish nor other-regarding, but as socialized. Experimental psychology and economics of the past 20 years have shown that in no society do subjects conform to the behavior of self-interested rational actors.[16] Patterns of trust, trustworthiness, conflict, and cooperation vary substantially across societies, and motivations and orientations toward cooperation or competition and conflict are endogenous to the institutional setting within which individuals engage each other.[17] In this volume, Henderson, Salter, and Schor and Eddy each offer interventions in organizational practices that harness the social-embeddedness of "preferences" for cooperation and depend on the possibility that a change in institutions will foster a change in levels of cooperation and trust.

Power and Conflict. The final major theoretical feature that the new political economy emphasizes is the need for a systematic integration of power into the analysis of economic relations. Again, Smith versus Marx is the basic framing, with Smith standing for a natural progression toward optimal division of labor through mutual coordination in the absence of coercive regulation, and Marx putting conflict at the heart of how social relations of production are created. Parallel to continued work in the Marxian tradition, the twentieth century saw sustained non-Marxian efforts to explain economic relations as shaped by the acquisition and use of power. In the 1920s and 1930s, some of the Legal Realists, most prominently Robert Hale and Morris Cohen, emphasized the central role of law in shaping power and exploitation in economic relations. In his 1936 *Black Reconstruction*, W. E. B. Du Bois explained the role of racism as a strategic investment by capital designed at once to undermine worker coalitions building economic and political power and to produce a steady flow of underpaid workers to put downward pressure on wages of all workers. This perspective was later taken up and extended by others, including Stuart Hall, Cedric Robinson, and Barbara Fields. Similarly, Ivy Pinchbeck's work in the 1930s formed the foundation of decades of work that emphasized the ways in which patriarchal relations in home and care work were translated into economic power. Work by Barbara Wertheimer, Angela Davis, Maxine Berg, Nancy Folbre, and Nancy Fraser developed historical, sociological, and economic understandings of how capitalists leveraged the status-subordination of women to create divisions within the workforce, providing a steady flow of both unpaid care work and low-paid workers to be used to ramp up production in times of war and tight labor markets and be pushed back to the home when demand for labor receded. To oversimplify drastically, in Marxian terms we can think of the Black Radical tradition anchored in Du Bois's *Black Reconstruction* as explaining how Western capital exploited Black and brown labor domestically and internationally as the quintessential stagnant reserve army of labor, while the feminist authors explained how women were forced to become the quintessential latent reserve army of labor. Both traditions insisted that while understanding gender and race was indispensable to understanding the operation of power in the economy, reducing race or gender domination purely to the economic dimension missed core aspects of power and domination in modern societies. Instead, as Hall put it, one needed to understand the "articulation between different modes of production, structured in some relation of dominance";[18] or as Fraser put it, feminism needed to integrate maldistribution and misrecognition as distinctive and mutually reinforcing systems of exploitation and domination.[19]

Within mainstream economics, the study of power was strictly cabined to the state. Markets were an arena where power occurred in well-defined exceptional circumstances, such as essential facilities or other sources of monopoly. The primary object of the state, however, was the deployment of power, and rational self-interested actors vied to maximize their own payoffs by capturing the institutions of the state. These efforts generally result in inefficient defeat of people's natural tendencies toward efficiently ordering their affairs. Hence, Buchanan or Stigler and even the more sophisticated and historically informed versions, like Acemoglu and Robinson, insist on state coercion as the primary source of extractive power and the locus of power-seeking, rather than integrating power into an analysis of the normal operation of the economy. The primary exception was Schumpeter, who based his theory of growth on continuous innovation (creative destruction), specifically aimed at creating market power, and who expressly credited Marx as having been the only classical economists who understood this fact. To this day, "neo-Schumpeterian economics" remains the leading discipline in the economics of innovation. But, following Schumpeter's example, this line of work has simply ignored the implications of the insight that power-seeking is the driver of innovation and hence the core dynamic of capitalism: continuous productivity growth. After Schumpeter, Marglin's *What Do Bosses Do?* and the work of Bowles and Gintis on contested exchange represent high points of efforts to integrate Marxian insights on the central role of conflict and power into mainstream economics. After the 1980s, most of the work in mainstream economics that reflected power in labor markets was focused on analyzing empirical evidence of the impact of union power on wages, following Freeman and Card, most prominently.

As with agency and structure, there is a long and rich tradition within cultural Marxism, from Benjamin to Adorno and Horkheimer to Althusser and Gramsci, that focuses on the production and maintenance of power in society, with a clear focus on class exploitation. And, as with agency and structure, both Foucault and Bourdieu developed their own distinctive version of the construction of power and domination in society, in institutions, in their habituation in body and disposition in ways that convert their mediation of agency and structure into a society that reproduces hierarchy and domination. Scholars who have dedicated their lives to one or another of these traditions or authors will undoubtedly treat my whirlwind tour and collapse of nuance, emphasis, and intellectual innovation with distaste. My purpose, however, is to identify opportunities for intellectual alliance across diverse and radically different traditions all of which, for all their differences, coalesce around core insights useful in diagnosing the flaws of, and providing alternatives to, neoliberalism.

A Model of Political Economy: Embedded Coordination, Cooperation, and Conflict

OVERVIEW

Synthesizing these diverse efforts to understand political economy allows us to outline a model of the economy as embedded coordination, cooperation, and conflict. Actors and organizations are always already embedded in a material (nature + technology) and social (institutions + ideology) context, in social relations inherited from prior rounds of political, social, and economic struggle.[20] There is no Archimedean point on which to perch microfoundational agents from whose universal, time-invariant nature (e.g., an imagined propensity to truck, barter, and exchange) social structures emerge. The social relations into which we are born shape our beliefs, preferences, constraints, but we nonetheless are not fully determined by this social structure: we struggle to understand our condition, imagine alternatives, diagnose intervention points, and struggle, alone and together, to change our social and material context. This microfoundational agent is not the presocial rational actor but the socialized individual. *Homo economicus* is replaced by *homo socialis*, whose motivations are diverse and socialized and whose decisions are situational and reasonable, not formally rational. Because *homo socialis* is already always embedded in a social and material context, the context sets the ratio of economic actors, organizations (firms and nonprofits), and individuals who pursue self-interest to those who pursue prosocial goals, and the extent to which discrete economic actors permit themselves to act purely on self-interested rather than constrained by prosocial considerations. Self-interested and prosocial actors interact to advance their individual or prosocial goals, trading off productivity for power as they act strategically within their institutional, ideological, and material context, and invest effort into shaping future contexts to increase their power in future interactions. Individuals and organizations do so not only at the micro-level but also at the meso-level, as organizations and individuals engage in collective action—the Business Roundtable or Chamber of Commerce, the Consumers Federation of America, unions like the AFL-CIO—similarly bargaining, lobbying, shaping social perceptions, and developing technologies that improve their short-term payoffs and long-term bargaining position.

It is critical to emphasize, though, that once market society emerges in the transition to capitalism, the dynamic of improved productivity through technological and institutional innovation is too powerful to permit incumbents to retain their position purely through power-seeking investments.

AT&T could not prevent the emergence of voice over Internet protocol any more than canal or turnpike companies could prevent railroads. But within a broad range, institutional power matters: craft producers in Lyon or Northern Italy did succeed in resisting Fordism and maintaining more flexible, less exploitative labor relations at the same technological and productivity frontier,[21] and Danish unions today urge adoption of robots, secure in their power to obtain a fair share of the productivity gains in a global marketplace. Under these realistic market conditions, firms and individuals mix strategies. They trade off investments in improving productivity to stay ahead of the competition for investments in obtaining power. They seek market power horizontally, against competitors and disruptive innovators to create larger rents, and bargaining power vertically, against workers, consumers, suppliers, and distributors to obtain a larger share of these rents from other claimants. And they trade off investments in short-term exploitation of the existing material and social context for investments in shifting the long-term context toward arrangements that increase their future power.

DEFINITIONS

Power is a property of a relationship between A and B, describing A's capacity to shape B's behavior, outcomes, or context so that the respective behaviors, outcomes, or context of A's and B's relations is closer to A's preferred relations than to B's, short term (within context) or long term (about context). "Context" is the social and material setting within which A and B act and relate to each other. The social context is made of institutions and ideology. The material context is nature and technology. The definition is meant to be general, describing power between a broad range of entities—individuals, organizations, classes or groups, states, and so on. It is intended to emphasize an understanding of power as a property of relations describing relative positions of entities within social relations.

Institutions are explicit or implicit instructions for *who should do what in which social relation,* serving as constraints and affordances on behavior for persons in the social relation to which they apply. Law is a system for producing such instructions susceptible to enforcement by legitimate violence. Social norms are systems of such instructions enforced through social coercion—gossip, shaming, ostracism—or internalized social conformism. Organizational or professional norms are explicit or implicit instructions produced by a given set of social actors to govern behavior (i.e., create affordances and constraints) in the social context for which they are developed so as to constitute the social relations they constitute—for example, the workplace or the profession.

Ideology is that subset of institutions that shape *how we understand the world, what causes what, what goes with what, what is valued and what is loathed.*[22]

Technology is *congealed practical knowledge embedded in material culture.*[23] "Practical knowledge," which is knowledge applied functionally to achieve desired outcomes, is a universally adopted element included in the definition of technology. I add the notion of "embedded in material culture" to distinguish technology from institutions and ideology, each of which is often treated as a form of practical knowledge (i.e., how to behave, how to interpret). While some definitions of technology treat any practical knowledge that allows us to do new things or old things more efficiently as "technology," and others emphasize "sociotechnical systems" to underscore that all technologies take their meaning from specific social relations, those definitions are less useful for distinguishing between institutions and technology. Emphasizing the material aspect of technology makes it easier to understand the difference between, say, the clothes dryer or the electronic spreadsheet, on the one hand, and Title VII of the Civil Rights Act or options theory, on the other hand, as contributing factors to the increase of women's labor force participation in the 1970s or financialization in the 1980s, respectively. Again, I rely not on claims of metaphysical truth but on practical utility for understanding the distinctive features of the contribution of technology to political economy, whose other major elements are institutions and ideology. "Congealed" underscores the friction and time associated with material embedding, which make technology a distinct battleground worth winning. Once narrow job definitions are built into the mechanical structure of a high-cost assembly line, for example, labor organizing is limited in its ability to demand a reorganization of work along craft structures; the bounds of feasible bargaining about shop-floor practices becomes limited for longer than it might be with more flexible workstations or machine tools.

In sum, power in social relations, its magnitude and distribution, is a function of institutions, technology, and ideology. Institutions are the "rules of the game"—that is, the instructions about who can do what in which context that define the relation and distribute power within it. The fact that you can touch the ball with your hands, cannot hold it for more than 3 seconds, and must dribble to advance makes basketball a distinct social practice from soccer. Technology describes the material conditions under which a practice so constituted is carried out. The fact that the hoop is of a certain size and located 10 feet off the ground means that taller players are more talented in basketball than they would have been had the same hoop been set at 2 feet. Ideology is the conception people have of what they are doing, the frame through which they understand the practice and define their preferences and beliefs and understand their constraints in the situation. Basketball is a competitive game, not a comic performance, and if the players imagined that it was the latter rather than the former, their behavior in the game would be different (think of the Harlem Globetrotters) even when the technology and formal rules are identical.

DYNAMICS

How the preponderance of agents and organizations act, what outcomes they obtain, and what practices form their competitive environment is shaped by the institutions, ideology, and technology that make up the context of the relation. Firms know this and act strategically in interactions both within markets and about the institutional, ideological, and technological determinants of power in market relations to increase their ability to extract quasi-rents in all their interactions—horizontally, against competitors or innovative disruptors, and vertically, against workers, consumers, suppliers, and distributors. Workers and consumers know this, so they organize to resist and reshape the power relationships, sometimes through market organizations like unions or cooperatives and often through nonmarket organizations and social movements.

Cyrus McCormick's reaper was a quintessential productivity-increasing technology, transforming American agriculture in the second half of the nineteenth century. But when Cyrus McCormick Jr. inherited his father's company, he harnessed technology in a very different way. Soon after inheriting the company, McCormick declared wage cuts, despite the firm's banner year in 1883. He had not counted on the iron molders union, whose unique craft skills made them irreplaceable and who had been the driving force of labor organizing in Chicago for 20 years. In 1884, McCormick lost a violent three-week strike against his arbitrary wage cuts. Almost immediately, the company invested in technology and politics to gear up for the next strike. It purchased pneumatic molding machines and replaced the entire workforce of craft molders with unskilled laborers working the new machines. The new machines produced low-quality castings and required attendance of many common laborers, actually increasing labor costs. But the technological investment served its long-term purpose: the iron molders union was defeated. When another strike erupted in 1886, the striking unskilled workers were easily replaced. McCormick also changed his political position. He supported

Chicago's mayor in exchange for the appointment of the new, anti-labor police inspector who would lead the 1886 Haymarket Massacre of protesters fighting for an 8-hour workday, still commemorated as May Day.[24]

More generally, firms deploy technologies that increase their bargaining power over labor in three primary ways—homogenization, monitoring, and fissuring.[25] Automation that standardizes and simplifies labor inputs weakens labor bargaining power, whereas automation that increases productivity more but requires experienced operators strengthens labor. Monitoring similarly alters bargaining power by removing workers' credible threat to slow down production if treated unfairly. When firms cannot perfectly observe effort or quality, they pay workers a premium to induce them to make firm-specific investments and work beyond what is observable. If technologies make effort more observable, workers' bargaining power declines, and with it wages. Technology that gives employers finely honed sticks reduces their dependence on carrots. Levy and Barocas, for example, show how retail firms repurposed data collection systems designed to monitor customers to homogenize experienced salespeople, making them more readily replaceable; monitor employees more finely to impose starker discipline; and externalize the risk of the ebb and flow of business onto workers by forcing algorithmically set "flexible" work schedules.[26] Finally, employers can deploy technologies that fissure the workplace and undermine worker collective action, as Rogers emphasized,[27] and which Gray and Suri demonstrated in their study of how contemporary "artificial intelligence" systems incorporate human "last mile" operations, harnessing individuals in the United States and India working behind a one-way mirror so that everything they do is observed and measured, while disabling worker coordination.[28]

Similar actions of individual firms abound throughout the history of modern market societies, not only with technology but with institutions and ideology as well. In the 1960s, Kelly Girls and other temporary personnel firms launched a campaign to circumvent then-still-powerful labor union's resistance to temporary workers. They framed their new employment model in patriarchal terms, recruiting married women "to make some pocket money" to fill the ranks of jobs in the new services industry, precursors of the fissured workplace.[29] Dubal's study of a century of labor struggle in the San Francisco taxi industry situates Uber's strategy of spending investor capital to monopolize the market in rider apps: Uber designed its app to evade regulators and control drivers and lobbied to undermine the municipalities' traditional jurisdiction over livery services and ensure the designation of drivers as independent contractors.[30] Schor examines how these strategies produced highly differential outcomes for occasional gig workers, mostly white and working for extra income, who benefit from opportunities to add income more than they lose from the power imbalance with the company, and gig workers who depend on platforms for a livelihood who are mostly minority and who see the power asymmetry cutting into their basic income.[31]

This microfoundational story (what individual firms or agents do) must be complemented by meso-level analysis of collective action, and both only happen in inherited macro-level institutions, ideology, and technology. The 1970s saw a dramatic increase of business lobbying efforts, which in turn supported institutions that weakened the power of government to constrain business and redirected government power toward weakening labor.[32] Unions had played a critical role for three decades during the postwar period, not only on wage setting and enforcement of compensation norms, including managerial compensation, but also as the central countervailing political power over broad questions of economic policy and redistribution.[33] A core focus of Organized Business since the 1970s was to undermine Organized Labor and harvest the rents from that transformation in bargaining power. Its decisive victory was President Ronald Reagan's breaking the PATCO (Professional Air Traffic Controllers Organization) strike in 1981. Declining union membership since then has been a major cause of median income stagnation in the United States. Broad, cross-industry collaboration among businesses on institutions like antitrust or labor law was complemented by industry-level collective action as a major determinant of market structure and both horizontal and vertical power in product and labor markets throughout the economy. The structures of the telecommunications industries, both wired and wireless, across the Organization for Economic Cooperation and Development (OECD) are the fossil record of the two-decades-long battles between firms and regulators.[34] So too the structure of the pharmaceutical, automobile, energy, and any other large-scale sectors. But collective action does not necessarily result in exploitation. Where power is symmetric and power-seeking offers few gains, coordination and cooperation between labor, management, and a well-functioning state actually help make high-productivity egalitarian arrangements work.[35]

These discrete political battles occurred on the background of a macro-level historical shift in institutions and ideology that responded to the political and economic shocks of the 1960s and 1970s. The ideological work had been in the works for decades, ready to coalesce when the postwar settlement was shocked out of equilibrium by the Great Inflation of the 1970s. Hayek and Friedman were both on the margins of academic and policy circles throughout the 1940s until the 1970s, but they built a network of academics and organizations that would be ready when the winds shifted. Initially funded by

ideologically committed individuals, the neoliberals built organizational capacity through think tanks and special-purpose programs within academia.
In some cases, as with Henry Manne's successes in fundraising for the law
and economics movement, there were direct appeals to the self-interest of
companies like ITT or US Steel, which wanted to loosen antitrust law to fund
a movement that would nudge law in that direction.[36] Subsequent study confirmed that these efforts were successful and that judges who participated
in Manne's Pareto in the Pines program rendered systematically more pro-
business verdicts and tended to rule against regulatory and tax agencies
more often for decades thereafter.[37] These appeals fit well the changed political program of business organizations in the 1970s and were foundational to
the victory of neoliberalism as the dominant economic theory of the 1980s
through the Great Recession. Some of these organizational beachheads were
located in traditional academic departments with a critical mass of members
who then influence future appointments to build a "school." The Chicago
economics department was one such place, as were Buchanan and Tullock
at the Virginia Polytechnic Institute and later George Mason University. So
too with the Olin Foundation's support of the establishment and expansion
of law and economics programs at law schools. To this "inside" strategy the
movement added think tanks that housed scholars focused on translational
work or academics translating their academic work for consumption by policymakers and elite opinion makers. The American Enterprise Institute and
Foundation for Economic Freedom were soon joined by the Heritage Foundation, the Cato Institute, and others that attracted funding to support a
steady flow of papers and events criticizing regulation and redistribution at
a detailed level of analysis of both policy and politics. To these think tanks,
the movement added public-facing programming to educate elites—such as
Manne's "Pareto in the Pines"—and mass audiences, as Milton Friedman's
Newsweek column and television show did so remarkably. By moving from big
ideas to technically well-worked-out details, from academia to think tank to
popular culture, and from idea development to education and training, the
movement was able to create a large cadre of elite actors who, some more
consciously than others, had come to adopt a worldview, a way of interpret-
ing the world, that saw markets as efficient and liberating and government
planning as doomed to fail, corrupt, and tending to tyranny.

   These institutional and ideological shifts of the 1970s were complemented
by broad technological deployments of information and communications
technologies that enabled offshoring and outsourcing of production. Then,
by the 1980s, computers and spreadsheets enabled ever-more complex financial products that led to financialization. In combination, these moves put

management and finance in a position to disinvest from labor, adopt short-termism, embrace the earnings game, and use the newly found legal freedom to suppress competition and extract a larger share of the resulting rents. Free trade agreements that emphasized investor protection and financial flows, but not labor or environmental standards, vastly expanded competition in the labor market between domestic and offshore labor and severely limited the power of labor domestically. Weakening antitrust enforcement since the Reagan administration, looser financial regulation, weaker labor regulation, and monetary policy aimed at keeping inflation in check by sticking to a relatively high "natural rate of unemployment" that kept labor markets relatively slack—all contributed to increased horizontal and vertical power in product and labor markets. These micro, meso, and macro dynamics combine to explain the observed patterns of the American economy over the past 40 years—declining business dynamism, increasing concentration and markups, slower productivity growth, and the particular pattern of American inequality—a top 1 percent and 0.1 percent takeoff coupled with broad-based income stagnation and economic insecurity.

The emergence of the Internet as the basic infrastructure of the twenty-first century, where I focused most of my research, is rife with examples of this dynamic. Microsoft's suite of antitrust cases in the 1990s revolved around technical choices (intentional incompatibilities with DR-DOS in the early 1990s; intentional incompatibilities with Java or HTML in the mid-1990s) and institutional strategies (licensing terms that made it impossible for PC manufacturers to replace Microsoft's products with competing operating systems without incurring huge costs) designed to build the firm's market power horizontally—against potential disruptive innovators or competitors—and vertically, against consumers, suppliers, and distributors. Apple's App Store is no more technically necessary for loading software on a mobile device than it had been for the PC. But it creates a bottleneck that allows Apple to extract rents from complementary app developers and delay or degrade apps that threatened to decrease its rents or bargaining power.[38] Cisco developed "policy routers" in 1999 to enable newly emerging cable broadband providers to extract rents from suppliers of complementary products. The result was two decades of political struggle and litigation over net neutrality. The dynamic is replicated in the advertising platforms of Google and Facebook and Amazon's relations with sellers in the Amazon marketplace.[39] As Julie Cohen masterfully showed, a series of strategic actions, in litigation and legislation, shaped intellectual property, on the one hand, and privacy and data protection law, on the other hand, to make data about individuals a "public domain" free for unconstrained harvesting by the major firms of our era, while making the data aggregations collected by these firms "private property" protected from both competitors and regulators.[40] And as Amy Kapczynski showed, transformations of trade secret and constitutional law since the 1980s have strengthened many companies' bargaining power in labor markets and increasingly hampered state regulation of firms across a broad range of industries.[41] In all these cases, firms engaged not only in technical changes but in extensive litigation and lobbying to create an institutional setting conducive to their continued power, and in extensive ideological work to reinforce the inevitability and benevolence of unconstrained technological change.

Throughout this period, individuals—acting alone or in networks, or collectively in civil society organizations—tried to push back in both institutional battles and by building technologies. Efforts by organizations like the Electronic Frontier Foundation (EFF), EPIC, Public Knowledge, Free Press, or Fight for the Future were conjoined with periodic mobilization efforts in the "copyright wars," encryption and privacy, access to knowledge, and more recently, fairness in algorithms. These institutional and ideological battles were complemented by technological interventions, such as strong encryption tools to protect privacy and decryption tools to circumvent digital rights management, each designed to defeat the efforts of companies and governments to impose arrangements that activists deemed oppressive. Nowhere was this dimension more clearly embodied in practice than in the free software movement.[42] Here, as in the free culture movement that followed it, we saw direct conflict between firms seeking to bring more of the economy into market relations and a social movement of people seeking to construct a context that allowed more of the economy to function on nonmarket models. Advocates of the commons (myself included) pointed to successful commons-based practices like free software and Wikipedia as existence proof that the economy need not be purely cleared by prices in markets supported by ever-more perfect deployment of property and contract. Indeed, we argued at the time, user innovation, socially motivated hacking, and norms-driven knowledge production offered important checks on purely market-based information, knowledge, and cultural production.[43]

Battles over privacy or algorithmic use of data are now the dominant front of consumer-oriented struggle in technology politics. Several of the world's most valuable companies are focused primarily on developing technologies whose core task is to extract information from and about, and run behavioral experiments on, consumers. One requires Panglossian optimism to imagine that pervasive surveillance and personalized, experimentally validated behavioral advertising was designed to inform rather than manipulate consumers. Successfully manipulating demand increases the value of quasi-rents by manipulating users' willingness to pay. It also increases the half-life of the quasi-rents by delaying competitive entry: manipulating information about substitutable products and magnifying perceived differentiation between the manipulator's product and substitutes. Applied to politics, the translation of this power into shaping the institutional dimension of power is obvious. While there is little quantitative evidence showing that these technologies work,[44] it is clear that their purpose is to develop such power over consumers and that, even without evidence, advertisers are buying enough of the promise to make these technology companies the most valuable in the world.

Most of the battles of the 1990s and 2000s focused on individual freedom and the market reach relative to nonmarket production, rather than on distributive justice. Nonmarket, nonproprietary production was celebrated largely as a degree of freedom from the power of market actors to invade our privacy and set the terms of information, knowledge, and cultural production. The Access to Knowledge movement was a first reorientation toward distribution-sensitive politics of technology, influenced by the Access to Medicines movement.[45] Since the Occupy moment we have seen more efforts to include concerns with economic power, insecurity, and inequality. Platform cooperativism,[46] the purpose-driven OuiShare festivals, the Sharing Cities Alliance, and the National Domestic Workers Alliance are all seeking to reorient technologically mediated economic practice toward egalitarian relations of production, using different mechanisms to embed production in solidaristic social relations (reflecting the focus of various chapters in this volume: cooperativism in Schor and Eddy; purpose-driven organization in Henderson; municipalism in Stears; and social mission-driven nonprofit in Shelby). In academia, leading examples of this reorientation are Cohen's work on the legal construction of informational capitalism;[47] Zuboff's on surveillance capitalism;[48] Schor's work on the sharing economy;[49] Kapczynski's analysis of the cost the price system to innovation and culture;[50] Levy on monitoring of truckers,[51] or her work with Barocas on the impact of consumer data collection on workers;[52] Ajunwa, Crawford, and Schultz's work on workplace surveillance;[53] Dubal's on the precarity of the gig economy drivers;[54] Pasquale's on algorithmic black boxes;[55] Barocas and Selbst's focus on big data's disparate impact;[56] and Rogers's work on the major dimensions of technological power employers seek as leverage over employees.[57] A distinctive feature of this newer work is a call for reviving state power as a counterbalance to market power—nowhere more forcefully than in Khan's work on antitrust[58] or Rahman's call for leveraging democratic governance to contain the domination of market actors.[59]

In contrast to this power-based story, the most influential neoclassical explanations of rising economic inequality centered on technology as an exogenous and politically neutral force: skills-biased technical change (SBTC)[60] and the economics of superstars in winner-take-all markets.[61] These explanations form the intellectual origin of current arguments that robots will create structurally high levels of unemployment and platforms will casualize work. Technology in these explanations develops exogenously, is roughly deterministic (some things are easier to automate, others harder), and interacts with efficient labor markets to change the relative value of different kinds of labor (skilled/unskilled workers; routine/nonroutine tasks). This interaction makes highly skilled workers valuable, the super-skilled few superstars, and relegates low- or mid-skilled workers to stagnant or declining wages. These technological explanations naturalize inequality as an inevitable function of the most distinctive dynamic in market society—productivity growth through technological change. Efforts to address inequality must therefore focus on fitting the poorly trained workers to inevitable technological change. The primary weakness of SBTC and winner-take-all theories is that they fail to explain how countries at the same technological frontier embrace these technologies with widely differing social consequences. The Nordic social democracies, Germany, France, and Japan all operate at the same technological frontier as the United States, yet they exhibit different patterns of inequality, and none exhibits the escape of the 1 percent that characterizes American inequality. Political economy offers a more plausible explanation of these divergent patterns than any generalized, apolitical, and ahistorical model.

The diversity among market societies at the production frontier is a product of the history of struggle in each society and its resulting social relations of production. These battles shaped how much happened in a market sphere as opposed to through nonmarket relations; how embedded those aspects that do occur in markets are in social relations of mutual obligation and solidarism; and how institutions that diverged between these clusters of democratic market societies shaped power in the economy, both within markets and between market and nonmarket spheres.[62] The differences in productivity and inequality in Demark and Mississippi are not usefully understood in terms of universals but in terms of specific historical struggles, over class, race, gender, and immigration, and how the social and material context inherited from these struggles determines current distributions of power within markets and dependence on and alternatives to markets for people satisfying their basic needs and developing basic capabilities. One cannot understand the relative weakness of labor in the United States, by comparison to Europe, or the relative stinginess of American social insurance without understanding the central role that enslaved Black workers played as the core workforce of America's leading export industry in its first seven decades and the role racial ideology has played as the central strategy for undermining labor mobilization and social insurance in America ever since.[63] Nor can one understand American capitalism without understanding how waves of immigration and anti-immigrant sentiment were used by capital to undermine labor organizing throughout the nation's history. It is to these dynamics that I turn next.

Status-Subordination and Economic Power in Market Societies

Central to the new political economy is a commitment to understanding the interaction between economic inequality and other dimensions of domination, most prominently race, gender, and other forms of atavistic status-subordination. As Dawson's *Blacks in and out of the Left* made eminently clear, the interaction between activists and scholars focused on racism and racial subordination and those focused on capitalism and economic exploitation has never been easy.[64] Nor will any reader of the debates between Butler and Fraser,[65] or of Williams's critique of how professional- and managerial-class feminists misunderstand the conditions and priorities of working-class women,[66] miss the challenges associated with producing a gender-class narrative. And yet, as the section on intellectual antecedents made clear, there is a century of rich work aimed at exploring the articulation of these different dimensions of exploitation and subordination, seeking, in the words of the Combahee River Collective, to develop an "integrated analysis and practice based upon the fact that the major systems of oppression are interlocking," referring to "racial, sexual, heterosexual, and class oppression."[67] I will not presume to offer an original intervention into these long-standing and rich debates. Rather, I sketch how such an integrated analysis could be used within the political economy model I outline here—built and synthesized from the framework that Du Bois, Hall, and Fields developed for race and racism, Davis for the intersection of racism and sexism, and Fraser and Folbre for gender—and extending it to immigration, the primary target of resurgent ethnonationalism in democratic market societies.

Recall that we start from the premise that actors and organizations are always embedded in a material and social context: social relations inherited from prior rounds of political, social, and economic struggle. At any given moment, therefore, there will be some people in society who occupy positions of status-subordination (borrowing, following Fraser, Weber's distinction between class (economically derived social hierarchy) and status (social hierarchy derived from noneconomic relations)). Status-subordinated people will have fewer and weaker political allies, and hence they will be more available for aggressive exploitation. This is, for example, Fields's explanation of why Black workers, wrenched from their social sources of counterpower, were unable to resist permanent enslavement in mid-seventeenth-century Virginia, as compared to English indentured servants whose position was anchored in the successful battles against serfdom in prior centuries in England. Status-subordinated people will have fewer alternatives and fewer kinship resources to fall back on, and observe lower benchmark wages among peers, and will therefore have fewer means to resist exploitative work conditions and lower pay. Women in particular, on the background of patriarchal norms, are forced to accept positions of lower commitment and greater "flexibility" in market relations in order to fulfill embedded expectations for care and reproduction work in the home. As Folbre explained, love and an ethic of care need not be seen as false consciousness, but their articulation in contemporary society has shaped conflict and cooperation in patriarchal market societies.[68] As Pinchbeck and Berg showed, this was as true for the different pathways of girls into service and boys into apprenticeships at the dawn of the modern era as it is for today's gender imbalance in "alternative work arrangements" typical of the fissured workplace.[69]

Every major transformation in the history of capitalism has in large part depended on harnessing status-subordinated workers to occupy the new positions that higher-status workers resisted. In Britain, before the eighteenth century Parliamentary Enclosures men were already heavily engaged in wage labor in agriculture, but women produced roughly half of household budget relying on commons-based production for both subsistence and income: dairying, harvesting wood and peat for energy, gleaning, and similar direct production for the household. Enclosure—the systematic use of lobbying to extinguish the legal use rights of the majority of workers in order to create exclusive rights in the hands of a minority of landowners—left women without productive opportunities and unmarried women and widows destitute. It rendered women the first fully proletarianized workforce.[70] The first industrial revolution, driven by water-powered cotton textile manufacture, harnessed them. Women and children became the majority of the workforce in the new factories of the 1790s, usually operating in units managed through patriarchal authority, often violently, by a male spinner, sometimes a relative.[71] As Berg showed, almost all labor productivity growth in the first decades of the nineteenth century in Britain, the world's emerging industrial power, came from industries where women's work predominated. Men were better able to resist the exploitative working conditions in the factories and remained primarily in craft manufacturing sectors. In the American South, the surge in British industrial demand for raw cotton, coupled with Whitney's cotton gin, drove a slew of legal changes designed to deepen enslavement of Black workers, make manumission harder and domestic slave trade from the border states to the empire of cotton easier, while reinforcing status degradation of free Black Americans toward the ultimate denial of humanity in *Dred Scott*.[72] In New England after 1820, the American factory system depended on girls and young women for labor. When these women began to organize unions in the 1830s, they were soon replaced by Irish immigrants who did not have the options to go back to the farm, or the political solidarity built over two decades of work in the mills.[73]

The classic case of the spinning mule offers an example of how technology too, like institutions and ideology, was oriented toward harnessing status-subordinated labor as a core workforce.[74] Early mechanization of textile spinning took "women's work" in the household and turned it into men's work, because of the physical strength necessary to operate the early spinning mules and a perception that men have the skill to maintain and repair the mule and manage the several women and children employed in supporting roles. By the 1790s, male mule spinners in England had organized into craft unions, and by 1810 they had become the most powerful craft union in England. Following strikes that decade, firms invested substantially to develop a "self-acting" mule—the first automated spinning mule. In 1834, a factory commissioner wrote of the self-acting mule that "[t]he introduction of this invention will eventually give a death blow to the Spinners' Union." Andrew Ure wrote in his 1835 *Philosophy of Manufactures* that the invention of the self-acting mule "would put an end . . . to the folly of trades unions," asserting that "when capital enlists science to her service, the refractory hand of labour will be taught docility." The goal of mechanization was to displace unionized adult men with teenagers and women, whose pay by convention at the time was two-thirds to one-half that of men, and whom the firms believed were more docile workers, less likely to organize. A second dimension of investment was the configuration of spinning mules. In Glasgow, the second largest center of cotton mills in Britain, a relatively tight-knit group of industrialists was able to circumvent the unions by replacing larger mules, usually operated by men, with rows of smaller mules operated by nonunionized women and supervised by a male supervisor. The Lowell Mills, set up in the 1820s without a generation of males organizing to contend with, immediately hired girls and young women working rows of smaller mules.

The pattern repeated itself throughout the history of industrial and postindustrial capitalism. In the US, the transition from cotton and water to coal, iron, and steam depended on Irish and German immigrants. Irish immigrants built the railroads from the East. Chinese workers built the railroads from the West.[75] Wages for these immigrants were below those of native-born workers and exhibited lower growth.[76] The next transition to high mechanization and unskilled labor associated with the second industrial divide depended on the mass migration from Southern Europe (Italians) and Eastern Europe (over 2 million Jews escaping pogroms in Russia). As World War I and fear of communism led to immigration exclusions, the pull of the new assembly lines for status-subordinated workers combined with the push of the second Klan's terrorism drove the Great Migration. This mass internal migration, in turn, triggered sustained efforts to maintain a racial caste hierarchy in the new urban, industrial setting. Be it zoning and restrictive covenants, racialized denial of access to the foundations of middle-class wealth through redlining in federal mortgage insurance, exclusion of historically Black occupations from labor protections, discriminatory denial of access to postwar educational opportunities, or weakening labor through the Taft-Hartley Act and the power it gave states to pass "right to work" laws, taken up throughout the South, anti-Black racial ideology and institutionalized status-subordination from the 1920s through the 1950s continued to play a central role in maintaining status-hierarchy and depressing the wages of Black workers throughout the "Golden Age of Capitalism."[77] And, during and after World War II until immigration reform in 1965, the Mexican braceros program filled the need for status-subordinated workers employed at substandard conditions in agriculture.[78]

During the neoliberal transformation, status-subordination continued to play a major role in weakening labor and providing the glue for the new coalitions that shaped the divergent patterns of liberalization across various market societies. In the United States, women and immigrants, newly admitted after 1965, formed the primary workforce of the shift to the postindustrial services economy. Labor force participation of married women increased dramatically in response to the successes of the women's movement, but male-dominated unionized workplaces in industrial sectors were blocked and experienced decline. Instead, women entered the expanding services industries at lower wages and with lower security, packaged as flexibility for workers already differentially burdened with care work and reproduction. At the same time, loose immigration enforcement contributed to a significant inflow of undocumented immigrants who filled the lowest rungs of agriculture and services with a steady flow of legally insecure workers with the least bargaining power. Both put downward pressure on wages and terms of employment in services. In Europe, as work by Esping-Andersen and Thelen suggests, patterns of integration of women and immigrants into the workforce during this transition were central to the divergence among the three major families of market democracies. By contrast to the broad insecurity that marked American labor, countries governed by coalitions anchored by Christian Democrats focused on maintaining the unionized male family wage in the industrial core of the economy and used Turkish and North African guest workers to create a dualized market system, one with a strong, protected native male industrial workforce and a periphery of insecure immigrant labor providing cheap services to that core. The Nordic social democracies, by contrast, adopted universal care programs that increased public-sector unionized jobs, filled mostly by women joining the paid workforce, and provided an expanded political foundation for strong unions. While work patterns were gendered, the class coalition strengthened and underwrote strong economic participation and political power for women by comparison to the other two models of market society.

Arguably, the most important political role that anti-Black racism in America played during this period was as the foundation of the new Republican coalition that Organized Business funded. President Richard Nixon's Southern Strategy, his "law and order" campaign, and the war on drugs legitimated white Southern backlash against the civil rights movement and made the GOP the new home for white identity voters. President Reagan's "Welfare Queen" bogeyman revived the racialized rejection of social safety net programs and underwrote the political coalition that eroded social welfare protection and rendered all workers more vulnerable[79] and less able to bargain. Combined with the newly emerging religious political identity of the fundamentalist backlash against the women's and gay rights movements in the 1970s, dog whistle racial politics and patriarchal religious fundamentalism continued to bring out the voting base in support of policies that directly contributed to the economic devastation of those same voters. These also formed a new media market that made the outrage industry of Rush Limbaugh and Fox News big business, and the propaganda feedback loop these developments created ultimately transformed the dog whistle of Nixon, Reagan, and former presidents George H. W. Bush and, later, George W. Bush into Donald Trump's bullhorn.[80]

Distinct from the wrongs of misrecognition, we can say that atavistic status-subordination plays two primary economic functions in the political economy of market societies. First, it is deployed to divide and conquer efforts to mobilize economic or political labor power. Second, it is deployed to harness labor at lower wages and under more insecure and dominated terms of employment than higher-status workers are willing to accept at the time. This pattern is sustained during periods of stability but plays a particularly critical role at moments of transformation, when status-subordinated workers and animus toward them from more politically powerful workers were harnessed to introduce new institutions and technologies that shaped the social relations of production in ways detrimental to labor power in the long term.

A Basic Programmatic Framework for a Post-Neoliberal Political Economy

Neoliberalism marked a high point in the extent to which markets were permitted to extend to every corner of production and to operate unmoored from solidaristic social relations. As it turned out, both productivity and justice suffered when agents and firms were left to pursue their self-interest in markets unfettered by mutual social obligation, and when access to basic goods and necessities came to depend ever more completely on earning money to buy them in labor markets in which workers' bargaining power eroded. Post-neoliberal political economy will have to embed more of our production system in relations of mutual solidarity and recalibrate power between present economic elites and the rest of the population by pushing on all three primary dimensions of context—institutions, ideology, and technology.

FIRST PILLAR: PARTIAL DECOMMODIFICATION OF BASIC NEEDS AND CAPABILITIES—FREEDOM FROM WANT

Understanding the political economy of market societies requires us to focus on market *reach* as much as on market *power*. Transformation requires partial decommodification of the basic necessities of life so that more people have a chance to keep body and soul together without being forced to sell their labor and maximize its monetary value.[81] The most comprehensive proposal for such a reform is Sitaraman and Alstott's synthesis of ongoing debates in American politics: over Medicare for all or a health care public option, free higher education, a jobs guarantee, postal banking, or increased public housing. All reflect a fundamental drive to shrink the domain of the market, particularly as it relates to provisioning of basic needs and capabilities.[82] These calls for state-centric alternatives to markets are complemented by calls for strengthening and expanding the role of nonprofit, commons-based, and cooperative enterprises, all of which are part of this broader push to expand the domain of nonmarket production and reduce the imperative to go to the market for everything.[83]

SECOND PILLAR: ACTIVELY COUNTERACTING STATUS-SUBORDINATION

The core lesson of the history of status-subordination in market societies is that no workers and working families are secure unless all are secure. In part, a programmatic focus on counteracting status-subordination depends on ideology. Current efforts at producing a race-class narrative that emphasizes precisely this dynamic—that race has long been used as a wedge to prevent labor mobilization and drive down wages—offer one example of such an ideology-shaping strategy.[84] In part, it requires that we understand how different policies will affect different populations differentially. As among possible jobs programs, funding a universal cradle-to-grave care commitment will have egalitarian and liberating benefits for women, who by social convention and practice continue to bear the brunt of unpaid care obligations. Policing and prison reform, whether abolition or less drastic approaches such as those Shelby discusses in this volume, are in part direct liberation from oppressive practices and in part a rejection of core legal and physical practices that embody the ideology of racism, the new Jim Crow, as Alexander puts it.[85] Immigration reform too falls into this pillar—for example, Allen's proposal in this volume to focus on moderating the stark division of membership that has so long marked immigrants as a subordinate class.

THIRD PILLAR: ACTIVE INSTITUTIONAL DESIGN TO REDISTRIBUTE POWER IN THE ECONOMY

A central implication of political economy is that institutions play a central role in shaping power in the economy, and power, in turn, determines productivity and justice in both the short and long term. Institutional design must therefore incorporate into consideration the coalitions it will bring into being and the configuration of power they will facilitate over time, rather than aiming purely at the end-state it seeks to enact. Efforts like the Clean

Slate Project to transform labor law, the Open Markets Institute to transform antitrust, or proposals from presidential candidates Senators Elizabeth Warren and Bernie Sanders to transform corporate governance with board labor representation or worker ownership, all represent the kinds of fundamental institutional transformations intended to redistribute power in economic relations.

FOURTH PILLAR: PARTIAL DECOMMODIFICATION OF LABOR AND CAPITAL AND EMBEDDING PRODUCTION IN SOCIAL RELATIONS OF SOLIDARITY AND MUTUAL OBLIGATION

Proposals to increase worker ownership and board representation are clear examples. These are complemented by efforts to leverage the state's fiscal power to support cooperativism, such as Senator Sanders's bill to create an employee ownership bank and employee ownership centers to provide both financing and mentorship. These state-led efforts should support the already-existing revival of interest in cooperativism, particularly efforts to leverage digital platforms, as we see in the platform and open cooperativism efforts that Schor and Eddy describe in their chapter. In parallel, we see alternative efforts to reshape the ideological bases of market production itself, emphasizing relations of mutual solidarity and obligation, as in efforts to revive stakeholder capitalism and establish a newly central role for firms as purpose-driven organizations, as Henderson's and Salter's chapters underscore.[86]

FIFTH PILLAR: REBUILDING STATE CAPACITY TO STEER AND BUFFER THE ECONOMY

The Green New Deal frame offers an example of redefining the state's role as central to macroscale steering of technological and industrial policy; other examples are proposals for a good jobs guarantee or universal care cradle-to-grave as a major intervention in gender equality. In this category we can think also of technology policy that aims to steer certain critical technologies: supporting the evolution of labor-complementing rather than labor-displacing automation, and reorienting algorithms and artificial intelligence (AI) toward instrumenting corporate accountability, monitoring and using the instrumented environment to deploy economy-wide exploitation detection and reporting. Rodrik and Sabel's chapter on good jobs and Rahman's chapter on building state capacity are the most obvious contributions in this volume along these lines.

SIXTH PILLAR: DEMOCRATIC ACCOUNTABILITY

Understanding the inherent fallibility of the market and the consequent embrace of revived public engagement in the economy should not come at the expense of preserving the hard-earned lessons about the major sources of state fallibilism—oligarchic capture, bureaucratic decay, and elite groupthink. Many contemporary proposals for democratic reform, such as ensuring proper political representation and significantly restricting the influence of money in politics, go directly to efforts to contain oligarchic capture. Dealing with bureaucratic decay and elite groupthink is marked by proposals such as Rodrik and Sabel's, as are experimentation with cooperative regulation combining civil society and public participation and various forms of municipalism of the type Stears describes. No revival of the state and the public will succeed if it does not assume fallibilism and build accountability, responsiveness, and adaptive learning into these newly revived public systems.

Notes

I owe particular acknowledgment to Talha Syed, whose work in progress on his draft manuscripts under the titles *Capital as a Social Relation* and *From Imperative to Opportunity: Radically Restructuring Markets* I have read and extensively discussed with him over the past three years. Central elements of the framework I outline here, as noted in specific footnotes, are based on or influenced by his arguments. I am also grateful to my coeditors for comments on this chapter and all the contributors to this volume during the Political Economy and Justice workshops, as well as to Sam Bowles, Oren Bracha, Alex Hertel-Fernandez, Amy Kapczynski, Bill Lazonick, Katrina Pistor, Brishen Rogers, Juliet Schor, Kathleen Thelen, and participants in the East Coast Political Economy Consortium and the Harvard Law School faculty workshop.

1. James C. Scott, *Seeing Like a State: How Certain Schemes to Improve the Human Condition Have Failed* (Yale University Press, 2008); Daniel Stedman Jones, *Masters of the Universe: Hayek, Friedman, and the Birth of Neoliberal Politics* (Princeton University Press, 2014).

2. Robert J. Gordon, *The Rise and Fall of American Growth: The US Standard of Living since the Civil War* (Princeton University Press, 2016).

3. Ufuk Akcigit and Sina Ates, "What Happened to US Business Dynamism?," NBER Working Paper 25756 (2019); Ryan Decker, John Haltiwanger, Ron Jarmin, and Javier Miranda, "The Role of Entrepreneurship in US Job Creation and Economic Dynamism," *Journal of Economic Perspectives* 28, no. 3 (2014): 3–24; Ian Hathaway, Ennsyte Economics, and Robert E Litan, "Declining

Business Dynamism in the United States: A Look at States and Metros," Brookings Institute, May 5, 2014.

4. Gustavo Grullon, Yelena Larkin, and Roni Michaely, "The Disappearance of Public Firms and the Changing Nature of US Industries," *SSRN Electronic Journal*, 2015, https://doi.org/10.2139/ssrn.2612047.

5. Jan De Loecker and Jan Eeckhout, "The Rise of Market Power and the Macroeconomic Implications," NBER Working Paper 23687 (2017).

6. Lawrence Mishel et al., *The State of Working America* (Cornell University Press, 2012).

7. Emmanuel Saez, "Striking It Richer: The Evolution of Top Incomes in the United States (Updated with 2012 Preliminary Estimates)," University of Berkeley, September 3, 2013, http://www.nuevatribuna.es/media/nuevatribuna/files/2013/12/20/saez-ustopincomes-2012.pdf.

8. Board of Governors of the Federal Reserve, "Report on the Economic Well Being of US Households in 2017" (Federal Reserve, May 2018).

9. Anne Case and Angus Deaton, "Mortality and Morbidity in the 21st Century," *Brookings Papers on Economic Activity*, Spring 2017, https://www.brookings.edu/wp-content/uploads/2017/08/casetextsp17bpea.pdf; Steven H. Woolf and Heidi Schoomaker, "Life Expectancy and Mortality Rates in the United States, 1959–2017," *JAMA* 322, no. 20 (November 26, 2019): 1996.

10. David Autor et al., "Importing Political Polarization? The Electoral Consequences of Rising Trade Exposure," NBER Working Paper 22637 (September 2016); Yann Algan et al., "The European Trust Crisis and the Rise of Populism," *Brookings Papers on Economic Activity*, 2017, 309–82.

11. Stuart Hall, "Race, Articulation, and Societies Structured in Dominance," in *Essential Essays, Stuart Hall, Selected Writings*, edited by David Morley (Duke University Press, 2018), 213.

12. Daron Acemoglu, James A. Robinson, and Thierry Verdier, "Asymmetric Growth and Institutions in an Interdependent World," *Journal of Political Economy* 125, no. 5 (October 2017): 1245–1305.

13. Jacob S. Hacker, Paul Pierson, and Kathleen Thelen, "Drift and Conversion: Hidden Faces of Institutional Change," in *Advances in Comparative-Historical Analysis*, edited by James Mahoney and Kathleen Thelen (Cambridge University Press, 2015), 180–208.

14. Thorstein Veblen, "The Limitations of Marginal Utility," *Journal of Political Economy* 17, no. 9 (1909): 620–36; Thorstein Veblen, "Why Is Economics Not an Evolutionary Science?," *Quarterly Journal of Economics* 12, no. 4 (1898): 373–97.

15. Walter W. Powell and Jeannette Anastasia Colyvas, "New Institutionalism," in *International Encyclopedia of Organization Studies* (SAGE Publications, 2019), 2:976–79; Walter W. Powell and Paul DiMaggio, eds., *The New Institutionalism in Organizational Analysis* (University of Chicago Press, 1991).

16. Joseph Henrich, ed., *Foundations of Human Sociality: Economic Experiments and Ethnographic Evidence from Fifteen Small-Scale Societies* (Oxford University

Press, 2004); Ernst Fehr and Herbert Gintis, "Human Motivation and Social Cooperation: Experimental and Analytical Foundations," *Annual Review of Sociology* 33, no. 1 (August 2007): 43–64.

17.   Samuel Bowles, *The Moral Economy: Why Good Incentives Are No Substitute for Good Citizens* (Yale University Press, 2016).

18.   Hall, "Race, Articulation, and Societies Structured in Dominance," 191.

19.   Nancy Fraser, *Fortunes of Feminism: From State-Managed Capitalism to Neoliberal Crisis* (Verso Books, 2013).

20.   The framework here is heavily influenced by reading and conversations with Talha Syed, as noted in the headnote.

21.   Michael J. Piore and Charles F. Sabel, *The Second Industrial Divide: Possibilities for Prosperity* (Basic Books 2000).

22.   Powell and Colyvas, "New Institutionalism," 976–79.

23.   This conception of technology as "congealed practical knowledge" is introduced by Talha Syed in a draft manuscript entitled *Capital as a Social Relation*.

24.   Robert W Ozanne, *A Century of Labor-Management Relations at McCormick and International Harvester* (University of Wisconsin Press, 1967), 20–27.

25.   Samuel Bowles, "Social Institutions and Technical Change," in *Technological and Social Factors in Long Term Fluctuations*, edited by Massimo Di Matteo, Richard M. Goodwin, and Alessandro Vercelli, vol. 321 (Springer Berlin Heidelberg, 1989), 67–87; David F. Noble, *Forces of Production: A Social History of Industrial Automation* (Knopf, 1984); Brishen Rogers, "Beyond Automation: The Law and Political Economy of Workplace Technological Change," *Harvard Civil Rights–Civil Liberties Law Review* 55 (November 18, 2019): 531–84.

26.   Karen Levy and Solon Barocas, "Privacy at the Margins | Refractive Surveillance: Monitoring Customers to Manage Workers," *International Journal of Communication* 12, no. 23 (March 2018).

27.   Rogers, "Beyond Automation: The Law and Political Economy of Workplace Technological Change."

28.   Mary L. Gray and Siddharth Suri, *Ghost Work: How to Stop Silicon Valley from Building a New Global Underclass* (Houghton Mifflin Harcourt, 2019).

29.   Erin Hatton, *The Temp Economy: From Kelly Girls to Permatemps in Postwar America* (Temple University Press, 2011).

30.   Veena Dubal, "The Drive to Precarity: A Political History of Work, Regulation, and Labor Advocacy in San Francisco's Taxi and Uber Economies," *Berkeley Journal of Employment and Labor Law* 38 (2017): 73–135.

31.   Juliet Schor, *After the Gig: How the Sharing Economy Got Hijacked and How to Win It Back* (University of California Press, 2020).

32.   Jacob S. Hacker and Paul Pierson, *Winner-Take-All Politics: How Washington Made the Rich Richer—and Turned Its Back on the Middle Class* (Simon & Schuster, 2010).

33.   Bruce Western and Jake Rosenfeld, "Unions, Norms, and the Rise in US Wage Inequality," *American Sociological Review* 76, no. 4 (2011): 513–37; Carola

Frydman and Raven Molloy, "Pay Cuts for the Boss: Executive Compensation in the 1940s," *Journal of Economic History* 72, no. 1 (2012): 225–51.

34. Yochai Benkler et al., "Next Generation Connectivity: A Review of Broadband Internet Transitions and Policy from around the World" (Berkman Center for Internet and Society, Harvard University, February 2010).

35. Kathleen Thelen, *Varieties of Liberalization and the New Politics of Social Solidarity* (Cambridge University Press, 2014).

36. Steven M. Teles, *The Rise of the Conservative Legal Movement: The Battle for Control of the Law*, chaps. 4, 6. (Princeton University Press 2008).

37. Eliott Ash, Daniel L. Chen, and Souresh Naidu, "Ideas Have Consequences: The Impact of Law and Economics on American Justice," July 25, 2020.

38. Jack Nicas, "Apple Cracks Down on Apps That Fight iPhone Addiction," *New York Times*, April 27, 2019, https://www.nytimes.com/2019/04/27/technology/apple-screen-time-trackers.html.

39. Lina M. Khan, "The Separation of Platforms and Commerce," *Columbia Law Review* 119 (2019): 973–1093.

40. Julie E. Cohen, *Between Truth and Power: The Legal Constructions of Informational Capitalism* (Oxford University Press, 2019).

41. Amy Kapczynski, *The Public History of Trade Secrets* (forthcoming, U.C. Davis Law Rev., 2022).

42. Richard Stallman, "The GNU Manifesto," (originally published in March, 1985) https://www.gnu.org/gnu/manifesto.en.html; Eben Moglen, "Anarchism Triumphant," *First Monday*, August 2, 1999, http://moglen.law.columbia.edu/publications/anarchism.html.

43. Yochai Benkler, *The Wealth of Networks: How Social Production Transforms Markets and Freedom* (Yale University Press, 2006).

44. Randall Aaron Lewis and Justin M. Rao, "On the Near Impossibility of Measuring the Returns to Advertising," *SSRN Electronic Journal*, 2013; Brett R. Gordon et al., "A Comparison of Approaches to Advertising Measurement: Evidence from Big Field Experiments at Facebook," *Marketing Science* 38, no. 2 (March 2019): 193–225.

45. Amy Kapczynski, "The Access to Knowledge Mobilization and the New Politics of Intellectual Property," *Yale Law Journal* 117 (2008): 804–97.

46. Trebor Scholz, "Platform Cooperativism: Challenging the Corporate Sharing Economy," Rosa Luxemburg Foundation, New York, 2016, https://rosalux.nyc/platform-cooperativism-2/.

47. Cohen, *Between Truth and Power*.

48. Shoshana Zuboff, *The Age of Surveillance Capitalism: The Fight for a Human Future at the New Frontier of Power* (PublicAffairs, 2018).

49. Schor, *After the Gig*.

50. Amy Kapczynski, "The Cost of Price: Why and How to Get Beyond Intellectual Property Internalism," *UCLA Law Review* 59 (2012): 970.

51. Karen E. C. Levy, "The Contexts of Control: Information, Power, and Truck-Driving Work," *The Information Society* 31, no. 2 (March 15, 2015): 160–74.

52. Barocas and Levy, "Privacy at the Margins | Refractive Surveillance."

53. Ifeoma Ajunwa, Kate Crawford, and Jason Schultz "Limitless Worker Surveillance," *California Law Review*, 2017.

54. Dubal, "The Drive to Precarity."

55. Frank Pasquale, *The Black Box Society: The Secret Algorithms That Control Money and Information* (Harvard University Press, 2015).

56. Solon Barocas and Andrew D. Selbst, "Big Data's Disparate Impact," Berkley Law Library Catalog, 2016, https://doi.org/10.15779/z38bg31.

57. Rogers, "Beyond Automation: The Law and Political Economy of Workplace Technological Change."

58. Lina M. Khan, "Amazon's Antitrust Paradox," *Yale Law Journal* 126 (2016): 710–805; Lina M. Khan and Sandeep Vaheesan, "Market Power and Inequality: The Antitrust Counterrevolution and Its Discontents," *Harvard Law and Policy Review* 11 (2017): 235–94.

59. K. Sabeel Rahman, *Democracy against Domination* (Oxford University Press, 2017).

60. Claudia Goldin and Lawrence F. Katz, *The Race between Education and Technology* (Belknap Press, 2010); Daron Acemoglu and David Autor, "What Does Human Capital Do? A Review of Goldin and Katz's *The Race between Education and Technology*," *Journal of Economic Literature* 50, no. 2 (June 2012): 426–63.

61. Sherwin Rosen, "The Economics of Superstars," *American Economic Review* 71 (December 1981): 845–58.

62. Gøsta Esping-Andersen, *The Three Worlds of Welfare Capitalism* (Princeton University Press, 1990).

63. W. E. B. Du Bois, *Black Reconstruction: An Essay toward a History of the Part Which Black Folk Played in the Attempt to Reconstruct Democracy in America, 1860–1880* (Harcourt Brace, 1935); Barbara Jeanne Fields, "Slavery, Race, and Ideology in the United States of America," *New Left Review* 181 (May 1, 1990): 95.

64. Michael C. Dawson, *Blacks in and out of the Left*, The W. E. B. Du Bois Lectures (Harvard University Press, 2013).

65. Judith Butler, "Merely Cultural," *Social Text*, no. 52/53 (1997): 265–77; Nancy Fraser, "Heterosexism, Misrecognition, and Capitalism: A Response to Judith Butler," *Social Text*, no. 52/53 (1997): 279.

66. Joan Williams, *Reshaping the Work-Family Debate: Why Men and Class Matter*, William E. Massey Sr. Lectures in the History of American Civilization 2008 (Harvard University Press, 2010); Joan Williams, *White Working Class: Overcoming Class Cluelessness in America* (Harvard Business Review Press, 2017).

67. The Combahee River Collective, *The Combahee River Collective Statement*, 1977, https://www.blackpast.org/african-american-history/combahee-river-collective-statement-1977/.

68. Nancy Folbre, *Who Pays for the Kids? Gender and the Structures of Constraint*, Economics as Social Theory (Routledge, 1994).

69. Ivy Pinchbeck, *Women Workers in the Industrial Revolution* (Taylor & Francis

Group, 2004); Maxine Berg, *The Age of Manufactures, 1700-1820: Industry, Innovation, and Work in Britain,* 2nd ed. (Routledge, 1994).

70. Pinchbeck, *Women Workers in the Industrial Revolution;* Jane Humphries, "Enclosures, Common Rights, and Women: The Proletarianization of Families in the Late Eighteenth and Early Nineteenth Centuries," *Journal of Economic History* 50, no. 1 (1990): 17–42.

71. Maxine Berg, *The Age of Manufactures* [this now reflects that I put Berg's first reference a little earlier, at your request]; William Lazonick, "Industrial Relations and Technical Change: The Case of the Self-Acting Mule," *Cambridge Journal of Economics* 3(3) (1979): 231–62; Claudia Goldin and Kenneth Sokoloff, "Women, Children, and Industrialization in the Early Republic: Evidence from the Manufacturing Censuses" (NBER 1981).

72. Fields, "Slavery, Race, and Ideology in the United States of America"; Winthrop D. Jordan, *White over Black: American Attitudes toward the Negro, 1550–1812* (University of North Carolina Press, 2012); Du Bois, *Black Reconstruction.*

73. Barbara M. Wertheimer, *We Were There : The Story of Working Women in America* (Pantheon Books, 1977); Angela Y. Davis, *Women, Race, and Class* (Vintage Books, 1983).

74. The case description is based on Berg, *The Age of Manufactures,* and Tine Bruland, "Industrial Conflict as a Source of Technical Innovation: Three Cases," *Economy and Society* 11, no. 2 (May 1982): 91–121.

75. Scott Alan Carson, "Chinese Sojourn Labor and the American Transcontinental Railroad," *Journal of Institutional and Theoretical Economics* 161 (2005): 80–102.

76. Christopher Hanes, "Immigrants' Relative Rate of Wage Growth in the Late 19th Century," *Explorations in Economic History* 33 (1) (1996): 35–64.

77. Ira Katznelson, *When Affirmative Action Was White: An Untold History of Racial Inequality in Twentieth-Century America* (W. W. Norton, 2006); Richard Rothstein, *The Color of Law: A Forgotten History of How Our Government Segregated America* (Liveright Publishing Corporation, 2017).

78. Julia G. Young, "Making America 1920 Again? Nativism and US Immigration, Past and Present," *Journal on Migration and Human Security* 5, no. 1 (March 1, 2017): 217–35.

79. Jacob S. Hacker, *The Great Risk Shift: The New Economic Insecurity and the Decline of the American Dream* (Oxford University Press, 2008).

80. Yochai Benkler, "A Political Economy of the Origins of Asymmetric Propaganda in American Media," in *The Disinformation Age,* edited by W. Lance Bennett and Steven Livingston (Cambridge University Press, 2020), 43–66.

81. Partial decommodification of basic needs is a central distinguishing feature of Nordic social democracies in Esping-Andersen, *Three Worlds of Welfare Capitalism.*

82. Ganesh Sitaraman and Anne Alstott, *The Public Option: How to Expand Freedom, Increase Opportunity, and Promote Equality* (Harvard University Press, 2019).

83.   Benkler, "Network Pragmatism."

84.   Ian Haney-López, *Merge Left: Fusing Race and Class, Winning Elections, and Saving America* (The New Press, 2019).

85.   Michelle Alexander, *The New Jim Crow: Mass Incarceration in the Age of Colorblindness* (The New Press, 2010).

86.   Rebecca Henderson and Eric Van den Steen, "Why Do Firms Have 'Purpose'? The Firm's Role as a Carrier of Identity and Reputation," *American Economic Review* 105, no. 5 (May 2015): 326–30.

2 Building a Good Jobs Economy

DANI RODRIK AND CHARLES SABEL

Statement of the Problem

Conventional models are failing throughout the world. In the developed world, the welfare-state compensation model has been in retrenchment for some time, and the drawbacks of the neoliberal conception that has superseded it are increasingly evident. Yet there is no compelling alternative on offer. In the developing world, the conventional, tried-and-tested model of industrialization has run out of steam. In both sets of societies, a combination of technological and economic forces (in particular, globalization) is creating or exacerbating productive/technological dualism, with a segment of advanced production in metropolitan areas that thrives on the uncertainty generated by the knowledge economy coexisting with a mass of relatively less productive activities and communities that neither contributes to, nor benefits from, innovation. The sizes of these two sectors and the trajectories leading into them may vary, but otherwise the nature of the underlying problem seems to have converged in the developed and developing worlds.

This productive/technological dualism is in turn responsible for many of the ills these societies face: inequality, exclusion, spatial/social segmentation, loss of trust in elites/governments/experts, the populist backlash, and authoritarian politics. Left to their own devices, globalization and new technologies look likely to aggravate these divisions and the pathologies that flow from them.

Much of our policy conversation today focuses on solutions that elide the true source of the problem. Ex post redistribution through taxes and transfers accepts the productive structure as given, and merely ameliorates the results through handouts. Investments in education, universal basic income (UBI), and social wealth funds seek to enhance the endowments of the workforce, without ensuring productive integration. Broadly speaking, the same can be said about the Keynesian approach to job creation, through aggregate demand management. Keynesianism aims at static efficiency—closing the gap between actual and potential output where the potential output is fixed enough to be precisely calculable. Dualism entrenched enough to shape long-term growth expectations—just the kind of structural deformation of the economy that most concerns us—cannot be addressed by demand management, short, perhaps, of mobilization for war. Though lax enforcement of antitrust laws may have contributed to the concentration of industry in recent decades, and exacerbated inequality by allowing oligopolists to increase their markups or use monopsony power in labor markets to drive down wages, redress through a new round of trust busting is at best a very partial solution to the larger problem, and then only in the long term.

What we seek to explore here is a set of interventions by the public sector—or its delegated agencies—directly in the productive sphere, and in direct collaboration with the most productive segments of the private sector. These interventions are targeted at expanding productive employment opportunities by supporting firms and workers in their efforts to acquire and extend the capacities needed to participate in the dynamic sector of the economy. We call it a strategy of "building a good jobs economy."

The definition of "good job" is necessarily slippery. We have in mind in the first instance stable, formal-sector employment that comes with core labor protections such as safe working conditions, collective bargaining rights, and regulations against arbitrary dismissal. A good job allows at least a middle-class existence, by a region's standards, with enough income for housing, food, transportation, education, and other family expenses, as well as some saving. More broadly, good jobs provide workers with clear career paths, possibilities of self-development, flexibility, responsibility, and fulfillment. The depth and range of such characteristics may depend on context: the prevailing levels of productivity and economic development, costs of living, prevailing income gaps, and so on. Further, a good job need not imply classical full-time employment and could permit job sharing and work flexibility. We expect each community to set its own standards and aspirations, which will evolve over time. In practice, the characterization of good jobs can be as "provisional" as many of the other features of the programs we will describe here.

Our approach has three, mutually reinforcing components: increasing the skill level and productivity of existing jobs, and the competitiveness of firms, for example through provision of extension services to improve management or cooperative programs to advance technology; increasing the number of good jobs by supporting start-ups, the expansion of existing, local firms or attracting investment by outsiders—what the many state and local programs (of greatly varying quality) currently directed to this last purpose refer to simply as "economic development"; and active labor market policies or workforce development programs to help workers, especially from at-risk groups, master the skills required for good jobs. Redistribution, Keynesian demand management, and antitrust policies can and should be important complements to such interventions, but alone or in combination, they cannot be a substitute for them.

Public-private collaborations are at the heart of this strategy. Our focus is on the design principles needed to govern these collaborations. Such principles do not need to be invented from scratch. We argue that they can be borrowed from existing innovative governance arrangements that firms, regulators, and other public agencies have already developed in response to the market and technological uncertainties they face. These arrangements have not been typically deployed in pursuit of good jobs, but they can be adapted to that end.

Active labor market policies have begun to receive considerable attention. A number of studies have reviewed development experience on the ground with some resemblance to the good jobs program. Austin, Glaeser, and Summers (2018) survey "place-based policies" such as regionally targeted employment subsidies and infrastructure investment; Miller-Adams et al. (2019) review a program focused on creating good jobs in communities that face economic challenges; and Autor, Li, and Notowidigdo (2019) summarize evidence on the impact of educational and other interventions. A common theme is the interrelated and conditional nature of the remedies: very few program elements work off the shelf and reliably across diverse settings. For example, Miller-Adams et al. (2019) recommend differentiated strategies that combine skill development strategies (targeted at the local workforce) with programs to attract businesses (targeted at employers). They emphasize the provision of customized services to firms tailored to local conditions.

In view of the inherent uncertainty about "what works," we focus here not on specific interventions or policies, but on a meta-intervention regime for generating good jobs in many different areas of economic activity. We describe a set of design principles for building dynamic governance arrangements that sustain public-private collaborations under conditions of uncertainty and learning, through ongoing review and revision of objectives, instruments, and benchmarks.

The most familiar variant of a "meta-regime" of this general type is collective bargaining, or some close social partnership or neo-corporatist analogue. The expectation is that, in return for a secure place in the constitutional order, labor and capital will bargain to achieve public-regarding outcomes. But for decades now such arrangements have failed because of some combination of inability to adjust to uncertain and diverse conditions and self-dealing by incumbents at the expense of outsiders. To address both failings, we found the meta-regime on governance principles subjecting all decisions to continuing mutual scrutiny by stakeholders under public oversight. These innovative modes of governance, we argue further, allow the parties, beginning with only a thin understanding of the substance and scope of their goals, to assess one another's capacities and good faith in the very process of refining ideas of what the eventual project should be. Trust and coalition building—the preconditions for meta-regimes built on social partnership—are the outcome of joint problem solving under this governance. The good jobs strategy can only succeed in the end with the support of a wide and robust coalition. We argue that building consensus through problem solving helps ensure that mobilization is put to effective use.

"Good Jobs" as a Source of Positive Externality

THE SOURCES OF THE EXTERNALITY

Producing good jobs is a source of positive externality for society. From an economic standpoint, the issues are analogous to those that arise in the cases of environmental externalities or research and development (R&D) externalities, two domains on which we will draw when we develop our organizational recommendations.

A firm considers labor as a production input, with the market wage as its cost. In the short run, the wage rate determines the firm's desired level of employment. In the medium run, it also determines the kind of technologies the firm invests in and the production technique—the mix between labor and various forms of capital. When wages rise, either because of greater productivity or enhanced bargaining power of labor, firms try to economize on the use of labor and adopt technologies that replace workers. From society's standpoint, the result is an undesirable trade-off between good jobs and the level of employment. Today's economies tend to manage this trade-off by allowing dualistic labor markets to become entrenched (Temin 2017): islands of productive, high-wage activities exist in a sea of poor jobs. Labor market and social policies generally determine the distance between working conditions in the two sectors. But a higher floor on economy-wide wages generally comes at the expense of higher unemployment and lower labor hours.

Some version of this trade-off has existed throughout history. In growing economies, the tension is typically alleviated by an economy-wide rise in productivity, which suppresses the distinction between insider and outsider jobs. For example, the mechanization of agriculture during the nineteenth and early twentieth centuries created a surplus of labor in the countryside. But the workers who flooded into urban centers could be absorbed into manufacturing activities (and related services) where productivity and wages were even higher. De-industrialization during the second half of the twentieth century led to a similar but more challenging dilemma. Rapid labor productivity growth in manufacturing (and import competition) resulted in a loss of production jobs and a shift to employment in services, where wages and employment conditions were often inferior. Today's technological trends—automation, the knowledge economy, digital technologies—are leading to a significant exacerbation of the problem. The productivity effects of these new technologies remain bottled in a limited number of sectors and metropolitan locations, generating relatively small numbers of good jobs, while the rest of the economy remains stagnant (Remes et al., 2018). "Where will the good jobs come from?" is perhaps the defining question of our contemporary political economy.

We do not view this simply as a problem of inequality and exclusion, but also as a problem of gross economic inefficiency—a case of operating deep inside the production possibility frontier, or in other economic terms, positive and negative externalities.

The central distinction in an externality is between private and social costs. When private costs of production of, say, a polluting firm do not take account of the costs to society of pollution, the result is a negative externality. When the social benefits of, say, a location decision exceed the gains to the investing firm, the externality is positive. Communities where middle-class jobs have gone scarce suffer from a variety of social ailments. Bad jobs, by undermining the social structures that underpin economic prosperity, create enormous negative externalities.[1]

In his pathbreaking book *When Work Disappears*, sociologist William Julius Wilson (1996) described at length the social costs of the decline in the number manufacturing and blue-collar jobs, ranging from broken families to drug abuse and crime. While Wilson's focus was on racial minorities living in inner-city ghetto neighborhoods, his argument applies more broadly. Autor, Dorn, and Hanson (2019) studied communities across the entire US, differentiating them by the degree to which they were affected by import competition with China. Communities where jobs came under greatest pressure from Chinese imports experienced an increase in "idleness" among young males (the state of being neither employed nor in school) and a rise in male mortality because of drug and alcohol abuse, HIV/AIDS, and homicide. Job loss also led to an increase in the fraction of unwed mothers, of children in single-headed households, and of children living in poverty.

These economic and social impacts of good jobs going scarce are compounded by the political consequences. There is by now considerable evidence from a number of advanced market economies that links the rise of nativist populist political movements to adverse labor market developments. In the United States, the China trade shock had a significant impact on political polarization (Autor et al. 2017). Holding constant initial political conditions in 2002, districts that experienced sharper increases in import competition were less likely to elect a "moderate" legislator in 2010. New legislators elected in hardest hit areas tend to occupy more extreme positions on the ideological spectrum, especially on the right. Districts initially in Republican hands were substantially more likely to elect a GOP conservative. What is perhaps the most intriguing implication of this research is that the labor market disruptions stemming from the China trade shock may have been directly responsible for Donald Trump's electoral victory in 2016. Autor et al. (2017) undertake a counterfactual analysis in which they assume the growth of Chinese import penetration is 50 percent lower than the realized rate over the 2002–2014 period. Their estimates on the electoral consequences indicate that a Democrat instead of a Republican presidential candidate would have been elected in 2016 in the swing states of Michigan, Wisconsin, and Pennsylvania. The Democratic candidate would also have obtained an overall majority in the Electoral College under this counterfactual scenario.

Another paper on Sweden traces out very similar political consequences, even though the shocks that led to labor market disruption were of a different nature (Dal Bò et al., 2018). A series of reforms after 2006 under a conservative-led coalition reduced social insurance and transfer benefits while lowering taxes, increasing the disposable income gap between "insiders" and "outsiders"—those with steady jobs and those who were either unemployed or relied on temporary jobs. The post-2008 financial crisis and recession helped widen the gap. The main beneficiary appears to have been the right-wing, anti-immigrant Sweden Democrats party. The authors show that the local insider-outsider income gaps and the share of vulnerable insiders are positively correlated with larger electoral gains by the Sweden Democrats. Exposure to immigrants, on the other hand, is not systematically associated with support for the political right. The fundamental cause of nativist politics seems to be decline in secure, good jobs rather than cultural or xenophobic preferences per se.

Similar results have been reported for other European countries. Analyzing the political realignment behind Brexit, Colantone and Stanig (2016) attribute a key role to the labor market impact of globalization. Using a China trade shock variable, similar to Autor et al., they show regions with larger import penetration from China had a higher Leave vote share. They corroborate this finding with individual-level data from the British Election Survey that shows individuals in regions more affected by the import shock were more likely to vote for Leave, conditional on education and other characteristics. A second paper by Colantone and Stanig (2017) undertakes a parallel analysis for 15 European countries over the 1988–2007 period, finding that the China trade shock played a statistically (and quantitatively) significant role across regions and at the individual level. A larger import shock was associated with support for nationalist parties and a shift toward radical right-wing parties. Guiso et al. (2017) look at European survey data on individual voting behavior and find an important role for economic insecurity—including exposure to competition from imports and immigrants—in driving populist parties' growth. Individuals who experience greater economic insecurity were also less likely to show up at the polls.

Perhaps the most concerning aspect of the political consequences of adverse labor market shocks is that such shocks weaken support for democracy and foster authoritarian attitudes. The association between economic crisis and the rise of fascism in interwar Europe is well known (Frieden 2006). More broadly, economic stagnation or decline among the middle classes undermines the set of moral values and beliefs that sustain liberal democracy (Friedman 2005). There is evidence from our current moment in history that some of the same tendencies are at play. In the United States, individuals located in local labor markets that were more substantially affected by imports from China appear to have developed more authoritarian values (Ballard-Rosa, Jensen, and Scheve 2018). Similarly, individuals living in European regions that received more negative globalization shocks were systematically less supportive of democracy and liberal values and more in favor of authoritarian leaders (Colantone and Stanig 2018).

In short, there are significant economic, social, and political costs of failure to generate good jobs. Bad jobs lead to lagging communities with poor social outcomes (health, education, crime) and social and political strife (populist backlash, democratic malfunction). A private employer fails to take these costs into account, unless prompted to do by the state. The empirical literature suggests that these negative externalities are substantial—perhaps so great that they threaten the economic order underpinning our form of government. Good jobs, conversely, have enormous positive externalities.

Our focus on the social externality of good jobs is a key difference from approaches that revolve around firm-level practices. For example, in her well-known book *The Good Jobs Strategy*, Zeynep Ton advocates a range of employment policies such as higher wages and benefits that she argues could help employers as well as employees. The argument, nicely encapsulated in her subtitle, is that smart companies can boost profits by investing in their employees. We do not deny that such opportunities exist, and that firms may do well by doing good for their workers. But as Osterman (2018) emphasizes in a review, the evidence that profit-maximizing firms can benefit from "high road" employment practices is limited and far from overwhelming. The vast majority of firms may not be inclined to offer or expand good jobs unless the strategy is part of a concerted collaboration with public agencies in which they are offered something in return. That something could be either carrots in the form of tailored public services or the withholding of a stick in the form of tax easements.[2] Put starkly, creating good jobs under current circumstances makes good sense for society as a whole, but not for many firms. Given the enormous costs of bad jobs, closing this gap seems almost self-evidently an urgent political task.

THE INADEQUACY OF STANDARD REMEDIES

Having established that good jobs are a source of positive externalities, we now explore why the standard remedies are inadequate. The conventional instrument for internalizing an externality is a Pigovian subsidy, which would be a generalized employment subsidy in this case. But successful administration of Pigovian subsidies requires sufficient information about the size of the externality and (what often amounts to the same thing) a relatively static environment. In a dynamic environment with substantial uncertainty, alternative regulatory arrangements are often preferable.

In a classic article, Weitzman (1974) showed that quantity targets may dominate price instruments (such as a subsidy) under such conditions. A price instrument (subsidy) minimizes the costs of achieving a certain target, at the risk of missing the target (because of uncertainty about supply and demand responses, say). Quantitative targets, on the other hand, achieve the requisite social outcome but potentially at greater economic cost than is necessary. When the risks of just missing the socially optimal target—making water drinkable, say—outweigh the risks of inadvertently imposing too high a cleanup cost on producers, quantity targets are preferable to Pigovian price instruments. The analogous argument in the present context is that the risk of failing to generate a sufficient number of good jobs in a particular community may dwarf the risk of imposing too high a burden on individual firms.

Uncertainty also increases the dimensionality of the policy space. In the standard conception of externalities, there is a single quantity, with an associated market price, that is responsible for the generation of the externality. The appropriate intervention consists of directly targeting that price (or quantity) and doing no more than that. But when there is uncertainty about behavior, technology, and the effectiveness of different policies, optimal policies—in the second-best sense of the term—will range over multiple margins of intervention and several different types of policy instruments. Learning about what works and what does not becomes an integral part of the policy process. Establishing mechanisms of feedback from firms to public authorities is critical to the regulatory apparatus. The relevant policy space is of much higher dimensionality.

Finally, an additional problem with standard regulatory remedies in the present setting is that they postulate clear goals ("objective functions," in economics jargon). As uncertainty increases, it becomes difficult to specify in advance not only the costs and benefits of regulation, but also its precise objectives. The government and its agencies will often have to go further and "negotiate" improvement targets with individual firms or clusters of firms. What is a good job, how many can be reasonably created, how do technological and other firm-level choices influence job creation, what are the complementary policy levers that are available, how can that set of instruments be expanded—these are necessarily local, contextual questions. They can be answered, and periodically revised, only through a customized, iterative process of strategic interaction between public agencies and private firms. This process is alien to the familiar, principal-agent framework of rulemaking, which assumes that goals and social benefits must be known in advance if public action is to be effective and accountable. But it is the hallmark of the new type of regulation to which we turn next.

Key Features of Regulation under Extreme Uncertainty

Consider first contracting under uncertainty between private parties (which as we will see in a moment closely approximates the ARPA case). Under stable conditions, each party can specify precisely what it expects in exchange with the other—*do ut des*. Precision, moreover, is often unnecessary, because in stable circumstances the same parties often contract repeatedly with each other, and these relations give rise to shared norms and expectations that guide performance even when there are gaps and ambiguities in formal agreements.

But under uncertainty, the very trajectory of technology is unforeseeable and solutions in any domain are often found by applying ideas that arise far afield. It is neither possible to specify obligations in advance nor to rely on shared norms as supplements or substitutes for detailed agreements. Operating at the edge of established solutions, neither party can say exactly what is feasible, let alone what the other should contribute to the joint effort. When solutions are in view, they will often involve collaboration not with familiar partners but with strangers, with norms and expectations of their own.

Under these circumstances, the nature of the contract itself changes. Instead of defining precisely each party's obligations, the agreement establishes broad goals and a regime for evaluating achievement of them. As observed in domains as diverse as biotechnology, information technology (IT), and advanced manufacturing, this regime establishes regular, joint reviews of progress toward interim targets or milestones, procedures for deciding whether and with what exact aim to proceed or not, and mechanisms for resolving disagreements. The information exchanged under such a regime allows the parties to develop a more and more precise idea of the shared goal while allowing each to assess with increasing reliability the capacities and good faith of the other: to observe if the capable stranger can become a reliable partner and the long-trusted partner is capable of innovative tasks. As collaboration progresses, each party comes to rely increasingly on the capacities of the other, deterring opportunistic defection and generating or activating norms of reciprocity. Joint regular review and deliberate consideration of the interim results thus create the conditions in which informal norms and self-interested calculations bind the parties to continue promising collaboration in good faith. Trust and mutual reliance are the result of agreement to collaborate, not its precondition, just as the precise aims of cooperation are the outcome, not the starting point of joint efforts (Gilson, Sabel, and Scott 2009).

Regulation under extreme uncertainty arrives at a closely related solution from a somewhat different starting point. Under stable conditions, mitigation of externalities is mandated by legislation and given precise form in consultation between the regulator and the regulated parties (subject to judicial review in case of continuing, insistent disagreement). The costs of mitigation are known to the regulated party but not (or at least not easily) to the regulator. Addressees of regulation try to use this information asymmetry to minimize their costs of adjustment while regulators devise ways of eliciting serviceable cost information without being captured by the actors that provide it. The upshot is a fixed set of limits on permissible behavior and a schedule of fines for exceeding them.

Under uncertainty, neither the regulator nor the regulated parties have reliable information on the possibilities and costs of adjustment in the medium term, and only conjectures regarding the possibilities that will open—or not—upon further investigation. Again the response—seen in food safety, civil aviation, and pharmaceuticals, among many other industries—is the creation of an information-exchange regime that ties ongoing specification of goals (here regulatory standards) to continuing exploration of new solutions. Typically the regulator, acting as before under a legislative mandate and after extensive consolations, establishes an ambitious, open-ended outcome: for example, "good water," as measured by minimal deviation from the pristine state of a particular type of body of water such as an alpine stream or Mediterranean river, or a dramatic reduction over an extended period in vehicular emissions from various sources. The regulated entities—private parties, states, or member states and their subdivisions in the US or the EU—are obligated to make plans to achieve the goals and to regularly report their results. Penalties in this regime are not calculated to deter infraction of clear rules but rather to incentivize cooperative production of the information from which standards will eventually be derived. Thus penalties are imposed as a rule only for failure to report or to report honestly, or for persistent failure to achieve results whose feasibility is demonstrated by the attainments of others in like positions; though infrequent, those penalties can be dauntingly severe, often amounting to exclusion from the market or (for public addressees) severe limits on decision-making autonomy. In contract law, such information-forcing sanctions are often called penalty defaults, and we adopt that term here.

The combination of ambitious and open-ended goals, planning obligations, and the threat of potentially draconian penalties for obstinately uncooperative behavior encourages investigation of new possibilities, including contextualized variants of general solutions and collaboration among regulated parties and between them as a group and the regulator. As long as some actors are looking to set new standards though their innovations—creating markets for innovative technology they develop, or simply putting competitors under pressure to match their performance—others will be less willing to cling to the status quo at the risk of being caught out when methods advance. In an environment where the development of technology is uncertain precisely because of the continually surprising abundance of opportunities it affords, the expansive search for innovation is likely to feed on itself, with inquiry generating more inquiry, if only to minimize the chances of being surprised by developments. Search is likely to be collaborative either because projects are interdisciplinary and require the combined efforts of different specialists or because any one approach, interdisciplinary or not, is likely to fail and many actors will consider it prudent to pool the risks of exploration through various forms of collaboration.

Taken together, many concurrent searches will yield a stream of surprises, unsettling the understanding of what is technically possible and raising questions about what regulation can and should reasonably require. "Notice and comment"—the one-time consultation of stakeholders required in rule-making by regulatory agencies in the US—gives way to regular, organized exchanges as regulators and addressees seek to establish common expectation in the face of rapidly evolving knowledge. Mutual ignorance and fear of surprises further bolsters information sharing between public and private actors. By making it risky to bet on the status quo and potentially rewarding to try to surpass it, this regulatory regime turns uncertainty itself from an obstacle to demanding standards into a spur to collective learning that shows, cumulatively, how to realize them.

The Environmental and R&D Analogues

There are two successful examples of regulation—understood in the broad sense of public measures addressing externalities—under dynamic and uncertain conditions. The first is the Defense Advanced Research Projects Agency (DARPA) and its offspring, the Advanced Research Projects Agency-Energy (ARPA-E). They respond to the characteristic learning externalities that arise at the far frontier of science and technology, where for now there may well be no solution at all to a particular problem, and the search for one will likely end in costly disappointment. Worse still for the private investor, even when the search is successful it is unlikely that the daring pioneer can appropriate the returns from the discovery. The predictable result is underinvestment, from the standpoint of society as a whole, in research and technology. The second example is regulation by the EU and Ireland of Irish water quality and the Irish dairy industry generally. This case illustrates the distinctive difficulties associated with mitigation of environmental externalities. Even when solutions can be developed in principle, it is difficult to estimate the costs of applying them, especially since, to be effective, general measures must be adapted to highly differentiated local circumstances. The familiar result is regulation that, for fear of imposing intolerable burdens on regulated parties, is often too timid to be effective, or when resolute, regulation that is ineffective for failure to take account of local particularity. Neither case is perfectly congruent to the "good jobs" challenge. But the success of both is due to the emergence of common mechanisms of governance under uncertainty that, we argue, can make the good jobs strategy workable and accountable.

DARPA AND ARPA-E

In discussions of industrial policy, DARPA, created in 1958 in response to the Soviet launch of the Sputnik satellite, is often and usefully invoked as a reminder that the knowledge economy was not created solely by private actors—entrepreneurs, venture capitalists, and technologists—responding only to opportunities signaled by markets. Far from being a mere bystander, the state, acting through DARPA and related agencies, played—and continues to play—a fundamental role in organizing the research from which are hewn the building blocks of the information economy. Among its iconic contributions are the computer network protocols underlying the Internet, precursors to the global positioning systems, and fundamental tools and devices for microprocessor design and fabrication. The accomplishments of DARPA have inspired a number of research agencies on similar lines, of which ARPA-E—a program created in the wake of the financial crisis to foster innovation in the energy sector—is both the most successful and the most faithful to the procedures of the original model.

Recent studies of ARPA-E examine in detail the institutional mechanisms by which such public entities can orient, coordinate, and discipline collaborative investigation at the outer edge of technical possibility. If those mechanisms are today commonplace or rapidly becoming so, it is not because DARPA's methods are widely emulated but rather because more and more organizations, public and private, are adapting to the high-uncertainty environment, once exotic, that shaped DARPA from the first.

ARPA-E's overarching goal in establishing programs is to eliminate "white spaces" in the landscape of technical knowledge: missing capabilities, just beyond the frontier of current technical possibility, which, if mastered, would clear the way for advances in an important domain. A program might, for example, aim to support the investigation of novel battery concepts with the potential to reduce storage costs by enough to make an environmentally attractive class of electricity grid designs economically feasible. At every stage in the organization of research—the definition of programs of investigation, the selection of a portfolio of projects advancing the program purpose, and the supervision of individual projects in the portfolio—ARPA-E treats goals as provisional, or corrigible in the light of experience. As with the contracts among innovating parties discussed above, precise goals are the result of a search, not fixed from the first.

ARPA-E's program directors (PDs) play a key role in the collaborative setting and revision of goals. PDs are hired largely on the basis of their promise in giving direction to an emergent area of investigation. For instance, a candidate with a background in geology will be hired to create a program in advanced geothermal energy. Once program goals have been framed, the PD does a "deep dive." PDs and ARPA-E technical staff supplement and correct their own background experience with reviews of the scientific literature, site visits to universities and companies, commissioned external studies, and consultation with Department of Energy (DOE) research managers. PDs then test the practicality of the emerging research area in technical workshops involving leading engineering, scientific, and commercial experts. If the research plan (adjusted to reflect the exchanges at the workshop) passes review, a project is formally created as a component of the developing program.

Proposals for research within the projects are developed and executed in the same manner, with goals open to recurrent challenge and revision. Applicants first submit a concept paper: a short document explaining why the proposal is superior to alternative approaches and how it responds to foreseeable technical and commercial risks. Proposals that survive a first round of external review are developed into full applications and reviewed again, with the difference that applicants may rebut criticism by external reviewers. The winners, designated "research partners" or "performers," then negotiate project milestones with agency staff.

The execution of the project is subject, in the argot of ARPA-E, to "active project management," a process with a strong family resemblance to the information-generating regime in contracting for innovation. Its most conspicuous feature is the quarterly progress report that research partners must provide for review by PDs and agency staff.[3] Missed milestones can touch off an intensification of site visits, conference calls, meetings, and written analysis of problems and possible solutions. When projects struggle, milestones can be reset to permit an alternative to the failed approach. Milestones are added or deleted in fully 45 percent of the projects, not counting substantive modifications, which are said to be frequent. If recovery efforts fail, the PD sends an "at risk" letter warning of the possibility of termination. In short, the agency rejects the model of hands-off, bet-on-the-person-not-the-project administration preferred by many established and successful research funders, public and private, in favor of the continuous, collaborative review and adjustment adopted in biotechnology, advanced manufacturing, and venture capital.

ARPA-E is too new to permit any evaluation of its long-term impact. The energy industry—where even demonstration projects require substantial investment, innovators immediately confront legacy providers, and regulation is more likely to constrain innovation than, as in pharmaceuticals, accommodate it—changes so gradually that large transformations only slowly become visible. But the available evidence does strongly suggest that ARPA-E is indeed choosing projects in the zone of uncertainty—where the positive externalities of research and development will be especially large—and using its information-generating regime effectively to make the most of its choices.

Expert disagreement about what is possible is a good working definition of uncertainty.[4] If ARPA-E funds uncertain projects, it should select projects whose prospects the best experts—its reviewers—disagree on. This is what we observe. There is a very slight correlation between reviewers' ratings of projects and the likelihood that they will be funded. Selection is not based on a consensus view of project prospects. Perhaps more tellingly, holding the rating constant, the agency picks the project where the range of reviewer rankings is the greatest—where judgments diverge the most. Plainly, the PDs and the selection committee are relying on other information—rebuttals, observation of the research in workshop dialogue with peers, and much else besides.

Project selection and governance, moreover, do not seem to favor either scientifically oriented projects doing basic research validated in journal publications or commercially oriented projects doing applied research validated by patents or market engagement. Compared to projects in other branches of the DOE doing either basic or applied research, ARPA-E projects have a higher rate of patenting and the same high rate of publishing. Most strikingly, they are more likely than the specialized projects to produce both a publication and patent (Goldstein and Narayanamurti 2018). A plausible interpretation is that they combine practical invention with scientific discovery on the model of use-inspired basic research made famous by Pasteur. As we will see next, commercial constraints and the penalty defaults imposed by EU environment law have made use-inspired research on similar lines central to the regulation of the water quality in Ireland and its dairy industry generally.

IRISH DAIRY FARMING

Regulation, and especially environmental regulation, differs from ARPA-E's contractual governance of research in two ways. First, agreements between the agency and award recipients are fully consensual (i.e., candidates compete for awards). Many addressees of regulation prefer no public constraints on their behavior; some even actively resist the imposition of rules. Penalty defaults therefore play an important role in inducing cooperation with the regulator, but none in the formation of award agreements. Second, ARPA-E faces the uncertainty that arises from manifest limits of our knowledge of science and technology: the "white spaces" mark the places where we do not know the laws of nature that apply to a particular problem. Environmental regulation encounters such frontier uncertainty as well, only it is often challenged instead or in addition by uncertainties arising from the singularities of place: the way known factors—familiar pollutant streams, types of subsoil and geology, for instance—combine in particular contexts to produce unforeseeable results. "White spaces" get filled in once and for all. Once we learn the electrochemistry of cutting energy storage costs by a certain amount, *that* problem is solved. But environmental problems typically have to be redefined and addressed place by place: they are more often white dots rather than white spaces, and filling in one is of limited or no help in filling in an adjacent one. In this regard, environmental regulation strongly resembles and can serve as a partial model for regulation of the "good jobs" externality. In both cases, a central task of governance is creating an information-exchange regime that induces the local actors to cooperate to contextualize solutions while enabling them to benefit from the pooled experience of others, and vice versa.

Within environmental regulation, nonpoint source pollution is the paradigmatic case of contextual uncertainty. The regular emissions of large polluters, such as power plants or sewage treatment facilities, are (relatively) easy to detect and control. Intermittent emissions from diffuse sources, such as the runoff from sporadic detergent use in scattered households, are not. Agricultural runoff is especially refractory because of the great variation in the pitch and absorptive capacity from field to field, the stark seasonal variations in weather and the rapid changes in the level and nature of productive activity induced by cycles of cultivation. We look to advances in the regulation of water pollution in agriculture to refine ideas about the governance of contextualization of the good jobs strategy, and to Ireland in particular, where pressures to reconcile demanding legal requirements to limit pollution with the needs of an expanding dairy industry have produced both an especially sharp understanding of the problem of contextual uncertainty and innovative reforms to address it.

The conviction that environmentally sustainable dairying could be a modern engine of growth came late to Ireland. Through much of the twentieth century, Irish dairy farming was dominated by extremely small holdings, with limited export opportunities and relatively low productivity and incomes. Membership in the European Economic Community (the predecessor of the EU) and its Common Agricultural Policy (CAP) together with imposition of EU milk quotas prompted consolidation, yielding a smaller but more efficient and capable cohort of specialized dairy farms that are still small—measured by farm acreage and herd size—in comparison to industrial producers. The Irish co-ops also consolidated and became first-tier suppliers of ingredients to global consumer food firms.[5] Ireland—which accounts for less than 1 percent of global milk output (Eurostat 2017; FAO 2018, 5)—supplies almost 10 percent of the world's infant formula market[6] and exports 90 percent of its dairy output.[7]

Grass is the source of the competitiveness of Irish dairy. The larger representative Irish dairy farm has the lowest cash cost-to-output ratio of the key international milk-producing regions, including the US, New Zealand, and Australia (Thorne et al. 2017, 70). Homegrown, grass-feed is much cheaper than purchased-feed concentrates; its price is relatively stable, sheltering Irish dairy farmers against a substantial risk. Cows that pasture on grass produce milk solids of superior quality; the grazing cow is, for watchful consumers in many parts of the world, the emblem of food production at its most natural.

For all these reasons the Irish dairy sector and its counterparts in various government departments have, since the turn of this century, come to see the national system of grass-based dairying on family farms as a model of production with a bright future and a central role in the overall development of the country—provided it can reconcile increasing efficiency with regulatory and consumer demands for environmental sustainability.[8]

EU law compelled Ireland to respond, haltingly and reluctantly, to agricultural pollution long before farmers, farm organizations, dairy co-ops, and the state extension service—Teagasc—became active advocates of sustainability. The Nitrates Directive of 1991 sets out precise concentration limits. Farms that fail to comply can be fined or disqualified from the EU single farm payment. Countries that fail to meet national limits must submit a plan for improvement to secure a temporary derogation of requirements or face potential draconian sanctions typical of penalty defaults.

The Water Framework Directive (WFD) of 2000 has, in contrast, extremely broad objectives: "good water" is defined for each type of water body (such as alpine streams or freshwater lakes) as minimal deviation from the chemical values and distribution and quantity of life forms associated with a pristine body of water of that type (Poikane et al. 2014). The basic unit of management is the river basin or catchment: the contiguous territory that drains into the sea at a single river mouth, estuary, or delta. Member states produce a six-year River Basin Management Plan (RBMP) for each basin using a collaborative process in which public officials, experts, and stakeholders specify objectives as well as procedures for translating them into concrete activities. Until 2027, counties[9] that fall short can submit a new RBMP at the end of each planning cycle by asserting that the earlier approach proved technically infeasible or disproportionately expensive. Thereafter, as a penalty default, cost and feasibility will not excuse noncompliance.

Implementation of both directives has proved frustratingly difficult. Adherence to "good practices" in agriculture has often failed to produce improvements in nitrate levels; effective, inclusive participation of local actors in the definition and continuing revision of the intentionally open-ended goals has been a major stumbling block in the application of the WFD. RBMPs, however made, have not achieved their objectives. Many member states will fail to meet the 2027 deadline. The directive was to be revised in 2019, but the revision postponed, among other reasons to reset the penalty default.[10]

In Ireland, compliance failures triggered a series of research programs to improve understanding and control of pollution flows at the catchment and field levels. These programs, linked with similar ones in other member states, have helped generate a web of institutions that is coming to function as an integrated system of local governance of water quality, greatly expanding public participation in environmental decision-making in the process.

In Teagasc's Agricultural Catchments Programme (ACP) of 2008, for example, six catchment areas, differing in soil types, geology, and types of farming, were selected to study the relations among farm management practices, flows of nutrients such as nitrogen and phosphorous, and the resulting changes in water quality. The ACP's key finding is that variations in soil and subsoil types and the underlying geology are in combination so influential in the absorption and drainage of nutrients that general rules of nutrient management, let alone plans based on them, will regularly fail. Poorly drained fields with environmentally innocuous phosphorus values may still pollute because of fast surface runoff while well-drained soils with alarming phosphorus concentrations may not pollute at all (Shortle and Jordan 2017, 17). The policy implication is that a nutrient management plan should be a starting point or provisional guide for joint investigation, by farmers and extension advisers, of environmental risks and how most economically to address them.

This kind of catchment program is part of a larger effort by the Environmental Protection Agency (EPA) and its partner institutions in water quality management to establish a cascading process of national, regional, and local consultation to select areas for intervention and to ensure full and effective participation of the affected local actors in the execution of projects that concern them. The selection process and new governance institutions come together in "local catchment assessments": field-level examinations by the local actors themselves of the source of pollution in water bodies identified as intervention priorities. This assessment determines the local work plan, specifying and prioritizing projects. Agricultural problems detected by field assessments are referred to specialist sustainability advisers who assist the implicated farmers to improve their nutrient management practices,[ii] linking contextualization of pollution mitigation measures on the farm to contextualization of water management at the catchment or territorial level.

We draw three lessons for the design of the good jobs strategy from the Irish and EU experience with environmental regulation of contextual uncertainty. First, while framework legislation (the WFD) and penalty defaults orient and incentivize the creation of new governance instruments for local adaptation of general policies, making those institutions actually work requires continuing revision of initial plans in light of—frequently disappointing— experience. The recent flurry of institution building in Irish water regulation is the culmination of systematic investigation and hard experience, punctuated by false starts and half measures. There are principles of design for these institutions, but no blueprints.

Chief among these principles—the second lesson—is that contextualization in the sense of recognition of the need for local solutions to idiosyncratic local problems is a corrective and supplement to higher-level decision-making and procedures, but not a substitute for them. Local catchment assessments modify the specifications of targets identified by national and regional review and the order in which they are approached. Local authorities and stakeholders are not free to disregard the national list of priorities. Lower levels correct higher levels and vice versa. We can think of contextualization of this kind as a variant of the reciprocal review of collaborators we encountered in contracting for innovation.

Finally, contextualization blurs the distinction between regulation, directed to ensure compliance with rules—order maintenance within a given system—and the creation of new institutional systems. Contextualization induces collaboration between regulators, other public officials, and regulated entities in the development of novel forms of capacity building and public participation in regulatory decision-making. Irish dairy farmers in the catchment projects prepare their nutrient management plans with the support of specialist extension agents, who consult with catchment specialists; farmers with environmental problems collaborate with newly formed catchment assessment teams, connected in turn to a new corps of specialist sustainability advisers. Traditional extension agents propagate consolidated expertise. In codeveloping improvement plans with individual farmers and each other, these new specialists are reconsidering and revising current understandings as much as applying them. Collaborative investigation is necessary precisely because current rules and best practices run out, and establishing what should be done goes hand in hand with understanding and building the capacity needed to do it. When we speak, as we do next, of regulation in relation to the good jobs strategy we mean the term in this enlarged sense of fixing (and revising) requirements and inducing the creation of novel institutions, with all their further spillovers, that enable the addressees of regulation to meet them.

Applying the Model to Good Jobs

The concept of "good jobs," like clean water, is imprecise and needs to be operationalized in a way that is both evolving and context-dependent. Reasonable, attainable targets for the creation of good jobs must remain provisional, to be revised under new information. We can think of them as rebuttable presumptions, mandating behavior except when there is compelling evidence that they demand the impossible or do not demand enough. Achieving the targets depends on decisions on investment, technological choice, and business organization, the consequences of which are unknowable ex ante. Governance under uncertainty takes as its starting point the provisionality of ends and means and the need for disciplined review and revision. Here we sketch what the model would look like when applied to the challenge of creating good jobs through public-private collaboration. We stress similarities, but also some differences.

Simplifying greatly, the uncertainty government agencies face in the ARPA-E case is principally about technological feasibility. The uncertainty in the dairy case derives largely from local adaptation. A "good jobs" program faces uncertainties of both kinds. Creating or preserving good jobs in a particular place often depends partly on extending technological capabilities: mastering techniques that are wholly novel (at least in some particular application) or so new to a given locale that they must almost be reinvented to be mastered. Here ARPA-E's experience with active project management and collaborative review and adjustment of milestones is directly relevant. But fostering good jobs depends at least as much on solving highly idiosyncratic, place-specific problems: failures of coordination between local firms and training institutions and between firms and their (potential) supply-chain partners, and the managerial breakdowns or skill gaps within individual firms and institutions to which the coordination problems point. Here the peer assessment of local problems and new forms of collaboration with networks of extension experts developed in Irish pollution control come into their own. There are many ways to imagine integrating or coordinating the operation of the two variants of the governance model in particular conditions; how precisely is a practical question, to be answered in context when the time comes, and provisionally—subject to correction—in accord with the precepts of the governance model itself.

An immediate question has to do with the timing, scale, and scope of the obligations (and penalty defaults) to be imposed on private firms. If there is a genuine good jobs externality, and a national or subnational mandate to address it, there is no reason, in principle, that the obligation to do so should not be applied immediately to all firms in the relevant jurisdiction. But as just noted, those obligations are inherently broad, open-ended, and at least initially, ill-defined. They would begin with the requirement to make plans to progress toward forms of organization and deployment of technology that in combination produce better jobs, and to make such plans in coordination with relevant peers and institutional partners. But this may well be a too draconian first step. Unless we assume extraordinary consensus in favor of addressing the jobs externality or a dangerously coercive state authority, we cannot really imagine the regulator imposing on all firms, or even all firms in certain sectors, the obligation to make such plans; and if we cannot imagine that, still less can we envisage penalty defaults for persistent failure to make good faith efforts to comply.

It is easier to imagine imposing such requirements and penalties on actors who volunteer to participate in government programs designed to achieve the same outcome and conferring benefits in the form of improved regulation, better coordination, extensive customized support services, or the like in return for participation. The framework goals, continuous monitoring and reporting requirements, and penalty defaults (in the form of exclusion) would apply in this setting, but they would be the mutually agreed, common governance mechanism of a whole portfolio of industrial policy measures addressing the good jobs externality. The voluntary and selective nature of the partnership with state agencies suggests that this start-up phase of the good jobs strategy could make use of ARPA-E's governance of program definition—proceeding incrementally and repeatedly exposing designs to objections and alternatives—and active project monitoring.

A key benefit of these voluntary arrangements over the medium term is to develop an inventory of "good practices"—a repertoire of contextualization measures variously suited to a wide range of settings—that can eventually guide application of the good jobs strategy to a larger set of firms, cutting the costs and increasingly the chances for early successes of broader coverage. Put differently, the initial, selective projects would serve as a pilot program for the new system of regulation, with the qualification that pilots are usually understood as practical tests of promising concepts, whereas in this case their purpose would be more to identify and begin to refine promising approaches under real-world conditions than subject them to definitive tests. As formal obligations are extended, the arrangements would come to resemble the European regulatory model, with a uniform requirement of participation but responses highly differentiated by locale. The need for contextualized support for the less capable actors drawn into the system would grow apace.

An intermediate arrangement might also be possible. Firms might be asked to make a choice between participation in customized compacts for good jobs with public agencies and submitting to a fixed regulatory regime that imposes a common, universal set of benefits and obligations linked to job creation: for example, a schedule of tax incentives/penalties in return for an increase of x percent per annum in the number of employees at wages at or above y percent of the local median, where the rate of job creation may be tied to the business cycle. Firms would then self-select into their preferred regime, providing information, by their choices, about the relative effectiveness of the alternatives and, in time, suggesting revisions to them.

With these design principles and staging practicalities in mind, an industrial policy on good jobs could be introduced in four steps. First the government commits in legislation or by other means to address the problem of bad jobs and no jobs as a constitutional externality that threatens the foundations of our democracy and requires for its solution concerted cooperation between regulators, service providers, and private actors. The framing legislation mandates regulators with relevant authority to put in place information-generating regimes that allow for standard setting and revision. The same legislation creates an interagency body to periodically review and prompt improvement of regulatory responses, and to resolve coordination problems arising from them, while also providing funds and authority for voluntary programs in anticipation of an eventual, step-wise extension of regulatory reach.

Regulators who currently have delegated authority for areas directly affecting job abundance and quality—vocation training, agricultural and manufacturing extension, standard setting, and the like—introduce, in a second step, innovation-inducing and contextualizing governance mechanisms where they are not already in place, anticipating the need for support services to help vulnerable actors comply with increasingly demanding requirements. The requirements can take different forms, including specific employment quantity targets and/or standards.

Where current regulatory authority does not reach, the government creates volunteer, public-private programs to advance the frontiers of technology and organization, or—and of equal and perhaps greater importance—provide support services and perhaps subsidies to help firms bridge the gap between their current low-productivity/low-skill position and participation in the advanced sector. These programs, in their ensemble, would have to combine services to workers as well as managers; they would have to be customized to the needs of particular sectors and locales, and probably both. They would adhere to the design principles of innovation-inducing governance; their performance would be accordingly reviewed and their goals adjusted by the responsible agency and then, if problems persist, the inter-agency body.

Finally, conditional on the success of voluntary arrangements, the scope of these practices would gradually be made obligatory for nonparticipating firms, starting with requirements for submitting credible plans for improving the quality and quantity of jobs they offer, along with their competitive position, by better organization and use of skill and technology. Where appropriate, plans should anticipate coordination with other firms and institutions. Penalty defaults would be imposed on laggard firms that, despite the availability of support services, persistently fail to comply.

To place our proposed framework in sharper relief, we discuss briefly how it relates to some existing initiatives for promoting manufacturing and job creation.

COMPARISON WITH CURRENT INITIATIVES

Of the three major components of the building good jobs program—extension services and cooperative research programs for existing firms; job creation and attraction policies; and active labor market policies or workforce development—it is to the last, workforce development, that the governance practices in advanced technology and European regulation (described previously) have been most consistently applied with demonstrable success. In the case of job attraction, the experience has been nearly the reverse. Local and state politicians outbid each other to win outside investments in new facilities, more often than not in deals that (in contrast to contracts for innovation) specify all terms of the exchange fully in advance: so much in subsidies for each job created at an agreed wage rate in a facility of an agreed type. Though there are important exceptions in conspicuous, recent cases, local learning is scarcely an afterthought. Extension services and cooperative research programs are an intermediate case, with successive waves of institutional innovation leaving the policy landscape dotted with small organizations that appear to do some good in their ambits but in their isolation do not much affect the course of development (Block, Keller, and Negoita 2018; Deloitte 2017). These different outcomes, as far as we can see, reflect the vagaries of policy choices and economic flux, not the inherent ease or difficulty of pursuing contextualization strategies in the various domains. To all appearances, in fact, workforce development should be the most refractory terrain, since programs must engage at-risk groups and address many of the compound problems—financial, educational, familial—that notoriously vex social welfare services. The focus here, therefore, is on workforce development to illustrate an important application of our general governance principles to building good jobs; we refer to some prominent, recent cases of job attraction to underscore the difference between an approach that is deliberately sensitive to the uncertainties of context and one that deliberately is not.

Many of the most successful workforce development programs trace back to Project QUEST (Quality Employment through Skills Training), founded in San Antonio in 1992,[12] in response to a wave of plant closings—an early portent of broader dislocations to come. The displaced workers lacked the skills for the new jobs being created in health care, IT, and other sectors; the service-sector jobs for which they were qualified paid too little to support a middle-class family. Two faith-based social movement organizations, seeing the urgent need for a program to equip the region's largely Hispanic population for good jobs, secured municipal funding to create Project QUEST (Warren 2011).

The new project faced a double challenge. On the one hand, it had to identify emerging opportunities on the local labor market, alert the city's community college system (then still inattentive to business needs) to them, and help shape the substance and timing of new courses to meet the needs of firms and students. On the other hand, it had to learn to support a population of high-risk learners, almost all of whom needed to pass difficult remedial courses to qualify for further study, and many of whom had family and financial burdens on top of anxieties about returning to school.

In facing these challenges, Project QUEST turned to former military members with long experience in workforce development. The first executive director was the former commander of the Air Force Recruiting Service; his successor, and many managers later hired, had a similar background. These managers brought with them not habits of military discipline and hierarchy but rather the culture of continuous improvement—the continuous monitoring of individual cases and rapid learning from disruptions at the core of our governance principles—that took root in many parts of the US military before it become standard operating procedure in much of the economy.[13] An expression of this culture was the early creation of a dedicated management information system, highly unusual for an organization like Project QUEST at the time, to track the performance of individual students, both to keep their counselors abreast of their progress and to allow continuing review of overall organizational performance.

To be eligible to participate in QUEST, students must demonstrate need (generally earnings of less than 50 percent of the local median wage) and levels of literacy and numeracy sufficient to ensure reasonable chances of succeeding at the intense remedial programs typically needed to prepare for the required, basic courses in community college programs. Once admitted, students design in collaboration with a counselor a bundle of "wraparound" services and supports to help them surmount stumbling blocks on the path to completing training, including subsides for tuition, child care, or rent or services to address problems of transportation, health, or domestic violence.

Counseling is continuous and intense. Students meet their counselors individually and in small, stable groups in weekly, hour-long sessions, where they share problems and devise mutual support strategies. A key purpose of these meetings is to identify and respond to emergent problems before they trigger a cascade of failure ending in withdrawal from the program. In effect, the counseling sessions in combination with information about students' class performance allows for continuous adjustment of the wraparound support bundle.

A recent randomized controlled trial (RCT) evaluation of the earnings of QUEST participants nine years after leaving the program demonstrates the effectiveness of the approach (Roder and Elliott 2019). QUEST participants earn roughly 10 percent more per year than the control group, and the gap does not diminish—and may be growing—over time. Crucially, the difference in earnings is the greatest for the most at-risk subgroups: students who took part in QUEST when they were older than the normal school-going age, with children and additional burdens.

In recent years, as community colleges are increasingly drawn into training partnerships with local firms, more students from more diverse backgrounds seek new qualifications, and the failures of limited, "light touch" interventions to increase completion rates become more conspicuous, the schools themselves are successfully providing many of the individualized services originally offered by QUEST. A leading example is the Accelerated Study in Associate Programs (ASAP) of the City University of New York (CUNY).

Like Project QUEST, ASAP provides financial support (to bridge the gap between the available aid and tuition and other fees) and wraparound services, above all a dedicated adviser for each student who furnishes frequent and comprehensive support. Again, a principal goal is to identify and resolve issues before a student drops out of school (Weiss et al. 2019). Cumulatively, over the course of the three-year program, these customized interventions have produced a striking increase in completion rates. Nearly 40 percent of the students in the program group in an RCT study graduated by the end of the program; the graduation rate for control group students was 22 percent. What makes ASAP uniquely successful, the authors of the study find, "is that its multiple, integrated, and well-implemented services address multiple prevalent barriers to student success, and those services are offered for three full years" (Weiss et al. 2019, 279): in our terms, continuing contextualization based on continuous monitoring.

We would expect a program designed to adjust to local circumstance to be scalable, and ASAP is proving to be. Since 2014, three Ohio community colleges have implemented ASAP, and early impact assessments show results comparable to those obtained in New York (Sommo, Cullinan, and Manno 2018). Community college leaders are following the success of ASAP closely and devising their own systems of comprehensive support, with the goal, in the words of one, of "making help unavoidable." In the most ambitious cases, growing confidence in the ability to train low-skill workers is encouraging community colleges to enter extensive partnerships with large firms such as Amazon, where the school offers customized training and student support and the company pays tuition expenses, synchronizes the work schedule of participating employees to mesh with school needs, and, perhaps most crucially, provides a career ladder from unskilled work into management for those who complete the program.[14]

If workforce development programs are increasingly aware of the need for continuous learning in response to the uncertainties of context, programs that directly target employment creation by attracting inward investment seldom are. The most visible of such programs, typically administered by states rather than the federal government, are tax incentives provided to large investors in return for specific commitments on job creation. The Foxconn and Amazon deals, in Wisconsin and New York, respectively, are recent high-profile examples. The Taiwanese company Foxconn had agreed to create 13,000 well-paying jobs in Wisconsin in return for more than $4.5 billion in government incentives. Amazon promised creating 25,000 jobs over a decade in return from an incentive package from New York valued at nearly $3 billion. Both arrangements have blown up amidst controversy; their failures are instructive in ways that demonstrate the superiority of the alternative approach we are suggesting here.

Essentially, the Foxconn and Amazon deals—as well as similar tax incentive programs—were predicated on ex ante contractibility (and hence a stable environment). With enough predictability about market and technology conditions, firms can make rational calculations about employment commitments. And the states have the assurance that firms will deliver. Once the contract is written down, the state remains at arms' length from the firm. In Amazon's case, the company said it wanted cities to "think big." In reality, as one commentator has noted, "the creative thinking was exclusively focused on incentive offers" (Jensen 2019). If the firm turns out to be unwilling or unable to carry out the terms of the contract—as was the case with Foxconn and Amazon, the former because of unforeseen changes in demand and technology and the latter because of unexpected political fallout—there is little room for revision or renegotiation.

Bartik (2018, 2019) has studied such tax incentive programs more broadly and concludes that, even when they work, they are not very cost-effective. This is especially true when local incentives have to be financed by cuts in public expenditures elsewhere (e.g., education or infrastructure). Bartik argues that the most effective employment programs focus specifically on local labor demand and supply conditions. He emphasizes three strategies in particular. The first—and, Bartik finds, by far the most cost-effective—is the provision of customized public services to small and medium-sized enterprises. These include job training tailored to local employers and run by local community colleges, and "manufacturing extension services" that provide marketing and technology advice. The second is targeted investments in workers' skills and training, ranging from preschool programs to wage subsidies, and the third is infrastructure programs that increase land supply and thereby lower business costs.

All three strategies are consistent with our emphasis on iterative fine-tuning and evolving standard setting in lieu of ex ante rules. The design of locally effective incentive packages along these lines obviously requires extensive information discovery and trial and error on the part of local development agencies, heightening the importance of organizational arrangements of the type we have discussed here. Note also that while Bartik's (2018) focus is on manufacturing employment, our proposals would apply to service sectors as well. This is important since it is unlikely that the long-term, secular decline in the share of manufacturing employment can be reversed.

More broadly, good practice in industrial policy has moved away from presumptive approaches that assume the government has a good fix on the underlying problem and the requisite solutions. For example, industrial parks of enterprise zones presume that the absence of good jobs is due to, say, high taxes and poor infrastructure, and they create spaces where neither is a problem. Such prepackaged solutions work poorly when firms face differentiated obstacles—lack of workers with appropriate skills or inadequate access to specialized technologies, for example. The collaborative framework we have outlined here has the advantage that it is explicitly diagnostic—that is, focused on information discovery.

A Reason Not to Despair and a Reason to Hope

In contrast to standard remedies that deal with the preproduction (e.g., schooling) or postproduction (e.g., taxation) stages of the economy, our approach directly targets production. The motivation is that private producers, left to their own devices, do not take the social costs of the scarcity of good jobs into account. In the absence of government action, production is not efficient. An important implication is that the traditional distinction between distribution and production no longer makes sense. Efficient production and distributive inclusion are two sides of the same coin. One cannot achieve one without the other. Questions of production—how goods and services are provided, which types of investments are made, what is the direction of technological change—are placed right at the heart of political economy and justice analysis.

We conclude on two positive notes. First, we argue that the prevailing academic pessimism about job-creating strategies may be misplaced as it is based on conflating treatments with meta-treatments. Second, we note the possibility that the governance arrangements we have sketched out may also help enlarge the constituency for acting on the problems they address.

Consider first the point about policy pessimism. The literature we have referred to when stating the problem suggests there are few, if any, policies that work reliably to expand good jobs. The conclusion that such findings often lead to is either some combination of agnosticism (as in Austin, Glaeser, and Summers 2018) or a call for more randomized evaluations (as in Autor, Li, and Notowidigdo 2019). Under our approach, these mixed results are not a surprise. The dual challenge of dealing with uncertainty and contextualization implies there are no fixed, clear-cut remedies. What is important is to get the governance regime right. With the appropriate regime in place, the hope would be that each locality can develop its own set of evolving practices. In the language of RCTs, our treatment is really a meta-treatment: a protocol for figuring out the treatment to apply in a particular setting. Correspondingly, proper evaluations would have to be carried out at the level of the governing regimes rather than individual policies.

Next, there is the point about building constituency. In many discussions of industrial strategy, the principal problem is creating a coalition of public and private interests in favor of development. The first task is rallying a national or local coalition of private and public actors in favor of a growth strategy with clear, immediate objectives. The formation of consensus and the clarification of objectives lead naturally to the creation of public-private partnerships to advance particular projects. The public actors contribute their expertise and authority in, say, regulation; private actors make complementary contributions with respect to markets and their firms. As long as the state retains sufficient autonomy to avoid capture, the governance of the industrial policy projects is part and parcel of the consensus that underpins the public-private partnerships.

We agree that building political will is a threshold condition for industrial policy. Full deployment of the good jobs strategy would eventually require national mobilization. But under current conditions—when development is as likely to depend on exploring and building domestic capacities as accumulating know-how and capital; when uncertainty makes the selection of goals necessarily provisional and the revision of ends and means routine—governance of a good jobs strategy can presume only a thin, initial, background consensus and does not grow directly from it. On the contrary, the fear that, under uncertainty, ambitious and urgently needed programs cannot be effectively and accountably administered could cast a shadow over consensus building, causing some potential members of a coalition in favor of a good jobs strategy to back away from a risky venture.

An attractive feature of the approach here is that the same institutions of interactive governance that enable the parties to specify and solve the problems they face under uncertainty also enable them to develop the trust and mutual reliance they need to deepen and broaden their efforts. The broad coalition needed for the good jobs strategy to succeed need not preexist; it can and will likely be the result of pursuing the strategy. Innovative modes of governance allow the parties, beginning with only a vague understanding of the substance and scope of their goals, to assess one another's capacities and good faith in the very process of refining ideas of what the eventual project should be. Trust and coalition building—the acceptance of mutual vulnerability—are as much or more the outcome of joint problem solving as its precondition.

A further advantage of this governance approach in coalition building is its compatibility, indeed natural affinity, with efforts at broad mobilization to address societal problems under uncertainty in other domains. The Green New Deal (GND) is the most prominent example. The GND goes beyond the classic remedy of carbon pricing to contemplate large-scale investments in green technologies and ambitious programs to foster greater economic opportunities. Every which way it turns—whether confronting environmental problems or creating employment and, most especially, doing both together—the GND will wrestle with the contextualization of familiar ideas to countless local settings and the collaborative exploration of the technological frontier that gave rise to the design principles of our good jobs strategy. At bottom, that strategy enlists some of the fundamental governance lessons of successful environmentalism in the service of employment creation. It would hardly be a surprise if the GND, combining goals that only recently seemed distinct, reached similar conclusions, creating the core of a broad coalition that helps respond effectively to the economic, social, and environmental externalities presently threatening our democracies and our planet.

Notes

We thank Tim Bartik, Josh Cohen, Paul Osterman, William Simon, and participants in the Political Economy and Justice workshop for very useful comments on an earlier draft.

1. Austin, Glaeser, and Summers (2018) consider three sources of economic externalities from nonemployment: fiscal costs on the state through the tax-transfer system, costs imposed on the family, and spillovers that encourage nonemployment by others in the community. They reckon these costs range 0.21 to 0.36 times the wage of low-income workers. Our focus here is on social and political costs that we believe are much higher.

2. A similar point applies to the relationship between this chapter and the arguments made in the chapters by Henderson and by Salter in this book. We give government agencies a larger role to play because we presume that there will be some but not complete overlap between what firms find to be in their enlightened, long-term interest and what is required for inclusive social prosperity more broadly. We also differ from Weyl (this volume) in advocating a specific kind of government activism, though our approaches are guided by many of the same principles. In particular, we agree with Weyl that we should move beyond a simplistic state-market dichotomy, favor emergent social organizations, and connect social and technological change.

3. Formally cooperation between ARPA-E and recipients of research awards is governed by a cooperation agreement that specifies that the "Prime Recipient . . . is required to participate in periodic review meetings [to] . . . enable ARPA-E to assess the work performed under this Award and determine whether the Prime Recipient has timely achieved the technical milestones

and deliverables" listed in an attachment. A sample agreement is available at https://arpa-e.energy.gov/?q=site-page/funding-agreements.

4. Frank Knight classically distinguished risk—where an outcome is unknown but its probability can be estimated—from uncertainty—where it is impossible even to estimate the probability of future states of the world.

5. Dairy Industry Prospectus Report 2003.

6. See Bord Bia (2016).

7. See Fitzgerald (2019).

8. The Food Harvest 2020 strategy, established in 2010, set a target by 2020 of a 50 percent increase in the volume of milk production over the average of 2007–2009 milk supply (4.93 billion liters). The volume of milk production in 2017 had reached 7.27 billion liters, an increase of 47 percent ("Milk Statistics: December 2017," Central Statistics Office of Ireland, statistical release, January 31, 2018, https://www.cso.ie/en/releasesandpublications/er/ms/milkstatisticsdecember2017).

9. WFD guidance documents from the European Commission are available at http://ec.europa.eu/environment/water/water-framework/facts_figures/guidance_docs_en.htm. For detailed discussion of the Common Implementation Strategy (CIS) as an experimentalist institution at the heart of the WFD, see Scott and Holder (2006).

10. On the possibilities for expanding the grounds for derogation beyond "natural conditions" while maintaining pressure to strive for compliance see Water Directors Meeting, "The Future of the Water Framework Directive (WFD)—Water Directors input to the fitness check process on experiences and challenges of WFD's implementation and options for the way forward," November 15, 2018.

11. On the Agricultural Sustainability Support and Advisory Programme (ASSAP), see https://www.teagasc.ie/environment/water-quality/farming-for-water-quality-assap/.

12. Unless otherwise indicated, this account of Project QUEST draws on Rademacher, Bear, and Conway (2001).

13. For the transformative effect of the introduction of a demanding variant of continuous improvement, developed in the US nuclear navy on the regulation of nuclear power generation, see Rees (1996).

14. Interview with David T. Harrison, president, Columbus State Community College, Columbus, Ohio, April 18, 2019.

References

Austin, Benjamin, Edward Glaeser, and Lawrence Summers. 2018. "Jobs for the Heartland: Place-Based Policies in 21st-Century America." *Brookings Papers on Economic Activity* (Spring): 151–232.

Autor, David, David Dorn, and Gordon Hanson. 2019. "When Work Disappears:

Manufacturing Decline and the Falling Marriage-Market Value of Men." *American Economic Review: Insights*.

Autor, David, David Dorn, Gordon Hanson, and Kaveh Majlesi. 2017. "Importing Political Polarization? The Electoral Consequences of Rising Trade Exposure," NBER Working Paper 22637, December.

Autor, Davis, Aaron Li, and Matthew Notowidigdo. 2019. "Preparing for the Work of the Future." Abdul-Latif Jameel Poverty Action Lab (J-PAL). https://www .povertyactionlab.org/sites/default/files/documents/work-of-the-future -literature-review-4.2.19.pdf.

Azoulay, Pierre, Erica Fuchs, Anna Goldstein, and Michael Kearney. 2018. "Funding Breakthrough Research: Promises and Challenges of the 'ARPA Model.'" NBER Working Paper 24674. National Bureau of Economic Research, June. https://doi .org/10.3386/w24674.

Ballard-Rosa, Cameron, Amalie Jensen, and Kenneth F. Scheve. 2018. "Economic Decline, Social Identity, and Authoritarian Values in the United States," October.

Bartik, Timothy J. 2018. "What Works to Help Manufacturing-Intensive Local Economies?" Upjohn Institute Technical Report No. 18-035. W. E. Upjohn Institute for Employment Research.

Bartik, Timothy J. 2019. *Making Sense of Incentives: Taming Business Incentives to Promote Prosperity*. Kalamazoo, MI: W. E. Upjohn Institute for Employment Research.

Berk, Gerald. 2018. "Building the Problem-Solving State: Bridging Networks and Experiments in the US Advisory Specialist Group in World War II." *Politics & Society* 46, no. 2 (June): 265–94. https://doi.org/10.1177/0032329218773711.

Block, Fred L, and Matthew R Keller. 2011. *State of Innovation: The US Government's Role in Technology Development*. London: Routledge.

Block, Fred, Matthew R. Keller, and Marian Negoita. 2018. "Network Failure and the Evolution of the US Innovation System," unpublished paper.

Bord, Bia. (2016). "Performance and Prospects 2015–2016, January 2016." https:// www.bordbia.ie/industry/insights/publications/performance-and-prospects -2015-2016/.

Colantone, Italo, and Piero Stanig. 2016. "Global Competition and Brexit." Bocconi University, September 28.

Colantone, Italo, and Piero Stanig. 2017. "The Trade Origins of Economic Nationalism: Import Competition and Voting Behavior in Western Europe." BAFFI CAREFIN Centre Research Paper Series No. 2017-49, January.

Colantone, Italo, and Piero Stanig. 2018. "The Economic Determinants of the 'Cultural Backlash': Globalization and Attitudes in Western Europe," August 4.

Dairy Industry Prospectus Report. 2003. "Strategic Development Plan for the Irish Dairy Processing Sector." https://www.agriculture.gov.ie/publications/2000 -2003/dairyindustryprospectusreport2003/.

Dal Bò, Ernesto, Frederico Finan, Olle Folke, Torsten Persson, and Johanna

Rickn. 2018. "Economic Losers and Political Winners: Sweden's Radical Right," August.

Deloitte. 2017. "Manufacturing USA: A Third-Party Evaluation of Program Design and Progress," January.

Eurostat. 2017. "Milk and Milk Product Statistics." https://ec.europa.eu/eurostat/ statistics-explained/index.php/Milk_and_milk_product_statistics.

FAO. 2018. "Dairy Market Review" Rome: Food and Agriculture Organization of the United Nations. http://www.fao.org/3/I9210EN/i9210en.pdf.

Fitzgerald, Ciaran. 2019. "Dairy in the Irish Economy!" *Irish Dairying: Growing Sustainably*, 46. Cork, Ireland: Moorepark Food Research Centre. https://www .teagasc.ie/media/website/publications/2019/Moorepark19-Irish-Dairying -booklet.pdf.

Frieden, Jeffry. 2006. *Global Capitalism: Its Fall and Rise in the Twentieth Century*. New York: W. W. Norton.

Friedman, Benjamin M. 2005. *The Moral Consequences of Economic Growth*. New York: Alfred A. Knopf.

Gilson, Ronald J., Charles F. Sabel, and Robert E. Scott. 2009. "Contracting for Innovation: Vertical Disintegration and Interfirm Collaboration." *Columbia Law Review* 109, no. 3 (April): 431–502.

Goldstein, Anna, and Michael Kearney. 2018. "Know When to Fold 'Em: An Empirical Description of Risk Management in Public Research Funding." NBER Working Paper. National Bureau of Economic Research, September 20. https://www .ssrn.com/abstract=3252548.

Goldstein, Anna P., and Venkatesh Narayanamurti. 2018. "Simultaneous Pursuit of Discovery and Invention in the US Department of Energy." *Research Policy* 47, no. 8 (October): 1505–12. https://doi.org/10.1016/j.respol.2018.05.005.

Guiso, Luigi, Helios Herrera, Massimo Morelli, and Tommaso Sonno. 2017. "Demand and Supply of Populism." CEPR Discussion Paper DP11871. Centre for Economic Policy Research, February.

Jensen, Nathan M. 2019. "Five Economic Development Takeaways from the Amazon HQ2 Bids." *Brookings*, March 4. https://www.brookings.edu/research/five -economic-development-takeaways-from-the-amazon-hq2-bids/.

Khosla, Pradeep K., Paul T. Beaton, Committee on Evaluation of the Advanced Research Projects Agency-Energy (ARPA-E), Board on Science, Technology, and Economic Policy, Policy and Global Affairs, Board on Energy and Environmental Systems, and Division on Engineering and Physical Sciences, eds. 2017. *An Assessment of ARPA-E*. Washington, D.C.: National Academies Press. https://doi .org/10.17226/24778.

Mazzucato, Mariana. 2014. *The Entrepreneurial State: Debunking Public vs. Private Sector Myths*. Rev. ed. Anthem Frontiers of Global Political Economy. London: Anthem Press.

Miller-Adams, Michelle, Brad Hershbein, Timothy J. Bartik, Bridget Timmeney, Amy Meyers, and Lee Adams. 2019. "Building Shared Prosperity: How Communities Can Create Good Jobs for All." Kalamazoo, MI: W. E. Upjohn Institute for Employment Research. https://research.upjohn.org/reports/235.

Osterman, Paul. 2018. "In Search of the High Road: Meaning and Evidence." *ILR Review* 71, no. 1 (January): 3–34.

Poikane, Sandra, Nikolaos Zampoukas, Angel Borja, Susan P. Davies, Wouter van de Bund, and Sebastian Birk. 2014. "Intercalibration of Aquatic Ecological Assessment Methods in the European Union: Lessons Learned and Way Forward." *Environmental Science & Policy* 44 (December): 237–46. https://doi.org/10.1016/j.envsci.2014.08.006.

Rademacher, Ida, Marshall Bear, and Maureen Conway. 2001. "Project QUEST: A Case Study of a Sectoral Employment Development Approach. Sectoral Employment Development Learning Project Case Studies Series." Economic Opportunities Program. Washington, DC: Aspen Institute.

Rees, Joseph V. 1996. *Hostages of Each Other: The Transformation of Nuclear Safety since Three Mile Island*. Chicago: University of Chicago Press.

Remes, Jaana, James Manyika, Jacques Bughin, Jonathan Woetzel, Jan Mischke, and Mekala Krishnan. 2018. "*Solving the Productivity Puzzle*." McKinsey Global Institute, February.

Roder, Anne, and Mark Elliott. 2019. *Nine Year Gains: Project QUEST's Continuing Impact*. New York: Economic Mobility Corporation.

Sabel, Charles, and Gary Herrigel. 2018. "Collaborative Innovation in the Norwegian Oil and Gas Industry: Surprise or Sign of a New Economy-Wide Paradigm?" In *Petroleum Industry Transformations: Lessons from Norway and Beyond*, edited by Taran Thune, Ole Andreas Engen, and Olav Wicken, 231–48. London: Routledge. https://doi.org/10.4324/9781315142456.

Scott, Joane, and Jane Holder. 2006. "Law and New Environmental Governance in the European Union." *Law and New Governance in the EU and the US*. Oxford: Hart Publishing, 211–242.

Shortle, G., and P. Jordan, eds. 2017. *Agricultural Catchments Programme: Phase 2 Report*. Wexford, Ireland: Teagasc.

Sommo, Colleen, Dan Cullinan, and Michelle S. Manno. 2018. "*Doubling Graduation Rates in a New State: Two-Year Findings from the ASAP Ohio Demonstration*." Policy Brief. MDRC, December.

Sabel, Charles, Gary Herrigel, and Peer Hull Kristensen. 2018. "Regulation under Uncertainty: The Coevolution of Industry and Regulation." *Regulation and Governance* 12, no. 3 (September): 371–94. https://doi.org/10.1111/rego.12146.

Temin, Peter. 2017. *The Vanishing Middle Class: Prejudice and Power in a Dual Economy*. Cambridge, MA: MIT Press.

Thorne, Fiona, Patrick R. Gillespie, Trevor Donnelan, Kevin Hanrahan, Anne Kinsella, and Doris Läpple. 2017. "The Competitiveness of Irish Agriculture." Carlow, Ireland: Teagasc. https://www.teagasc.ie/media/website/publications/2017/The-Competitiveness-of-Irish-Agriculture.pdf.

Ton, Zeynep, *The Good Jobs Strategy*. Amazon Publishing, 2014.

Warren, Mark R. 2011. *Dry Bones Rattling: Community Building to Revitalize American Democracy*. Princeton, NJ: Princeton University Press.

Weiss, Michael J., Alyssa Ratledge, Colleen Commo, and Himani Gupta. 2019. "Supporting Community College Students from Start to Degree Completion: Long-Term Evidence from a Randomized Trial of CUNY's ASAP." *American Economic Journal: Applied Economics* 11, no. 3 (July): 253–97.

Weitzman, Martin L. 1974. "Prices vs. Quantities." *Review of Economic Studies* 41, no. 4 (October): 477–91.

Wilson, William Julius. 1996. *When Work Disappears: The World of the New Urban Poor*. New York: Alfred A. Knopf.

3 *The Political Philosophy of RadicalxChange*

E. GLEN WEYL

What the inventive genius of mankind has bestowed upon us in the last hundred years could have made human life care free and happy if the development of the organizing power of man had been able to keep step with his technical advances. As it is, the hardly bought achievements of the machine age in the hands of our generation are as dangerous as a razor in the hands of a 3-year-old child.
—ALBERT EINSTEIN, "STATEMENT ON THE 1932 DISARMAMENT CONFERENCE"

A common pattern in mainstream Western political discussions is to imagine an ideally just society and seek to correct deficiencies of our present society relative to this benchmark. Implicitly this assumes we can easily know what such an ideal political economy would look like and that all we need do is correct a few injustices of present democracy or "market failures" to arrive there. This attitude differs profoundly from the way the same culture approaches technology, where no one believes we are even close to imagining much less achieving perfection. Einstein's words invite us to a similar ambition in reimagining our social institutions to that we bring to physical technology.

Over the past centuries, communications technology has advanced dramatically with the invention of the telegraph, telephone, television, videoconferencing and more. Each generation of technological development made more aspects of in-person human communication accessible at long distances. We can think of the primary tokens of our present formal political economic systems, money and state-issued individual identities, as the telegraph of political economy, conveying as they do so little of the richness that constitutes informal social relations and value creation.

The RadicalxChange (RxC) movement is a community of artists, researchers, entrepreneurs, and activists working to imagine, design, experiment with, and build political change based on radically innovative political economies and social technologies truer to the richness of our diversely shared lives. The diversity that the movement aspires to and has begun to instantiate requires frequent code switching, expressing ideas in the idioms and values of a range of social groups and holding itself accountable to those value systems. For all its attitudinal differences from analytical political philosophy at a broad level, this is one of the many languages RxC must speak to be effective.

As such, this chapter aims to express many of the political values central to the social innovations RxC has promoted and with which communities have begun to experiment. These include a social data and identity structure known as Intersectional Social Data (XSD); a voting system known as Quadratic Voting (QV); a computation-facilitated platform for democratic deliberation referred to as Crowd Law (CL); a matching-based framework for funding organizations called Quadratic Finance (QF); a property regime/asset management system, or Self-Assessed Licenses Sold by Auction (SALSA); and a framework for data governance known as Data Dignity (DD). Readers interested in the details of these specific designs and how they work should visit http://www.radicalxchange.org. Those inclined to think in terms of political philosophy should read on.

Introduction

In his 1854 *Fragment on Government*, Abraham Lincoln wrote, "The legitimate object of government, is to do for a community of people, whatever they need to have done, but can not do, at all, or can not, so well do, for themselves—in their separate, and individual capacities." The possibility that many people, working together, can achieve more than the total of what each could achieve separately is what economists call the phenomenon of "increasing returns." The greatest chance of enabling broad human flourishing lies in understanding increasing returns and structuring markets and governance to unleash their shared value to humanity while avoiding the ills they can provoke— monopoly, opportunity hoarding, majoritarian exclusions, tragedies of the commons. A central goal of any effort to build a new political philosophy or fresh paradigm for political economy should be to lay out approaches to markets, governance, and community that capture the benefits of increasing returns without falling into the traps that the increasing returns phenomenon can generate.

A historical name for this philosophy is Liberal Radicalism, though the

RxC neologism may be more appropriate given the misunderstandings that crop up around the word "liberal" in the United States. Liberal Radicalism was a philosophical tradition that took "radical" critiques of liberalism's limits seriously and sought to design a liberalism that can work in a fundamentally diverse but social world. It attempted, wherever possible, to combine the flexibility and dynamism of capitalism with democracy's public spirit and inclination toward the common good. Classical liberalism was instantiated by capitalism and the one-person-one-vote concept, but no equally simple, formal institutional ideas have, as of yet, instantiated Liberal Radicalism. A core goal of the RxC movement is to develop such institutions.

This manifesto begins by laying out why increasing returns are so important and explains how reigning paradigms of capitalism, populism, nationalism, and technocracy, fail to deliver on the value for human well-being of increasing returns while also generating a range of problems—from failures of freedom to poor economic outcomes—because of their mode of handling the increasing returns phenomenon. Finally, it ends with an attempt to articulate a set of principles to guide the alternative to institutional design that we advocate.

Why Are Increasing Returns So Important?

Civilization is definitionally about increasing returns. Through organizational forms like cities and complex economies, we increase what is available for all of us to consume—whether it is food, water, or other goods. We could all live in isolated huts or villages and be just as well off as we are today absent increasing returns. Cities, which are etymologically joined to the foundations of modern society through terms like "citizen" and "bourgeoisie," are increasing returns phenomena.

The power of human cooperation to generate increasing returns should be harnessed for the general well-being of those who participate in such processes. Instead, many of our most significant contemporary political problems are all failures to harness the power of increasing returns for the social good. Sometimes the increasing returns structure generates monopolies; sometimes it undermines investment in crucial infrastructure; sometimes it leads to failures of governance over matters of common concern. Here are some examples of the problems:

- Network and data economies of scale are classic increasing returns phenomena and are widely seen as the reason for extreme market power in technology. Treating such systems as private property inevitably leads to monopoly.

- There are huge economies of scale in portfolio management that are responsible for the horrific institutional investor monopoly problem.
- The issues around zoning and land use on which so many left-libertarians focus these days are largely disputes over complementarities across plots' use and spillovers at different levels.
- Insurance pools have increasing returns because of selection dynamics, and many of the issues around social insurance of various sorts should be thought of as issues of increasing returns.
- Investment in information goods, whether "innovation" or news quality, is an extreme example of increasing returns where the cost to create news for one person to consume is the same as the cost to produce it for all to consume, but the benefit to consumption of high-quality news by all produces a phase shift in value to the society.
- Most environmental issues are best seen as resources that bring benefits to many people if preserved. Global change is the most extreme example, where anything we do to the climate affects the welfare of literally everyone living on the planet.

These challenges show how our reigning paradigms of the economy and of governance have failed us because they are not equipped to cope with the challenge and opportunity of increasing returns. It is time for radical change in those paradigms. What follows is a critique of the reigning economic paradigm of capitalism and the dominant majoritarian, nation-state-based, populist alternative typically ranged against it.

Beyond Capitalism

The default politico-economic ideology of today's elites is capitalism—or what is sometimes called neoliberalism. While many of the core arguments for capitalism are well- expressed by thinkers such as Milton Friedman (for example, in his classic *Capitalism and Freedom*), the target here is not some caricatured or extreme form of capitalism. Moreover, the critique here is offered in the language of economics that is central to the traditional formulation and justification of capitalism, as it is most useful to critique a worldview as much as possible on its own terms. Nor do we treat all the problems with capitalism. Instead, we focus here simply on the fundamental inability of capitalism's core concepts to grapple productively with the issue of increasing returns.

Most capitalists would agree with the argument above, that increasing returns are the central theoretical problem of political economy, in addition to being, as a practical matter, at the heart of many of our day's major political questions. Yet capitalism offers no coherent framework for grappling with increasing returns.

An endless stream of work shows that markets based on private property and competition—the type of markets that capitalism utilizes—do not work well in contexts with increasing returns. Classic results include the inefficiency of average cost pricing under increasing returns, famously associated with Harold Hotelling, and the free-rider problem associated with Paul Samuelson. There are different ways to phrase it: with increasing returns, marginal cost pricing does not cover average costs; there is natural monopoly with increasing returns; there is a free-rider problem; private provision of public goods leads generically to only one contributor.

The basic problem is that capitalism is based on the principle that every contributor should be paid their marginal contribution. Yet the key feature of increasing returns is that everyone together achieves much more than all can achieve individually. This implies that everyone's marginal contribution, once all others are participating, is far greater than their proportional share of the total produced, and thus everyone can "claim credit" for more than can, in total, possibly be paid out. In such situations, capitalism simply outputs an error. If you want a capitalist system based on private property you have to decompose the final product into the components of what each person contributed, at least on the margin, but the definition of increasing returns phenomena is that such decomposition is impossible.

The point can be made the other way around as well, by focusing not on the production of increasing returns goods but on their consumption. Consider the common rhetoric from technologists that "the internet is the best deal we have ever gotten." Most of us pay, so the argument goes, only hundreds of dollars each year, while most of us would be willing to pay $10k–20k to maintain access. Regardless of whether these numbers are precisely right, one must immediately ask what else that we pay little for we would be willing to pay a lot for. As examples, consider running water, sewage, electricity, vaccines, city streets (yes, it is not hard to find historical and present times and places without safe sidewalks), and, for that matter, livable weather and air to breath. If you added our willingness to pay for all of these things, you would arrive at far more than any of us have available to pay for them. Asking for an accounting of the fraction of value in our lives attributable to these various causes is like asking what fraction of a body's life depends on the heart, lungs, or brain. Matters grow yet worse if we recognize that each of these technologies and elements constituting our well-being itself grew out of the increasing returns collaboration of millions of people who, for example, created the websites that built search engines and so on to make the modern Internet possible.

Such is always the case with increasing returns phenomena. Private ownership is economically incoherent because of the collective nature of value creation in modern economies. The best deal we have ever gotten is the possibility of civilization, powered by increasing returns, and which makes such a linear accounting for the sources of our well-being on which capitalism relies impossible.

Now the problem with capitalism's failure to grapple with phenomena that cannot be decomposed into individual contributions of production or consumption is that goods that depend on a costly upfront investment (for instance, news) can fail to be produced in a capitalist environment, can be co-opted into monopoly power and thus their availability restricted. You can put a Band-Aid on this problem—a little tax-funded research and development here, a bit of social insurance there, a sprinkling of anti-monopoly policy—but ultimately these are all precisely the sort of unsystematic and often discretionary state interventions that capitalists tend to fear. To the extent that there is any method behind all of this, it is statist, an expectation that nation-state investments can compensate for the failures of market capitalism to deliver public goods. If such Band-Aids are the capitalist answer to the problem of political economy, capitalism itself does not really offer an answer. Capitalist thinking as currently constituted, because of the previous points, is an intellectual cul-de-sac and a dangerous distraction from the serious project of responding to the challenges of our time. Political economy still has a theoretical and practical question to resolve.

Beyond Populism

This basic critique of capitalism is far from new. It is at the core of many arguments for socialism. During the twentieth century, many nation-states experimented with lodging the collective nature of value (hopefully democratic) in nation-state governments. While out of fashion for some time, this approach has reemerged prominently in recent years through "populist" movements that see the fulfillment of the interests of majorities within such states as the path for resolving the problems of capitalism

The problem with such populism is not the collective or "socialist" conception or value, evident in increasing returns phenomena. It is instead the valorization of the majority will within "The State"—or more generally, some historically derived but ultimately quite arbitrary polity, as the locus of collective action—and the effort to lodge authority and responsibility to govern increasing returns phenomena in this imagined actor. Many ideas for increased collective action at the level of the state (such as much higher marginal income or carbon tax rates funding a social dividend or free university tuition) may be more or less appealing, but they are not at the core of problematic populism. The subset of really concerning ideas are those policies that aim to transfer significant discretionary power of often unprecedented scope to currently existing nation-states. The relevant transfers of power are bound to interact with preexisting mechanisms of governance intended to hedge unchecked power, yet little attention is given to the question of whether these new grants of power will obliterate those hedges or whether they ought themselves to be hedged for the sake of preserving liberties, both negative and positive.

Examples of problematic populism grants of power include:

- Calls for nationalizing, placing under detailed discretionary state regulation, or creating "national champion" versions of social media platforms like Facebook and Google
- Plans to create a single-payer health system for the entirety of the US that would administer prescription drug prices
- Many of the vaguer and more ambitious proposals labeled "Green New Deal"
- A Social Wealth Fund (SWF), managed by the US federal government

The last example, especially in the version proposed by leading contemporary populist thinker Matt Bruenig, makes the problem particularly clear. An SWF, managed by the US federal government would come to be the dominant voting shareholder in most publicly traded American corporations. Either a democratically chosen administrator or the public directly would vote the shares (which would be held, roughly, equally by all Americans) and the fund would come to manage something like 30 to 70 percent of US public equities. To be clear, this SWF policy on which much of the critique below will focus is not the same as one where, say, 30 percent of equities are owned by a Social Wealth Fund and are passively managed with shares not being voted on and no corporate governance involvement. Populists usually explicitly oppose this option. They focus on the importance of nation-state-based majoritarian control over corporate governance and the economy. But giving dramatically increased discretionary powers to existing simple democratic states to address collective action problems is dangerous. These difficulties could be overcome by codesigning new governance structures (as Rodrik and Sabel imagine) along with these increased powers that would help ensure they are used rather than abused.

But populism as critiqued here does not focus on this design and hopes that the state, controlled by some form of democracy, will act as a *deus ex machina* to solve large-scale social problems. Just as capitalist economists have failed to come to grips with the phenomenon of increasing returns at either a theoretical or practical level, political scientists with their focus on national-level democracy have also failed to come to grips with the relation between governance and increasing returns at either a theoretical or practical level.

What political scientists have failed to grapple with is that the phenomenon of increasing returns often leads to a separation between natural polities (NPs), which are sets of people affected by and knowledgeable about a set of decisions, and actual polities (APs), which are the electoral polities of the democratic states. Many of the collective action problems we face today have an NP that lines up poorly with existing states, being smaller, larger, or most commonly cutting across state borders. The examples invoked above also pertain here: new drug development, technology, news production, immigration, global inequality, and environmental questions are all phenomena where the increasing returns dimension of the good also disregards currently existing nation-state borders. In fact, it is challenging to find examples of increasing returns phenomena where current nation-states *are* a good match to the NP.

When is it reasonable to expect a democratic state to succeed at governing an increasing returns phenomenon? We should expect simple democracy, based on some version of one-person-one-vote (1p1v) and without extensive "liberal" constraints (such as federalism, checks and balances, strong protections of individual rights, international treaties), to lead to good outcomes exactly when "the majority is right." Majority rule is appropriate on issues where the preferences and knowledge of a typical citizen are reasonably representative of the overall good of society. This is commonly the case in reasonably homogeneous societies, where differences of interest and opinion are relatively "randomly distributed," or on issues where this is the case assuming that all the relevant individuals for a decision are enfranchised. It will tend to fail dramatically when there are deep, consistent, and politically salient "fractures" that divide societies, at least on certain important issues, into aggrieved minorities. These minorities are either divided against the majority or are disenfranchised, such as in cases where many of the individuals most affected by important political decisions do not have a vote.

To formalize this, we can say that if the AP diverges in a severe way from the NP, we should expect simple democracy to lead to very bad outcomes. To keep matters simple, the focus here is on inclusion or exclusion from the polity as a 0–1 variable. In most cases in practice, the AP and NP will both be weighted (some will have a more effective voice than others and some will be more or less affected by a decision), but this complication only further strengthens the argument because simple democratic mechanisms based on 1p1v have a hard time dealing with this subtlety.

Importantly, the failure of simple democracy when actual and natural polities diverge is one of the most persistent themes of political history. It is useful to divide historical cases into three buckets:

1. AP > NP: this is the case of minority or local group oppression, when the actual polity is much larger than the natural polity for an issue.
2. NP > AP: this is the case where important individuals are disenfranchised from the decision.
3. NP ≠ AP: this is the generic case when the natural polity cuts across the boundaries of the actual polity and is neither smaller nor larger; some but not all members of the actual polity are in the natural polity, and there are members of the natural polity disenfranchised from the actual polity.

Some examples of extreme failures of democracy under these conditions are listed below. They are chosen to be particularly salient and persuasive to those who have populist inclinations. However, nearly endless examples, contemporary and historical reaching back to the dawn of democracy, exist. Disastrous examples of AP > NP:

1. The Rohingya genocide: The end of military and the brief emergence of democratic rule in Myanmar was widely celebrated around the world. But, as has been widely noted, it appears to have only fueled long-standing sectarian divisions between the Buddhist majority and the Muslim Rohingya minority, precipitating an ongoing genocide. Here the NP is local Rohingya communities and the AP is the Burmese nation-state.
2. Underrepresented communities in US cities: Many US cities have a variety of substantial minorities (namely, African American, various immigrant communities, artist communities, and so on) that are systematically underrepresented and neglected by majority-elected city administrations. Here the NP is these communities and the AP is the city.

Disastrous examples of NP > AP:

1. Global change: Anthropogenic climate catastrophe is one of the greatest threats facing the world. Yet the effects being global, many nation-states have strong incentives to free-ride on mitigation efforts, leading to our present stalemate. Here the NP is essentially the cosmopolis and the APs are a bunch of nation-states.

2. Migration and global inequality: Inequality across countries is two to three times greater, depending on how you measure it, than is inequality within countries, and millions of people around the world would be willing to take a substantial chance of death to have the opportunity for safety and economic advancement that wealthy countries offer. Yet wealthy countries are increasingly and violently slamming their doors shut not just against the desperately and unjustly impoverished but even against those fleeing mass murder. Here the NP is the set of people who would like to live in wealthy countries, and the AP is those currently living there.

Disastrous examples of NP ≠ AP:

1. International waterways: Nature does not respect the arbitrary boundaries of nation-states. Two of the largest rivers in the world, which supply crucial public goods and can easily be degraded by exploitation, are the Amazon and Nile, which each cross at least a half dozen countries. The free-riding by, and conflicts among, the nation-states that lie along these rivers has contributed to systematic degradation, poisoning, and deforestation. Yet the NP here is not simply the whole of these states but instead those who live along and directly benefit from the river, which in most cases is a minority or even a small minority of each polity. Thus, the NP is the union of several national minorities, while the APs are a collection of national polities.

2. The war on drugs: The war on drugs in the Americas has been roughly a war waged against poor and especially Black and brown citizens, allegedly for the benefit of these same groups. Putting aside the opioid crisis (the policy response to which has been, unsurprisingly, very different), it would not be far off to argue that there has been virtually no drug enforcement against the well-off white Americans who, many studies suggest, are the main consumers of most cocaine. Bearing the brunt of the drug war are Black and brown US citizens, who have been incarcerated at literally record-setting levels, and the tens of millions in Central and

South America whose lives have been shattered by drug violence. The NP here is the Black and brown minorities of the US plus the sometimes minority, sometimes majority (depending on country) of Latin Americans. Yet the AP of American citizens has consistently supported doubling down on policies that destroy the lives of the NP.

In short, it seems quite clear that not just in theory but in practice, significant divergences between the AP and NP tend to lead to very poor outcomes from populism.

Some claim that modern democratic states can avoid the fundamental problem of populism. One version of this argument sees this improvement over time resulting from the process of democratic dialogue. Another version sees this improvement coming from the training of a mission-driven and expert bureaucratic technocracy. There is a great deal that could be said historically and empirically about these claims. But the primary problem is more abstract: they do not allow one to distinguish among different forms of governance in the first place.

Perhaps the leading contention of neoreactionary thinkers is that good governance will come from the appointment of a benevolent autocrat in the mold of Lee Kuan Yew, who will then create a mission-driven and efficient administrative bureaucracy beneath him (and it is almost always a him, in their imagining). A leading contention of many religious conservative defenders of capitalism is that capitalism will allow a space for the emergence of a benevolent civil society discourse and public-spirited business leaders who will elevate moral culture and address the failures of capitalism. A central argument among less democratically inclined members of the contemporary global elite is that the quality of their discourse and reflection on global challenges is likely to lead to policies that better serve the average citizen of the globe than would arise from distributing voice broadly. And, indeed, there are historical examples of these things occurring, as demonstrated by Lee's case and many generous and effective philanthropists and moves by elites to establish supranational institutions with limited direct democratic involvement. In other words, contemporary defenses of democracy often slip into defenses of bureaucracy and technocracy, not of democracy itself.

Yet policymakers who claim that the modern democratic state has distinctive virtues would vehemently reject these arguments. They appear to think there is something about the formalism of democracy and the vision of some sort of equal voice and power for citizens that is critical to will formation, establishment of a legitimate and successful bureaucracy, and productive collective decision-making. Otherwise they would not be arguing for the assumption of power by such preexisting democratic polities. Instead of arguing for the establishment of a SWF that owns most of the American corporate economy, they could simply focus on improving any of the plentiful bureaucracies or already existing opportunities for public discussion. But this leads one naturally to the question of what those distinctive virtues of democracy are. Formal rights to vote for some portion of a polity's population, and democratic participation by those with voting rights, as well as their participation in a functioning civil service cannot suffice to deliver what those who defend democracy promise.

The experience of the twentieth century with nation-states, and the hope that democratic but exclusionary forms within them will lead through a process of bureaucratization and democratic dialogue toward justice, is an unhappy one. Zionists who escaped (originally democratically elected) Nazi terror hoped to establish a Jewish democratic state. That state excluded from political influence most of the Arab people whose ancestral lands it occupies. Every year of the boisterous democratic debate in Israel, more vital than anywhere in the world, seems to be leading *Hatikvah bat shnot 'alpayim* (the hope of 2,000 years) ever more in the direction of oppressive and exclusionary ethnonationalism. This is clearly not a result of an insufficiently active democracy or an incompetent civil service; quite the reverse. It seems quite clearly a result of an exclusionary construction of the polity. And with increasing returns phenomena that cross the borders of APs, we have new levels of exclusion to contemplate. Given the tremendous effects each nation has on others—for example, through global warming and the war on drugs— any policy focused on empowering current nation-states simply deepens the problem of APs dominating NPs whose members they exclude.

Still, we need not abandon the concept of democracy, just its tight connection to the existing nation-state framework. In contrast, to majoritarian democratic nation-states that have perfected the politics of exclusion, a specific set of nations and regions have made progress in developing democratic and civil service cultures of the "progressive" sort that proactively seek inclusion and alignment of APs with NPs. Despite their differing individual political histories, Singapore, Scandinavia, Switzerland, Estonia and Taiwan were all deeply influenced by the Liberal Radical tradition and by ideas about decentralization of power. Henry George and other radical political economists were central to the canon shaping thought in these locations in a way they were not to the same extent anywhere else in the world. These countries and regions have exceptionally efficient bureaucracies, use market mechanisms of an enlightened community-oriented variety extensively, and have (except for Singapore) among the best democratic cultures and most vital civil societies in the world. This suggests that the same types of institutions that effectively decentralize power may also be conducive to, in other less clear and formal ways, improving democracy and governance. Importantly, we will see in the final section on imagining alternatives that mechanisms for governance by decentralization need not be limited in their function to geographies that align with nation-state boundaries. Instead, these mechanisms can be deployed for use across the public sphere created by NPs.

Successful exercises of state power have coevolved tightly with detailed governance structures that help align actual polities and natural polities through checks and balances. While such systems are described by extreme capitalists as "populist" or "central planning" they are not populist in the sense here: they involve simple, transparent, widely understood legal or quasi-legal regimes that decentralize power in a way that is quite different from and much more effective than simple capitalism. They constrain the discretionary power of the democratic state, as well as that of private wealth. There are also international equivalents, such as restraints on nuclear weapons, rules of war, and trade barriers, that try to deal with NP > AP and NP ≠ AP cases; while these have been relatively ineffective, there are increasing experiments with creative new means of international cooperation, such as blockchains and open-source software collaborations. Such systems are precisely what we need to build.

The important point, coming out of the Georgist tradition, is that social institutions need to be worthy of the trust we place in them to deliver good governance while protecting freedom roughly in parallel to our entrusting them with powers based on that trust. We should not entrust power to social institutions that have proved themselves unworthy of our trust or where no work has been done to assess their trustworthiness from the point of view of governance and results. Trust can be earned based on clear arguments about why power is appropriately distributed, by good empirical performance on average, by clearly visible experiments, and so forth. Along all these dimensions, we have little reason to trust in the likelihood of success for policies that rapidly give great amounts of power to majoritarian states with few predesigned checks and balances. Many of the sort of disasters that have occurred in previous mismatches between NP and AP are likely to occur if the discretionary authority of actual polities is dramatically increased in the ways that current statists are advocating. We have no more reason to trust democratic populism on matters of governance than to trust neoliberalism on economic policy.

It is worth concluding this section by returning to the example of the SWF to draw out in more detail the likely failures of governance we should expect from such a policy. As a detailed example, consider the SWF where, remember, either a government-appointed board or a democratic majority would effectively become the controlling shareholders of most US public companies. The natural polity here would be the workers and product consumers of these corporations and the actual polity would be the US electorate. What could go wrong from this divergence?

Many employees and customers of US companies are abroad. Given extreme nationalism and protectionism, it seems quite likely that US national democratic control of these companies would lead to protectionism by owner preference, probably of such an extreme form that the US's status as a "market economy" under World Trade Organization (WTO) rules would be suspended. Observe the behavior, prior to checks from the European Union, of European state-owned national champions.

- Public companies would probably do everything within existing laws to stop hiring undocumented and perhaps even certain types of documented migrants.
- Efforts of US companies to combat climate change, which are increasingly gaining steam, would probably be stopped in their tracks given the widespread skepticism of the American public about climate change.
- Efforts at diversity and inclusion by corporations would probably be significantly reduced, based on current public opinion on these issues.
- Investments in research and development on speculative or unpopular projects would likely be squashed, while investment in wasteful white elephant schemes that are attention-grabbing would probably be greatly increased.

In short, the corporate sector would come to inherit all the dysfunctions of the public sector (though, admittedly, some of the dysfunctions of the corporate sector, such as chronically low investment, low wages, and exploitation of US consumers, would thereby be eliminated). But now, rather than these two dysfunctions checking and balancing each other, every US company would come to look like the current US government and would be roughly equally likely at any time to be ruled by a nativist protectionism, capitalist conspiracies, or a moderately progressive agenda.

This seems disastrous. For all the monopolization and cruelty of the current corporate economy, at least companies seek workers and customers in a reasonably flexible and adaptive manner that makes the base they serve (even if poorly) somewhat heterogeneous and diverse. Furthermore, to the extent that not all companies have precisely the same set of investors, the capitalists in control, while all wealthy elites, at least come from a range of different power centers rather than a single actual polity. Effectively nationalizing all of these would eliminate that tendency and homogenize the control of much of the world's economy under a single wildly unrepresentative AP.

A natural response would be, "If it works in Alaska and Norway, why not in the US?" The answer should be obvious: those communities are a tiny part of the global economy while the US is a huge part. Thus, effectively those vehicles are purely for investment, and they are small investment funds relative to any of the problematic funds like those mentioned above. Their NP is thus their investors (the Alaskan and Norwegian polities) and pure investment services (with limited voting power) have the property that they are reasonably scale invariant. To the extent that there are harms from this concentration, they are felt by consumers and workers around the world who experience reduced competition, not by Alaskans and Norwegians in particular, so even if there are large harms, they would be hard to see. In short, the fact that things have gone reasonably well for Alaskans and Norwegians because of their large SWFs is simply a non-sequitur with regards to the key problems with a US SWF.

Other examples of recent statist ideas pose quite clear similar risk. Placing global platforms like Facebook and Google under the discretionary control of the US democratic polity would likely result in far more rampant politicization of content (such as news), further erode civil society, and could even be used as a weapon against unfriendly but democratic governments. A single-payer system for the entire US economy, which provides most of all funding for pharmaceutical research, would be qualitatively different from systems in other countries. Such a system would very likely be able to regulate drug prices down to levels like those in other single-payer systems and thus cut off most of the funding for pharmaceutical research at present. A "Green New Deal" could easily become a protectionist football, used to favor domestic green projects over Chinese ones that are more efficient, further escalating trade tensions with China. Of course, none of this should prejudice us against carefully designed institutions that adopt these labels.

Championing idealistic schemes to address public goods like inequality and the environment without parallel developments in effective governance mechanisms endangers both liberty and prosperity. If this approach captures the popular imagination, it will not solve the primary collective action problems we are facing. Instead, it will further entrench the nonalignment of

APs and NPs, fostering resentment in those who are excluded from decision-making and oppressed as a result. This will only worsen existing conflicts.

Imagining an Alternative

So, if we are to reject capitalism and populism (and related approaches of nationalism and technocracy discussed elsewhere), what's left? The RadicalxChange movement has produced several designs that steer away from these pitfalls and illustrate a different approach to social imagination and to harnessing increasing returns for the good of humankind. Many of the designs are quite specific, however, and it is easy to get lost in the details. The focus here is therefore on broader principles, with brief mentions of illustrative formal designs. These principles are broader in their application than any specific design, as specific designs may succeed or fail in instantiating the broader principles depending on social and historical context. For example, some instantiations may be more appropriate to a longer-term, more fundamental redesign of social institutions, while others may work better in the near term. All can be derived, however, from the same underlying philosophy—**the power and public goods created by increasing returns phenomena require governance mechanisms that align natural polities and actual polities; this in turn typically requires pluralism.**

Many thinkers and social systems have tried to piece together, in a time and place, institutions that capture this core philosophical tenet of Liberal Radicalism or RadicalxChange. Core examples include:

· The system of checks and balances in the US Constitution, defended in *The Federalist Papers* by Alexander Hamilton and James Madison, and the similar Girondin constitution of the Marquis de Condorcet
· The diverse system of different levels of government and civil society that sustained American democracy, according to Alexis de Tocqueville
· The emergence of democratically governed labor unions and worker board representation to combat the problem of corporate power, as celebrated and theorized by Beatrice and Sidney Webb
· Antitrust policies aimed at combating monopoly power and taxes on land rents created by urbanization, as promoted by Henry George
· The "council system" of self-selection into political leadership proposed by Hannah Arendt and Rosa Luxemburg
· The liberal and social democratic welfare states of the mid-twentieth century in Europe and the US

- The liberal international order of restraints on the power of nation-states that emerged especially in the wake of the Second World War

These examples are diverse in a variety of ways, and there are many things on which the relevant thinkers and actors who advocated them would disagree. Yet the core idea of RxC is to try to build formal institutions that roughly have the character of the above examples and are as clearly articulated and as broadly applicable as "capitalism" and "populism." We therefore recommend a form of institutional design for increasing returns phenomena that adheres to the following principles:

1. **Beyond capitalism versus populism**: Both capitalism and populism are fundamentally flawed. At minimum, they must check and balance each other. Yet, wherever possible, we should strive not just for a compromising middle path between them but for institutions that genuinely combine their strengths. We should seek to combine the entrepreneurial spirit of capitalism in generating new technologies and creating organizations that supply emergent demands based on these technologies, on the one hand, with the ongoing responsiveness to the community served, on the other, which democratic nation-states allow. The QF public matching fund system offers one formal structure for creating such institutions.

2. **Beyond individualism versus collectivism**: Both atomic individualism and hegemonic collectivism (such as nationalism) are flawed visions of personal identity. In a vibrant society, identity is constituted not overwhelmingly by membership in a single group or mostly by a vision of autonomy/self-reliance, but instead by memberships in a unique and evolving pattern of social commitments to a variety of communities. The sociology of Georg Simmel and the XSD built to formalize it offer a data structure instantiating this social theory.

3. **Against isolation and totalitarianism**: The ultimate evils of a society are isolated individualism and totalitarianism. While these may seem opposites, they are ultimately two sides of the same coin, as both erase the diversity of social commitments that make an individual life rich and the diversity of individuals that make social life rich; think of the way that solitary confinement replicates many features of totalitarianism. Their opposite is diverse, overlapping, and interweaving forms of social life.

4. **Emergent, responsive social organization**: New, emergent, responsive forms of social organization should be fostered to gradually replace increasingly irrelevant historical forms of organization, without abruptly

discarding the past. Entrepreneurs who challenge business incumbents, new forms of governance (such as subnational, supranational, and cross-cutting governance) that supplement incumbent governments, and a wide range of civil society all deserve support, but none is a panacea. Democratic and accountable forms of organization that seek to maximize the benefits accruing to those they serve should be fostered wherever possible to supplant plutocratic, autocratic, or profit-oriented organizations. The organizations most to be admired are those that are responsive, fitted to their time and social circumstances, and democratically accountable to those they serve. At the same time, attempts to suddenly "build a new world" and wipe away past institutions that are still relevant should be resisted as they usually aim at totalitarian enslavement of individuals in the name of liberation from existing institutions. The combination of QF and the SALSA system, with a mandatory sale requirement at the self-assessed value, would help to formalize the idea of emergent, gradually decaying social structures.

5. **Aligning social and technological innovation**: Social and technological innovation are both desirable and should progress as much as possible in parallel. When social innovation runs ahead of the technologies needed to instantiate it, it usually fails and leads to violence. For example, new modes of governance usually require new information and communications technologies to support and formalize them or they can degenerate into dictatorship, as happened during the French Revolution and in the case of the Soviet Union. When technological innovation runs ahead of social innovation, it becomes the basis of dangerous private concentrations of power and erodes democracy. For example, heavy industrialism requires labor organization to avoid the domination of capital and a level of global governance to avoid climate catastrophe. Modern information technologies and transportation technologies that allow globalization require new forms of governance corresponding to the patterns of collaboration they allow. The idea of DD, that data producers should organize collectively to bargain for the value of the data they create, is an example of an attempt to update social organization to new production modes.

6. **Equilibrium between individuals and communities**: Communities and individuals should each flow from and be in equilibrium with the other. Community identity and interest should be derivable from an interaction of preferences, knowledge, and interests of the individuals that make them up. Individual identities and interests should be derivable from the emergent culture of communities. Monopolies by individuals over communities and commonwealth should be feared and fought, but

so too should a monopoly by a single community over the identity of an individual. Duality theories between groups and individuals help formalize this concept.

7. **Diversely shared property**: Absolute private property and absolute national sovereignty are both, and roughly equally, to be avoided. Both the financial benefits and the prerogative to use capital should appropriately be shared across many levels of community, roughly in proportion to the needs of those different communities to use them and the contributions their efforts made to create them. Freedom of movement within nations, across territory, including land typically considered "private property," and freedom of movement across nations, including across typically closed borders, are both desirable, at least under some conditions, but neither should be absolute, free, or possible with unlimited "private property" in tow. SALSA and variations on it, which share property across many levels, help instantiate this idea.

8. **Equal but flexible voice**: A narrow vision of democracy as absolute equality of influence, vote, or voice on every issue within a fixed polity is undesirable. Instead, we should seek a process by which the political leadership of a diverse range of polities emerges through the bottom-up desire for engagement of citizens in these different polities to which they are committed to different degrees. While equality of dignity and voice overall is a central value, individuals will and should choose different leadership paths, some focusing on leadership within one community, others participating more lightly in several. Some of these communities will be narrower but deeper, others broader but shallower. QV, a system in which citizens are allocated equal budgets of voice credits that they can spend on a variety of issues and candidates as they see fit, is a formalizations of this ideal, especially in combination with technologies for large-scale deliberation like CL.

9. **Democratizing capitalism, blurring the state**: Wherever feasible, we should seek to democratize agglomerations of private power and capital through a combination (based on efficacy in the circumstance) of preventing or breaking up these agglomerations, democratizing them internally, or creating countervailing power to restrain them. Wherever feasible, we should seek to make the use of state power more flexible and responsive by using a combination (based on efficacy in the circumstance) of decentralization, enfranchising those without a voice in the exercise of state power, and the creation of cross-national democratic institutions. Economic democracy reforms and non-state-based visions of democracy may help formalize this goal.

10. **Subsidiarity beyond geography**: Rather than either centralization or decentralization, a diverse ecosystem of polities should emerge based on the principle of subsidiarity. This principle can be stated either as "everything should be handled at the lowest level of government capable of capturing the crucial necessary spillover effects associated with that domain of policy" or "everything should be handled at the highest level of government capable of flexibility accommodating important local differences and information." These may seem like opposite principles, but in practice they are overdetermined, as any structure will end up straining both local knowledge and the ability to incorporate relevant interactions. Given this, to form the best levels of organization, we should avoid focus exclusively on physical locality and seek forms of organization that respond to the patterns of interaction and commitment (linguistic, cultural, social, network-based, interest-based, occupational, relation to environmental features) that are relevant to the common interests at hand. Again, more flexible substrates for democratic participation, not based on nation-states, may help formalize this principle.

11. **Social plasticity**: Human conceptions of community are plastic to changing social dynamics; we should not be excessively attentive to the forms of social organization that characterized the past, especially when these do not themselves have deep historical roots. On the other hand, attempts to impose rather than to allow new forms of social structure to emerge should be resisted as authoritarian and forms of tradition with enduring value to the individuals who participate in them should be maintained and affirmed. We should seek formal polities that respond to social evolution at the same time as they shape it without seeking to monopolize the process of identity formation. Again, QF and SALSA together may help formalize this principle.

12. **Political economy, not economics and politics**: Sharp divides between the economic/private and the political/public should be avoided wherever possible. Agency, flexibility, and choice of issues and communities to prioritize are important political values; reason, equality, and cooperation deserve attention in the economy. Sharp divides between exit and voice should also be avoided and replaced by more gradual processes of shifting commitments. QF offers a natural formalization of this principle.

13. **Erosion and taming, not revolution or disruption**: While the concentrations of power in institutions like states and corporations are to be resisted, attempts to rapidly change power structures without clearly tested alternative bases of legitimacy have typically ended up recentral-

izing power in more dangerously concentrated forms. Breaking existing power structures therefore requires a careful combination of concerted and growing bottom-up experimentation that can gradually replace existing power structures ("erosion") and action through existing power structures to restrain and check the excesses of other such structures and to bring attention to alternatives ("taming"). The dual focus of RxC on entrepreneurial efforts to build local and voluntary experiments in radical new political economy structures and on pursuing at a broad political scale more modest regulatory constraints on capitalism and checks and balances of the state spring from this principle.

14. **Work within the system to replace it**: To the maximum extent possible, erosion should occur in ways that harness and beat existing power structures at their own game, rather than through extra-system means that could precipitate violence. Within the democratic politics of nation-states, this means building political movements capable of winning widespread political assent and healing existing political divisions. Within capitalism, it means building more-productive-than-capitalism entrepreneurial organizations that through their greater productivity accumulate capital that can be used to bring more resources under more just management. Only once such forms have robustly proved their legitimacy and the ability to offer sustainably liberal structures for social organization should they be formalized by supplanting existing capitalist and democratic institutions. Again, much of the structure of RxC, from its focus on art as a way to build legitimacy, its attempt to form new political coalitions with nearer-term policies, and its small-scale but radical experiments structured often as for-profit start-ups spring from this principle.

15. **Collaborate with power to contain it**: Efforts to tame existing concentrations of power must naturally run through existing institutions, through mechanisms like showing private companies how they can improve their profit by competing more vigorously or avoiding regulatory sanction, organizing politically for regulations that break concentrations of private power, and encouraging private companies to resist attempts by authoritarian states to concentrate power over information. These efforts will require collaboration with problematic existing power structures, which are often worthwhile as long as excessive legitimation of those power structures compared to the reforms thereby achieved can be avoided. RxC's cooperation with a range of existing nation-states, political parties, and large corporations, all of which differ from RxC values on many dimensions, spring from this principle.

16. **Live your values**: The most important goal of social reform should be to build new, widely shared visions of legitimacy that underpin a society in which violence is therefore of minimal importance. Building a widely shared notion of legitimacy requires a broad social conversation and imagination, something impossible without incorporating a diversity of means of communication and community organization. Art, education, entertainment, and connections to a wide range of preexisting civil society will be critical to facilitating such a conversation. Such approaches can build broad-based social movements capable of not just exercising power but instantiating in their practices new forms of legitimacy. Such a diverse interlinking of social forces in turn mirrors fundamental RxC values. As such, building an RxC society requires living the values described here and, while constantly experimenting with how these can be formalized at smaller scales, formalizing them in the large only when they have pervaded social life. Internal RxC efforts to "eat our own dog food" on everything from publication structures to internal governance and the emphasis on diversity and inclusion instantiate this principle.

While still quite broad, these principles may well give sufficient clarity to inspire the social action RxC will need to provide answers to the puzzles associated with increasing returns—puzzles that ideologies like capitalism, populism, nationalism, and technocracy have left unsolved to the detriment of humanity. If RxC succeeds, it will replace these failed paradigms with a pathway to a diversity of free and equal communities on a healthy, prospering planet.

4 On Flourishing: Political Economy and the Pursuit of Well-Being in the Polity

DEVA WOODLY

Philosophical liberals and modern conservatives have long used Aristotle's thoughts on *eudaemonia*, or flourishing, as a justification for a limited state and the primacy of negative liberty because they read the Nicomachean Ethics as a treatise on the possibilities of individual moral development (Aristotle 1893). On this account, people are best able to achieve their highest good without the interference of the state. However, if we take Aristotle seriously and respect his methodological edict that we must begin philosophical inquiry with "what is known to us," then we must acknowledge that in assessing the flourishing of a polis, we cannot look at the isolated individual but must instead observe the individual-in-context. The context of the individual includes the home, family, community, and nation that they are born into, the physical environment that they exist in, and the structural conditions that link them to socially intelligible categories and political history, therefore organizing the consequences of their being in the world. Preserving, maintaining, or changing the conditions extant in the world is the subject of politics. Given that this is so, I contend that we must examine the conditions that prevent most people in modern society from flourishing and begin to conceptualize a political remedy.

The task before us in the twenty-first century is to figure out how to create and maintain flourishing polities. In order to conceptualize what would be required for such a polity, this chapter proceeds in several parts. First, I discuss the concept of flourishing, exploring its definitions in philosophy and psychology as well as the corollary concept of well-being in economics. Second, I discuss the political and economic commonsense beliefs that we must chose to break from in order to move toward a polity in which ordinary people can expect to live and thrive. Then, I explain why the flourishing subject, the unit of analysis for a flourishing polity, must be the *individual-in-context* rather than an isolated, autonomous, and implicitly raced "economic man." Taking into account the reality of context necessitates that we wrestle with the systematic power asymmetries that structure the world we share, which then requires us to account for how a political economy toward flourishing can acknowledge, take into account, and seek to mitigate the effects of oppression and domination. Finally, I review the ways that economists have wrestled with the concept of flourishing, recounting their empirical findings on what factors increase well-being in the polity and noting the ways that measuring and keeping track of those indicators of quality of life can inform a politics that prioritizes people and their lived experience over mere charts recording the infinite increase of the gross national product.

What Does It Mean to Flourish?

On the question of how to decide what counts as flourishing, let us take as our rubric one that is, improbably, shared by both the father of capitalism, Adam Smith, and the contemporary American Left—that is, "no society can surely be flourishing and happy, of which the far greater part of the members are poor and miserable. It is but equity, besides, that they who feed, clothe, and lodge the whole body of the people, should have such a share of the produce of their own labor as to be themselves tolerably well fed, clothed, and lodged" (A. Smith 1977, B1, chap. 8).

Political conservatives tend to argue about what counts as "tolerable" whereas I will argue that the rule on which our judgment must be based is the prevalence of "misery." The reality is that in the world as it is the vast majority of people report that they are miserable—dealing with precarity in every aspect of life—and those of us who are concerned with either justice and/or the preservation of democracy must seek to understand and implement the changes of perspective, practice, and policy required to diminish the structural reality of misery that conditions so many lives. Our understanding of the nature and purpose of political economy has a large part to play in mitigating misery and enabling flourishing.

But what counts as flourishing? Psychologists define it as a state of well-being in which a person "lives within an optimal range of human functioning" which means that people experience "positive emotions, positive psychological functioning, and positive social functioning most of the time" (Fredrickson and Losada 2005, 678). Flourishing is a broader category of well-being than "happiness," which is usually used to describe immediate feelings or, as Daniel Kahneman puts it, "what I experience in the here and now," and it does not always take into account the balance of affect and satisfaction that characterizes a person's lived experience from day to day (Mandel 2018).

Flourishing is the opposite of both psychopathology like depression and a nonclinical yet unhappy state called "languishing," a kind of misery that causes people to describe their lives as "hollow" or "empty," which is characterized by prolonged, low-level distress brought about by chronic neglect, inactivity, and decreasing vitality and/or inability to thrive.

Flourishing is important, for our purposes, not only or primarily because it is a pleasant state but instead because flourishing people are more able to engage in focused attention, creative problem solving, inventive planning, and resilient follow-through. A flourishing person is able to "broaden and build" their "thought-action repertoires," or the range of cognitive, physical, and social possibilities that an agent can conceive and execute in given circumstances. This allows people to discard time-tested or automatic "action tendencies" and pursue novel, creative, and unscripted courses of thought and action. These are characteristics that are not only nice to have but, more importantly, critical to cultivate in democratic citizens, particularly in the current moment, when large-scale solutions and changes in societal, cultural, and individual habits are necessary for the survival of democracy and the continued, long-term human habitation of the planet. While psychologists normally measure flourishing at the individual level and most economists think of flourishing as the mean of aggregate individuals, I contend that the more accurate and useful measure of flourishing must locate the individual-in-context. This means that we must think of flourishing as a proportion rather than a mean (Sechel 2019) and that a polity's flourishing can only be observed by taking into account what proportion of individuals are flourishing and attending to whether and what demographic and structural characteristics accord with flourishing and why.

It is important to note that while a politics toward flourishing is ambitious, it is neither utopian nor absurd. Not every individual can be made happy or well. However, our current politics and political economy forces choices that make *most people miserable most of the time*. This reality may not be unique in the history of human civilization, but the nesting of this misery within the doctrine of the American Dream or the more widely Western doctrine of liberal-capitalist development is particularly brutal, as it causes people to not only experience misery but to feel that their misery is either groundless or solely a result of their choices and actions. The result is that people feel "gaslighted," or manipulated into questioning their own experience and sanity by the dominant ideology. This causes a despair that manifests at all levels, causing individual- and community-destroying behaviors as well as democracy- and polity-destroying actions.

We find evidence of despair in individual-level data regarding the shocking decrease in life expectancy among American adults (Devitt 2018), the deterioration of happiness all over the developed world, with particular drops in populous rich countries (Helliwell, Huang, and Wang 2019), and the decrease in reported interpersonal and institutional trust in democracies (Meer 2017). These dynamics have been accompanied by a popular clamor for the leadership of bombastic authoritarians in many locations across the globe. Donald Trump's institutionalization of concentration camps for immigrant children in the United States, Jair Bolsonaro allowing Brazil to burn in order to line the pockets of agribusiness, Boris Johnson championing the withdrawal of Britain from Europe, Recep Erdogan purging Turkish universities of those who dissent from his regime, Andrzej Duda enacting fundamentalist Christian nationalism in Poland, Viktor Orban promoting white supremacist policies in Hungary, and Narendra Modi's Hindu nationalism, relegating the 14.2 percent of India's population who are Muslim to second-class citizenship—it is a worldwide carnival of despair. This despair is not only personal but also, and quite devastatingly, political.

Political despair is a lack of efficacy brought on by an (often accurate) assessment of current conditions that views social and political ills as innumerable and natural—forces of (human) nature that cannot be combated, only avoided or girded against. It is the experience of social groups (similarly situated persons who recognize themselves as such) with a profound constraint on their lives and life chances that seems to come from everywhere and nowhere, impacting their ability to both develop themselves (oppression) and determine the trajectory of their own lives (domination) (Young 1994). In sum, it is the feeling that nothing can be done, that politics itself is a dead end, and that whatever remedies there are for human suffering and political injustice must be carved out piecemeal by individuals who are either lucky or blessed with unusual gifts.

Relegating much-needed political and social change to hero tales is what we do when democratic politics and our belief in our own citizenship fails. This is why the members of the polity pushing toward authoritarianism and away from democracy seem less interested in their own material interests than in the frank, public declamation that their reality—and that of most people they know—is characterized by languishing. So much the better if the politicians that acclaim these desperate political feelings promise to punish some undeserving *other* for the despair that has been growing for decades, unacknowledged and unaddressed.

While the wave of political despair sweeping the globe caught many unaware, believing that the late twentieth century had brought "the end of history," with economic development and pluralist tolerance on an inevitable, global spiral upward (as dominant discourse and what I have elsewhere called neoliberal common sense would have it), most people have had reason to doubt the efficacy of modern liberal democracy for some time (Woodly 2015). The form of capitalism that is now dominant—variously called neoliberal capitalism, corporatism, or crony capitalism—takes the logic of the hyperefficient, profit-maximizing rational person (either individual or corporate) as the relevant agent in all aspects of life and has spawned ways of reasoning that devalue all aspects of human life that cannot be properly categorized by price or efficiency.

This means that areas of life that support the human body (health care), human connection (voluntarism, nonprofessional clubs and associations, child and elder care), or human spirit (leisure time, vocation) have been increasingly unsupported by public resources and priced at a premium that most people either cannot or struggle to afford. We are told that this grueling setup is simply the nature of "the economy" and/or that striving with anxiety, depression, and ill health is good for our character. In the US, we are taught that this suffering is actually key to any patriotic identity. It is fine, we are to believe, that in the richest country in human history, 1 in 5 children are too poor to have stable housing and seasonal clothing, and that 1 in 12 is in extreme poverty—that is, too poor to eat regularly. For those who are not poor, scrambling to remain in the "middle class," or the 51 percent of Americans who make between $45,000 and $125,000,[1] they can expect to see between 30 and 50 percent of their income (depending on geography) go to housing costs that have inflated four times faster than income from wages (which have remained stagnant for 40 years) and health care, education, and child care costs that have each doubled in average price since 1996 (Desilver 2018). Indeed, according to a 2017 Urban Institute study that surveyed 7,500 people, 4 in 10 Americans are struggling to pay for their basic expenses: food, housing, utilities, and health care (Michael Karpman 2018). Alissa Quart argues that these realities have given rise not only to a precariat, as Guy Standing dubbed working-class people saddled with temporary, low-paying, and part-time jobs, but also to a "middle precariat" who are at the upper end of the middle distribution and "believed that their training or background would ensure that they would be properly, comfortably middle class, but it has not worked out that way" (Quart 2018). Quart's vivid account of the state of affairs boils down to a misery born of having lost "the narrative of their lives and futures," not only dealing with the material reality of struggle but also the philosophical and psychological question: "Who are [we] and what will [we] become?" A fair question since "their incomes have flatlined [and] many are 'fronting' as bourgeois while standing in a pile of debt" (Quart 2018).

We are supposed to tolerate this hardship because "the economy," we imagine, *naturally* produces winners and losers. The winners, we are told, win because they have worked hardest—despite ample evidence that the surest way to win is to be born winning (Hess 2019). We are to believe that "the economy" necessarily blows people to and fro in accordance with its anthropomorphized whims, which are only able to be divined—with limited accuracy and questionable ethics but boundless faith—by credentialed aco-lytes steeped in the mysteries of supply and demand curves and the variously meaningful shapes they may take.

The premodern sense of "economy," which simply meant the prudence and frugality with which tasks for living are carried out, has fallen out of usage and now the word almost always carries the personifying article "the," creating an invisible hand of god where one of many useful characteristics of human behavior once resided. My purpose here is not to mock modernity or to recall us to the "true" meaning of economy, but to highlight that we have, through our language and ideology, put most of the activities that organize human life out of our own control because of a belief in a mysticism that seems modern only because it is mathematical. This ideology has prevented us from rearranging the priorities and organization of our systems of care, exchange, and governance in accordance with the things we say we value, both as individuals and collectively.

The ideology, institutional policies, and social practices that characterize the current political economy ensure that resources accrue disproportion-ately and almost exclusively to those who already occupy the highest decile of income and wealth while the vast majority face the reality that there are astounding and nearly insurmountable institutional barriers to creating a stable economic foundation for their families and communities. This grim reality is systematically more forbidding when disaggregated by race, region, and country, making the progress that exponential capital growth has prom-ised a punishingly illusive mirage (Bourguignon 2015; Coyle 2011; Piketty 2013; Skidelsky and Skidelsky 2012; Standing 2011; Wilkinson and Pickett 2009).

Economists J. Allister McGregor and Nicky Pouw put the matter this way: "As we are aware from recent major contributions to the literature . . . , the primacy given to the pursuit of private wealth and the ways that govern-ments sanction and support this has served to strengthen the economic and political power of those who are already in a privileged position, while people at the bottom of the income distribution receive limited benefits and are marginalized from the development process" (McGregor and Pouw 2017, 1126). Phillip Smith and Manfred Max-Neef state things more bluntly, argu-ing that we are "under the spell of a dehumanized economy" in which "there is never enough for those who have nothing, but there is always enough for those who have everything" (Smith and Max-Neef 2012, 128–29).

Soaring inequality and the precarious instability that is its most telling hallmark have been the topic of increasing concern in a variety of domains, from academic economics to the political agendas of social movements and politicians, but the dominant perspective, policies, and practices that have enabled market logic to colonize almost all areas of life have yet to change. As a result, last century's economic ideas carry us unhappily forward with a momentum that can only be broken by the repetition of a clear and resonant theory that prioritizes the well-being of the individual-in-context over efficiency, endless growth, and maximal profit.

The good news is the efficiency and austerity economy can be remade into the well-being economy. We can create conditions under which many more or even most people can attain a flourishing life. In order for this to be possible, we have to change our minds about what counts and what to count, then make judgments about the political and economic infrastructure based on new commonsense priorities. To this end, our politics must concern itself with identifying, acknowledging, and attempting to remedy oppression and domination and preventing new forms (or reinscriptions of old forms) from becoming embedded in perspective, practice, and policy. Such an aim can only be facilitated if the health of the polity is judged based on the assessment of the lived experience of those whose misery is most palpable—that is, from the bottom up and from margin to center.

Oppression, Domination, and the Misery of the Polis

The individual-in-context has their own perceptions, dreams, desires, and agency, but individuals are nevertheless born into a world that is a given, and that givenness includes power asymmetries rooted in and reproduced by unjust inequality. Therefore, an account of flourishing that is grounded in what we know must begin with the acknowledgment that individuals are never wholly autonomous, self-reproducing, utility-maximizing agents who begin in a state of universal human equality. The natural equality that obtains at birth is immediately supplanted by the realities of a world that is already built—a world that has a history and structuring forces that condition but do not fully determine the individual's place in it. This means that observing characteristics of individuals alone cannot tell the whole story of the well-being of the polis; instead, we must observe how groups of individuals who are similarly situated may systematically differ in their ability to flourish.

We do not often talk about the ways that oppression and domination have conditioned not only the political economy as it is, but the possibilities extant in the understandings of that economy. The dominant understanding of individuals as ever-productive autonomous entrepreneurs and the perspectives, practices, and policies that flow from this understanding was famously called *neoliberalism* by Wendy Brown. She contends that this ideology has been a constructive project, a marked shift from the classical liberalism that reigned during most of modernity, in that the neo ideology refuses to acknowledge and, indeed, seeks to smother all domains, logics, and values that refuse or exceed market logic (Brown 2003). While I think Brown's observations about the changes in the liberal paradigm are largely accurate, it is a term that is too colloquially fraught and conceptually limited for our purposes. Instead, I take up Iris Young's notion of "the distributive paradigm," which refers to not only the totalizing market logic that has infected commonsense thinking since the middle of last century, but also to the "decision-making power and procedures, division of labor, and culture" that adaptively reproduce conditions that enable and preserve that logic. Like Young, I contend that the distributive paradigm encompasses the thinking of both neoliberals and their class-first or class-only critics, joining her in observing that "even explicitly socialist or Marxist discussions of justice under socialism . . . assume the primary difference between socialist justice and capitalist justice is in their principles of distribution" (Young 1994, 17).

Neoliberalism is also fundamentally characterized by oppression and domination, often excused as the risks and remainders of liberty given luck, divergent commitments to moral austerity, and freedom of choice. But critiques of neoliberalism that concede the logic of the distributive paradigm cannot answer the intersectional reality of oppression with only the blunt instrument of welfare or the guarantee of material goods—whether it is offered as a perk of ethical capitalism or a mandate of moral socialism. This is because oppression is a "family of concepts" with five aspects: exploitation, marginalization, powerlessness, cultural imperialism, and violence. Oppression cannot be reduced to the economic inequality that neoliberalism creates because oppression always "involves social structures and relations beyond distribution" (Young 1994, 9).

While the distributive paradigm does not by itself produce the misery of the polis, the atomism and autonomy (an autonomy that slides dangerously into an impossible expectation of sovereignty) of its social ontology does. This is because, regardless of the American social theology of "personal responsibility," in what Nancy Fraser has called the "actually existing world," people arrive, from the moment of their birth, into a context, and that context is structured—meaning that many of the personal characteristics observed or bequeathed to them at birth (race, gender, family, region, nation) will shape (though not fully determine) the way that they experience the rest of their lives as surely as the structuring laws of physics do. It is for this reason that conceptions of justice based on or unreflectively embedded in the distributive paradigm can only, as Machiavelli says, come to grief.

This is because justice is not quantifiable. It is not definite. It is not certain. It is, in much the same way that human beings are, the product of context, negotiation, and action. A social ontology (neoliberal individualism) and politics (interest group pluralism) that ignores context and discourages action through the production of despair is one that can only produce an apportioning justice—one that seeks to make laws about what people ought to have and by what rules, rather than how people can be supported in their efforts as "doers and actors" (Young 1994, 37).

The oppressive structuring of power and privilege in race, gender, and class hierarchies is relevant for a full accounting of this despair because what politics can promise those who are languishing, in lieu of deep and difficult restructuring of the political economy, are scapegoats: the promise that some group ascribed as *other* is responsible for the general misery and will be punished. That most people, including those who vote for and/or support neoliberal authoritarians will be harmed by their policies, is not the relevant decision rule. The mythologized autonomous individual is not, it turns out, a universal character. Instead, this individual is raced and gendered, a white man who by the commonsense logic of the myth, deserves, by virtue of his values and value, to be at the top of the human hierarchy. In the United States, this phenomenon is vividly illustrated in Jonathan Metzl's important book, *Dying of Whiteness*. Metzl relates the story of Trevor, an uninsured working-class white Tennessean, who at age 41 was dying of the debilitating effects of the hepatitis C virus. Hepatitis C is curable. In his interview with Trevor, Metzl pointed out that if he lived only 40 minutes away, in the state of Kentucky, he would have access to life-saving drugs because that state chose to set up insurance exchanges and expand Medicaid in compliance with the Affordable Care Act while Tennessee had not. But, as Metzl writes:

> Even at death's doorstep, Trevor wasn't angry. In fact, he staunchly supported the stance promoted by his elected officials. "Ain't no way I would ever support Obamacare or sign up for it," he told me. "I would rather die." When I asked him why he felt this way . . . he explained, "We don't need any more government in our lives. And in any case, no way I want my tax dollars paying for Mexicans and welfare queens." (Metzl 2019, 3)

Metzl was shocked that Trevor "voiced a literal willingness to die for his place in [the racial] hierarchy." Metzl went on to interview many people across the American Midwest and South, writing:

> [They] were dying in various overt or invisible ways as a result of political beliefs and systems linked to the defense of white "ways of life" or concerns about minorities or poor people hoarding resources. People like Trevor who put their own bodies on the line, rather than imagining scenarios in which diversity or equity might better the flourishing of everyone. (Metzl 2019, 5)

The logics that excuse or ignore oppression harm us all because they make us believe that it is OK for some people to suffer. And, more insidiously, if you are one of the suffering, it is very likely your own fault or, at least, a necessary sacrifice to the social hierarchy. This view rests on the idea that there is nothing but rights (executable or not) that we deserve, and that freedom and autonomy principally mean being left alone. These kinds of beliefs have begun to harm even people of relative privilege. The cultural hunger for exploring "mindfulness," "work–life balance," and "self-care" is a symptom, a cultural response to a political economy that is punishing, approaching impossible, for most people most of the time. The poor and historically marginalized are most inhibited from flourishing via oppression, but even the relatively privileged are increasingly structurally vulnerable to three of the four miseries that characterize languishing—poverty, isolation, poor health, and precarity. This is because a distributive paradigm posits people as atomistic and autonomous but paradoxically politically passive agents. It imagines the world as full of individuals gifted with inherent powers that they simply *have* and ought to be left free to use, rather than as people in diverse contexts who *can do* a variety of things and may, indeed, be made capable of learning and creating still more. Young calls her theory "the politics of difference."

Amartya Sen articulates a similar view with his capabilities approach. He writes, "In contrast with the utility-based or resource-based lines of thinking, individual advantage is judged in the capability approach by a person's capability to do things he or she has reason to value. . . . The focus here is on the freedom that a person actually has to do this or be that—things that he or she may value doing or being" (Sen 2009, 231–32). Further, "the Capability approach focuses on human life, and not just on some detached objects of convenience, such as incomes or commodities that a person may possess, which are often taken, especially in economic analysis, to be the main criteria of human success. Indeed, it proposes a serious departure from concentrating on the *means* of living to the *actual opportunities* of living" (233).

Sen writes that capabilities are heterogenous rather than homogeneous and cautions that "we cannot reduce all things we have reason to value into one homogenous magnitude" (239). And he calls out utilitarian theories, the most popular philosophical arguments in economics, for institutionalizing this mistake:

> The utilitarian tradition which works toward beating every valuable thing down to some kind of allegedly homogenous magnitude of "utility," has contributed most to this sense of security in "counting" exactly one thing. . . . If the long tradition of utility has contributed to the sense of security in commensurable homogeneity, the massive use of gross national product (GNP) as the indicator of the economic condition of a nation has also made its contribution in that direction. Proposals for weaning economic evaluators away from exclusive reliance on the GNP have tended to generate worry that with diverse objects to judge we shall not have the sense of ease that goes with just checking whether GNP is higher or lower. (Sen 2009, 239)

Sen understands that "by proposing a fundamental shift in the focus of attention from the *means* of living to the *actual opportunities* a person has, the capability approach aims at a fairly radical change in the standard evaluative approaches" (253). However, that radical shift seems warranted given the great incommensurability of mass misery with democratic governance.

Sen's conception of capabilities accords with Young's politics of difference in that his ideas about how to evaluate the progress and success of people in the world is not by measuring what they have, but by taking account of what structural conditions allow and/or enable them to do. While the distributive paradigm points to whether one *has the appropriate amount* of nonmaterial social goods, the tack taken by Young and Sen, what I will call the liberatory paradigm—the one we need to facilitate a political economy toward well-being—points to whether one can take advantage of, or exercise and enact the activities associated with, living well. In this way, the distributive paradigm imagines people and their just portion as being determined by what characteristics they are said to possess, the liberatory paradigm, to what evidence shows they are able to do. Further, since the distributive paradigm asks only "What do you have," the only referent is the individual—no context, other than the rules that have been deduced, is necessary. For the second way of seeing the world, the context is essential to the assessment of capability and justice and to the ability toward flourishing polities. Since the liberatory paradigm relies on situated individuals and cannot be deduced from behind a veil or any other Archimedean point, it takes the asymmetrical positions of social groups seriously and takes the recognition of patterned asymmetry (systemic injustice) to be politically essential.

This meaning-giving social context is organized in and through institutions and structured by the habits, rules, norms, and law that characterize the condition of their enactment. What we find is that this social, institutional, and structured context may, and empirically often does, prevent people from exercising or enacting their claim to social goods even when they may be said to *have*, or be possessors of, those goods according to rules and law. This happens because while individuals exist in the world as irreducible pluralities, the world cannot and does not apprehend them that way. From the moment of their birth, people are in relation—situated with regard to the other things in the world. And they share similar (though never identical) situations with others. Which of these situations are deemed significant are matters of custom and negotiation, but the fact of this situatedness is inescapable. Furthermore, we find, those who are similarly situated often have similar chances to exercise their capabilities with regard to social goods. A paradigm that concerns itself only with what people *have*, rather than with what people *can do*, is unrealistic and eventually fails to help people make sense of their realities because it is a conception that ignores the world, even as it attempts to order it. The political upheaval of the first two decades of the twenty-first century gives an inkling of the political danger that obtains when dominant paradigms no longer help people make sense of the world, their place in it, and what they can do to maintain and improve it.

One limitation of Sen's approach compared to Young's is that he does not take asymmetrical power, and the oppression and domination it evinces, seriously enough. Sen insists that the capability approach is not methodological individualism, although "capabilities are characteristics of individual advantages" (Sen 2009, 296). Still, he contends, "the capability approach does not assume . . . detachment, its concern with people's ability to live the kind of lives they have reason to value brings in social influences both in terms of what they value . . . and what influences operate on their values" (244). Sen ultimately argues that groups rely on the value judgments of individuals to figure out what is valuable for the group, and further asserts that "the increasing tendency toward seeing people in terms of one dominant 'identity' . . . is not only an imposition of an external and arbitrary priority, but also the denial of an important liberty of a person who can decide on their respective loyalties to different groups" (246–47). This ignores the fact that there are groups in which ascribed membership—in itself—limits one's capabilities because of systemic injustice, not only the false consciousness of internalized oppression. You need not feel loyal to the group in order to be affected by its status. Groups that experience oppression are not usually voluntary associations. If you are Black, for example, it does not matter one whit the affinity you feel for Black people as a group; statistics show that if a law enforcement officer encounters you and, for whatever reason, fears for their life, you are more likely to end up dead than those otherwise ascribed. Young does a much better job of acknowledging the reality of these asymmetries and the ills that they produce, chiefly the politics of despair that we are wrestling with globally. The remedy for this despair is to embrace a liberatory paradigm that can give rise to more accurate assessments of reality and forms of political action and policy that put the cultivation of human life rather than the efficiency of markets and maximization of growth at its center.

Economics and Well-Being

The idea that the political economy needs a massive overhaul toward well-being is not a new one. At least since the Great Recession, many economists have been calling for reform in their discipline at the same time that people have filled the streets around the globe in movements demanding a reckoning and governing bodies and political candidates have scrambled for regressive (fascist), radical (socialist), or retrenched (liberal) rhetorical cover for the fact that there is wide acknowledgment of a fundamental common problem with no consensus solution. In 2009, leading economists Joseph Stiglitz, Amartya Sen, and John Paul Fitoussi produced a report for the French Commission on the Measurement of Economic Performance and Social Progress. In it, the authors argue that economists and states have been measuring social progress in the wrong way, narrowly focusing on gross domestic product (GDP), an indicator of the growth of the size of the economy, while ignoring or failing to collect data on indicators that more accurately measure people's ability to thrive. They quite reasonably point out that "we often draw inferences about what are good policies by looking at what policies have promoted economic growth; but if our metrics of performance are flawed, so too may be the inferences that we draw" (Stiglitz, Sen, and Fitoussi 2009, 7). Economic growth and quality of life do not necessarily correlate, particularly in view of environmental degradation, and the practice of assuming the former indicates the latter is a fundamental mistake with pernicious and increasingly devastating consequences. Economists J. Allister McGregor and Nicky Pouw point out:

While economic growth is vital at different stages of development to provide the food and incomes to bring populations out of absolute poverty, when we delve deeper into the historical and present day effects of growth, it is apparent that it does not always equate with improvement in our broader conception of well-being. While material conditions may improve, other aspects [of] well-being may suffer (e.g. the quality of the environment that one is able to live in, work–life balance, the social institutions of neighborhood and community). Both the relational and subjective quality-of-life outcomes of well-being are often reduced during development processes that are myopically focused on growth. (McGregor and Pouw 2017, 1134)

They propose that our assessment of economic progress must change its focus from prioritizing the "growth paradigm" to "how to protect and promote sustainable human well-being apriori" (McGregor and Pouw 2017, 1125). This requires a fundamental reorientation of how most people think of the economy. They argue that the foundational metaphor of neoclassical economics of the "auctioneer" who moves agents to the optimal efficiency of rational action is flawed because there are many optima, not one, as Aristotle pointed out 3,000 years ago. Even so, in an attempt to make this inaccurate model work, economists have employed the idea of average optima, cutting out data that evinces the reality of heterogenous and endogenous preferences. Further, this model refuses to account for the reality that there are many situations in which *only suboptimal* options present themselves. As McGregor and Pouw put it: "The optimal point at which the economic agent is behaving rationally and, in a cost-optimizing manner (efficiently) may not be among the possible alternatives. If the person wants to survive in the short run, then it is possible that only suboptimal solutions will be available, for example when people are forced to accept below-minimum wages or inferior/harmful working conditions that are detrimental to their health" (1127).

In sum, in the world as it actually exists, the economy is not an objectively observable set of phenomenon but instead a socially and politically instituted process of resource allocation in which power differences between resource agents matter profoundly and decision-making is characterized not by uninflected rationality but "by a sense of identity, community and their relationships to others and their environment." Understanding that what we call the economy is emergent, or the contingent product of interaction within a wider system, helps us to reason from the reality that "resource exchange between agents is driven not only by relative prices within the narrowly defined system, but by a wider range of forces, including: power differences in resource and market access and control; people's culture and social habits; legal rules about factor payment; and concerns about the relationship between the natural environment and production processes" (McGregor and Pouw 2017, 1129).

Well-being, then, should be judged by the combination of "what [people] have (material), how they are able [to] use what they have (relational) and the level of satisfaction or subjective quality of life that they derive from what they have and can do" (McGregor and Pouw 2017, 1125). It is important to underscore that well-being is plural. If people are institutionally enabled to author their own thriving, they will choose to pursue different forms of satisfaction in different ways. Unlike the neoclassical stick figure approximation of the human who is only a rational economic agent pursuing utility maximization of optimal outcomes in accordance with self-interest, an economics toward well-being understands that "what is an optimal choice for one human being at one point in time is not necessarily an optimal choice for the other," and that "well-being cannot be achieved by people in isolation; it is achieved through their relationships to others in society" (1132). This insight highlights an important point about the need for a view of economics that accounts for the necessity of cooperation and social integration, on the one hand, and power asymmetry, on the other. In the contemporary political landscape, liberal pluralists tend to downplay power asymmetry and the ways that their historical legacies compound, shaping current relations, while Marxists (though not Marx) tend to downplay the need to respect and encourage plurality in the pursuit of multiple goods in multiple ways, rather than one universal good pursued by methods dictated by states, parties, and regimes.

Answering this skewed view can no longer be achieved by promoting "welfare" as was done in the mid-twentieth century because the logic of social welfare still gives the growth paradigm pride of place. In the twentieth-century reformist view, economic growth is seen as the main provider of improvements in welfare. Growth is seen as providing jobs that increase incomes that can be invested in consumption, health, and education while at the same time providing the tax base to fund services. In the tradition of nineteenth-century welfare states, social welfare is then provided to those who, for one reason or another, are not able to benefit from economic growth (McGregor and Pouw 2017, 1134).

Therefore, it is not welfare (tolerable material sustenance only) but well-being (flourishing—material sustenance, social connection, subjective assessment of well-being) that must be the foundational concept for the transformation of our understanding of the economy and its purpose and possibilities. As Amartya Sen has noted, it is not the things that we have that make us well, but what we can do and achieve with those things (Sen 1985). In point of fact, it is not only what we can do with things that make us well, but also our connections to other people. Economists interested in well-being's effects on organizations and nations, including Alan Krueger, Ed Diener, and John Helliwell, among others, have found that "much of what contributes to well-being happens outside markets" (Crabtree 2008).

Empirical research in both psychology and economics has shown that "although at low levels of economic development, income does indeed predict subjective well-being, at somewhat higher levels (say above the median for OECD countries) material well-being has a quite modest effect" (Helliwell and Putnam 2004, 1436). That is, above a modest threshold, more money cannot buy you more happiness. The three things that most consistently impact subjective well-being are material well-being, family circumstances, and health (Easterlin 2004). Interestingly, although our common sense is oriented toward ever-more acquisition, after our basic needs are met with some comfort (at a rate of about 20 percent above the median income of the nation we happen to be in), we experience "hedonic adaptation" to greater sums. That is, we simply adapt to making more money and our happiness level does not increase. With family and health, however, our happiness levels continue to increase as we get more good things in those realms (and decreases if we get bad things). Economist Richard Easterlin writes that "each of us has only a fixed amount of time available for family life, health activities, and work. Do we distribute our time in the way that maximizes our happiness? The answer, I believe, is no, [because] we decide how to use our time based on the false belief that more money will make us happier" (32). Easterlin calls this the "money illusion," which causes people to "allocate an excessive amount of time to monetary goals and shortchange nonpecuniary ends such as family life and health," even though social connections and self-care have more potential for increasing our sense of well-being (32). Put more succinctly: "most people could increase their happiness by devoting less time to making money, and more time to nonpecuniary goals such as family life and health" (33).

Paying attention to the life satisfaction of the individual-in-context matters at the level of society as well. Helliwell and Putnam (2004, 1437) write that "a common finding from research on the correlates of life satisfaction is that subjective well-being is best predicted by the breadth and depth of one's social connections. In fact, people themselves report that good relationships with family members, friends or romantic partners—far more than money or fame—are prerequisites for their happiness. Moreover, the 'happiness effects' of social capital in these various forms seem to be quite large, compared with the effects of material affluence." Of course, this is not just a matter of individual choice. Our political economy is structured such that if one works for a living (and could not live off the capital gains of investments), one's grasp on material comfort is always precarious. This reality obtains for a number of reasons, chief among them that firms, as employers, increasingly have monopsony or concentrated buying power. This means that even when labor markets are tight, workers cannot command the wages or working conditions that would allow flourishing lives. Combine this with a work culture in many parts of world that insists one should always be available for work and, if employed, should never complain (unless wages are not paid). But firms are not the only or even primary villains in this state of affairs. The monopsony-creating practices that have become commonplace have been allowed by federal governments that simply look the other way as people who work for a living are bled dry by the collusion and outsized political power of those few who do not have to work (Ghilarducci 2019; Naidu, Posner, and Weyl 2018; and Weil 2018).

This work culture has, of course, developed on the foundation of a neoliberal common sense in which market logic is suitable for all ends and firms and their interests are perceived to be self-evidently more important than workers and their needs, because firms are lionized as "job creators" on whose fate the capacity for endless growth rests. That the empirical picture seems to show that the astronomical growth in economies around the world has not corresponded to a concomitant widespread prosperity and has, in the last two decades, corresponded with a precipitous drop in people's sense of well-being has, until recently, been ignored by those with decision-making power.

As it turns out, participating in the maintenance and governance of their communities is something that contributes to people's sense of well-being. As Helliwell has observed, "People directly value their engagement with others, including their involvement in the process making public decisions and delivering public services" (Helliwell 2006, C43). For example, psychologist Laura Wray-Lake and her coauthors have found that civic engagement is associated with well-being in US adolescents, particularly civic engagement that causes people to meet and help each other in settings that bring them face-to-face and activities that they perceive to be improving their environment or the environment writ large (Wray-Lake et al. 2017). Likewise, Rashmi Choudhary and Deepali Sharma Gupta, in a study of Indian adolescents, found that civic engagement was tightly correlated with subjective well-being, with a youth's level of civic engagement explaining 58 percent of the variance in the subject's reported well-being (Choudhary and Gupta 2017). Economists Bruno Frey and Alios Stutzer found that among adults, subjective well-being is higher in Swiss cantons that had more frequent consultations with their electors (Frey and Stutzer 2000). Elsewhere, psychologists Michael Chandler and Christopher Lalonde found that several measures of community-level self-government were associated with dramatically lower suicide rates among indigenous communities in British Columbia (Chandler and Lalonde 1998).

Helliwell further observes that social context makes a definitive difference in all areas of people's lives. "Whatever their personality type, they value trust in their neighbourhoods, their workplaces, their public services and their public servants" (Helliwell 2006, C43). More pointedly:

Once the importance of trust and engagement are digested, they might be expected to inform almost every policy decision about the form and delivery of public services. We might expect to see more provision of multi-use public spaces; more linkage among generations in the provision of care, education and leisure; provision of better ways for community newcomers to give as well as get public services and social contacts; meshing of voluntary and professional workers in more effective ways; and changing the nature of the lessons and myths that inspire education. In particular, it is incumbent on economists especially, who have been responsible for propagating the myth of economic man, to at least consider the costs of policies that rely too much on its assumed truth. (Helliwell 2006, C43)

As Julie Rose points out in her chapter in this book, it is time to consider that "beyond some level of wealth, people may be better off in a society that ceases to pursue economic growth." My brief review of the literature on well-being in economics suggests that we should not be investing in the acquisition of things (past a certain level of comfort) but should instead be investing in structuring society such that people are able to spend time on their relationships and participate in activities that build and engage with their communities. The key takeaway here is that contrary to the doctrine of the autonomous individual, happiness is not only or primarily an individual trait; it is a characteristic of the individual-in-context, produced by feelings of self-esteem, efficacy, and satisfaction that are fashioned in relation with others. Our current political economy inhibits our relations with others with both structural barriers and a commonsense paradigm that privileges growth at the economy-wide level and a desperate (and for most people) never-ending push for material sustenance at the individual level. Ordering society in this way makes for a miserable situation for most people most of the time. We can and should do better.

We can begin to do so by incorporating measures of well-being into the data that we collect to inform us about our political economy. Daniel Kahneman and Alan Krueger have developed a method of measuring well-being in the populace using "hedonic" time-allocation surveys, which ask a representative sample of people to keep diaries of their activities during a two- or three-day period and record their subjective reaction to those activities. The data can then be averaged across individuals for a national-level measure of well-being or disaggregated for population-specific measures (Krueger 2006, 5). Such accounts can give policy analysts objective measures of average or median subjective states. In other words, "national accounts of subjective well-being can reflect many different aspects of quality of life beyond the economy, and thus serve as an efficient way to assess many different aspects of quality of life" (Diener, Oishi and Lucas 2015, 234).

A Political Economy Toward Flourishing

At this historical moment, we are at what political scientists call "a critical juncture." Paul Pearson writes that "junctures are 'critical' because they place institutions on paths or trajectories, which are then very difficult to alter" (Pearson 2004, 135). The dissolution of and disillusionment with the dominant ideology of the last century has been unsettling, but the upside of being unsettled is the opportunity to think anew, to consider not only how we understand the world but also how many of us have misunderstood it, granting us the opportunity to reconceive the principles and parameters of the world we share. We are in a unique period when we have an opportunity to not only pay attention to the empirical reality of the increasing misery of the polis but also to make moral choices and institutional changes that aim to alleviate some of that misery and, more boldly, to reimagine and restructure the economy toward the end of enabling most people to live well. This requires letting go of some of the notions that have been regarded as common sense for (at least) the past century: that the autonomous individual is best conceived as unbound by context and unfettered by social ties and that profit and efficiency represent the highest economic goods. We have to come to believe that people deserve to live well simply because they are people and that our society ought to be geared toward making that both possible and probable. We can do so by displacing profit, efficiency, and austerity from the center of the catechism of late-capitalist virtue and instead placing the lived experience of the least well off as the touchstone at the foundation of twenty-first-century political economy. We must do this not only because it is a good in itself, but also because it is necessary for the health and likely the survival of democracy.

Notes

1.   Dollar amounts are based on a family of three.

References

Aristotle. 1893. *The Nicomachean Ethics of Aristotle,* 5th ed. Translated by F. H. Peters. London: Kegan Paul, Trench, Truebner.

Balko, Radley. 2014. "How Municipalities in St. Louis County, Mo., Profit from Poverty." *Washington Post,* September 3. https://www.washingtonpost.com/ news/the-watch/wp/2014/09/03/how-st-louis-county-missouri-profits-from -poverty/?utm_term=.8baf968b716a.

Bourguignon, F. 2015. *The Globalization of Inequality.* Woodstock, UK: Princeton University Press.

Brown, Wendy. 2003. "Neoliberalism and the End of Liberal Democracy." *Theory and Event* 7, no. 1.

Chandler, Michael, and Christopher Lalonde. 1998. "Cultural Continuity as a Hedge against Suicide in Canada's First Nations." *Transcultural Psychiatry* 35:191–219.

Choudhary, R., and Gupta, D. 2017. "Civic Engagement a Precursor to Well-Being." *Indian Journal of Health and Wellbeing* 8, no. 2: 152–156. http://www.i -scholar.in/index.php/ijhw/article/view/147206.

Cohen, G. A. 1994. "Amartya Sen's Unequal World." *New Left Review,* January/February. https://newleftreview.org/issues/i203/articles/g-a-cohen-amartya-sen-s -unequal-world.

Colander, D., M. Goldberg, A. Haas, A. Kirman, K. Juselius, B. Sloth, T. Lux. 2011. "The Financial Crisis and the Systematic Failure of Academic Economics." In *Lessons from the Financial Crisis: Causes, Consequences, and Our Economic Future,* edited by Robert Kolb, 427–36. New York: John Wiley & Sons.

Coyle, D. 2011. *The Economics of Enough: How to Run the Economy as if the Future Matters.* Princeton, NJ: Princeton University Press.

Crabtree, Steve. 2008. "The Economics of Happiness." *Gallup,* January 10. https:// news.gallup.com/businessjournal/103549/economics-happiness.aspx.

Desilver, Drew. 2018. "For Most U.S. Workers, Wages Have Barely Budged for Decades." Pew Research Center, *FactTank: News in the Numbers,* August 7, 2018. https://www.pewresearch.org/fact-tank/2018/08/07/for-most-us-workers-real -wages-have-barely-budged-for-decades/.

Devitt, Michael. 2018. "CDC Data Show US Life Expectancy Continues to Decline."

American Academy of Family Physicians, December 10. https://www.aafp.org/
news/health-of-the-public/20181210lifeexpectdrop.html.

Diener, Ed, Shigehiro Oishi, and Richard E. Lucas. 2015. "National Accounts of
Subjective Well-Being." *American Psychologist* 70:234–42.

Easterlin, Richard. 2004. "The Economics of Happiness." *Daedalus* 133, no. 2
(Spring): 26–33.

Fredrickson, Barbara, and Marcial Losada. 2005. "Positive Affect and the Complex
Dynamics of Human Flourishing." *American Journal of Psychology* 60, no. 7 (October): 678–86.

Frey, Bruno S., and Alois Stutzer. 2000. "Happiness, Economy and Institutions."
Economic Journal 110:918–38.

Ghilarducci, Teresa. 2019. "How Big Firms Keep Wages Low." *Forbes*, January 21.
https://www.forbes.com/sites/teresaghilarducci/2019/01/21/uncovering-the
-mystery-of-your-sluggish-paycheck/#3cc6f16e1d79.

Helliwell, John F. 2006. "Well-Being, Social Capital and Public Policy: What's New?"
Economic Journal 116, no. 510 (March): C34–C45.

Helliwell, John F., Haifang Huang, and Shun Wang. 2019. "Changing World Happiness." *World Happiness Report*, March 20. https://worldhappiness.report/ed/
2019/changing-world-happiness/.

Helliwell, John F., and Robert D. Putnam. 2004. "The Social Context of Well-Being."
Philosophical Transactions of the Royal Society London 359 (September): 1435–46.

Hess, Abigail Johnson. "Georgetown Study: 'To Succeed in America, It's Better to Be
Born Rich than Smart.'" *CNBC*, May 29, 2019. https://www.cnbc.com/2019/05/
29/study-to-succeed-in-america-its-better-to-be-born-rich-than-smart.html.

Kahneman, Daniel, and Alan B. Krueger. 2006. "Developments in the Measurement
of Subjective Well-Being." *Journal of Economic Perspectives* 20, no. 1 (Winter): 3–24.

Karpman, Michael, Stephen Zuckerman, and Dulce Gonzalez. 2018. "Despite Labor
Market Gains in 2018, There Were Only Modest Improvement in Families'
Ability to Meet Basic Needs." Urban Institute. https://www.urban.org/sites/
default/files/publication/100216/despite_labor_market_gains_in_2018_there
_were_only_modest_improvements_in_families_ability_to_meet_basic_needs
.pdf.

Krugman, Paul. 2011. "Presidential Address: The Profession and the Crisis." *Eastern
Economics Journal* 37: 307–12.

Mandel, Amir. 2018. "Why Nobel Prize Winner Daniel Kahneman Gave Up on Happiness." *Haaretz*, October 7. https://www.haaretz.com/israel-news/.premium
.MAGAZINE-why-nobel-prize-winner-daniel-kahneman-gave-up-on-happiness
-1.6528513.

McGregor, J. Allister, and Nicky Pouw. 2017. "Towards an Economics of Well-Being."
Cambridge Journal of Economics 41, no. 4 (July): 1123–42.

Meer, Tom Van Der. 2017. "Political Trust and the 'Crisis of Democracy.'" *Oxford
Research Encyclopedias*, January. https://oxfordre.com/politics/politics/view/10
.1093/acrefore/9780190228637.001.0001/acrefore-9780190228637-e-77.

Metzl, Jonathan. 2019. *Dying of Whiteness: How the Politics of Racial Resentment Is Killing America's Heartland*. New York: Basic Books.

Naidu, Suresh, Eric Posner, and Glen Weyl. 2018. "More and More Companies Have Monopoly Power of Workers' Wages. That's Killing the Economy." *Vox*, April 6. https://www.vox.com/the-big-idea/2018/4/6/17204808/wages-employers -workers-monopsony-growth-stagnation-inequality.

Pearson, Paul. 2004. *Politics in Time*. Princeton, NJ: Princeton University Press.

Piketty, Thomas. 2013. *Capital in the 21st Century*. Cambridge: Cambridge University Press.

Quart, Alissa. "There's a Reason Why You Can't Afford to Live in America." *Guardian*, June 18, 2018. https://www.theguardian.com/money/2018/jun/18/middle -class-debt-squeezed-alissa-quart-extract.

Sechel, Cristina. 2019. "Happier than Them, but More of Them Are Happy." Working Papers 2019, University of Sheffield, Department of Economics.

Sen, Amartya. 1985. "Well-Being, Agency and Freedom: The Dewey Lectures 1984." *Journal of Philosophy* 82, no. 4 (April): 169–221.

———. 2009. *The Idea of Justice*. Cambridge, MA: Harvard University Press.

Skidelsky, R., and E. Skidelsky. 2012. *How Much Is Enough? The Love of Money, and the Case for the Good Life*. London: Allen Lane.

Smith, Adam. 1976. *The Theory of Moral Sentiments*. Oxford University Press.

———. 1977. *An Inquiry into the Nature and Causes of the Wealth of Nations*. University of Chicago Press.

Smith, P. B., and M. Max-Neef. 2012. *Economics Unmasked: From Power and Greed to Compassion*. Cambridge, UK: Green Books.

Standing, G. 2011. *The Precariat: The New Dangerous Class*. New York: Bloomsbury Academic.

Stiglitz, J. E., A. K. Sen, and J.-P. Fitoussi. 2009. *Measuring Economic Performance and Social Progress*. Paris: Commission on the Measurement of Economic Performance and Social Progress.

Stiglitz, Joseph. 2012. *The Price of Inequality: How Today's Divided Society Endangers Our Future*. New York: Norton.

Weil, David. 2018. "Why We Should Worry about Monopsony." *Institute for New Economic Thinking*, September 2. https://www.ineteconomics.org/perspectives/ blog/why-we-should-worry-about-monopsony.

Wilkinson, R. G., and K. Pickett. 2009. *The Spirit Level: Why More Equal Societies Almost Always Do Better*. London: Allen Lane.

Woodly, Deva. 2015. "Seeing Collectivity: Structural Relation Through the Lens of Youngian Seriality." *Contemporary Political Theory* 14: 213–33.

Wray-Lake, Laura, Cody DeHaan, Jennifer Shubert, and Richard Ryan. 2017. "Examining Links from Civic Engagement to Daily Well-Being from a Self-Determination Theory Perspective." *Journal of Positive Psychology* 14:166–77.

Young, Iris Marion. 1994. *Justice and the Politics of Difference*. Princeton, NJ: Princeton University Press.

5 Beyond the Perpetual Pursuit of Economic Growth

JULIE L. ROSE

Introduction

Though economic growth is a leading policy goal of nearly all contemporary governments, with quarterly changes in gross domestic product (GDP) widely reported as a barometer of a society's health, skepticism about the pursuit of economic growth is increasingly prominent.[1] Challenges to growth first peaked in the 1970s[2] and have risen again today, with a political and social movement questioning the "growth paradigm,"[3] as well as the development of alternative indicators of social progress "beyond GDP."[4] Many critics object to how economic growth is unsustainably pursued and how its gains are inequitably distributed. Others, however, go further and challenge the pursuit of indefinite economic growth itself. These critics reject the idea that a society ought to aim for economic growth without end, arguing that there is a point at which a society is wealthy enough. A society's economy ought to be "based on *enough*" instead of one that "forever chases *more*." Beyond some threshold level of wealth, they argue, a society need not and should not aim endlessly for further economic growth in pursuit of ever-higher levels of income and wealth.[5]

Though objections to how economic growth is pursued and distributed may be readily understood and granted, to reject the continued pursuit of economic growth itself is a more difficult proposition. Even if a society has attained high levels of income and wealth, continued economic growth, if sustainable and broadly shared, on its face could make everyone, including the worst off, still better off.

While any engagement with the question of whether a society ought indeed to perpetually pursue economic growth, or whether at some point it may or should cease to do so, undeniably must draw on a set of empirical considerations, the question is at bottom a normative one. To address it fully depends on an account of the aims and values that should guide a society. Yet contemporary theories of justice have given this question little sustained attention. To the extent that they do provide guidance on the question of whether a society should perpetually pursue economic growth, contemporary theories of justice primarily suggest two possible approaches.

The first approach denies that a society may cease to pursue economic growth. On this view, a society should aim to make its members (or people more generally) indefinitely better off, and to do so it ought to aim to increase their shares of income and wealth. The second approach instead implicitly or explicitly treats the question of whether a wealthy society should aim for further economic growth, or further gains more broadly, as a matter of societal discretion, on which principles of justice are silent or indifferent. This view focuses on the demands of meeting and maintaining sufficiency thresholds and egalitarian principles and leaves open whether and what further gains a society should pursue.

These two approaches, taken together, suggest either that a society is obligated to aim to make its members (or people more generally) indefinitely better off, and that even wealthy societies must perpetually pursue economic growth, or that a society is not obligated to do so and accordingly may cease to pursue economic growth.

Earlier arguments against the perpetual pursuit of economic growth, however, suggest an alternative approach. Two of the most prominent and generative sets of arguments against the perpetual pursuit of economic growth—those in John Stuart Mill's chapter on "The Stationary State" in *Principles of Political Economy* (1848) and John Maynard Keynes's "Economic Possibilities for Our Grandchildren" (1930)—instead suggest that, beyond some level of wealth, it is by ceasing to pursue economic growth that a society may make its members better off. This approach, distinctively, does not dispute that if it is possible for a society to make its members genuinely better off it ought to do so, but denies that this entails that a society must indefinitely pursue economic growth.

Mill's and Keynes's arguments are richly suggestive, but they merge the political and the ethical, tying their arguments to particular views of the good life. While some may welcome arguments against the perpetual pursuit of economic growth on such grounds, they are in tension with contemporary liberal principles of justice that preclude the justification of a society's basic political and economic institutions and public policies on perfectionist judgments about better and worse ways of living.

Yet the core insight of Mill's and Keynes's arguments—that people may be better off in a society that does not continue to pursue economic growth—

need not rest on such perfectionist grounds, as examining this claim within the terms of John Rawls's theory of justice as fairness suggests. Rawls's principles of justice provide particularly productive terrain to pursue this idea because Rawls, most notably within contemporary liberal theories of justice, denies that a society must indefinitely pursue economic growth. Though Rawls's argument is not explicitly developed and is indeed "puzzling," reconstructing his position that the principles of justice as fairness are "compatible" with Mill's "just stationary state" demonstrates how, without necessarily relying on perfectionist premises, a society may arrange its institutions and policies such that they do not pursue or realize further economic growth, on the grounds that it is under such arrangements that its worst-off members are better off.[6]

Developing this alternative approach drawn from Mill's, Keynes's, and Rawls's arguments more broadly within the contours of contemporary liberal principles of justice supports, I argue, a *just agrowth* position.[7] On this view, a society should open-endedly aim to make people better off, insofar as is possible and consistent with a theory of justice's other principles, by fairly and reliably expanding their effective opportunities.[8] Continued economic growth may, or may not, contribute to this aim, and so a society should neither reject nor endorse the pursuit of economic growth itself. It is beyond the scope of this chapter to fully develop and argue for this alternative position; rather, the aim here is instead to show how Mill's, Keynes's, and Rawls's prominent arguments against the perpetual pursuit of economic growth can illuminate and support a just agrowth position and to advance it as an alternative approach.[9]

Before proceeding, it is important to clarify a conceptual question about the definition of economic growth that arises in parallel with the normative question about whether it makes people better off, which Mancur Olson, writing in the introduction to a volume on "The No-Growth Society" in 1973, puts well. If, following Lionel Robbins's canonical definition, one sees economics expansively as the "relationship between ends and scarce means which have alternative uses," then, as Olson sees it, there is "economic growth whenever existing wants are satisfied to a greater degree than they were in a previous period." If this definition of economic growth as simply an increase in preference-satisfaction is accepted, Olson presses, then the call for the cessation of economic growth "comes down simply to saying that people should have no more of anything they want," even a "cleaner environment," or more "cathedrals and art galleries," or whatever else the critic might prefer. But, Olson argues, this raises a contradiction, because when proponents "advocate zero economic growth, they do not mean that we should not be better off; on the contrary, they mean that if what they understood to be economic growth were to cease, we would be better off." As Olson then recognizes and grants, contrary to the economist who holds that "the economic dimension has no logical outer limit," critics of economic growth reject its identification with an increase in preference-satisfaction, or overall well-being or quality of life. They instead take economic growth to have a more circumscribed meaning, such as an increase in income and wealth, capital accumulation, or material throughput, and the conventional definition of economic growth as an increase in real GDP per capita generally serves as a practical referent for both its defenders and challengers.[10]

It is also important to note that the examination of Mill's, Keynes's, and Rawls's arguments considers whether a society may or should cease to pursue economic growth and whether in doing it may make its members better off, without directly considering how economic growth in one society affects or is affected by other societies, or whether a society has an open-ended obligation to make people in other societies better off, because their arguments examined here proceed within this societal frame. I do not, however, maintain this restricted scope when turning to the just agrowth position in concluding.

The remainder of the chapter examines Mill's, Keynes's, and Rawls's arguments in turn, before concluding by showing how the alternative approach they suggest may be developed to yield a just agrowth position.

Mill and the Progressive Stationary State

Mill's chapter on "The Stationary State" in *Principles of Political Economy* provides a clear vision of what we may call the progressive stationary state, in which a society, while ceasing to aim for economic growth, continues to pursue and realize gains on other dimensions. Beyond some level of wealth, Mill suggests that people may be better off in a society that ceases to pursue economic growth, and indeed that they may be continuously better off, without continued economic growth, as a society can still attain ongoing gains on other, relatively more valuable dimensions.[11]

Mill's vision of such a progressive stationary state was a radical departure from the view of the classical political economists, who saw the stationary state, a condition in which economic growth ceases, as an unwelcome state of stagnation in which most people's lives would be "pinched and stinted."[12] Though they saw the process of economic expansion as constrained by inevitable limits, they nonetheless sought and recommended measures—such as restraints on population growth, expansion of foreign commerce, and technological improvements—by which a society could attempt to continuously postpone the stationary state's arrival.[13]

Although Mill, too, believed that an increase in wealth was not "boundless" or "in its nature unlimited," he did not share the perspective of the "political economists of the old school" who regarded the stationary state with "unaffected aversion." Rather, Mill argues, he is "inclined to believe that it would be, on the whole, a very considerable improvement on our present condition." Indeed, rather than recommending that societies unceasingly seek to defer the stationary state, he hopes that they "will be content to be stationary, long before necessity compels them to it."[14]

Mill argues that it is a mistake to assume that people must live in poverty in a society in which economic growth—which he treats as the "mere increase of production and accumulation"—has ceased. A society, having developed its technology, security, and cooperation to a degree that allows for abundant production and accumulation, can maintain a high standard of living in a stationary state if it distributes wealth more equally and voluntarily restrains population growth. Under "this two-fold influence," Mill writes, such a society would have certain characteristics:

> A well-paid and affluent body of labourers; no enormous fortunes, except what were earned and accumulated during a single lifetime; but a much larger body of persons than at present, not only exempt from the coarser toils, but with sufficient leisure, both physical and mental, from mechanical details, to cultivate freely the graces of life, and afford examples of them to the classes less favourably circumstanced for their growth.[15]

"This state of things," he continues, "which seems, economically considered, to be the most desirable condition of society, is not only perfectly compatible with the stationary state, but, it would seem, more naturally allied with that state than with any other."[16]

Having recast what is economically possible consistent with a stationary state, Mill makes a series of arguments against the continuous pursuit of economic growth. First, Mill contends that the social relations that the pursuit of economic growth depends on and fosters are its "disagreeable symptoms." He is, he writes, "not charmed with the ideal of life held out by those who think that the normal state of human beings is one of struggling to get on." The "trampling, crushing, elbowing, and treading on each other's heels" associated with the "struggle for riches"—the "existing type of social life"—is far from the "most desirable lot of human kind." Rather, "the best state for human nature" is one in which "while no one is poor, no one desires to be richer, nor has any reason to fear being thrust back, by the efforts of others to push themselves forward."[17]

Mill further argues that increases in production and consumption have diminishing value, to a point at which they indeed might provide no additional value. He suggests that, above some threshold, consumption no longer serves to meet important interests and instead serves only as a means of expressing one's wealth: "I know not why it should be matter of congratulation that persons who are already richer than any one needs to be, should have doubled their means of consuming things which give little or no pleasure except as representative of wealth." In the "most advanced" societies, "increased production" is no longer "an important object."[18]

Moreover, Mill argues, beyond some degree of industrial progress, further increases in wealth are of diminishing value relative to other rival goods.[19] The competing goods to which Mill gives particular emphasis are solitude and nature. Mill argues that if the increase of wealth and population were to be unlimited, the "earth must lose that great portion of its pleasantness":

It is not good for man to be kept perforce at all times in the presence of his species. A world from which solitude is extirpated, is a very poor ideal. Solitude, in the sense of being often alone, is essential to any depth of meditation or of character; and solitude in the presence of natural beauty and grandeur, is the cradle of thoughts and aspirations which are not only good for the individual, but which society could ill do without. Nor is there much satisfaction in contemplating the world with nothing left to the spontaneous activity of nature. . . .[20]

In addition to solitude and nature, this argument applies to any good that is more valuable than additional wealth and that further economic growth might limit, including leisure time, "to cultivate freely the graces of life."[21]

Finally, Mill stresses that people could still be continuously better off without continued economic growth:

A stationary condition of capital and population implies no stationary state of human improvement. There would be as much scope as ever for all kinds of mental culture, and moral and social progress; as much room for improving the Art of Living, and much more likelihood of its being improved, when minds ceased to be engrossed by the art of getting on. Even the industrial arts might be as earnestly and as successfully cultivated, with this sole difference, that instead of serving no purpose but the increase of wealth, industrial improvements would produce their legitimate effect, that of abridging labour.[22]

A society would continue to realize improvements, and indeed when people are no longer driven by the pursuit of wealth's "coarse stimuli," these improvements would take more valuable forms.[23]

Taken together, Mill's case against perpetually pursuing economic growth is, first, that contrary to the claims of the earlier classical economists, the stationary state could be a condition of secure and shared abundance; second, that the pursuit of economic growth itself depends on and fosters undesirable social relations; third, that beyond some level of economic development, additional wealth and consumption have little value and are less valuable than competing goods; and finally, that a stationary state would continue to be one of progress, and its continued improvements would be realized in and directed toward more valuable domains. Accordingly, rather than seeking to continuously postpone the end of economic growth, such a just stationary state ought to be regarded and aimed toward as a social ideal.

Beyond the particulars of Mill's arguments on behalf of the stationary state, in view of the aim here of drawing from these arguments an alternative approach to the question of whether a society must indefinitely pursue economic growth, the central idea that his vision provides is this: beyond some level of wealth, people may be better off in a society that ceases to pursue economic growth, and furthermore, they may be continuously better off as a society can continue to realize gains on other, more valuable dimensions.

Keynes and the Complete Stationary State

In the years after Mill's *Principles of Political Economy*, the idea of the stationary state as the welcomed end of economic growth was absent from economic thought until it was resuscitated by Keynes in "Economic Possibilities for Our Grandchildren."[24] Like Mill, Keynes provides a vision of the stationary state that suggests how, beyond some level of wealth, people may be better off in a society that does not continue to pursue economic growth. But his account goes further to suggest that people may be best off in a society that—because of the disvalues associated with perpetually aiming to be better off—does not continue to pursue improvements more generally. Keynes's vision requires more interpretive reconstruction than Mill's, but from this examination, it is possible to discern an ideal of what we may call the complete stationary state, in which a society ceases to aim not only for further economic growth but further gains on any dimension.

Keynes's essay opens by considering the long-run trend of "economic progress" and then "takes wings into the future" to ask what we can expect the "level of our economic life" to be in another century. He predicts that, owing to "science and compound interest," the standard of living in "progressive" societies will be four to eight times higher. Assuming that in a hundred years, people will be on average "eight times better off in the economic sense," he comes to this "startling" conclusion:

> Assuming no important wars and no important increase in population, the *economic problem* may be solved, or be at least within sight of solution . . . This means that the economic problem is not—if we look into the future— *the permanent problem of the human race.*[25]

Keynes defines the economic problem as "the struggle for subsistence" and its solution as the point at which our "needs are satisfied" and our energies can be devoted to "non-economic purposes." Though Keynes acknowledges that there are "relative" needs, or positional desires, he sees the solution to the economic problem as the point at which our specifically "absolute needs"— those felt "whatever the situation of our fellow human beings may be"—are met.[26] Further, due to "revolutionary technical changes," these absolute needs can be fully met with little "human effort." The solution to the economic problem will then bring an "age of leisure and of abundance."[27]

Keynes predicts that this transformation will happen gradually, and indeed had already begun, and that it will be realized as there are ever more "people from whom problems of economic necessity have been practically removed." Since "it will remain reasonable to be economically purposive for others after it has ceased to be reasonable for oneself," the pivotal point will be when the freedom from economic necessity is so widespread that "the nature of one's duty to one's neighbor is changed."[28]

When this point is reached and the economic problem is solved, humankind will then face "his real, his permanent problem—how to use his freedom from pressing economic cares, how to occupy the leisure . . . to live wisely and agreeably and well." All of society will then be in the position of the "wealthy classes" or the "wives of the well-to-do" who, without the "spur of economic necessity," struggle to find "amusing" ways to spend their time. In the same way, without the need to work for subsistence, "mankind will be deprived of its traditional purpose."[29]

Keynes argues that if a society is to benefit from solving the economic problem and to realize the possibilities of leisure and abundance, there must be a widespread transformation in people's values and social and economic practices.[30] Because humanity's "primary, most pressing problem" has always been the economic problem, "we have been trained too long to strive and not to enjoy." Existing values and practices have been maintained, "however distasteful and unjust," because they are "tremendously useful in promoting the accumulation of capital"—"foul is useful and fair is not." But without the need for further economic growth, "we shall be able to rid ourselves of many of the pseudo-moral principles which have hag-ridden us for two hundred years, by which we have exalted some of the most distasteful human qualities into the position of the highest virtues."[31]

Keynes focuses on two principles whose errors we will finally be able to see properly and "at last, to discard." The first, more narrowly economic principle, is the "money-motive"—the "love of money as a possession" rather than as a "means to the enjoyments and realities of life." Reflecting his interest at the time in Freud, he argued that the "detestable" love of money "will be recognized for what it is, a somewhat disgusting morbidity, one of those semi-criminal, semi-pathological propensities which one hands with a shudder to the specialists in mental disease."[32]

The money-motive (which, along with the principle of compound interest, Keynes sometimes equates with "avarice and usury") is an aspect of the second, broader principle, which Keynes labels "purposiveness." For Keynes, purposiveness "means that we are more concerned with the remote future results of our actions than with their own quality or their immediate effects on our own environment." This purposiveness, which almost everyone has to some extent, is ultimately irrational. "The 'purposive' man is always trying to secure a spurious and delusive immortality for his acts by pushing his interest in them forward into time." By perpetually acting for the sake of the future results of our actions, we deprive ourselves of enjoyment in the present. The purposive man "does not love his cat, but his cat's kittens; nor, in truth, the kittens, but only the kittens' kittens, and so on forward for ever to the end of cat-dom."[33]

Ultimately, these principles can "lead us out of the tunnel of economic necessity into daylight," and "we can reach our destination of economic bliss." Led into the daylight, and now facing the permanent problem of occupying our leisure and living well, how then does Keynes propose that we ought to meet this true challenge? Keynes does not provide a full account of what it means "to live wisely and agreeably and well" but does provide suggestive remarks. Following his rejection of purposiveness, he contrasts "the activities of purpose" with "the arts of life" and argues that "it will be those peoples, who can keep alive, and cultivate into a fuller perfection, the art of life itself and do not sell themselves for the means of life, who will be able to enjoy the abundance when it comes." Rather than continuously looking to the future results of one's actions, the person who cultivates the art of life itself enjoys the present: it is those "who take the least thought for the morrow" who "walk most truly in the paths of virtue and sane wisdom." We should emulate "those who can teach us how to pluck the hour and the day virtuously and well, the delightful people who are capable of taking direct enjoyment in things, the lilies of the field who toil not, neither do they spin." Along with taking "direct enjoyment in things" without "thought for the morrow," we should, most fundamentally, "value ends above means and prefer the good to the useful." It is in this way that we can live well and realize the "real values of life."[34]

Keynes does not, in this essay, provide an account of the "real values of life" or what constitutes the "arts of life," but understanding what he means by these values, and their distinction from "activities of purpose," is central to reconstructing Keynes's account of the stationary state. To develop Keynes's account of what ways of living are truly valuable, the argument in "Economic Possibilities" can be read in the context of his lifelong commitment to the philosophy of G. E. Moore. While a student, Keynes attended Moore's lectures on ethics and became an active member of the Apostles, a society that included Bertrand Russell, Henry Sidgwick, and Moore.[35] As he recalled in "My Early Beliefs," an essay read at a Bloomsbury group meeting that included many from this society in 1938, Moore's *Principia Ethica* profoundly shaped his views: "I went up to Cambridge at Michaelmas 1902, and Moore's *Principia Ethica* came out at the end of my first year . . . of course, its effect on *us*, and the talk which preceded and followed it, dominated, and perhaps still dominate, everything else." Keynes became a close student of Moore's *Principia Ethica*, and in 1905 he wrote "Miscellanea Ethica," an extended sketch of a "complete ethical treatise," in which he embraced the central claims of Moore's ethics on the nature of the good. As Keynes wrote in 1906 to Lytton Strachey, "It is impossible to exaggerate the *wonder* and *originality* of Moore . . . How amazing to think that only we know the rudiments of a true theory of ethic; for nothing can be more certain than that the broad outline is true." In his 1938 essay, Keynes remained faithful to Moore's philosophy: "It remains nearer the truth than any other that I know, with less irrelevant extraneous matter and nothing to be ashamed of. . . . It is still my religion under the surface."[36]

In the final chapter of *Principia Ethica* on "The Ideal," Moore sets out his account of what it is that is intrinsically good in a passage Keynes cites in

"My Early Beliefs": "By far the most valuable things, which we can know or can imagine, are certain states of consciousness, which may be roughly described as the pleasures of human intercourse and the enjoyment of beautiful objects." Moore argued that "it is only for the sake of these things—in order that as much of them as possible may at some time exist—that any one can be justified in performing any public or private duty." It is, Moore argued, the existence of these goods—the states of consciousness experienced in love, friendship, and the appreciation of beauty—that "form the rational ultimate end of human action and the sole criterion of social progress."[37]

The goods Moore identified as intrinsically valuable connect to the Bloomsbury ideal of life dedicated to friendship and beauty, and indeed *Principia Ethics* was a "sacred text" among the group of writers and artists united by their shared values. Keynes lived in Bloomsbury for several years with Vanessa and Clive Bell and remained a member of its circle, and as his biographer Robert Skidelsky describes, "they were not just his friends but his ideal."[38]

Reading "Economic Possibilities" in the context of Keynes's abiding commitment to Moore's ethics and the ideals embodied by his Bloomsbury friends provides grounds to develop Keynes's account of what it would mean to meet the permanent problem of living well.[39] First, when Keynes holds that we ought to "value ends above means and prefer the good to the useful," this can be read not only as a general appeal for ultimate over instrumental values but specifically for Moore's understanding of intrinsic good. Second, and more concretely, the content of the good can be filled in, from Moore, as the states of mind experienced in love and friendship and the enjoyment of beauty. The "art of life itself" is, then, not to be concerned with pursuing the means to some future good but, like those "delightful people," to take "direct enjoyment" in the goods of human relationships and aesthetic appreciation. Upon solving the economic problem, we ought to cast aside not only the love of money but all purposiveness and occupy our newfound leisure with the enjoyment of relationships, community, and beauty. Keynes's ideal then reverses the tendency "to strive and not to enjoy," as people reject purposiveness in favor of taking direct enjoyment in these goods without regard for the future. Because enjoying the "real values of life" is in conflict with perpetually seeking improvement, people may be best off, on Keynes's account, by forgoing the continuous pursuit of further gains.

Both Mill's and Keynes's visions of the stationary state suggest that beyond some level of wealth, people may be better off in a society that forgoes further economic growth. The structures of Mill's and Keynes's accounts illustrate two ideals of the stationary state: one in which a society ceases to pursue economic growth but continues to aim for gains on other dimensions, and one in which a society ceases to aim for further gains on any dimension. In the progressive stationary state, because the society continues to pursue gains on other, relatively more valuable dimensions, people are continuously better off, while in the complete stationary state, because of the disvalue of continuously aiming for improvement, people are best off without being continuously better off.

Rawls and the Possibility of the Stationary State

In the most notable endorsement of the stationary state in contemporary theories of justice, Rawls argues that the principles of his theory of justice as fairness do not require a society to perpetually pursue economic growth.[40] Rawls's position is, however, not explicitly developed and requires reconstruction. In developing Rawls's argument here, I take up an interpretation provided by Samuel Freeman and build on it to show how Rawls's position may be extended in a way that furthers the tracks set by Mill and Keynes. This position provides grounds, without necessarily relying on perfectionist judgments about better or worse ways of living, to develop the approach indicated by Mill's and Keynes's suggestions that, beyond some level of wealth, people may be better off in a society that does not continue to pursue or realize further economic growth, or indeed they may be best off without any further gains.

Rawls argues that neither justice as fairness's intergenerational nor intragenerational principles entail that a society must indefinitely aim for further economic growth. The intergenerational just savings principle requires each generation to "put aside in each period a suitable amount of real capital accumulation," but it does not require perpetual accumulation. The savings principle has an ultimate "objective," which is the point at which "just institutions are firmly established and all the basic liberties effectively realized." When this cutoff point is reached, justice does not require a generation to continue accumulating capital to further improve the prospects of future generations. As such, the just savings principle does not require "maximizing indefinitely," a point Rawls reiterates in *Law of Peoples* and there connects to Mill.[41] The principle's "aim is to realize and preserve just (or decent) institutions, and not simply to increase, much less to maximize indefinitely, the average level of wealth, or the wealth of any society or any particular class in society."[42] He continues, in a footnote:

I follow Mill's view that the purpose of saving is to make possible a just basic structure of society; once that is safely secured, real saving (net increase in real capital) may no longer be necessary. "The art of living" is more important than "the art of getting on," to use his words. The thought that real saving and economic growth are to go on indefinitely, upwards and onwards, with no specified goal in sight, is the idea of the business class of a capitalist society. But what counts for Mill are just basic institutions and the well-being of what Mill would call "the labouring class."[43]

Moreover, he argues, the realization of just institutions does not depend on having "great abundance," as "it is a mistake to believe that a just and good society must wait upon a high material standard of life."[44] As such, the just savings principle does not require a society to aim indefinitely to make future generations better off and, taken on its own, suggests that a society that has met the cutoff point may then cease to pursue further economic growth.

But, for Rawls, the route to justifying the stationary state is not so direct. Though the just savings principle specifies a cutoff point for justice between generations, it is only one component of Rawls's full theory of justice, and the theory's central intragenerational principles do not have the same structure. Of greatest relevance here, consistent with the satisfaction of the theory's prior principles, the difference principle holds that "social and economic inequalities are to be arranged so that they are . . . to the greatest benefit of the least advantaged."[45] As Rawls explains, what this entails is that "we are to compare schemes of cooperation by seeing how well off the least advantaged are under each scheme, and then select the scheme under which the least advantaged are better off than they are under any other scheme," and then within this scheme, to aim to maximize the expectations of the least advantaged.[46]

The difference principle itself contains two conditions, as Rawls indicates in his discussion of the distinction between a "just throughout" and a "perfectly just" society. The first condition is that social and economic inequalities are permissible only to the extent that they are to the greatest benefit to the least advantaged. The second condition is that inequalities ought to be arranged so that they maximize the expectations of the least advantaged. A society that meets the first condition but not the second is "just throughout." It is not unjust, as it would be if inequalities exceeded their permissible bounds, but it is not "the best just arrangement." In a "perfectly just" society, both of the difference principle's conditions are satisfied, as "the expectations of the least advantaged are indeed maximized . . . No changes in the expectations of those better off can improve the situation of those worst off."[47] As such, the difference principle both limits the extent of permissible inequality and directs a society ideally to maximize the expectations of the least advantaged.

Given that Rawls often refers to the expectations of the least advantaged in terms of their "prospects of income and wealth over a complete life," on its face, it then seems that the difference principle directs a society to indefinitely pursue economic growth to maximize, within generations, the lifetime expectations of the least advantaged.[48] Yet, in clarifying the meaning of the difference principle in his later works, Rawls makes plain that the difference principle does not require indefinite economic growth. Repeating and elaborating on a footnote in *Political Liberalism* that the difference principle is "compatible with Mill's idea of a society in a just stationary state where (real) capital accumulation is zero," Rawls writes in *Justice as Fairness*:

> The difference principle . . . does not require continual economic growth over generations to maximize upward indefinitely the expectations of the least advantaged (assessed in terms of income and wealth). That would not be a reasonable conception of justice. We should not rule out Mill's idea of a society in a just stationary state where (real) capital accumulation may cease. A well-ordered society is specified so as to allow for this possibility.[49]

Rawls continues, explaining how the difference principle is compatible with the cessation of economic growth:

> What the difference principle does require is that during an appropriate interval of time the differences in income and wealth earned in producing the social product be such that if the legitimate expectations of the more advantaged were less, those of the less advantaged would be less. . . . Permissible inequalities (thus defined) satisfy that condition and are compatible with a social product of a steady-state equilibrium in which a just basic structure is supported and reproduced over time.[50]

Rawls here suggests that the difference principle is compatible with the cessation of economic growth because it is possible that a society could be at a point at which any additional inequality, though it would incentivize greater production and so result in economic growth, would not benefit the least advantaged (e.g., if the marginal increase in the social product would be consumed entirely by the more advantaged's incentive). This inequality would not be permissible, and so the society would remain at an equilibrium with a zero growth rate.

When here clarifying that the difference principle does not require perpetually pursuing economic growth, Rawls makes reference only to the least advantaged's shares of income and wealth, or shares of a society's productive output as realized in wages and salaries.[51] Yet, within this focus on income and wealth, the argument only narrowly establishes the possibility of a just stationary state. As long as inequalities earned in producing the social product are restricted to those that are to the greatest benefit to the least advantaged, the difference principle would still direct a society, within its constraints, to institute an economic arrangement that allows for maximal economic growth and then to aim to continuously maximize productive output.[52]

There are two ways to reconstruct Rawls's account to more robustly reconcile the difference principle with the stationary state. The first focuses on the difference principle's limitation on the extent of permissible inequality and holds that, on its best interpretation, the difference principle does not require a society to indefinitely maximize the expectations of the least advantaged. It would then not direct a society to aim to make the least advantaged indefinitely better off, and so would not require a society to perpetually pursue economic growth.[53]

The second does not question the difference principle's directive ideally to maximize the expectations of the least advantaged, but instead broadens the difference principle's focus beyond income and wealth. Though Rawls often treats income and wealth as a proxy, the expectations of the least advantaged are more accurately assessed with reference to their expected shares of a bundle of primary goods, weighted in an index, over a complete life. Primary goods are the social conditions and all-purpose means that are generally necessary to develop and exercise one's moral powers and to pursue one's particular conception of the good. The difference principle applies not only to the primary goods of income and wealth, but also to the powers and prerogatives of offices and positions of authority and responsibility, and the social bases of self-respect.[54]

Freeman proposes such a reconstructive argument to square Rawls's claim that the difference principle is compatible with the stationary state.[55] Some economic arrangements, such as those in which workers have cooperatives or partial ownership in their workplaces and more control over production and their work conditions, may provide the least advantaged with greater shares of the powers and prerogatives of office and the social bases of self-respect. Yet, such arrangements may provide the least advantaged with less income and wealth than other economic arrangements, such as those of the capitalist welfare state, and it is possible that such arrangements might dramatically dampen or entirely cease economic growth. Nonetheless, such arrangements may indeed be to the greatest benefit to the least advantaged, depending on how the different primary goods are weighted in the index.

As such, considering the difference principle's directive to maximize the expectations of the least advantaged within this appropriately broad focus reveals wider grounds on which it is compatible with the stationary state. Following Mill's and Keynes's suggestions that people may be better off in a society that ceases to aim for further economic growth, the least advantaged's expectations may be maximized, in terms of the full bundle of primary goods, under arrangements that do not pursue or realize economic growth.

Moreover, broadening the range of the difference principle to apply not only to Rawls's listed primary goods but a fuller set of the social conditions and all-purpose means that citizens generally require to develop and exercise their capacities and pursue their conceptions of the good provides even wider scope for the stationary state, either progressive or complete, to be to the greatest benefit to the least advantaged. Further, the argument that the difference principle is compatible with the stationary state need not rely on perfectionist judgments about better or worse ways of living, as long as the index is composed of such generally required resources and conditions and the weights in the index are not determined on the basis of such judgments.[56] The fuller set of resources and conditions also ought to include the temporal resource of free time (understood as time not committed to meeting basic needs) and the social bases of health and longevity (in the form of both health care and measures for public health) and other internal resources. The list should also include access to relational goods and environmental goods (both as instrumental resources and as components of conceptions of the good).[57]

The possibilities for how arrangements that cease to pursue or realize economic growth may still be to the greatest benefit to the least advantaged are significantly extended if the index of resources and conditions to which the difference principle applies is composed of such a multidimensional set, and given that economic and social arrangements can affect shares of these goods in both beneficial and burdensome ways. Depending on how the goods are weighted in the index and a society's circumstances, it may be the case that the lifetime expectations of the least advantaged are greatest under arrangements that cease to pursue or realize economic growth, while continuously increasing their free time, the social bases of health and longevity and other internal resources, and their access to relational and environmental goods. But it may also be the case that, if realizing gains on some dimensions could only be achieved in ways that produce outweighing losses on other dimensions, the least advantaged are best off under arrangements that cease to pursue or realize not only economic growth but gains on any dimensions.

The result is that, while Rawls's difference principle directs a society to arrange its social and economic institutions such that they are to the greatest benefit to the least advantaged, it is potentially compatible with both the progressive and complete stationary states suggested by Mill and Keynes. Depending on circumstances and how goods are weighted in the index, the least advantaged may be best off under arrangements that *continue* to pursue and realize economic growth or under arrangements that *cease* to pursue or realize gains in income and wealth, or further gains on any dimensions.

Conclusion

To return, then, to the opening question: Must a society perpetually pursue economic growth, or may it cease to do so? Contemporary theories of justice suggest two possible approaches to this question: either a society is obligated to aim to make its members (or people more generally) indefinitely better off and even wealthy societies must perpetually pursue economic growth, or a society is not so obligated and so may cease to pursue economic growth.

Yet, Mill's and Keynes's earlier arguments against the perpetual pursuit of economic growth suggest an alternative approach. Both centrally argue that, beyond some level of wealth, people may be better off in a society that ceases to pursue economic growth. Mill's vision of the stationary state suggests that because a society can continue to realize improvements on other dimensions, people may be continuously better off without the continued pursuit or realization of economic growth. Keynes's vision instead suggests that, because of the disvalues associated with perpetually pursuing improvements, people may be best off without the continued pursuit or realization of further gains on any dimension. Their accounts support ideals, respectively, of progressive and complete stationary states.

While Mill's and Keynes's arguments depend on particular ideas of the good life, as the reconstruction and extension of Rawls's difference principle demonstrates, it is possible to develop their central claim without necessarily relying on such perfectionist judgments. That is, the principle that a society ought to aim to arrange its institutions and policies such that they are to the greatest benefit to the least advantaged is compatible with the stationary state, in both its progressive and complete forms. Depending on a society's circumstances, and on how the multidimensional resources and conditions that people require to develop their capacities and pursue their ends are weighted, people may be best off in a society with institutional arrangements that continue to aim for economic growth or with arrangements that do not.

Developing these arguments more broadly within contemporary liberal egalitarian principles of justice suggests and supports an alternative position. This just agrowth position comprises, first, the principle that a society ought to open-endedly aim to make people better off (insofar as is possible and consistent with a theory of justice's other principles) and, second, the contention that this principle is compatible with a society continuing or ceasing to pursue or realize further economic growth.

While it is beyond the present scope to fill in an account of such a just agrowth position, in general form this position holds that a society's aim to make people better off must be constrained and guided by a broader set of principles of justice setting the terms of this aim. These broader principles must centrally address the international and intergenerational scope, the individual liberty constraints, and the distributive principles within which a society ought to pursue the aim of making people better off.[58] Then, within the terms set by these broader principles of justice, a just agrowth position requires an account of the standard by which a society ought to aim to make people better off, and such an account may take a range of forms. Central liberal egalitarian commitments to effective freedom and respect for pluralism, however, suggest, again in general form, that a society should aim to expand people's effective opportunities to form, revise, and pursue their individual and collective ends, and to do so in a way that respects the diversity of people's ends. Such an account, in this general form, then guides a society to open-endedly aim to make people better off, insofar as is possible and consistent with broader principles of justice, by fairly and reliably expanding their effective opportunities.

A society should, accordingly, neither reject nor endorse the pursuit of economic growth itself. Rather, a society ought to aim to fairly and reliably expand people's opportunities. Because economic growth may or may not contribute to the realization of this principle, a society should treat economic growth as at most a subsidiary aim, pursued only if, and to the extent and on terms such that, it is consistent with the realization of this principle.

Such a just agrowth position, if developed within a full account of the principles, values, and aims that ought to guide a society, provides an argumentative framework within which the normative and empirical evaluation of a society's continued pursuit of economic growth may then more constructively proceed.

Notes

I am grateful to all of the participants in the Political Economy and Justice working group for their insightful and constructive comments. Previous versions of this chapter were presented at Harvard University, the University of Montreal, and Stanford University, and at conferences of the American Political Science Association, Association for Political Theory, Association for Social and Political Philosophy, and Ethics and Economics Network. I thank participants in these events, and Danielle Allen, François Claveau, Eric MacGilvray, Herschel Nachlis, Heather Pincock, Emma Saunders-Hastings, and Juliet Schor for their helpful comments.

1. See Heinz W. Arndt, *The Rise and Fall of Economic Growth: A Study in Contemporary Thought* (Melbourne: Longman Cheshire, 1978); Robert A. Collins, *More: The Politics of Economic Growth in Postwar America* (Oxford: Oxford University Press, 2000); Matthias Schmelzer, *The Hegemony of Growth: The OECD and the Making of the Economic Growth Paradigm* (Cambridge: Cambridge University Press, 2016).

2. Influential critiques from this period include E. J. Mishan, *The Costs of Economic Growth* (London: Staples Press, 1967); Donella Meadows et al., *The Limits to Growth* (New York: Universe Books, 1972); Herman E. Daly, ed., *Toward a Steady-State Economy* (San Francisco: W. H. Freeman, 1973); E. F. Schumacher, *Small Is Beautiful: Economics as If People Mattered* (2010 repr., New York: Harper Collins, 1973); Richard A. Easterlin, "Does Economic Growth Improve the Human Lot? Some Empirical Evidence," in *Nations and Households in Economic Growth: Essays in Honor of Moses Abramovitz*, edited by Paul A. David and Melvin W. Reder (New York: Academic Press, 1974), 89–125; Fred Hirsch, *Social Limits to Growth* (Cambridge, MA: Harvard University Press, 1976); Tibor Scitovsky, *The Joyless Economy: The Psychology of Human Satisfaction* (Oxford: Oxford University Press, 1976).

3. Valérie Fournier, "Escaping from the Economy: The Politics of Degrowth," *International Journal of Sociology and Social Policy* 28 (2008): 528–45; Federico Demaria et al., "What Is Degrowth? From an Activist Slogan to a Social Movement," *Environmental Values* 22 (2013): 191–215.

4. Marc Fleurbaey and Didier Blanchet, *Beyond GDP: Measuring Welfare and Assessing Sustainability* (Oxford: Oxford University Press, 2013); Joseph E. Stiglitz, Amartya Sen, and Jean-Paul Fitoussi, *Mismeasuring Our Lives: Why GDP Doesn't Add Up* (New York: The New Press, 2010).

5. Rob Dietz and Dan O'Neill, *Enough Is Enough: Building a Sustainable Economy in a World of Finite Resources* (Abingdon, Oxon: Routledge, 2013), 15; see also Rob-

ert Skidelsky and Edward Skidelsky, *How Much Is Enough? Money and the Good Life* (New York: Other Press, 2012); Peter A. Victor, "Questioning Economic Growth," *Nature* 468 (2010): 370–71; Tim Jackson, *Prosperity without Growth: Economics for a Finite Planet* (London: Earthscan, 2009); James Gustave Speth, *The Bridge at the Edge of the World: Capitalism, the Environment, and Crossing from Crisis to Sustainability* (New Haven, CT: Yale University Press, 2008); Clive Hamilton, *Growth Fetish* (Sydney: Allen & Unwin, 2003). I examine whether a society must indefinitely pursue economic growth in Julie L. Rose, "On the Value of Economic Growth," *Politics, Philosophy & Economics* 19 (2020): 128–53.

6.   John Rawls, *Political Liberalism*, expanded ed. (New York: Columbia University Press [1993], 2005), 7n5. Both Samuel Freeman and Andrew Williams describe Rawls's position as "puzzling." Samuel Freeman, *Rawls* (New York: Routledge, 2007), 112; Samuel Freeman, *Justice and the Social Contract: Essays on Rawlsian Political Philosophy* (Oxford: Oxford University Press, 2007), 106; Andrew Williams, "Linguistic Protectionism and Wealth Maximinimization," in *Arguing about Justice: Essays for Philippe Van Parijs*, edited by Axel Gosseries and Philippe Vanderborght (Louvain-la-Neuve: Presses universitaires de Louvain, 2011), 395–402.

7.   On the agrowth idea more generally, see Jeroen C. J. M. van den Bergh, "Green Agrowth: Removing the GDP-Growth Constraint on Human Progress," in *Handbook of Growth and Sustainability*, edited by Peter A. Victor and Brett Dolter (Cheltenham, UK: Edward Elgar, 2017), 188–90; see also Peter A. Victor, *Managing without Growth: Slower by Design, Not Disaster* (Cheltenham, UK: Edward Elgar, 2008), 2.

8.   Effective opportunities are here understood broadly, encompassing the ideas of real or effective freedom, capabilities, and genuine opportunities. See John Rawls, *A Theory of Justice*, rev. ed. (Cambridge, MA: Belknap Press of Harvard University Press, 1999), 179; Philippe Van Parijs, *Real Freedom for All: What (If Anything) Can Justify Capitalism?* (Oxford: Clarendon Press, 1995), 21–24; Martha C. Nussbaum, *Women and Human Development: A Capabilities Approach* (Cambridge: Cambridge University Press, 2000); Amartya Sen, *Development as Freedom* (New York: Anchor Books, 1999); Jonathan Wolff and Avner De-Shalit, *Disadvantage* (Oxford: Oxford University Press, 2007); Elizabeth S. Anderson, "What Is the Point of Equality?," *Ethics* 109, no. 2 (1999): 315–21. For related ideas, see Allen's account of empowerment and Woodly's account of flourishing in their chapters in this book.

9.   The just agrowth position may be specified in a range of ways. I develop one way of specifying this position in "The Evenhanded Gains Approach," chapter in progress in *The Ends of Growth* (book manuscript in progress), where I draw on the capabilities approach. The capabilities approach—developed most notably by Amartya Sen and Martha Nussbaum, and from which Nussbaum in particular has built a partial theory of justice—has been central to challenging ideas of development that focus on growth in GDP per capita. Capabilitarian theories of justice have, however, thus far generally followed

the second approach described above, attending primarily to the demands of sufficiency and equality and leaving open, as a matter of societal discretion or as a question still to be addressed, whether and on what dimensions a wealthy society should pursue further gains. As such, a just agrowth position, though specifiable in a range of ways, can be understood and developed to build on the capabilities framework. On the capabilities approach generally, see, for instance, Sen, *Development as Freedom*; Nussbaum, *Women and Human Development*; Martha C. Nussbaum, *Creating Capabilities: The Human Development Approach* (Cambridge, MA: Belknap Press of Harvard University Press, 2011); Ingrid Robeyns, *Wellbeing, Freedom and Social Justice: The Capability Approach Re-Examined* (Cambridge: Open Book Publishers, 2017); Ingrid Robeyns, "The Capability Approach," in *The Oxford Handbook of Distributive Justice*, edited by Serena Olsaretti (Oxford: Oxford University Press, 2018), 109–28. More specifically, on GDP-focused approaches to development, see Martha C. Nussbaum, "Tell Narendra Modi: Human Development Is More than GDP," *Boston Review*, June 18, 2014; Nussbaum, *Creating Capabilities*, 46–50, 56–58. On other questions of justice to be addressed, see Nussbaum, *Women and Human Development*, 75; Nussbaum, *Creating Capabilities*, 40.

10. Lionel Robbins, *An Essay on the Nature and Significance of Economic Science (1932)*, 2nd ed. (London: Macmillan, 1935), 16; Mancur Olson, "Introduction," in *The No-Growth Society*, edited by Mancur Olson and Hans H. Landsberg (New York: Norton, 1973), 4–5. Material throughput, a concept from ecological economics, measures the economy's biophysical scale, as the "flow beginning with raw material inputs, followed by their conversion into commodities, and finally into waste outputs." Herman E. Daly, *Beyond Growth: The Economics of Sustainable Development* (Boston: Beacon Press, 1996), 28.

11. This section follows closely my discussion of Mill's progressive stationary state in Rose, "On the Value of Economic Growth," 131–33.

12. John Stuart Mill, "Principles of Political Economy," in *Principles of Political Economy and Chapters on Socialism*, edited by Jonathan Riley (Oxford: Oxford University Press, 1994), 125. This edition uses the seventh and final edition version of Mill's text from 1871; the passages cited here, except where noted, are the same in the original 1848 and final 1871 versions.

13. On the classical political economists' view of the stationary state, see Murray Milgate and Shannon C. Stimson, *After Adam Smith: A Century of Transformation in Politics and Political Economy* (Princeton, NJ: Princeton University Press, 2009), 191–99; E. A. Wrigley, "The Limits to Growth: Malthus and the Classical Economists," *Population and Development Review* 14 (1988): 30–48; Lisa Herzog, "The Normative Stakes of Economic Growth; Or, Why Adam Smith Does Not Rely on 'Trickle Down,'" *Journal of Politics* 78, no. 1 (2015): 50–62.

14. Mill, "Principles of Political Economy," 124, 126, 129. For discussion of Mill's view of the stationary state, see Jonathan Riley, "Mill's Political Economy: Ricardian Science and Liberal Utilitarian Art," in *The Cambridge Companion*

to Mill, edited by John Skorupski (Cambridge: Cambridge University Press, 1998), 293–337; Nadia Urbinati, "An Alternative Modernity: Mill on Capitalism and the Quality of Life," in *John Stuart Mill and the Art of Life*, edited by Ben Eggleston, Dale E. Miller, and David Weinstein (Oxford: Oxford University Press, 2011), 236–63.

15.   Mill, "Principles of Political Economy," 127–28.

16.   John Stuart Mill, "Principles of Political Economy, Books III-V," in *The Collected Works of John Stuart Mill*, edited by J. M. Robson, vol. 3 (Toronto: University of Toronto Press, 1965), 755. In the 1871 version, this sentence begins: "This condition of society, so greatly preferable to the present, is not only. . . ." (Mill, "Principles of Political Economy," 128).

17.   Mill, "Principles of Political Economy," 126–27. Mill's view of this sort of economic competition as undesirable bears a connection to the closing paragraph of *Principles of Political Economy*, where he writes of the government's role in limiting conduct that is "clearly injurious": "Even in the best state which society has yet reached, it is lamentable to think how great a proportion of all the efforts and talents in the world are employed in merely neutralizing one another. It is the proper end of government to reduce this wretched waste to the smallest possible amount, by taking such measures as shall cause the energies now spent by mankind in injuring one another, or in protecting themselves against injury, to be turned to the legitimate employment of the human faculties, that of compelling the powers of nature to be more and more subservient to physical and moral good" (Mill, 367).

18.   Mill, "Principles of Political Economy," 127.

19.   On this point, more broadly, see Deva Woodly's chapter in this book discussing the plural dimensions of well-being.

20.   Mill, "Principles of Political Economy," 128–29.

21.   Mill, "Principles of Political Economy," 128.

22.   Mill, "Principles of Political Economy," 129.

23.   Mill, "Principles of Political Economy," 127.

24.   Skidelsky and Skidelsky, *How Much Is Enough?*, 54; see also Milgate and Stimson, *After Adam Smith*, 216. There are some references to Mill's *Principles of Political Economy* throughout Keynes's writings, as Thomas Baldwin notes, so it is likely that Keynes read Mill's chapter on the stationary state. But, as Baldwin notes, Keynes did not otherwise engage with his political or moral philosophy, and this likely owes to G. E. Moore's critique of Mill as "naïve and artless." See Thomas Baldwin, "Keynes and Ethics," in *The Cambridge Companion to Keynes*, edited by Roger E. Backhouse and Bradley W. Bateman (Cambridge: Cambridge University Press, 2006), 240.

25.   John Maynard Keynes, "Economic Possibilities for Our Grandchildren (1930)," in *Essays in Persuasion* (New York: Norton, 1963), 365–66; emphasis in original.

26.   Keynes defines relative needs as those felt "only if their satisfaction lifts us above, makes us feel superior to, our fellows," and grants that they "may

indeed be insatiable" (Keynes, "Economic Possibilities," 365), but he does not consider their significance in the remainder of the essay. For critical discussions on this point, see, for instance, Robert H. Frank, "Context Is More Important than Keynes Realized," in *Revisiting Keynes: Economic Possibilities for Our Grandchildren* (Cambridge, MA: MIT Press, 2010), 143–50; Stephen A. Marglin, *The Dismal Science: How Thinking Like an Economist Undermines Community* (Cambridge, MA: Harvard University Press, 2008), 207–22; Skidelsky and Skidelsky, *How Much Is Enough?*, 33–42.

27. Keynes, "Economic Possibilities," 358–68.

28. Keynes, "Economic Possibilities," 372.

29. Keynes, ""Economic Possibilities," 366–68.

30. Keynes grants that, "for many ages to come," we will not have complete leisure, as "the old Adam will be so strong in us that everybody will need to do *some* work if he is to be contented." He suggests that 15 hours of work per week should be sufficient (Keynes, "Economic Possibilities," 368–69).

31. Keynes, "Economic Possibilities," 366–69.

32. Keynes, "Economic Possibilities," 369–70; Robert Skidelsky, *John Maynard Keynes, Volume II: The Economist as Saviour, 1920–1937* (London: Penguin Books, 1992), 234; John Forrester and Laura Cameron, *Freud in Cambridge* (Cambridge: Cambridge University Press, 2017), 485–86.

33. Keynes, "Economic Possibilities," 370–72.

34. Keynes, "Economic Possibilities," 366, 368, 372–73. For rich connections to these ideas, see Deva Woodly's analysis of the concept of flourishing and Marc Stears's discussion of the everyday "unforbidden pleasures" in the chapters in this book.

35. Tiziano Raffaelli, "Keynes and Philosophers," in *The Cambridge Companion to Keynes*, edited by Roger E. Backhouse and Bradley W. Bateman (Cambridge: Cambridge University Press, 2006), 160; Roger E. Backhouse and Bradley W. Bateman, "A Cunning Purchase: The Life and Work of Maynard Keynes," in *The Cambridge Companion to Keynes*, edited by Roger E. Backhouse and Bradley W. Bateman (Cambridge: Cambridge University Press, 2006), 1.

36. Skidelsky, *John Maynard Keynes, Volume II: The Economist as Saviour*, 56–57, 408 emphasis in original; Baldwin, "Keynes and Ethics," 237, 240–46; Raffaelli, "Keynes and Philosophers," 160.

37. Baldwin, "Keynes and Ethics," 238; Skidelsky, *John Maynard Keynes, Volume II: The Economist as Saviour*, 64; Raffaelli, "Keynes and Philosophers," 160; Craufurd D. Goodwin, "The Art of an Ethical Life: Keynes and Bloomsbury," in *The Cambridge Companion to Keynes*, edited by Roger E. Backhouse and Bradley W. Bateman (Cambridge: Cambridge University Press, 2006), 219.

38. Goodwin, "The Art of an Ethical Life," 220; Skidelsky, *John Maynard Keynes, Volume II: The Economist as Saviour*, 10–13.

39. Crauford Goodwin argues that "Economic Possibilities" should instead be read as influenced by Roger Fry, an artist and critic and member of the Bloomsbury group who argued that as society progressed, it should increas-

ingly focus on the "imaginative life"—the arts, literature, and pure science and inquiry (Goodwin, "The Art of an Ethical Life," 219–22).

40. On the development of Rawls's ideas on this point, see Katrina Forrester, "The Problem of the Future," in *In the Shadow of Justice: Postwar Liberalism and the Remaking of Political Philosophy* (Princeton, NJ: Princeton University Press, 2019), 172–203. See also Alyssa Battistoni, "The Limits to Justice: John Rawls and Herman Daly at the End of the Golden Age," unpublished manuscript, October 2019.

41. Rawls, *A Theory of Justice*, 252–58.

42. John Rawls, *The Law of Peoples* (Cambridge, MA: Harvard University Press, 1999), 107. The same is true of the international duty of assistance—which, as Rawls notes in *The Law of Peoples* (106–107), is structurally analogous to the intergenerational duty of just savings.

43. Rawls, *The Law of Peoples*, 107n33.

44. Rawls, *A Theory of Justice*, 257.

45. Rawls, *A Theory of Justice*, 266.

46. John Rawls, *Justice as Fairness: A Restatement* (Cambridge, MA: Belknap Press of Harvard University Press, 2001), 59–60, 63; see also Rawls, *A Theory of Justice*, 175; Samuel Freeman, "Rawls on Distributive Justice and the Difference Principle," in *The Oxford Handbook of Distributive Justice*, edited by Serena Olsaretti (Oxford: Oxford University Press, 2018), 19–24.

47. Rawls, *A Theory of Justice*, 68; see Freeman, "Rawls on Distributive Justice and the Difference Principle," 24–29; Williams, "Linguistic Protectionism and Wealth Maximinimization."

48. Rawls, *A Theory of Justice*, 175, see also 83; Rawls, *Justice as Fairness*, 62, see also 59–63.

49. Rawls, *Political Liberalism*, 7n5; Rawls, *Justice as Fairness*, 63–64, repeated at 159–60.

50. Rawls, *Justice as Fairness*, 63–64, repeated at 159–60.

51. Rawls, *Justice as Fairness*, 61–64.

52. See Freeman, *Rawls*, 112.

53. Williams, "Linguistic Protectionism and Wealth Maximinimization." Freeman has also offered an interpretation of the difference principle that rejects the "mandatory maximizing" view, developing a "qualified optional inequality" view that is similarly compatible with ceasing to pursue economic growth. Freeman, "Rawls on Distributive Justice and the Difference Principle," 24–34. Another view holds that, on its best interpretation, the difference principle does direct a society to maximize the expectations of the least advantaged and, in particular, their shares of income and wealth, and so it should not be compatible with ceasing to pursue economic growth; see John Tomasi, *Free Market Fairness* (Princeton, NJ: Princeton University Press, 2012), 184–96; John Tomasi, "Market Democracy and Meaningful Work: A Reply to Critics," *Res Publica* 21 (2015): 446–48. See also Steven Wall, "Rescuing Justice from Equality," *Social Philosophy and Policy* 29 (2012):

180–212. I discuss these two interpretations more fully in Rose, "The Even-handed Gains Approach."

54. The primary goods included in the index also include "non-basic rights and liberties," that is, those that are not covered by the theory's prior principles; see Freeman, *Rawls*, 113. On the primary goods more generally, see Rawls, *Justice as Fairness*, 57–61.

55. Freeman, *Rawls*, 111–14, 133–34; Freeman, *Justice and the Social Contract*, 106–8; Samuel Freeman, "Capitalism in the Classical and High Liberal Traditions," *Social Philosophy and Policy* 28 (2011): 47–52. See also Samuel Arnold, "The Difference Principle at Work," *Journal of Political Philosophy* 20 (2012): 113–14; Samuel Arnold, "Right-Wing Rawlsianism: A Critique," *Journal of Political Philosophy* 21 (2013): 398–404; Matthew Clayton and David Stevens, "Is the Free Market Acceptable to Everyone?," *Res Publica* 21 (2015): 367–70. I also develop this position in Rose, "On the Value of Economic Growth," 136–38.

56. Rawls's own remarks that "great wealth" is "more likely to be a positive hindrance, a meaningless distraction at best if not a temptation to indulgence and emptiness," may provide such objectionably perfectionist grounds to determine the weight of income and wealth in the index (Rawls, *A Theory of Justice*, 257–58). He also made reference to "a civil society awash in meaningless consumerism" in a letter to Philippe Van Parijs; see John Rawls and Philippe Van Parijs, "Three Letters on the Law of Peoples and the European Union [1998]," *Autour de Rawls, Special Issue of Revue de Philosophie Économique* 7 (2003): 7–20. However, the argument in its general form does not and need not draw on such perfectionist judgments.

57. Julie L. Rose, *Free Time* (Princeton, NJ: Princeton University Press, 2016); Chiara Cordelli, "Justice as Fairness and Relational Resources," *Journal of Political Philosophy* 23 (2015): 86–110; Kristin Shrader-Frechette, *Environmental Justice: Creating Equality, Reclaiming Democracy* (Oxford: Oxford University Press, 2002); Rosa Terlazzo, "Entitlement and Free Time," *Law, Ethics and Philosophy* 5 (2017): 91–104. As Rawls notes, the list of primary goods, which are to be specified in full detail at a society's legislative stage, is open to extension and might include leisure time and health care and public health goods. Rawls, *Justice as Fairness*, 168–72, 179.

58. The form these broader principles take will determine how such a just agrowth position bears on and addresses an important set of concerns that arise within discussions of the value and imperative of economic growth—in particular, related to international geopolitical stability and security, international distributive obligations, and climate change. The focus here is to begin at a prior step: to show how a society can be committed to making its members indefinitely better off and at the same time cease to pursue economic growth.

Part 2

NEW ASPIRATIONS FOR FIRMS
AND OTHER ORGANIZATIONS

6 What's Wrong with the Prison Industrial Complex?

Profit, Privatization, and the Circumstances of Injustice

TOMMIE SHELBY

The central concern of this chapter is with the call to dismantle the prison industrial complex. I argue that this form of prison abolition, while in many ways insightful and appealing, also has serious weaknesses as a moral critique. After outlining these limitations, I defend the use of nonprofit prison privatization in limited contexts—that is, in societies that, while maintaining some measure of legitimacy, are marred by serious structural injustices.

I focus on the work of Angela Davis, who is a leading scholar-activist in the abolitionist movement and an influential social philosopher. In books, essays, speeches, and interviews spanning nearly 50 years, she has defended a world without prisons (whether public or private) as a morally required and realistic political goal. One of Davis's core objections to incarceration is that, as generally practiced, it is an immoral fusion of ineffective state crime-control measures, the privatization of public functions, and the maximization of corporate profit. Davis seeks to abolish prisons partly because she views them as components of a vast and destructive "prison industrial complex."[1] This designation, she tells us, is meant to draw attention to the fact that prison construction, prison ownership, prison administration, prison services, and inmate labor attract large amounts of private capital and that commercial profit from the practice of imprisonment is a driver of mass incarceration. Davis also views prison abolition as a necessary component of resistance to "neoliberalism" and a key demand in a democratic-socialist movement.[2]

Some who are otherwise sympathetic to the abolitionist cause stop short of calling for a complete ban on prisons. They allow that incarceration, whether as detention, rehabilitation, or punishment, has (or at least could have) a legitimate public function. Yet they are deeply troubled and often outraged by the many ways that privatization, commerce, and profit figure in some prison systems, particularly those in the United States. Thus, taking inspiration from Davis, they call for an end to the prison industrial complex, though not necessarily to prisons as such. Others see the complete abolition of prisons as a long-term objective but treat the abolition of the prison industrial complex as an intermediate goal. Decoupling incarceration from capitalist enterprise is, for them, a necessary step toward a prison-free world.

Philosophers have written extensively about punishment and its moral justification. They have proposed and criticized theories based on retribution, deterrence, consent, forfeiture, fairness, reconciliation, rehabilitation, moral education, and other things. However, these theories typically abstract away from the concrete realities of imprisonment. They also ordinarily abstract away from related questions of political economy and public finance. Moreover, philosophers usually assume, in the context of their theorizing, that the society within which imprisonment occurs is just (or nearly so) and that the governing authority (usually a state) is fully legitimate. But what has to be shown (if it can be) is that imprisonment is morally permissible and cost-effective in our own unjust society and world, or at least that it could be so justified under better social conditions that we can feasibly bring about. Davis raises serious doubts about whether this kind of justification is possible.

Incarceration, Detention, and Punishment

US federal, state, and municipal prisons are often grossly unjust and inhumane, and they contain many who have been confined for far too long and many who should never have been imprisoned at all. Indeed, elsewhere I have questioned the legitimacy of the American criminal justice system.[3] Yet because some prisons are better than others, in deciding whether to be a reformer or an abolitionist, we need to know what a "prison" is and not just what some existing prisons are like. Both reformers and abolitionists seek social "change"—sometimes the same changes, in fact. But the reformer thinks the necessary changes are consistent with preserving core features of the practice of imprisonment, while the abolitionist believes the requisite changes require doing away with the practice completely or so transforming the practice that it would no longer be apt to call it "imprisonment." So, to resolve the disagreement, we need to understand which features are *constitutive* of prisons and which can be discarded or altered without eliminating prisons entirely. I will not pretend that there is some ideologically neutral conception of a prison. But I do hope to offer a conception that reformers and abolitionists can accept so that the issue turns not on contentious or question-begging definitions but on whether the familiar practice of imprisonment is one that, on moral grounds, should be abandoned.

I treat "incarceration" as my general category and regard "imprisonment" (and thus "prisons") as a type of incarceration. Incarceration, broadly conceived, has at least five elements. It entails *involuntary confinement*—restriction to a limited space with no right to leave without permission from authorities. This socio-spatial site of confinement is an *enclosed space* with a physically secure perimeter—walls, fences, guards, and locks—to prevent escape and unauthorized entry. Incarceration is a *hierarchical institutional practice* defined by a set of rules, roles, and goals. It is not just a building with people locked inside. These rules and roles vary with the overall justificatory aims of the institution (and sometimes with the covert purposes of its officials). Those confined to carceral spaces ("inmates") are *isolated from the general public*—separated from others in the outside world (and sometimes from one another) and with highly restricted (if any) rights to visitation and communication with those outside (and sometimes within) the facility. Importantly, inmates are in the *custody* of carceral authorities. Custody is a form of guardianship, which includes providing necessary shelter, care, and protection from harm (including self-harm). If inmates are a known danger to others or to themselves, then they must sometimes be deprived of anything that could inflict serious bodily harm. Providing adequate protection will sometimes require surveillance, searches, and the enforcement of rules of order.[4]

Incarceration, so understood, can be used for a variety of purposes. Some are legitimate. For instance, incarceration can be used to quarantine those with highly infectious and dangerous diseases or to hold enemy combatants in times of war. Some uses of incarceration are clearly illegitimate: to keep a population available for exploitation, to repress political dissent, to torture inmates, or to use them for medical experiments.

Even within the context of crime control, incarceration can have a number of purposes. For example, there is pretrial detention, or what might be better called "preconviction detention." Such detention raises a number of issues for the reform-versus-abolition of the prison industrial complex.

Let us distinguish two pretrial periods. First, there is the period directly after arrest, when law enforcement agents take a suspect (perhaps against their will) into custody for questioning or to face formal charges but before formal charges are brought and before a formal plea on the part of the accused. The accused will be incarcerated during this period, which ideally should be brief (hours or days, not weeks or months, and certainly not years). Second, there is the period directly after a formal plea of "not guilty" but before a trial to determine guilt. (This is "pretrial detention," strictly speaking.) There are two plausible justifications for detention in jail. The first is that there are strong reasons to believe that the accused will not appear for trial or (what amounts to the same) will refuse to voluntarily submit to accountability measures. The second is that there are strong reasons to believe that the accused is a serious danger to others and therefore incapacitation is warranted.

It is worth noting that to completely abolish incarceration as pretrial detention would mean that the public would have to rely solely on voluntary compliance with court orders and that the police would be prohibited from forcibly arresting suspects, even those accused of the most serious crimes and those known to be highly dangerous. If there are less harmful alternatives that would adequately ensure that the accused will submit to accountability measures (for instance, bail or electronic monitoring), then generally these should be chosen. There may be some question about the costs of these alternatives (and who should pay for them) that would make incarceration preferable and defensible. But I will largely leave this issue aside.

Now these non-carceral alternatives could lead to economic exploitation in commercial bail and profit from electronic monitoring technology. There are critics of the prison industrial complex who want to abolish commercial bail services. This could lead, if not to more people in jail (and for longer), to greater electronic monitoring and thus greater state surveillance, which some abolitionists, including Davis, also oppose. Some might argue that prohibiting commercial bail would be an unfair interference with personal liberty. Why shouldn't the accused (or their family or friends) be permitted to make a contract with another private actor to share the cost and risk of bail?

If bail were always set at a cost the accused could be expected to pay relying solely on their own personal financial resources (cash bond), commercial bail would not be necessary. Bail might be reasonably set, though, on the assumption that friends or family will help with the costs. When such voluntary financial assistance is forthcoming, this not only communicates that the accused has strong ties to the community (and so is unlikely to flee the jurisdiction) but also that friends or family members are confident that the accused will appear for trial (or could be brought to do so through persuasion or informal sanctions). If the default assumption is that friends and family will help, then it is not unreasonable (and perhaps wise) to sometimes set bail somewhat beyond the personal means of the accused.

Yet, the fact that a person lacks friends or family with the resources or requisite trust does not mean the person won't show up for trial. I am inclined to think that such a person should probably be permitted to use commercial bail services, as this may be their only means to ensure the court that they will appear for trial. It is important to note, though, that a bail-bond agent would be unlikely to make such an agreement if they lacked the power of arrest (or at least of electronic monitoring). Otherwise, commercial bail service companies would run an unreasonably high risk of default, perhaps making the enterprise unprofitable or very likely to fail. These companies are effectively assuring the court that they will ensure, by force if necessary, that the accused will appear in court. They are thereby exercising the equivalent of policing powers, despite being a private organization.

The advocate for the abolition of the prison industrial complex might insist that the public fully cover the costs of electronic monitoring and law enforcement to ensure that the accused appears in court. This would eliminate the need for pretrial detention and bail (though some among the accused may prefer bail to electronic monitoring), therefore limiting the financial burdens on the accused and their loved ones and reducing the extent to which criminal justice is a commercial enterprise.

Indeed, the abolitionist could go further. Where the criminal justice system is fair and widely believed to be so, we should expect citizens to appear for trial when the public (through its official representatives) has accused them of committing crimes. It should be mutually understood to be their civic responsibility and moral duty. Accordingly, it could be argued that since the accused has yet to be convicted, the presumption of innocence suggests that neither jail nor bail nor electronic monitoring is warranted unless there are strong reasons to believe the accused represents a grave danger to the public and thus needs to be incapacitated.

There is still the question of flight. If the worry is that the person will leave the country, then border enforcement (assuming this is sometimes justified), extradition agreements, and electronic monitoring should be sufficient to deal with this risk. One might nonetheless worry about the person who does not leave the country but does leave the relevant jurisdiction. Should the public accept the financial costs of ensuring that such a person will appear in court through the use of electronic monitoring? Or is it fair to expect the accused to cover the costs of this assurance, and if so, should they be permitted to make use of commercial services or private loans to cover the costs? These are challenging questions, and a full assessment of the prison industrial complex would need to answer them.

I focus, however, on incarceration when its official purpose is *punishment*—a penalty for committing a crime. In fact, Davis uses the phrase "punitive incarceration" to differentiate it from incarceration as pretrial detention.[5] We can call an incarceration facility whose primary purpose is rehabilitation a *penitentiary*. An incarceration facility that aims to treat and house those who suffer from serious psychological disorders is a *psychiatric hospital*. An incarceration facility that functions to impose punishment is a *prison*. These aims can be, and often are, combined within the same facility. Davis opposes both the penitentiary and the prison. Accordingly, I refer to both practices as "imprisonment" and to their corresponding facilities as "prisons."

Let me say a brief word about *incapacitation* through incarceration. It is sometimes necessary or prudent to rely on incarceration to incapacitate dangerous individuals. There is an analytical and moral difference between incarcerating persons to physically *prevent* them from harming others (by restricting their movement to a guarded and enclosed space) and incarcerating persons to *punish* them. Yet when carceral incapacitation is imposed in response to a criminal offense, it is practically indistinguishable from punishment. To the incarcerated, both will naturally feel like punishment even if that is not the aim. The same can be said when carceral incapacitation is combined with moral rehabilitation or psychiatric treatment. These are all ways of using incarceration to control and respond to crime, where the hard treatment of offenders is triggered by a criminal offense. The same cannot be said of carceral incapacitation when it is used for the quarantine of those with deadly communicable diseases, the involuntary commitment of mentally ill patients who have not perpetrated crimes, or the confinement of enemy combatants in wartime. These inmates are regarded as dangerous enough to warrant incarceration, but their confinement is not punishment or even akin to punishment.

Prison, Privatization, and Profit

One way to argue for the abolition of the prison industrial complex is to focus critical attention not so much on prisons but on capitalism. For instance, the critic of the prison industrial complex could argue that capitalism is an oppressive social system—say, unjust, undemocratic, dehumanizing, or exploitative—and so its basic institutions (e.g., private ownership of productive assets, wage labor, markets, and private finance) should be dismantled and replaced. If one is already opposed to capitalism, it would also be natural to oppose the prison industrial complex, as it necessarily relies on and is enmeshed with capitalist practices and products. In this way, there is a direct road from a critique of capitalism to the demand to abolish the prison industrial complex.

But this ground of opposition would apply to *many* institutions and organizations—not only prisons and the military but also schools, hospitals, banks, news organizations, communication networks, mass transportation, homes for the elderly, and even the family. The thesis that the prison industrial complex should be abolished would then just be a theorem derived from the more general claim that *capitalism* should be abolished. An institution that necessarily depends upon and operates through an inherently unjust practice could never be fully legitimate and would be morally tainted by its association with the oppressive practice. Prisons would not be special in that regard, though, and the primary critical task would be to convince skeptics that no form of capitalism is compatible with true human freedom—which, on one plausible interpretation, was Marx's aim in *Capital.*

Yet Davis and other abolitionists have objections to the prison industrial complex apart from their general objections to capitalism. They are also concerned with how prisons interact with or are shaped by capitalism, and these concerns will be my focus. To isolate these specific worries, keeping them distinct from a rejection of capitalism itself, I shall assume that capitalism is not inherently unjust. To be clear, I am not assuming that *existing* capitalist practices are just. Far from it. I assume only—and here primarily for the sake of argument—that there is a realistic form of capitalism that would be compatible with a stable, just, and democratic society.

To gain further clarity about what, morally speaking, is at issue, we need to make explicit the meaning of some relevant terms. *Privatization* is the process by which a property or enterprise goes from being government owned to being privately owned. Privatization can involve two types of rights transfer: the transfer of *ownership rights* to assets (such as land, facilities, vehicles, or machinery) and the transfer of *operating rights* to an enterprise (say, the prerogative to provide certain goods or services). Sometimes a public function (for instance, law enforcement, education, transportation, or sanitation) is carried out, at least in part, by a private organization rather than by a government agency or public-service employees. This *outsourcing* arrangement is facilitated by public-private contracts and need not involve the transfer of ownership rights. Public institutions also often make use of *private suppliers* for goods and resources needed to carry out relevant public functions but without turning over any ownership or operating rights.

Private organizations can be for-profit or nonprofit. *Profit* is a financial benefit that is realized when the amount of revenue gained from a business enterprise exceeds the costs (including taxes) needed to sustain the enterprise. The primary purpose or goal of for-profit organizations is to secure profit. If we rely on capitalist principles, any profit that is gained through the enterprise belongs to the business's owners, who are free to decide what to spend it on (e.g., reinvestment in the enterprise, other stocks or bonds, personal consumption, donation, and lobbying) and free to save it for future use.

A nonprofit private organization exists for purposes other than generating profit, such as serving a community, advancing a cause, or benefiting the general public. Although the organization's members may be concerned with revenue, costs, debts, and efficiency, they are concerned about these financial matters only insofar as they bear on keeping the organization operating, expanding it, or making it operate better. Members of a nonprofit do not own stock in the organization and thus have no claim on financial benefits based on ownership rights.

Labor compensation is different from profit. Although both can serve as motives and rewards, labor compensation is a financial benefit derived from providing a service or doing some task. It is payment in exchange for actual work. Such payment can be given to a public-service employee working for a government agency or to an employee working for a private organization (profit or nonprofit). Employees are free to decide what to spend their compensation on (e.g., stock, consumption, gifts, lobbying) and may save it for future use. The distinction between commercial profit and labor compensation is meant to mark the difference between deriving a financial benefit from *ownership* and deriving it from *work*.

With these distinctions in mind, we can more readily see that objections to the prison industrial complex can take a variety of forms. I leave aside objections on grounds of cost-effectiveness and focus on moral objections. For instance, a concern could be that some private organizations are wrongly earning (or attempting to earn) profit from prisons. Or the objection might be to granting administrative power over prisoners to private organizations. Or perhaps the issue is which specific prison functions are being outsourced to the private sector. Or the concern may be over ownership rights, which is its own form of power—a type of power that, when it comes to prisons, is perhaps only legitimately held by the public.

Corruption, Wrongful Gain, and Perverse Incentives

I shall assume, with Davis, that *retribution* for wrongdoing is not a legitimate public function. That is, I will not rely on the premise that those who commit crimes *deserve* to suffer and that the state has a right to use incarceration to ensure they endure this suffering. But, on one influential view, and the one I favor, the official function or principal purpose of prisons (like other law enforcement institutions) is to provide security to the general public by preventing and controlling crime—that is, by keeping crime within tolerable levels so that everyone's basic liberties and property are adequately secured. The provision of this essential public good is a fundamental state responsibility. Indeed, on some accounts, it is the primary justification for governmental authority and for the state's claim on a monopoly over the use of coercion.

Davis claims, however, that for-profit companies in the prison industry do not actually seek to provide security but only to make money for shareholders. The real or latent function of these institutions is to amass private wealth under the ideological cover of providing a necessary public good.[6] Prison privatization is, in effect, a *scam*—a way to accumulate private capital using public funds (and sometimes using prison labor) and on the pretext of making an essential contribution to public safety.

This critique reaches beyond the familiar charge that capitalists are greedy and indifferent to the human costs of their enterprises. It is an objection to neoliberal governance, in particular to public-private contracts to carry out public functions. Governments make contracts with private companies in prison-related industries. Presumably, these contracts would not be renewed unless government officials were satisfied with the services provided (assuming there is sufficient competition for government contracts). This suggests that these officials (and perhaps the institutions of which they are a part) are *corrupt*, that they are colluding with businesses that profit from public revenue without providing the relevant public good. For-profit companies often engage in lobbying efforts that exacerbate the problem of corruption among public officials. They also sometimes participate in misinformation campaigns to mislead the public and thereby sway it in their favor. I have no doubt about the reality or seriousness of these problems of corruption. Yet here authorities clearly *misuse* carceral institutions and *abuse* their power to make and implement crime-control policies. Something similar happens in the arenas of education, health care, and housing.

However, a similar form of corruption can occur within a wholly public prison system. Public officials, too, can be indifferent to whether prisons help to secure public safety. Their chief concern is sometimes keeping their jobs (along with the compensation, power, and status attached to their positions). And it is not just high-level public officials who have motives that could undermine public functions. Lower-level public-service employees may be similarly motivated. For instance, prison-guard unions have a financial stake in keeping prisons open and full regardless of whether this would prevent crime or rehabilitate inmates. Consequently, they may be tempted to defend the need for draconian sentences. They also have an incentive to resist managerial or technological innovations that would reduce the need for correctional officers.

Unfortunately, the broader public often fails to check these abuses. Citizens might not hold these officials and public employees accountable for their poor performance and unethical conduct because of limited collective efficacy, or because they do not know about the corruption, or because they are insufficiently concerned about the problem, perhaps because they lack sympathy for those convicted of felonies.

The vice of being indifferent to whether a public good is adequately provided can afflict public institutions and private organizations. Whenever it is possible to continue acquiring benefits no matter the quality of the goods or services provided, we should not be surprised if some fail to carry out these responsibilities in a conscientious way. Private organizations hardly have a monopoly on institutional corruption. Such corruption should be exposed and ended, which requires being vigilant in both the public and the private sector.

But let us suppose the relevant private organizations actually provide adequate services and products in a cost-effective way. Would the fact that profit is their motive and reward be sufficient reason to prohibit the practice of privatizing prisons? Davis thinks so, and for two reasons. She objects to the *source* of these profits—namely, the intentional deprivation of freedom and imposition of hardships on inmates and their families. She also thinks that the *profit-motive* undermines the effective provision of public goods (in this case, security) and is a strong incentive to maintain horrid prison conditions (as a cost-cutting measure to maximize profit).

The first concern—the unsavory source of profit—suggests that the relevant principle is that *no one should gain financially from the suffering caused by imprisonment.* Yet even if prisons were constructed, maintained, and administered solely by public-service employees, these employees' labor would be (and should be) compensated and so they would gain financially from the suffering of inmates and their loved ones.

Perhaps the objection is not to fair compensation for necessary work but rather to profiting from ownership of prison-industry firms. The distinction between profit and labor compensation does not appear to help, though, because at least some financial gain from property rights would appear to be permissible in this domain. For example, prisons need supplies and resources—food, clothes, bedding, medical supplies, equipment, technology, toiletries, fuel, and so on—that, in a capitalist society, will be provided, at least partially, by for-profit organizations. The owners or shareholders of these companies will therefore profit from prisoners' suffering and curtailed freedom. Indeed, incarceration makes capital gains possible for at least some employees of public prisons, for they (at least the more highly paid among them) can use a portion of their pay to buy shares in companies and this ownership may yield financial benefits. Although somewhat indirect, this too would be profiting from the suffering caused by incarceration.

A slightly different underlying principle is this: *no one should profit from the harmful wrongdoing of others* (in this case, from the serious crimes of prisoners). Again, this is overly broad and for the same reasons. Medical personnel and hospitals do no wrong when they expect to be paid for treating victims of serious crimes. And a private company reasonably expects to turn a profit from the sale of its goods and services used in such medical treatment.

It could be maintained that one is permitted to profit from others' harmful wrongdoing but *only if in so doing, one also contributes to repairing the harm, redressing the wrong, or preventing further such wrongdoing.* This might explain the moral acceptability of the medical case. But a private prison that contains convicted serious offenders will usually satisfy this condition as well.

A sounder principle would be something like this: *one should not seek to profit from suffering caused by injustices one has perpetrated.* In other words, it is wrong to act so as to profit from one's *own* harmful wrongdoing. One might inadvertently profit from a wrong one has committed, but one may not act wrongly so as to profit from the wrong. This is widely and rightly regarded as impermissible. I believe Davis is on firm ground here.[7] To the extent that a corporation is blameworthy for creating or perpetuating crime, it should not turn this wrongdoing to its advantage by profiting from prisons. I will return to this point.

Davis's second concern with profit from prisons is that it creates *perverse incentives*—namely, practical reasons to lock up people and to impose long sentences even when it won't prevent crime.[8] It is a morally unacceptable situation when there exist operative reasons to impose unnecessary suffering. In response to this legitimate worry, reformers could insist that arrests, indictments, verdicts, sentencing, parole, and release decisions be made only by those without a financial stake in the outcome of those decisions (and perhaps who cannot be hired or fired by someone with such a stake). They might also maintain that government officials who regulate or oversee the prison industry should be prevented from having a financial stake in that industry. These reform efforts would be directed toward reducing conflicts of interest between actors in prison-related firms and the aim of fair and humane crime prevention. No reasonable and honest defender of prison privatization believes that the corrections industry should be free to operate without public oversight and government regulations.

This response, however, is not entirely adequate, as the problem runs deeper. There is in fact a second perverse incentive: to keep the costs of prison administration as low as possible so as to increase profits. This incentive can lead to limiting or cutting educational, vocational, health care, psychiatric, or rehabilitation services. It can lead to unsanitary environmental conditions, low-quality or unhealthy food, and inmate overcrowding. It can lead to reducing correctional staff to dangerously low levels or to hiring the cheapest workers available without due regard for their competence and commitment to doing the job well.

The cost-cutting problem can negatively affect the administration of public prisons, too. Public revenue is limited. Budgetary considerations (including public debt and deficits) can lead to the elimination of important prison programs and the hiring of inadequate staff. And the public, given its usual contempt for prisoners and embrace of retributive attitudes, may not support greater spending or higher taxes to improve the lives and safety of prisoners, thus placing a democratic constraint on what public officials may do to improve prisons. So the incentive to keep costs down (whether to increase profit margins or to stay within budgetary constraints) is powerful and present for public and private organizations.

However, the incentive to cut costs, even for vital goods and services, is *inherent* in for-profit enterprises. There is no way to eliminate it. The public can only try through government oversight and regulation to prevent corporations from acting on the incentive in ways that compromise the provision of adequate public goods and services. By contrast, the public could be convinced—on grounds of justice, human rights, or public safety—to spend more money on prisons and prison services. This is one reason to prefer public prisons over privatized for-profit prisons.

And there is another. Not only do for-profit private prisons have no incentive to rehabilitate prisoners or to reduce recidivism. They have an incentive to *promote* crime and criminality. Creating prison conditions that make prisoners more likely to reoffend once released or more likely to violate prison rules that extend their prison stay is actually good for business. Insofar as they exacerbate the crime problem in this way, they profit from suffering caused by their own unjust actions. (Recall our earlier principle: *one should not seek to profit from suffering caused by injustices one has perpetrated.*) The injustices at issue are encouraging criminal activity and complicity in any subsequent crime. The temptation to engage in such wrongdoing might be so strong and the resulting harms so enormous that it would be better not to run the risk of using for-profit private prisons. The general public is not subject to such temptation. It seeks cost-effective ways to limit crime. Efficient crime control means not only greater public safety but also more public resources for things like schools, hospitals, and parks.

It could be argued that the problem is not so much profiting from prison ownership or prison administration as it is profiting from prison *labor*. Private companies do sometimes contract with the state to gain access to cheap prison labor (whether in a public or private prison). Yet where inmates can refuse to work for private companies without incurring penalty, the fact that a private company profits from prison labor is not in itself unjust—*unless capitalism is unjust*. Many nonincarcerated persons, to meet their material needs, seek employment from for-profit companies that pay low wages.

Perhaps Marx was right that wage labor under capitalism is a form of slavery—dehumanizing servitude under despotic rule. But if so, prison labor that benefits private firms would be an instance of a much more widespread unjust practice that occurs inside and outside prison walls, not a distinctive form of oppression. And, again, our call should therefore be for the abolition of *capitalism*, not the abolition of prisons. In any case, profit can be secured from prisons without extracting it directly from the labor of prisoners.[9] Thus, ending prison labor or raising prisoner wages, though perhaps welcome on other grounds, will not abolish the prison industrial complex.

One motive for the privatization of a public function is to weaken organized labor, which keeps wages low. This is an objectionable way to reduce public expenses, for it leaves workers vulnerable to exploitation and wrongly reduces the value of their basic liberties. It is clear that government can save money by relying on private companies partly because these companies unfairly squeeze labor (including prohibiting or undermining unions). But reform seems possible here, too. Government could get some of the advantages of agreements with private companies (for example, efficiency due to specialization and economies of scale) while only contracting the services of vendors with fair labor practices, including respecting the right of workers to organize and strike.

Now, Davis opposes public prisons that rely on for-profit companies for *any* goods and services.[10] And she extends her critique to domains beyond law enforcement. She argues that there are certain vital public goods—security, education, shelter, and health care—that should be available to everyone on the basis of *need* alone and that providing these goods should not depend on whether doing so would also turn a profit. Private for-profit companies should play no role in the provision of these public goods, on her account. Therefore, these public services, she argues, must be moved entirely to the public sector.

I find this idea appealing, yet it is difficult to see how a nonsocialist government could ensure universal access to education, health care, and housing without extensive reliance on for-profit companies. Some of the personnel, supplies, technology, vehicles, and facilities needed to provide these goods and services would have to come from the for-profit private sector. Just consider what it takes to build and maintain a single high school—one or more buildings, hundreds of books, computers, desks, chairs, electricity, food, clean water, sporting equipment, art supplies, cleaning supplies, maintenance equipment, medical supplies, and so on. To avoid reliance on for-profit companies completely, government would have to take over almost the entire economy just to ensure that all children have access to a decent school. At the very least, government would have to enable, support, and rely exclusively on nonprofit worker cooperatives. However, this would make Davis's opposition to privatization—whether of prisons or anything else—just a consequence of her opposition to capitalism. It would not have to do with prisons per se.

Nonprofit Prison Privatization?

The critique of the prison industrial complex—again, when not simply an expression of anti-capitalism—is best regarded as principled opposition to structural injustice. That is, it is concerned not about privatization of carceral functions as such, but about privatization in the context of a wide range of serious social injustices, from economic and racial injustice to gender injustice and undemocratic practices. Under current unjust social conditions, a scheme of cooperation between the public penal system and the corporate world is deeply worrisome, even frightening. Such a collaboration has many perils that are difficult, if not impossible, to contain adequately through government regulation and public accountability measures. Moreover, continuing reliance on for-profit private prisons would likely further erode public trust in the criminal justice system, which needs to be widely accepted as legitimate if it is to be effective at crime control. To maintain or regain political legitimacy, criminal justice must not only be done but must be *seen* to be done. Transparency and accountability are crucial here, and commercial mechanisms and the profit-motive can inhibit these democratic ends.

Notice, however, that the choice is not limited to either publicly owned, fully government-operated prisons or private for-profit prisons. There is also the possibility of a nonprofit private organization administering and perhaps owning a prison facility.[11] Prison privatization *without profit* could be a viable option under certain special, though not uncommon, circumstances.

Such an unusual proposal immediately raises three questions. First, how, practically speaking, would such an arrangement work? Second, why think this arrangement would be better, from a moral point of view, than the alternatives—public prisons, private for-profit prisons, or no prisons at all? And third, under what circumstances would this public-nonprofit arrangement be justified?

A well-funded private organization concerned with protecting the interests of a vulnerable population or promoting the public good could make a contract with a government (local, state, or federal) to take over some core carceral functions. Among these functions are ensuring prisoner safety (from others' aggression and self-harm), health care (including mental-health care), nutrition and physical fitness, maintenance and sanitation, inmate supervision and perimeter security, discipline for prison-rule violations, facilitating in-person and remote interaction between prisoners and their families and friends, and educational and vocational services.

A nonprofit private incarceration facility could also be used to hold those charged with crimes but not yet convicted. Again, pretrial detention is overused, and bail is sometimes set too high and often unnecessary. But to the extent that such measures are needed to ensure accountability or incapacitation, private jails could be used when bail is denied, cannot be raised, or is refused by the accused. The private organization could be held responsible for custodial care and for ensuring that inmates appear for trial. This would be functionally equivalent to holding a private party financially liable (through forfeiting their bond payment) for when the accused fails to appear in court.

Some might object to permitting private agents to use coercion or violence against prisoners, insisting that the use of force should never be delegated from the public to a private actor. Let us assume this position is sound. It would not rule out nonprofit, private prison administration and services. The enforcement of a prison's perimeter (to prevent escape and unauthorized entry) and the use of force to ensure safety, order, and discipline could remain exclusively in the hands of state agents—that is, public employees trained and officially authorized to play this role. The remaining functions would be in the hands of a private organization and its employees and volunteers, subject of course to public rules and accountability. This would be similar to other private organizations (e.g., private universities and hospitals) that rely on the police for certain purposes or under certain circumstances.

Now let us assume that some coercive functions can be legitimately outsourced or privatized. (After all, physical force *is* sometimes used in private psychiatric hospitals and schools.) To the extent that private security is relied on, such personnel could be required to receive specialized and publicly approved training and to go through psychological evaluation and background checks. Perhaps all correctional officers in the private organization should be required to pass certain tests and to secure a license to serve in this capacity. This is already true of medical personnel who work in prisons (public or private).

To reduce reliance on coercion and violence in the facility, it might be wise to permit only nonviolent offenders to be admitted to a private prison. Or inmates convicted of violent offenses could be permitted, but only if (given an objective risk assessment) they are appropriate for a minimum- or medium-security prison. All prisoners who, for reasons of custodial care or security, are best held in a maximum-security facility could be excluded from private prisons.

If the major administrative and service roles within the prison were undertaken by the nonprofit organization and the prison itself was owned either by the organization or the public, this would effectively eliminate the problems of wrongful financial profit and profit as a perverse incentive. The organization would not be in violation of the principle that no one should seek to profit from suffering caused by their own unjust acts, because it would not be seeking to profit from the enterprise at all. Neither those who own nor those who run the prison would have a right or duty to maximize profit or shareholder gains. Unlike the for-profit prison industry, nonprofit prisons would have no financial incentive to increase crime rates, recidivism, or societal punitiveness. They could concern themselves with money matters only insofar as this was necessary to ensure the continuance of the prison. They could carry out the entire operation at cost, folding any budget surplus into improving prison conditions, services, and administration.

To reduce the risk of impropriety and corruption, the private organization could have an all-volunteer board with no members who have a stake in prison-related industries. Paid staff could be kept to a minimum. Participation from affected communities could be encouraged or even required. Of course, it might be difficult for a nonprofit organization (or even a group of such organizations) to raise sufficient funds to build a prison facility or to buy or rent the land on which a prison would sit. However, the public could own the land and facilities and the prison could be operated (in whole or in part) by a private organization. The public-private arrangement would concern prison administration and services on public property, not prison construction or the renting of private property. This, too, should reduce concerns about intrusions from corporate actors and the corrupting influence of the profit-motive.

A nonprofit private prison would secure part of its funding from the public and so would be subject to public accountability measures. But it would also secure some of its funding from private donations. This would allow concerned members of the community to help shape the leadership, goals, and operation of the institution, rather than relying exclusively on state bureaucracy and business interests. These private donors could, for example, aim to satisfy higher standards for custodial care than public prisons are required to. They could offer more or better services to prisoners, including educational, vocational, medical, drug treatment, and reentry services.

For those deeply concerned about the plight of disadvantaged Black, Latinx, and Indigenous peoples in the United States (social groups who are disproportionately incarcerated) but skeptical that existing governments can be trusted to secure adequate custodial care for prisoners from these populations, this public-private arrangement could be an avenue for community control over central elements of law enforcement. It could also be a way to address unacceptable prison conditions. If this is correct, then some outsourcing of penal functions could be beneficial to the oppressed.

Those who call for affected communities to play a significant role in crime control, including civilian oversight of the police, cannot consistently maintain that law enforcement functions, to be legitimate, must be carried out entirely by public-service employees. If unjustly disadvantaged communities are to be truly empowered in the arena of criminal justice, then they must possess effective private organizations that can counteract abuses of state power and reduce institutional corruption. A nonprofit, justice-promoting organization that could win a bid to run a jail or prison could play this role.

In suggesting a role for private nonprofit prisons, I am *not* claiming that a just society would permit these public functions to be moved to the private sector. This is a tentative proposal for *nonideal* conditions—for the circumstances of *injustice*. When social conditions are grossly unjust and the state lacks legitimacy in the eyes of the most disadvantaged, private interventions are sometimes justified, even required. Systemic state failure can necessitate aggressive actions from civil society. The argument that punishment, to be legitimate, must be imposed through the collective *agency* of the public and in *name* of the public and so administered solely by public-sector employees democratically authorized to play this role is not applicable under conditions of intolerable injustice.[12] Given that the state operates with a serious deficit of legitimacy, the question under these conditions is what practical measures of crime control, whether public or private, can be justified to those affected by them, particularly those among the oppressed.

An example of a related and necessary civil society intervention into law enforcement under unjust conditions is the use of bail-fund organizations. These organizations raise money from private donors to bail out low-income inmates who cannot afford to pay their bail costs. Sometimes disadvantaged persons are charged with minor crimes but cannot raise the money for bail. Stuck in jail until trial, they risk losing their jobs, they are unable to care for dependents, and they are needlessly separated from their families and friends. Support from a nonprofit bail-fund makes such persons less likely to be exploited by for-profit bail-bond companies.

Many in unjustly disadvantaged and racially stigmatized communities need protection against wrongful aggression and violence—murder, rape, and aggravated assault. Some of the perpetrators of these wrongful harms are, tragically, themselves members of such communities. So, although members of these communities want these crimes prevented and highly dangerous persons incapacitated, many (including some victims) are reluctant to hand over (some) criminal offenders to a state responsible for racialized mass incarceration and inhumane prison facilities. In the right hands, nonprofit private prison administration and services could be a viable, if temporary, alternative.

Conclusion

I do not know whether the public-nonprofit arrangement I have described is *economically* feasible. That is, it may be unrealistic to expect private actors, though trustworthy and genuinely concerned with the plight of prisoners, to be able to raise the necessary funds to operate a prison on a nonprofit basis. Perhaps such nonprofit organizations would always be outbid by for-profit firms. The arrangement could also be *politically* unfeasible, in the sense that there may be no practical path to wrestling prison administration away from the state or from public correctional officers' unions. Or perhaps there is no regulatory regime that can effectively monitor a private prison, whether for-profit or nonprofit. My aim here has been merely to establish the principle that the temporary, nonprofit privatization of central prison functions is morally defensible and indeed could advance the ends of justice and reduce the burdens on the oppressed under nonideal conditions.

I also contend that acceptance of this principle is compatible with the abolitionist critique of the prison industrial complex, at least insofar as that critique does not rely on the premise that capitalism is inherently unjust. In addition, the principle is consistent with resistance to neoliberal governance, at least insofar as such resistance is primarily to public contracts with for-profit companies and not to all public-private partnerships. Moreover, limited private nonprofit prison administration is, in principle, consistent with the fundamental aims of prison abolitionists. Few, if any, would insist that all prisoners should be immediately released and that, henceforth, there must be no new prisoners regardless of the risks or costs. A world without prisons would have to be a long-term goal, which will require broad structural transformation before prisons are truly obsolete. In the meantime, some limited use of prisons is, regrettably, a necessary evil. Yet abolitionists do not trust the state to incarcerate in a way that is humane and safe and that treats prisoners with dignity. Nor do they trust the corporate world to fill the gap. A nonprofit private entity could be the best option and is in keeping with the spirit of experimentalism that is at the heart of the abolitionist ethos.

Notes

For comments on previous drafts of this chapter, I thank the editors and the participants in the Political Economy and Justice Workshops at Harvard. I'm also grateful to Lidal Dror, Bréond Durr, Carol Gould, Wendy Salkin, Lucas Stanczyk, Brandon Terry, Iakovos Vasiliou, and the students in my Punishment and Incarceration seminar. A version of the chapter was delivered as the Marx Wartofsky Memorial Lecture at the CUNY Graduate Center. I thank the audience for their feedback. Generous support for this research was funded by the Andrew Carnegie Foundation.

1. Angela Y. Davis, *Are Prisons Obsolete?* (New York: Seven Stories Press, 2003), chap. 5; Angela Y. Davis, *The Meaning of Freedom* (San Francisco: City Lights Books, 2012), chap. 2; Angela Y. Davis, *Freedom Is a Constant Struggle: Ferguson, Palestine, and the Foundations of a Movement* (Chicago: Haymarket Books, 2016), chap. 4.

2. Davis, *Freedom Is a Constant Struggle*, 7.

3. See Tommie Shelby, *Dark Ghettos: Injustice, Dissent, and Reform* (Cambridge, MA: Belknap Press, 2016), chaps. 7–8.

4. The small-occupancy cell (one to two persons) is not essential to incarceration. The cell does, however, lessen the need for supervisory personnel and so may save money. It can also reduce the need for constant surveillance (to prevent harm or escape) and so could also provide some privacy for inmates.

5. Davis, *Are Prisons Obsolete*, 41–43.

6. Davis, *Freedom Is a Constant Struggle*, 5–6.

7. Davis, *Freedom Is a Constant Struggle*, 65, 107.

8. Davis, *Are Prisons Obsolete*, 36–37. Also see Davis, *Freedom Is a Constant Struggle*, 24.

9. See Ruth Wilson Gilmore, *Golden Gulag: Prisons, Surplus, Crisis, and Opposition in Globalizing California* (Berkeley: University of California Press, 2007).

10. Davis, *Are Prisons Obsolete*, 90–91, 98–100.

11. For a defense of the nonprofit alternative, with a focus on its possible contribution to prisoner rehabilitation, see Daniel L. Low, "Nonprofit Private Prisons: The Next Generation of Prison Management." *New England Journal on*

Criminal and Civil Confinement 29 (2003): 1. Also see Richard Moran, "A Third Option: Nonprofit Prisons," *New York Times*, August 23, 1997, sec. 1, p. 23.

12.   Compare Avihay Dorfman and Alon Harel, "The Case against Privatization," *Philosophy and Public Affairs* 41, no. 1 (2013): 67–102. Also see Chiara Cordelli, "Privatization without Profit," in *Privatization: NOMOS LX*, vol. 29 (New York: NYU Press, 2018).

7 Firms, Morality, and the Search for a Better World

REBECCA HENDERSON

A World on Fire

Could the private sector play a significant role in the struggle to build a just and sustainable world? At first sight, the idea might seem preposterous. We face a series of enormous and seemingly intractable issues—from climate change to accelerating inequality to continued racial exclusion—that are clearly public goods problems and that in many cases have been exacerbated by the ruthless push for profit that has characterized much of the last 50 years.

Since December 2015, for example, when the Paris Climate Agreement was signed, the world's fossil fuel companies have spent more than a billion dollars lobbying against controls on greenhouse gas (GHG) emissions. As Salter (chapter 8 in this book) suggests, a commitment to maximizing shareholder value at almost any cost has led them—and too many of the world's firms—to what can appear to be an almost complete moral disengagement with the society around them.

Turning things around will require sweeping, systemic reform and the rediscovery of the critical role of government in constraining the free market in ways that ensure that competition is genuinely "free" and genuinely fair. This implies that we will not be able to solve the great problems of our time without renewing the power of democracy, rebuilding a strong voice for labor, strengthening the power of independent media, and creating a shared sense of common citizenship and social solidarity—and we are not going to be able to do any of these things without building strong social movements rooted in popular participation and a renewed commitment to civic society.

But none of this will be easy. Our public institutions are struggling. In many countries the labor movement has been almost totally destroyed, and both democracy and the free media are under widespread attack. Rebuilding our communities and our political systems in ways that are transparent, inclusive, and responsive is surely the royal road to change. But progressives need allies. Trust in government—following 30 years of sustained attack on the idea that government can be a force for good—has fallen to an all-time low. One 2015 Gallup poll suggested that 69 percent of Americans believed that "big government" was the biggest threat to the country's future (Riffkin 2015). Those younger than 30 cannot remember a time when government "worked," and many of them have come to believe that it is incapable of doing so. Relying on political action alone to address the problems that we face may be a recipe for disaster.

Given this context, this chapter makes the argument that "authentically purpose driven" firms—those that explicitly embrace a prosocial goal beyond profit maximization and that routinely sacrifice short-term profits in the service of these goals—may be crucial allies in the pursuit of a just and sustainable society. They can serve as living demonstrations of alternative ways of structuring economic activity, providing conclusive proof that it is possible to create decent jobs that pay well in workplaces where employees are treated with dignity and respect. Building a more sustainable society requires not only the complete restructuring of the power, transportation, construction, and agricultural sectors but also profound changes in consumer behavior. Purpose-driven firms have the courage and the vision to catalyze the profound innovation that is required to drive this kind of transformation and to sustain the levels of trust and commitment internally that is required to operationalize them.

Purpose-driven firms may also have an important role to play beyond their own boundaries. They are already acting as catalysts for cooperation across industries and regions, attempting to make commitment to the public good "precompetitive." As they cooperate—and as they build business models dependent on successful cooperation—they are learning that it is immensely easier to make progress if these kinds of moves are supported by the capital markets—and by local governments. In ways that we have not seen for 50 years, global business leaders are speaking out in favor of strengthening the social safety net, regulating carbon emissions, and protecting the democratic purpose. "Purpose" is fashionable.

It is easy to be skeptical, of course. Much of this is probably just greenwashing. Indeed, the idea that business could hold to any normative commitment—and that such commitments might shape action—may seem deeply counterintuitive. Many people consider the idea deeply eccentric and potentially dangerous. When Larry Fink, the CEO of BlackRock, the largest asset manager in the world, suggested that business might have a "social responsibility," he was widely attacked. Nearly every manager at every firm feels constrained by the pressure of competition and how so many investors focus only on short term results. The idea that business should take on responsibility for solving public goods problems, and that it might be a powerful agent of positive change if it did, can seem deeply eccentric.

Those on the right fear any talk of purpose or a broader mission for firms as at best a distraction and at worst both illegal and immoral—something designed to provide cover for policies that will shield mediocre managers from the rigors of an efficient capital market. The left views the private sector with deep suspicion. They fear that talk of purpose is at best greenwashing and at worst a cynical attempt to seduce employees and to forestall serious regulation. When I told Ed Balleisen, one of the great economic historians of self-regulation, that I thought that cooperation across firms could help solve the great problems of our time, he laughed out loud and referred me to his research (Balleisen 2007).

It is certainly true that throughout history the quest for profits and power has led many firms to do terrible things. When the Dutch first discovered the Spice Islands, they were dismayed to find that the local inhabitants could not be forced to work sufficiently long or sufficiently hard to be usefully enslaved. They killed them all and replaced them with Africans. The Barclay brothers, the founders of Barclays Bank, one of the largest banks in the UK, traded in enslaved people. So did at least two of JPMorgan Chase's predecessor banks. Firms have machine-gunned their own workers, polluted on a grand scale and then tried to hide it, and cheerfully subverted governments.

More recently, American business has come close to destroying the US labor movement, while the Chamber of Commerce has led the push to hold down the minimum wage and resist the regulation of greenhouse gases. The arrogance and negligence of the world's banks led to the Great Crash of 2008. Wells Fargo lied to its customers and set up millions of fake accounts in the pursuit of the bottom line. Facebook failed to tell the American government that a foreign power was using its product to influence elections. More than 40 million people continue to be enslaved, 71 percent of them women and girls, 25 percent of them children (Council on Foreign Relations, n.d.). But the fact that businesses and businesspeople sometimes behave dreadfully does not mean that businesspeople never think about ethics or that morality has no place in business. Throughout history, business people have grappled with the morality of what they were doing and they continue to do so today.

It Was Never Just about Profits

People have questioned the morals and goals of private corporations for hundreds of years. Some commentators have celebrated trade and industry as a source of prosperity and markets as sources of innovation and opportunity, while others have wondered whether any institution motivated almost entirely by greed can be moral and whether and when managers should focus on their responsibilities to society as well as on their own profits. Our society's current obsession with shareholder value is just one swing of a pendulum that has been swinging for a long time.

Under the Sung dynasty (960–1279), for example, great fleets of ships left China carrying porcelain, paper, and silk to Southwest Asia, India, and the Arab world. They returned with cotton, horses, spices, medicines, and other luxury goods. But in the 1430s, a coalition of conservative landowners and Confucian civil servants were able to capitalize on what one historian called "the ever-present mistrust of commerce and capital accumulation" to shut the trade down (Kocka, 2016, 29–30). China turned its back on the sea and allowed the fleet to deteriorate.

In thirteenth- and fourteenth-century Italy, the great merchant companies of Florence, Venice, and Genoa laid the foundations for the diffusion of capitalism across Europe, generating enormous wealth in the process. But many merchants struggled with their conscience as a result. Money lending—"usury"—was considered a sin, something equivalent to robbery or lying—and in 1179 the Roman Catholic Church denied Christian burial to usurers. Fra Jacopo Passavanti, one well-known preacher of the time, described the "commerce of money," as it was called, as "abominable." Filippo degli Agazzari, a fourteenth-century Augustinian monk, told the story of a usurer whose corpse was placed in a mortuary chapel that his heirs had built for him. "On the night after the funeral," he wrote, "all the devils of Hell surrounded the chapel wheren he lay, with so much noise and clamour that for miles around no man could sleep; and in the morning it was seen that the chapel had been uprooted and cast into the river nearby (Origo 2017, 152).

The tension that this created in many successful merchants of the period is evident in the letters of Francesco Datini, one of the richest men of his time. Datini made his fortune in international trade, dealing in armor, cloth, enslaved people, spices, wine, and olive oil. He left a fortune of 100,000 florins, a small fortune at a time when a pig cost 3 florins, a maid's wages for a year were 10 florins, and a female enslaved person—one of which Datini owned and by whom he had his only recognized child—cost between 50 and 60 florins (Soll 2014).

Datini appears to have liked not only money, but all the things that money could buy: fine clothes, large houses, great banquets, guests with titles to their names, and a crest to put over his doorway. But he was consumed by the thought that he was missing his life. Lapo Mazzei, one of his closest friends, spent many years trying to persuade him to step back a little from his constant search for gain, writing to him once that:

> It grieves me that you should take these enterprises of yours . . . with too much avidity, desire, solicitude and anguish. It is not good. A wise man should learn to bridle himself and not thus follow his desires, but behave with moderation and temperance. . . . You know men are not pleased with a house wherein the maid rules her mistress; even so the soul in which reason is ruled by the will, is displeasing to God. (Origo 2017, 155)

Again and again in his letters, Datini promises that he will moderate his desires, wind up his business, and have time for thoughts of God. "May God give me grace, if it be His pleasure, to lead a better life than in the past, for it is a dog's life—and it is all through my own fault" (Origo 2017, 156). When he died in 1410, he left his money to the clergy of Prato. His massive fortune was used to found a hospital for the poor—the Casa del Ceppo dei Poveri di Francesco di Marco. The hospital still stands, and over its door is an inscription calling Datini "the Merchant of Christ's Poor" (Sull 2014).

The belief that the pursuit of profit for its own sake might run counter to the will of God and one's duty to the community remained a live issue for at least the next 200 years. In 1639, for example, a Mr. Robert Keayne, who "kept a shop in Boston," was fined 200 pounds for charging unreasonable prices, and thereby making unreasonable profits, despite "being an ancient professor of the gospel, a man of eminent parts (and) having been formerly dealt with and admonished, both by private friends and also by some of the magistrates and elders, and having promised reformation" ("Admonishment and Reconciliation of Robert Keayne with the Church 1639–1640").

John Cotton, who was the leading Puritan minister in the early decades of the Massachusetts Bay Colony, preached against Keayne, once summarizing in a sermon why this kind of behavior was unacceptable and laying out some "false principles," among them "that a man might sell as dear as he can, and [buy] as cheap as he can" and that "if a man lose by casualty of sea, etc., in some of his commodities, he may raise the price of the rest" (Winthrop 1853, 1:377–82).

As firms began to play an increasingly important role in European commercial life, the philosophers of the enlightenment squared this particular circle by proposing that the greedy businessperson might—paradoxically—increase the general good, as long as firms competed fairly and honorably with each other. Adam Smith's *Wealth of Nations*, together with its lesser known but equally important counterpart *The Theory of Moral Sentiments*, were the key texts in this conversation, but as Albert Hirschman's book *The Passions and the Interests* suggests, it was by no means the only one. Hirschman's central point is that this literature solved a moral problem—replacing the imperative to pursue honor with the imperative to pursue material gain—by transforming greed from a vice into a virtue that could enrich the entire society. This solution was not taken to release businesspeople from the need to have a strong sense of personal morality. *The Theory of Moral Sentiments*, for example, insisted that humans had to pay great attention to matters of personal ethics—and indeed that society could not survive if they did not.

The idea that business was potentially a source of enormous social benefit was taken up particularly enthusiastically in the United States. In the words of Gordon Wood, a prize-winning historian of the American Revolution:

> Most of the Americans' defenses of interest and money as the best connecting links in society were thus not cynical or reluctant concessions to reality; they were not made obliquely or in embarrassment. Quite the contrary: these defenses were made proudly and enthusiastically, as if interest and the making of money through trade had become deserving of as much acclaim and admiration as republican virtue traditionally had been given. Interest and moneymaking after all were egalitarian and democratic. When people related to each other only through interest, there was no obligation, no gratitude required; the relationship was to that extent equal. (Wood 1993, 337)

Samuel Blodget, who wrote extensively about the American economy in the first decade of the nineteenth century, suggested that commerce was the major source of cohesion in the society—that commerce and business were the "golden chains" that held the society together, creating "the best social system that ever was formed." The principle of commerce was "the most sublime gift of heaven wherewith to harmonize and enlarge society." Similarly, the French theorist Comte Destutt de Tracy, whose works Thomas Jefferson translated and prepared for publication in America, wrote that "commerce, that is exchange, being in truth society itself, it is the only bond among men; the source of all their moral sentiments; and the first and most powerful cause of the improvement of their mutual sensibility and reciprocal benevolence" (Wood, 1993).

The turn to the free market was seen as a powerful anecdote to traditional hierarchical relationships based on patronage and deference. Instead of relationships based on trust or on personal or familial relationships, relationships were structured by cold, hard cash. Caesar Rodney, who became attorney general under Jefferson wrote that, in the old world, "statutable provisions fix and regulate the price of everything," but in the US, "honesty and industry are sure to meet a due reward" and "the poorest individuals can claim the full price of his labor." "In America," said William Findley, who fought in the American Revolution and who retired in 1817 as the longest-serving member of the US House of Representatives, "no man has a greater claim of special privilege for his £100,000 than I have for my £5" (Wood, 1993).

In the nineteenth century, a number of highly successful businesspeople built their firms on the idea that the goal of the firm was not to maximize profits but to sell useful, high-quality products produced by well-treated, well-paid employees. Take, for example the case of Cadbury, the British confectionary giant. George and Richard Cadbury took over their father's failing tea and coffee business in 1861. They were Quakers or, as they preferred to be called, members of the Society of Friends. As a community, the Quakers were suspicious of profit, believing that the function of commercial activity should be to serve the community as a whole and that conflict between labor and management should be resolved through open conversation and goodwill. George was an active teacher in the Quaker Adult School Movement and had spent years teaching in Birmingham's worst slums. The brothers explicitly rejected Frederick Taylor's approach to management and its implicit assumption that employees were merely things to be manipulated. "Even if on the productive side"—one of them remarked in a 1914 paper entitled, "The Case Against Scientific Management"—"the results are all that the promoters of scientific management claim, there is still the question of the human costs of the economies produced." George Cadbury claimed that "the status of a man must be such that his self-respect is fully maintained, and his relationship with his employer and his fellow-workmen is that of a gentleman and a citizen" (Smith, Child, Rowlinson, and Cadbury 2009).

The Cadbury brothers invested heavily in their beliefs. The firm, for example, required that every employee take an introductory training course and gave employees the option to take further commercial or technical training at company expense. It provided sports facilities, sick pay, and a (men's) pension fund and experimented with worker participation in the running of its plants. The Works Committee included both staff and foremen and was responsible for factory conditions, quality control, and welfare work. In 1919, the company began to experiment with full-fledged industrial democracy, creating a three-tiered structure of Shop Committees and Group Committees reporting to a Works Council. There is no evidence that this method of management placed the firm at a competitive disadvantage. Indeed, rather the reverse. By the 1930s Cadburys was the 24th largest manufacturing company in England and had created a portfolio of brands that remain global powerhouses today.

The sense that business was at heart a moral enterprise was reinvented in a particularly powerful way by Milton Friedman and his colleagues. The advent of neoliberalism is often framed as a movement that took its power from neoliberal economics. But it was also an explicitly moral movement.

Friedman's suggestion that the "social responsibility of business is to increase its profits" is first and foremost a *moral* injunction, deeply rooted in the belief that well-functioning capitalism is a critical source of economic prosperity and economic and political freedom and that for managers to do anything other than maximize profits is to invite them to betray the trust of their investors and reduce the efficiency of the market. Friedman and his colleagues suggested that, under a number of well-defined conditions, including free competition, nonconstant returns to scale, the absence of collusion, the mitigation of information asymmetries, and the presence of proper accounting for both positive and negative externalities, maximizing shareholder returns maximizes public welfare. (For an early articulation of this model, see Stigler 1952.) In modern business, executives who talk about their duty to maximize shareholder value thus often experience themselves as acting from a deep sense of moral responsibility.

Indeed, one way of thinking about the current move toward prosocial purpose is that it represents a natural evolution in this kind of moral thinking. For if markets are not genuinely "free"—if, for example, firms are free to influence the political system in ways that shape the rules of competition to benefit themselves, or if prices do not reflect real costs because firms can legally emit huge quantities of greenhouse gases that cause enormous social harm, then there is no reason to believe that maximizing shareholder value will maximize either welfare or freedom.

Paul Polman, the former CEO of the European consumer-goods giant Unilever, is one of the most prominent exponents of this idea. On his very first day in the job, he announced that Unilever would no longer issue either quarterly earnings guidance or quarterly earnings reports. (He later joked that it was the first thing he did because he did not think the board would fire him on his first day.) Instead, Unilever would focus on the long term and on solving the great problems of the world. He even went as far as to urge shareholders to put their money elsewhere if they did not "buy into this long-term value creation model, which is equitable, which is shared, which is sustainable." Six months later he announced the Unilever Sustainable Living Plan, under which the firm committed to halving the size of its environmental footprint while doubling its output. In the years that followed, he claimed repeatedly that his responsibility was to multiple stakeholders, including consumers in the developing world and climate-change activists. Regarding shareholders, Polman said, "I'm not just working for them. . . . Slavery was abolished a long time ago" (Boynton 2015).

Many people continue to believe that it is illegal for a firm to embrace a purpose beyond profitability, but in general business leaders do not have a fiduciary duty to maximize profits—except in the highly exceptional circumstances that trigger "Revlon" or "Unocal" duties (Henderson and He 2018). Managers owe duties of care, candor, and loyalty to both the corporation and its investors, but that's it. It is probably illegal for the board of a publicly traded company to announce that any particular course of action will certainly significantly reduce short-term profits, but if the board believes that adopting a purpose beyond profit maximization is consistent with the long-term health of the corporation, doing so is entirely legal (Henderson and He 2018). Indeed, the first dean of the Harvard Business School suggested that the purpose of the corporation was to "make a decent profit, decently" and in August 2019, 181 members of the Business Roundtable—an organization composed of the CEOs of many of the largest and most powerful American corporations—released a statement redefining the purpose of the corporation to be "to promote an economy that serves all Americans" and committing to lead their companies for "the benefit of all stakeholders: customers, employees, suppliers, communities, and shareholders" (Business Round Table 2019).

Running an authentically purpose-driven company is thus both ethically required and entirely legal. This does not mean, of course, that it is practical! Here the evidence is mixed but encouraging. While there is no guarantee that embracing purpose will lead to long-term competitive advantage, and ruthlessly managed companies focused on the bottom line are often very successful, there are many reasons to believe that well-managed purpose-driven companies can compete successfully with more traditional rivals—and indeed that in some circumstances they can be extraordinarily successful.

In the first place, many of the most successful firms of the last 50 years have been demonstrably driven by purpose. Walmart's founder aimed not to make himself rich but to bring a much wider selection of products to customers who had historically been chronically underserved. Toyota's incredible success was built on the idea that the role of the firm was to create great jobs and serve Japanese society. Southwest Airlines insists—on its investor relations site, no less—that its purpose is to "be the world's most loved, most efficient, and most profitable airline."

In the second, an outpouring of research in psychology and behavioral economics has suggested that while people like money, and while in some situations offering employees additional compensation can be a powerful motivator, beyond the critical threshold at which people believe they have "enough," relying on monetary incentives can be ineffective and even counterproductive—and that companies motivated by purpose who treat their employees with dignity and respect and give them significant autonomy and agency in their jobs are likely to be significantly more productive and innovative than their conventional rivals (Henderson 2020a, 2020b).

Most human beings are driven by a deep need for some sense of meaning, by the desire to be autonomous and competent at work, and by the need to be in relationship with others (Pink 2011). Shared purpose creates a sense that one's work has meaning, and in authentically purpose-driven firms, the combination of a strong mission and the decision to treat employees with dignity and respect often creates ideal conditions for this kind of intrinsic motivation to flourish (Henderson 2020). It also creates a strong sense of identity, persuading people to go the extra mile in the service of the firm (Henderson and Van Den Steen 2015). When employees are empowered to be their authentic selves at work, they are also more likely to find work satisfying and interesting in itself, rather than approaching work as an instrument toward some other goal. This in turn leads to positive emotions like happiness and self-confidence, which in turn make it easier to build new skills, to bounce back after difficult times, and to be more resistant to challenges or threats.

This research has focused almost entirely on the level of the individual, but there is also increasing evidence that the embrace of purpose can drive performance at the firm level. In the US, for example, on average the most productive plants in any given industry make almost twice as much output *with the same measured inputs* as the least productive. In China and India, the best plants outperform the worst by an average of 5:1. I spent 20 years in windowless conference rooms full of economists trying to make these results go away. But they would not. Even with the inclusion of careful controls for factors like the age and quality of capital equipment, the nature of the firm's governance structure, the education and experience of workers and managers, and the pricing power of the firm, there are still "persistent performance differences across seemingly similar enterprises" (Gibbons and Henderson 2013; Syverson, 2004a, 2004b).

High productivity turns out to be correlated with differences in the adoption of high-performance management practices, where "high performance" is measured by the degree to which firms pay sustained attention to skills development, implement incentive systems that use more than simple quantitative metrics to measure performance, and use self-directed teams to manage work and create widespread opportunities for distributed communication and problem solving (Bloom and Van Reenen 2007, 2010, 2011; Bloom et al. 2019; Jon, Ichniowski, and Shaw 2002; Ichniowski and Shaw 1999).

These practices do not readily diffuse, suggesting that they are deeply rooted in the history and culture of the firm. It took General Motors nearly 20 years to come close to imitating Toyota—one of the best documented examples of a firm whose success is deeply rooted in its use of high commitment practices—despite the thousands of articles and the hundreds of the book that had been written about the firm (Helper and Henderson 2014). Some scholars believe that this enduring heterogeneity is rooted in the slow diffusion of information. One study in the Indian textile industry, for example, showed that the adoption of high-performance practices was accelerated by exposure to management consultants (Bloom et al. 2013). This is certainly plausible in some situations but cannot explain cases like GM, in which firms are aware of the superior practices and strongly motivated to adopt them but nonetheless find it immensely difficult. My own belief is that in many cases, slow diffusion reflects the fact that high-road firms are characterized by very high levels of trust between management and employees, and that this trust takes time and trouble to build (Gibbons and Henderson 2013; Henderson 2020).

Studies of the relationship between purpose and financial performance have generated mixed results, partly because it has proved difficult to develop credible measures of the degree to which a firm is purpose driven and partly because even when the embrace of purpose increases productivity and creativity, in many firms the benefits of these improvements are largely devoted to the very real costs of being purpose driven. Zeynep Ton's pioneering work, for example, suggests that in the retail sector, purpose-driven firms succeed by paying over the odds and redesigning work to give significantly more autonomy to floor-level employees. This allows purpose-driven firms to survive and even thrive, yet they do not seem to consistently outperform their more conventional rivals (Ton 2014). That said, Gartenberg, Pratt, and Serafeim (2019) use measures of purpose derived from more than 4 million individual employee surveys to show that the embrace of purpose is correlated with financial outperformance when there is a tight link between the firm's purpose and its strategy, and Alex Edmans (2020) summarizes much of the quantitative data suggesting that the embrace of purpose is increasingly linked to superior competitive performance.

In summary, there is ample reason to believe that authentically purpose-driven firms can survive, even in the face of intense competition. They may also be crucially important allies in the drive to build a just and sustainable economy.

Purpose-Driven Firms Are Catalysts

Most obviously, purpose-driven firms often have an immediately positive impact on their employees, customers, communities, and suppliers. Walmart claims that its commitment to energy efficiency and renewable energy has reduced greenhouse gas emissions by millions of tons (Walmart, 2019). When Mark Bertolini, Aetna's CEO, discovered that nearly 12 percent of the company's workforce were being paid minimum wage and, consequently, were having a great deal of difficulty making their lives work, he insisted that the firm pay them a living wage and increased their average cash compensation pay by more than 30 percent.

Purpose-driven firms are also ideally situated to act as catalysts for innovation within their industry.

It is tempting to believe that there is a bright line between business decisions that are profitable and those that are not. But in reality, most major decisions come freighted with significant risk, leading different firms to value them very differently. The decision to invest in new technologies or entirely new business models, for example, is fraught with enormous uncertainty. Things that look obviously profitable in retrospect rarely look so before the fact. Well-established and highly profitable firms often find it very difficult to believe that the future will be different from the past, and they frequently have trouble exploiting new innovations even once it is clear that they will be profitable.

A commitment to purpose provides both the strategy vision to identify these kinds of opportunities and the organizational capacity required to exploit them successfully. A commitment to a common purpose greatly increases strategic alignment within the firm, making it much more likely that employees will work hard and that their efforts will be mutually aligned (Henderson, 2020b). Purpose-driven firms are likely to select for employees who share the firm's values and for those who have prosocial preferences. In combination, these qualities are likely to create a preference for cooperation within the organization, greatly increasing the ability of the firm to pioneer disruptive or "architectural" innovation (Henderson 2020).

I have had the good fortune to meet many entrepreneurs who are trying to make a difference in the world. They begin by outlining the astounding new business they have in mind—one firm I know of, for example, is planning to invest more than $4 billion in mining mineral nodules from the floor of the Pacific Ocean—but then they unfailingly transition to telling me about the purpose that drives them to pour both their lives and their hearts into the venture. A brand-new idea may be profitable—or it may not—but if you believe strongly that it will make a real difference against the big problems, at the margin you are more likely to take the risk inherent in trying to make it happen. Purpose is the fuel that can drive change at scale.

This dynamic is evident inside much larger firms. When Unilever committed itself to making 100 percent of its tea brands sustainable, for example, it was not at all clear exactly how such a move was going to be profitable. Tea bags are a commodity business in which it is impossible to raise prices. But Michiel Leijnse—a relatively low-level employee—was able to pull together a coalition within the firm that was able to push the decision through. He and his team pointed to a variety of business models that might make the decision profitable—but their primary motivation was their deeply held belief that making the business sustainable was simply the right thing to do.

The move significantly increased Unilever's market share, and every other major branded tea company was forced to follow suit, tipping the entire industry toward sustainable production. Ex post, the decision is now viewed as a brilliant strategic move, but ex ante it was driven by the passion of the leaders of the tea business, who were able to translate their deep concern for the long-term sustainability of the business and the well-being of their employees into a convincing business case.

The US solar business is now a $84 billion industry and employs more people than coal, nuclear, and wind combined. The alternative meat business is expected to be a $140 billion industry within the next 10 years. The automotive industry is in the midst of a multibillion-dollar transition to electric vehicles. In each case the business was catalyzed by purpose-driven leaders willing to take the risks necessary to explore entirely new ways of doing things.

An equally important consequence of the willingness and ability of purpose-driven firms to challenge the status quo is the fact that their success—and the escalating commitment to solving the world's big problems that this success nearly always entails—often leads them to realize that there are many problems that they *cannot* solve—or at least that they cannot solve alone.

Take, for example, the case of palm oil. Palm oil is the world's most widely produced and consumed vegetable oil. Land planted with palm yields 5 to

10 times more oil, on average, than land used to produce other oils like soybean or rapeseed (canola), and it is both largely tasteless and highly stable. Thousands of products, including food, detergents, cosmetics, and biofuels, contain palm oil or its derivatives. But conventional palm oil production comes with heavy environmental and social costs. Clearing forest for palm oil production is a major source of greenhouse gas emissions and also reduces biodiversity and drives species extinction. New plantation development also frequently forces indigenous communities from their land, compelling locals to take on work as low-wage laborers on palm oil plantations, often under dangerous and abusive conditions (Henderson, Yew, and Baraldi 2016).

Unilever is the world's largest purchaser of palm oil, and in 2008—under significant pressure from activists—committed itself to buying only sustainably grown oil. But this commitment proved impossible to keep since sustainable palm oil is significantly more expensive than conventionally grown oil, and most consumers were unwilling to pay a premium for products that contained it.

In response, Unilever helped to found the Roundtable for Sustainable Palm Oil and was then able to persuade the Consumer Goods Forum—a trade association that includes nearly all of the major Western manufacturers of consumer goods and nearly all of the major retailers—to commit to purchasing only sustainably grown oil. Since together the group purchased roughly 60 percent of the world's traded palm oil, Unilever believed that these commitments could tip the entire industry toward the use of sustainable oil—thereby ensuring that no single firm would be at a competitive disadvantage despite its higher price.

This kind of industry-wide cooperation is emerging across a wide variety of industries. Many fisheries can be almost completely regenerated within a couple of years if left unfished for two or three years, for example, so fisher people that can jointly agree to restrain themselves are usually much better off than those who cannot, and a significant share of the world's inshore fisheries are now sustainably fished. In the apparel industry, it proved to be impossible for individual firms to force child labor out of their supply chains. In response, a group of firms together founded the Sustainable Apparel Coalition, a group committed to disseminating (and auditing) better labor standards across the entire supply chain, and the group has attained some success in improving conditions across the worldwide apparel industry. Cooperative arrangements to address the problems of sustainability are springing up not only in palm oil but also in crops like beef, soy, timber, and cocoa.

Here again, it is tempting to believe that building cooperation is simply a matter of economics. But it is not. Just as in the case of the decision to invest in significant innovation, the decision to enter a cooperative agreement— and to continue to conform to its provisions as it evolves—is fraught with uncertainty and as such often relies on the combination of economics and purpose-driven commitment that is fueling so much innovation. Many of the key quantities are socially determined and evolve endogenously as the various firms learn more about their own payoffs and those of their collaborators. Merely being able to demonstrate on paper that everyone would be better off if everyone cooperated is not sufficient to put a collaboration in place or to sustain it over time. Any single firm's decision to collaborate is shaped by its beliefs about how other firms are likely to behave.

Purpose-driven firms are thus particularly well suited to initiating these kinds of collaborations. They are likely to have already invested heavily in making credible commitments to behaving "well," so they are much less likely to take advantage of short-term temptations to cheat. This makes them much better partners. They have strong incentives to punish badly performing firms and have often built strong connections to the nongovernmental organizations (NGOs) whose activism is often one of the best means of bringing defecting firms into line. Moreover, building these kinds of collaborations is an intensely personal exercise as well as an economic one, requiring that the participants build a complex network of shared relationships and mutual trust. Purpose-driven firms like Unilever are uniquely suited to initiating such groups and to persuading others to join them because they have made costly commitments to behaving well and to following through on their commitments.

Of course, as Ed Balleisen reminded me, voluntary cooperative agreements are inherently fragile since they often present a classic prisoner's dilemma. Individual firms may promise to do the right thing but often face a significant temptation to fail to follow through, leaving the defectors with a short-term cost advantage and those that chose to cooperate feeling like (angry) patsies. It has become very clear that—as the work of Eleanor Ostrom and her collaborators has long suggested—the ability to sanction or to punish is critical to sustaining long-term cooperation (Ostrom 1990).

Sometimes voluntary private associations can find a way to put this capacity in place. The Institute of Nuclear Power Operations (INPO), for example, was founded in 1979 following the disastrous nuclear reactor meltdown at Three Mile Island. It develops operating standards and procedures for the nuclear industry and supports their adoption through an aggressive program of training and plan visits. Each plant is extensively evaluated each year and publicly ranked against its peers, and in the case of bad performance, INPO first contacts the utility's board and then reaches out to the relevant regulators. INPO is entirely industry funded and participation in its work is entirely voluntary, but between 1980 and 1990, the average rate of emergency plant shutdowns fell more than fourfold, and the INPO is widely credited with making an order of magnitude improvement in the safety of the US nuclear power industry. This is perhaps not surprising since the benefits it offers to the industry are tangible and immediate and the temptation to cheat is very small. Moreover, "defection" can be both easily observed and routinely punished.

But in many other cases, while ongoing collaborations have succeeded in making major gains they have not (yet?) achieved their original objectives. In the palm oil industry, a significant fraction of the supply chain is now sustainably certified—but marginal players desperate for short-term gains who are willing to sell to Indian and Chinese buyers are continuing to drive high levels of deforestation. In textiles, basic improvements have been achieved in some areas (e.g., health and safety) but not in others (e.g., freedom of association, excessive working hours) (Locke 2013).

The good news is that in many cases the effort to collaborate has created a network of firms that have built their business models—and recruited their employees and their customers—on the basis of an implicit promise to "do good." They now have strong incentives to support the creation of entities that have the power to sanction those firms that will not cooperate. These incentives are driving them to seek help from two powerful groups—so-called universal investors and governments.

The world's largest asset owners are now so wealthy that they are effectively forced to hold all the world's assets. They are increasingly coming to believe that problems like inequality and climate change are not, for them, "externalities" that can be diversified away but instead critical determinants of future performance. For example, Hiro Mizuno, who was until recently the chief investment officer of the Japanese Government Pension Fund, the world's largest pension fund, came to believe that climate change and social exclusion were the largest risks to the fund's ability to meet its long-term obligations to Japanese pensioners, and that his fiduciary duty required him to tackle them. These "universal investors" face their own free-riding problem, of course, but there are so few of them that it may well be that they can form a sufficiently powerful coalition that they can reshape the behavior of the firms in which they invest (Henderson 2020; Serafeim 2018). An NGO called Climate Action 100+, for example, includes more than 400 investors who together control more than $40 trillion in assets. They are committed to pushing the world's 100 largest GHG emitters to transition to a carbon-free economy and have proved to be willing to vote against boards they believe are not moving sufficiently fast.

Purpose-driven firms on the leading edge are also rediscovering government. In both palm oil and textiles, for example, the purpose-driven firms that have pioneered cooperation and bet their strategies and their brands on it have begun to look to local regulatory authorities as critical partners in achieving fully sustainable supply chains. For example, in palm oil, members of the Consumer Goods Forum have been meeting regularly with a broad range of stakeholders to explore productive ways forward. One possibility is to move to a "jurisdictional" approach—to build partnerships with local politicians, NGOs, and communities in an attempt to build a business case for converting entire regions to sustainable palm. Similar conversations are happening in the textile business in the context of some promising early success. One study of the Indonesia apparel industry, for example, found that self-regulatory efforts were significantly more likely to increase wages when the self-regulating body worked closely with the state and when local unions were mobilized to push for state action. As Rodrik and Sabel suggest in their chapter in this book, these kinds of public-private partnerships are starting to emerge in many industries.

Allies in Building Inclusive Institutions?

In short, purpose-driven firms are beginning to learn that the easiest way to solve the big problems—and to ensure that they themselves are profitable—is to support smart, well-run government. Could they be allies in the fight to rebuild our institutions and our democracy?

Historically, dramatic social change and, in particular, the dissolution of concentrated wealth and power has been most often accomplished by violent upheaval—by revolution, war, or famine. But profound change is not always cataclysmic. In Denmark in the 1890s, for example, the Danish business association reached out to Denmark's major labor association, suggesting that there had to be a better way to run Denmark than through endless labor unrest—and the Danish system was born. In Germany in the 1940s, German business—facing the ruin of all their hopes and the threat of communism—likewise reached out to German labor, proposing a system of industry-wide collective bargaining and a nationwide apprentice program. In Mauritius in 1968, as ethnic riots led to the death of hundreds of people, the head of the newly elected (largely Hindu) Labor government reached out to the recently defeated (largely francophone) party—the home of Mauritius's sugar barons—to suggest taking a new road to development, one in which business worked as hard to grow the supply of good jobs as it did do grow revenues. Together, they initiated a partnership that has endured to the present day. In South Africa, De Klerk's Afrikaner party yielded power peacefully to Nelson Mandela's African National Congress, following years of struggle that most observers had expected would end in bitter civil war. While much of his success was a result of more than 50 years of courageous struggle on the ground, it was almost certainly helped by the support of South Africa's white industrialists (Acemoglu and Robinson 2019).

In each case, it was clear ex post that working together to build a more inclusive society was good for all the parties concerned. But there have been many situations in which there is a clear collective case for action and the relevant actors have been unable to realize it. I believe that the current move to purpose greatly increases the odds that in the face of our current problems we may be able to build these kinds of coalitions. Purpose can be as catalytic for cooperation in the service of the public good as it is for innovation within the firm and cooperation across industries.

The world's largest firms are larger than many economies. By some measures, the 1,000 largest firms together control over 70 percent of the world's gross domestic product (GDP); more economic activity takes place within the world's firms than in the free market. If even a relatively small fraction could be persuaded to argue that justice (as well as self-interest!) requires a remaking of the international economic and political order, they could prove to be powerful allies.

Are they sufficient to drive the changes we need? Surely not. But they could be very helpful. US CEOs have pushed local politicians to respect gay and transgender rights. NGOs like "We Are Still In" draw on the support of hundreds of firms to push for local action on climate change. Many of the firms attempting to increase diversity and inclusion within their ranks are discovering that really moving the ball forward will require tackling structural racism in the broader society. The 2020 election in the United States saw many of the country's largest firms speak out publicly in support of the democracy and the peaceful transition of power.

None of these moves are enough to change the world. But they are important steps in the right direction, and they might well have broader implications. Firms are increasingly the place where people spend most of their time and are often the institution that employees trust the most. Could purpose-driven firms become a site for the development of civic consciousness? I have only anecdotal evidence on this front, but I know of more than one firm where the embrace of purpose has led to employees whose lives are now characterized by greatly increased agency becoming active in local politics.

Most fundamentally, the emergence of purpose-driven firms has the potential to normalize the idea that the purpose of business is not to increase its profits—indeed that it never was. The purpose of business is to help build prosperous, just, sustainable societies rooted in genuine freedom of opportunity and mutual respect. No one now argues in public that employing child labor is a good idea. It should be as unacceptable to emit greenhouse gases, to pay less than a living wage, or to lobby to subvert either the free market or democracy. Purpose-driven businesses have the potential to help drive a profound normative shift, making it much, much harder for firms whose profits are rooted in the destruction of our environment, our society, or our politics to hide behind the claim that they are simply maximizing shareholder value.

Several policies can help to support the emergence of this new approach. Reforming the governance of corporations so as to make it significantly easier for firms to commit to doing the right thing over the long term is undoubtedly important; see, for example, Mayer (2019). There are a raft of sensible proposals in this space, including accelerating the adoption of the "Benefit" corporate form, explicitly changing the responsibilities of the board, making it easier to form firms that are owned by their customers and their employees, and supporting the creation of sources of long-term or "stewardship" capital (Strine 2019). But it will also be crucially important to develop auditable, replicable, reliable measures of the degree to which firms are indeed "doing good" in the world. If we are to trust firms, we must be able to verify their behavior. In this context, the gathering strength of the so-called ESG movement—a movement pushing for the mandatory reporting of environmental, social, and governance metrics—is a hugely welcome development.

Let me close by coming back to the question with which I opened— namely, whether firms that are genuinely committed to doing the right thing can survive in the context of a system premised entirely on self-interest. I could tell you many stories, but I will close with one of my favorites.

In February 2017—eight years after Paul Polman had taken the helm and announced his commitment to purpose—Kraft Heinz, a large consumer-goods company controlled by Warren Buffett's Berkshire Hathaway Holdings, and 3G Capital, a large Brazilian private equity firm, made a hostile bid for Unilever. (Kraft Heinz was offering $143 billion for the company, an 18 percent premium over Unilever's market value. Unilever had announced lower than expected fourth quarter sales just three weeks before, sending its shares down by 4.5 percent.) 3G had a reputation as an aggressive cost cutter, and Unilever's stock jumped 13 percent on the announcement.

Unilever's board immediately turned down the bid, claiming that it grossly undervalued the company. This in itself was not unusual. What was out of the ordinary was the way in which the company's supporters mobilized in protest.

One group pulled together 100,000 signatures on an online petition in less than three days. Bono, the rock singer and campaigner, reached out offering to write a song. And a number of carefully selected people—we don't know exactly who or how many—called Mr. Buffett. "Warren was approached by probably more people than he expected," Polman later said. "As soon as (he) discovered that this was a hostile takeover, the tone of the conversation became different." Three days later, Kraft Heinz withdrew the bid.

Unilever has since emerged as one of the world's most successful consumer-goods companies. The company claims that in 2018, its purpose-driven brands grew 69 percent faster than its more conventional brands, generating 75 percent of the firm's overall growth (Unilever 2019). Unilever's new CEO, Alan Jope, remains deeply committed to purpose—and to changing the world.

Polman, Jope, and other business leaders like them believe—and are increasingly saying in public—that to continue on our current course is deeply immoral. They use the language of justice and equity as justification for business decisions—and they are thriving. We live in a desperate time. Perhaps they can be helpful.

References

Acemoglu, Daron, and James A. Robinson. 2012. *Why Nations Fail: The Origins of Power, Prosperity, and Poverty*. Crown Books.

———. 2019. *The Narrow Corridor: States, Societies, and the Fate of Liberty*. Penguin Press.

"Admonishment and Reconciliation of Robert Keayne with the Church, 1639–1640." https://teachingamericanhistory.org/library/document/admonishment-and-reconciliation-of-robert-keayne-with-the-church-1639-1640/.

Balleisen, Edward J. 2017. *Fraud: An American History from Barnum to Madoff*. Princeton University Press.

Bloom, Nicholas, Erik Brynjolfsson, Lucia Foster, Ron Jarmin, Megha Patnaik, Itay Saporta-Eksten, and John Van Reenen. 2019. "What Drives Differences in Management Practices?" *American Economic Review* (May).

Bloom, Nicholas, Benn Eifert, David McKenzie, Aprajit Mahajan, and John Roberts. 2013. "Does Management Matter? Evidence from India." *Quarterly Journal of Economics* 128, no. 1 (February): 1–51.

Bloom, Nicholas, and John Van Reenen. 2007. "Measuring and Explaining Management Practices across Firms and Countries." *Quarterly Journal of Economics* 122:1351–1408.

———. 2010. "Why Do Management Practices Differ across Firms and Countries?" *Journal of Economic Perspectives* 24, no. 1 (February): 203–224.

———. 2011. "Human Resource Management and Productivity." In *Handbook of Labor Economics*, edited by Orley Ashenfelter and David Card, vol. 4, 1697–1767. Amsterdam: Elsevier and North-Holland.

Boynton, Andy. 2015. "Unilever's Paul Polman: CEOs Can't Be 'Slaves' to Shareholders," *Forbes*, July 20, 2015. https://www.forbes.com/sites/andyboynton/2015/07/20/unilevers-paul-polman-ceos-cant-be-slaves-to-shareholders/#593e468e56le.

Business Roundtable. 2019. "Business Roundtable Redefines the Purpose of a Corporation to Promote 'an Economy That Serves All Americans.'" August 19, 2019. https://www.businessroundtable.org/business-roundtable -redefines-the-purpose-of-a-corporation-to-promote-an-economy-that-serves -all-americans.

Council on Foreign Relations. n.d. "Modern Slavery." *CFR InfoGuide*, accessed July 9, 2021. https://www.cfr.org/modern-slavery.

Edmans, Alex. 2020. *Grow the Pie: How Great Companies Deliver Both Purpose and Profit*. Cambridge University Press.

Gant, Jon, Casey Ichniowski, and Kathryn Shaw. 2002. "Social Capital and Organizational Change in High-Involvement and Traditional Work Organizations." *Journal of Economics and Management Strategy* 11:289–328.

Gartenberg, Claudine, Andrea Prat, and George Serafeim. 2019. "Corporate Purpose and Financial Performance." *Organization Science* 30, no. 1 (1–18).

Gibbons, Robert, and Rebecca Henderson. 2013. "What Do Managers Do? Exploring Persistent Performance Differences among Seemingly Similar Enterprises." In The *Handbook of Organizational Economics*, edited by Robert Gibbons and John Roberts, chap. 17, 680–731. Princeton, NJ: Princeton University Press.

Helper, Susan, and Rebecca Henderson. 2014. "Management Practices, Relational Contracts and the Decline of General Motors." *Journal of Economic Perspectives* 28, no. 1 (Winter): 49–72.

Henderson, Rebecca. 2020a. *Reimagining Capitalism in a World on Fire*. Hachette Public Affairs.

Henderson, Rebecca. 2020b. "Innovation in the 21st Century: Architectural Change, Purpose, and the Challenges of Our Time." *Management Science*, October. https://pubsonline.informs.org/doi/10.1287/mnsc.2020.3746.

Henderson, Rebecca, and Tony L. He. 2017, "Shareholder Value Maximization, Fiduciary Duties, and the Business Judgement Rule: What Does the Law Say?." Harvard Business School Background Note 318-097, January.

Henderson, Rebecca, and Karthik Ramanna. 2015. "Do Managers Have a Role to Play in Sustaining the Institutions of Capitalism?" *Brookings*, February 9.

Henderson, Rebecca, and Eric Van Den Steen. 2015. "Why Do Firms have Purpose?

The Firm's Role as a Carrier of Identity and Reputation." *American Economic Review*, Papers and Proceedings, May 2015.

Henderson, Rebecca, Hann-Shuin Yew, and Monica Baraldi. 2016. "Gotong Royong: Toward Sustainable Palm Oil." Harvard Business School Case No 1-316-124.

Ichniowski, Casey, and Kathryn Shaw. 1999. "The Effects of Human Resource Systems on Productivity: An International Comparison of US and Japanese Plants." *Management Science* 45:704–22.

Kocka, Jürgen. 2016. *Capitalism: A Short History*. Kindle ed. Princeton University Press.

Locke, Richard. 2013. *The Promise and Limits of Private Power: Promoting Labor Standards in a Global Economy*. Cambridge University Press.

MacDuffie, John Paul. 1995. "Human Resource Bundles and Manufacturing Performance: Organizational Logic and Flexible Production Systems in the World Auto Industry." *Industrial and Labor Relations Review* 48:197–221.

MacDuffie, John Paul, Kannan Sethuranman, and Marshall Fisher. 1996. "Product Variety and Manufacturing Performance: Evidence from the International Automotive Assembly Plant Study." *Management Science* 42:350–369.

Mayer, Colin. 2019. *Prosperity: Better Business Makes the Greater Good*. Oxford University Press.

Origo, Iris, 2017. *The Merchant of Prato: Daily Life in a Medieval Italian City*. Penguin Modern Classics.

Ostrom, Elinor. 1990. *Governing the Commons: The Evolution of Institutions for Collective Action*. Cambridge University Press.

Pink, D. H. 2011. *Drive: The Surprising Truth about What Motivates Us*. Penguin.

Riffkin, Rebecca. 2015. "Big Government Still Named as Biggest Threat to US." *Gallup*, December 22. https://news.gallup.com/poll/187919/big-government-named-biggest-threat.aspx.

Stigler, George. 1952. *The Theory of Price*. Macmillan.

Syverson, Chad. 2004a. "Product Substitutability and Productivity Dispersion." *Review of Economics and Statistics* 86:534–50.

———. 2004b. "Market Structure and Productivity: A Concrete Example." *Journal of Political Economy* 112:1181–1222.

Serafeim, George. 2018. "Investors as Stewards of the Commons." *Journal of Applied Corporate Finance* 30, no. 2 (Spring/Summer): 8–17.

Smith, Christopher, John Child, Michael Rowlinson, and Sir Adrian Cadbury. 2009. *Reshaping Work: The Cadbury Experience*. Cambridge University Press.

Soll, Jacob, 2014. *The Reckoning: Financial Accountability and the Rise and Fall of Nations*. Basic Books.

Stigler, G. 1952. *The Theory of Price*. London: Macmillan.

Strine, Leo E. Jr. 2019. "Towards Fair and Sustainable Capitalism." Research paper No 19-39, Institute for Law and Economics, University of Pennsylvania Law School. https://papers.ssrn.com/sol3/papers.cfm?abstract_id=3461924.

Ton, Zeynep. 2014. *The Good Jobs Strategy: How the Smartest Companies Invest in Employees to Lower Costs and Boost Profits*. New Harvest.

Unilever. 2019. "Brands with Purpose Grow—and Here's the Proof," November 6. https://www.unilever.com/news/news-and-features/Feature-article/2019/ brands-with-purpose-grow-and-here-is-the-proof.html.

Walmart. 2019. "Walmart on Track to Reduce 1 Billion Tons of Emissions from the Supply Chain by 2030." https://corporate.walmart.com/newsroom/2019/05/ 08/walmart-on-track-to-reduce-1-billion-metric-tons-of-emissions-from-global -supply-chains-by-2030.

Winthrop, John. 1853. *The History of New England from 1630 to 1649*, 2 vols. Boston.

Wood, Gordon S. 1993. *The Radicalism of the American Revolution*. Vintage Books.

8 Corporate Purpose in a Post-Covid World

MALCOLM S. SALTER

Summary

The canonization of shareholder wealth maximization as the only legitimate expression of corporate purpose has contributed to a widening gulf between what the capital market values and what people value. Narrowing this gulf in a post-Covid world—where long-standing social inequities and injustices have been dramatically exposed—requires a very different conception of corporate purpose based on moral and economic principles that challenge the theory underlying shareholder wealth maximization. To this end, I first explain what the theoretical underpinnings of the shareholder wealth maximization doctrine are, how this doctrine has become so deeply ingrained in our capitalist system, and what practical and conceptual problems this doctrine presents. I then propose an alternative guideline for corporate purpose rooted in Aristotle's theory of reciprocal justice and compatible theories of business organizations as cooperative systems. This guideline—referred to here as *ethical reciprocity*—focuses on the utility of cooperation in transactional settings and the efficiencies flowing from cooperation, neither of which are a priority in a shareholder wealth maximization regime. Based on these ethical and economic underpinnings, the concept of ethical reciprocity offers a practical framework for balancing the dissimilar interests of shareholders and other corporate constituencies. I end by addressing (a) how "reciprocity practitioners" can survive in a world dominated by shareholder wealth maximizers and (b) what those with the most power to foster change in corporate purpose and governance—namely, large asset holders and asset managers—can do, and increasingly are doing, to encourage public corporations to retreat from their singular focus on shareholder wealth maximization.

Introduction

In April 2020, the former governor of the Bank of England, Mark Carney, predicted that "value will change in the post-Covid world . . . the traditional drivers of value have been shaken, new ones will gain prominence, and *there's the possibility that the gulf between what markets value and what people value will close*" (italics added).[1]

The possibility of our capitalist economy yielding more to human values is surely to be wished for. But narrowing the gulf between what markets value and what people value will be as difficult as it is necessary.

It is pretty clear, for example, what the capital markets value: increasing returns to shareholders. Despite the vast academic literature and many management testimonials advocating broader conceptions of corporate purpose, shareholder wealth maximization remains the de facto expression of corporate purpose for most publicly listed companies, especially in the US and UK, where this value-maximizing doctrine offers strong protection from the relatively unconstrained market for corporate control.[2]

While it is less clear what the general public values most, maximizing shareholder returns is not at the top of the list. More likely, especially in the aftermath of the Covid-19 pandemic that exposed and magnified long-standing social inequities, matters related to income security, economic opportunity, and social justice are top of mind.

The inconsistency that currently exists between what markets value and what people value has become increasingly more troublesome over the past 40 years as shareholder wealth maximization has been canonized as the only legitimate expression of corporate purpose. Aggressive pursuit of this foundational doctrine has left a well-documented trail of corporate conduct and consequence that is incompatible with what many people consider to be the well-being of society.

The adverse effects of this incompatibility include major increases in income inequality and insecurity in an economy experiencing one of the fastest growth rates in our history; persistent neglect of the natural environment and sustainability of the entire economy; rampant cronyism involving collusion among firms, their regulators, and Congress, resulting in policies and regulations that serve private shareholder interests at the expense of the society's well-being; widespread gaming of legislated rules and regulations that benefit corporate shareholders but offer few compensating public benefits; and inattention to the plight of capitalism's "losers," such as the underpaid and the forced unemployed—just to note a few.

Not surprisingly, the damaging side effects of relentless shareholder wealth maximization have contributed to a remarkable decline of public trust in large corporations—arguably one of America's most representative social institutions—and capitalism as a system of economic governance. Over the last decade, surveys by Gallup, Frank Luntz, Harvard's Institute of Politics, and the Edelman Trust Barometer have all shown that only about one in five respondents trust US big business and that throughout the industrialized world only 20 percent of those surveyed feel that the current system of political economy is working for them. It is highly unlikely that these opinions will change in a post-Covid world.

Before the onset of Covid-19, many parties in both the business and academic communities had become well aware that reform of American-style capitalism was becoming an ethical and political necessity. This realization has led more and more business leaders, including the Business Roundtable, to claim that shareholder profits can no longer be the primary goal of their large, public corporations.

For US companies that have somehow not heard this message, they are now hearing it loud and clear from both large asset holders (such as pension funds, insurance companies, sovereign funds, and endowments) and large asset managers (such as BlackRock, Vanguard Group, and State Street Corp.) who collectively own one in five shares of the Standard & Poor's 500 (S&P 500). With the objective of improving the long-term financial sustainability of the funds they manage—by reducing the risk of their investments and increasing their resilience to changes in the political and regulatory environment—there is a surge underway in the amount of funds invested by large asset holders and managers on the basis of how they handle environmental, social, and governance (ESG) matters. In response to increased investor attention to the broad impact of corporations on society and the environment, ESG-oriented investing now tops $30 trillion—up 68 percent since 2014 and tenfold since 2004. The current capitalization of the global equity market is in excess of $80 trillion.

Central bankers are also beginning to assert themselves in the matter of long-term financial sustainability. The Bank of England and the central banks of France, the Netherlands, and Singapore have introduced "stress tests" on commercial banks seeking to discover climate-related credit risks embedded in their loan portfolios. In response to these tests, banks need to establish how their borrowers are managing current and future climate-related risks. This new discipline will have the inevitable effect of shifting the attention of corporate borrowers toward improved environmental sustainability and away from unconstrained shareholder wealth maximization.

This is promising news for those interested in closing the value gulf, and the trend may well be accelerating. In the same week Carney's column appeared in *The Economist*, the head of equities at Fidelity International wrote in a message to clients that "the silver lining to this unfortunate crisis is that society's focus on sustainability is about to go parabolic, not just in relation to dealing with climate change and reducing poverty, but in how companies treat all stakeholders, and critically their own employees."

For such a shift in investment priorities to spread further through the public company economy, three matters need to be addressed straight on. As a first step, we need to understand why the shareholder wealth maximization doctrine is not appropriate, either theoretically or practically, as a principal guideline for the espoused purpose of publicly listed companies.[3]

Second, we need to consider an alternative guideline for corporate purpose, which can replace, or at least supplement, the shareholder wealth maximization doctrine. This guideline needs to meet the twin tests of (a) satisfying both what markets value and what people value and (b) serving practical business interests. The alternative guideline that I suggest is based on the moral principle of "ethical reciprocity," an idea rooted in Aristotle's theory of reciprocal justice. In public corporations where the principle of ethical reciprocity is adopted as a guideline or moral constraint for corporate purpose, shareholders continue to hold a preeminent position in the hierarchy of corporate stakeholders with expectations of a return on their investment sufficient to compensate them for the uncontrollable and often unknowable risks that they bear. This expected return is, of course, shareholders' reserve price for participating in the enterprise. But reciprocity practitioners also recognize that many who participate in the life of a corporation are not the only party with a legitimate claim of fair exchange with the corporation. Other parties—such as employees, suppliers, customers, creditors, neighbors, and guardians of the environment—are recognized as having their reserve prices, too, related in part to the risks that they bear through their voluntary and sometimes involuntary participation in the life of the enterprise. Their continued participation in, and support for, the enterprise is dependent on a surplus of benefits for their participation and support or, at the very least, a level of valued benefits above breakeven exchange. In this context, the principle of ethical reciprocity offers adopters a practical guideline for balancing the conflicting interests of various participants in the enterprise who hold nonidentical goals and conflicting preferences. Similarly, it provides a principled framework for working with corporate stakeholders on shaping a social contract based on cooperation rather than domination and discord—where cooperation involves some measure of shared of control over the institutional policies and procedures that affect stakeholder interests. And, finally, adopting ethical reciprocity as a guideline for corporate purpose liberates executives to pursue a wide diversity of business purposes that are only constrained by the need to pay the reserve price required by parties participating in the life of the enterprise.[4]

Third, two practical matters related to the adoption of ethical reciprocity as a guideline for corporate purpose also need to be addressed: how can "reciprocity practitioners" survive in a competitive world currently dominated by shareholder wealth maximizers, and what can those with the most power to determine the success or failure of any such reform effort do to change the behavior of executives and investors who may be deeply hostile to any retreat from shareholder wealth maximization. In the absence of any new statutory or regulatory interventions (which would travel a slow and rocky road of re-legislation, re-regulation, and re-litigation), the most powerful source of influence for such reform are large asset holders and asset managers.

The Problematic Canonization of Shareholder Wealth Maximization

The evolution of shareholder wealth maximization as the only legitimate expression of corporate purpose can be traced directly to the proposition that shareholders own their corporations and that corporate executives should therefore run the corporation in their interest, meaning that their primary mandate is to maximize the value of the company's shares. And since shareholders are the residual bearers of risk in corporate activity—meaning that they could lose all their money without any recourse or appeal—corporate executives have an ethical obligation to protect shareholders from the "unusual degree of exposure" that they have to the corporation.

By the early 1970s, however, there was increasing concern among economists and finance scholars that what managers actually sought to do was to maximize their own self-interests before attending to the value of the firms for which they worked. But did managers actually revert to maximizing their own self-interest? Conversely, to what extent were managers truly loyal to shareholders?

In 1976, Michael Jensen and William Meckling addressed these questions in a landmark paper addressing the "agency relationship" that existed between shareholders and managers as agents of the shareholders. They also laid out a theory of the firm based on agency theory, which, among other major contributions, made the economic case for shareholder wealth maximization as the only legitimate expression of corporate purpose and the most effective tool for managing the agency relationship between shareholders and managers.

The Jensen and Meckling paper reflected a rich intellectual background that extended back in the history of economic thought to the self-interested model of humankind assumed by Jeremy Bentham and to Richard Coase's conception of the modern corporation as a "nexus of contracts," or series of transactions bound by "contracts" with suppliers, customers, and other parties that agree to work together for mutual benefit. In the words of Jensen and Meckling:

> It is important to recognize that most organizations are *simply legal fictions which serve as a nexus for a set of contracting relationships among individuals. . . .* The private corporation or firm is simply one form of a *legal fiction which serves as a nexus for contracting relationships and which is also characterized by the existence of divisible residual claims on the assets and cash flows of the organization which can generally be sold without permission of the other contracting individuals."*[5] (original italics)

What is most notable about this theory of the firm is that it stands in sharp contrast to the older conception of the corporation as an entity cocreated by public authority (through state charter), which grants corporations and their managers the right to make money and operate within the constraints of certain rules of game.

According to this new theory (and echoing the work of Nobel Laureate economist Oliver Williamson), firms are created when internalizing contracts between owners and various factors of production into a hierarchy is efficient—that is, when the benefits of coordinating these implicit and explicit contracts and related activities in a hierarchy are greater than the costs of coordinating them through market-based transactions and when the value of the goods and services sold by the firm exceed the costs of the inputs used.

This basic idea about the nature of firms was at the core of Jensen and Meckling's theory, and it was very effectively enhanced and publicized by Jensen in a series of academic papers and management articles spanning 20 years of original thinking and scholarship. Jensen's theory posits that the efficient performance of this contractual firm requires the recognition that the primary interest of shareholders (principals) is the maximization of their wealth by professional managers (agents)—to whom significant decision rights have been delegated. The theory also argues that efficient performance requires that firms adopt a system of internal governance and control that supports this primary interest.

According to Jensen, the objective of such an internal governance and control system is minimizing whatever agency costs exist when agents (directors and managers) behave in opportunistic ways that do not fully satisfy the interests of the principals (shareholders). These agency costs—equal to the sum of the costs of monitoring managers incurred by principals, the costs of bonding managers' interests to those of shareholders incurred by the agents, and the residual losses from agency costs that cannot be controlled—arise naturally, the argument goes, because in real organizational life, managers of publicly owned firms, who possess substantial decision and control rights over corporate resources, are rarely "perfect agents" for dispersed shareholders. This is because they do not receive the full benefits of the profits earned and therefore have incentives to extract perquisites from the firm at the expense of the firm's true owners. In other words, the incentives of managers and owners are not naturally aligned. Minimizing such agency costs therefore logically involves paying corporate managers in ways that tie their pay increases with share value, thereby aligning management incentives with the primary interests of shareholders—namely, the value of their investment expressed in stock price.

Agency theory immediately attracted enormous attention. Thirty years after its publication, the Jensen-Meckling article was the third most cited in major economics journals, and today more than 2,000 papers on the Social Science Research Network have "agency" in their title. The most significant management implication of this theory—that long-term wealth maximization for shareholders needs to be the primary metric for assessing the performance of business enterprise—also found a great deal of support in the financial and business communities and among faculty members in many leading business schools. Despite Michael Jensen's observation in the *Business Ethics Quarterly*—25 years after his pioneering 1976 paper appeared—that shareholder wealth maximization is not a vision or even a purpose and that wealth (or value) maximization is only a standard for measuring corporate success, the performance measurement element of his management theory was, and remains, foundational to the "shareholder primacy" theory of the firm.

Much of the appeal of this new theory of the firm and its implications for corporate purpose was undoubtedly created by the widely read, practitioner-oriented articles published by Michael Jensen, all of which were backed up by more than 100 scientific papers addressing, one way or another, what he referred to as "the struggle for organizational efficiency." By the start of the new millennium, Jensen was one of the best-known and influential business economists, even as his work was being challenged by academic colleagues and students who had entirely different conceptions of what role corporations served, and needed to serve, in contemporary society. To many audiences, however, Jensen's ideas about the coordination, control, and management of organizations "made sense." And, in many respects, they did.

For example, many of Jensen's students and fans in industry were just as concerned as he was about failure of the internal control systems of large, public firms, which was the subject of his 1993 presidential address to the American Finance Association. After analyzing the performance of large public firms from 1980 to 1990 in preparation for this address and its accompanying paper, Jensen discovered that a large proportion were unable to earn their cost of capital on a sustained basis (due to major inefficiencies in their capital expenditures and research and development spending). From these findings of low investment returns and the widespread destruction of economic value in large firms (particularly those without monopoly power) during the 1980s, it seemed straightforward that Jensen's advocacy for aggressive pursuit of shareholder wealth maximization, coupled with compatible governance reforms, was the proper antidote for the large number of underperformers. Many in academia and the business community agreed.

In addition, Jensen's concerns about underperforming firms coincided with the development of the market for corporate control, which blossomed in the 1980s, and his arguments in favor of hostile takeovers as a disciplining device for inefficient firms immediately found support from buyout firms, whose widely debated and oft-criticized takeover strategies suddenly found an elegant, academic validation. Starting in the 1980s, almost a quarter of public firms in the US were the target of attempted hostile takeovers opposed by a firm's management and another quarter received takeover bids supported by management. In this environment, Michael Jensen's rationale for shareholder wealth maximization and equity-based pay (as a way of reducing agency costs) was quickly picked up and embraced by buyout firms and takeover specialists seeking economic justification for their supposedly value-creating strategies.

Another source of popularity of this new theory of the firm and expression of corporate purpose was that it offered corporate executives and financial analysts a single, theoretically justifiable performance measure (stock price) that captured the present value of all future effects—namely, firm value. As Jensen famously wrote in 2002:

> Any organization must have a single-valued objective as a precursor to purposeful or rational behavior. . . . It is logically impossible to maximize in more than one dimension at the same time. . . . Thus, telling a manager to maximize current profits, market share, future growth profits, and anything else one pleases will leave that manager with no way to make a reasoned decision. In effect, it leaves the manager with no objective.[6]

From here, it was an easy step to place firm value and shareholder wealth at the center of corporate conscience.

Finally, the contractual theory of the firm, buttressed by agency theory, was a timely reinforcement of the Friedman doctrine, as described by Nobel Laureate Milton Friedman in *Capitalism and Freedom* in 1962 and his famous 1970 article in *The New York Times* that grabbed the attention of the business community and continues to resonate today in many classrooms and boardrooms. Friedman argued that a manager's primary duty is to maximize the value of shareholders' capital because it maximizes the chance of capitalism to allocate capital freely in the service of individual needs, promotes economic efficiency, preserves individual freedoms, and maintains the trust that shareholders place in managers to serve their interests. At base, this was a normative, ethical argument. In this way, the concept of shareholder wealth maximization was cobranded by two of the leading lights of the Chicago school of economics (where Freidman was a professor and Jensen received his doctorate).

Criticisms of this revisionist conception of the firm and corporate purpose have persisted for many reasons. To start, the well-functioning of market economies and firms requires more than shareholder wealth maximization as a motivating principle, as business school professor Edward Freeman and law school professor Lynn Stout have long argued. To operate functionally, firms need to work hard at building and retaining the mutual trust and confidence of constituencies beyond shareholders. Entrepreneurship, which involves the assembly of complementary resources and skills, cannot be practiced in the absence of cooperation and mutual trust among enterprise members. And apart from entrepreneurial start-ups, shareholders are rarely the sole group providing specialized inputs to corporate production and making essential contributions to an enterprise's success. Executives, rank-and-file employees, creditors, even members of a local community also make essential contributions. For all these reasons, in the absence of cooperation and mutual trust, the costs of coordination and commitment will skyrocket, and the social legitimacy of market-based institutions will be under relentless challenge.

Second, the striking metaphor of the firm as a "nexus of contracts" with attendant principal-agent problems that only a focus on shareholder wealth maximization can mitigate is too simple an analogy. Corporations, in their everyday operation, are far more than a "nexus of contracts" through which business transactions are carried out—although associating with a corporate entity through contracts and law to pursue self-interest is certainly part of the creation story. But contracts do not exhaust the reciprocal understanding on which the productivity of firms rests. As philosopher Elizabeth Anderson pointed out in her 2015 essay on the business enterprise as an ethical agent, supracontractual understandings or voluntary reciprocal exchanges with stakeholders are also required for corporations to be successful. For example, relationships with internal stakeholders (directors, executives, and employees and their unions) comprise the teamwork necessary for production and the mutual benefits flowing from that production, and in this production team the contributions of each manager and worker are difficult to observe and ascribe to specific bits of production. Since it is impossible to contractually specify all the ways team members need to cooperate for efficient production, and since excessive monitoring is likely to depress morale and breed "reciprocal distrust," well-managed firms develop norms or trust and reciprocity among members in return for contractually unguaranteed rewards such as bonuses, promotions, better working conditions, family leaves, and so forth. For similar reasons, relationships with "external stakeholders" (suppliers, customers, and communities in which the corporation does business) also require reciprocal understandings beyond contractual guarantees.

On this basis alone, it does not make much sense to view the firm as a nexus of contracts. Rather, it makes more sense to view the firm, in Anderson's words, as follows:

> [It is] a joint enterprise constituted by a nexus of cooperative relationships in which internal stakeholders commit firm-specific assets to relatively long-term team production arrangements, submit to common governance, and repeatedly interact on the basis of norms of trust and reciprocity, all for mutual and reciprocal benefit, the terms of which are not exhausted by law and contract. The firm also typically enters into protracted reciprocal relationships with external stakeholders . . . which are supported by normative expectations of trust, reciprocity, and mutual gain, not all of which are defined in explicit contracts.[7]

The most important implication of this conception of the firm is that directors owe a fiduciary duty to the corporation itself, not to the shareholders exclusively, and that shareholder wealth maximization as a singular definition of corporate purpose is inappropriate.

Third, there are other problems with principal-agent and agency cost theories derived from the nexus of contracts conception of the firm. In considering the firm to be an instrument of its owners, who employ agents to operate on their behalf, agency cost theory assumes that these agents (managers) are, to a notable extent, shirkers or disloyal to the firm's principals (shareholders). It is by no means clear, however, that this assumption holds up in real life. Jensen's 1993 study revealing the systematic inability of large public corporations to earn their cost of capital during the 1980s can only *imply* that agency costs are a driver of his computations of value destruction. There have been very few other attempts to measure agency costs directly, and it is probably impossible to do so because the definition of agency costs lacks the kind of specificity that can be converted into easily measurable, organizational, or behavioral characteristics. So the premise of agency costs, while conceptually plausible, remains to be proved.

Fourth, the shareholder-primacy conception of the firm assumes that all shareholders are alike in their personal goals and values. But can we assume that all retail investors, family offices, mutual funds, pension funds, private equity funds, hedge funds, governments, foundations, and universities, have the same goals? What if some—but not all—institutional investors seek to maximize financial returns for their investors; what if families seek to maximize their "socio-emotional wealth"; what if governments seek to improve social welfare of their citizens? This assumption seems to be an oversimplification of shareholder and investor motives that both reduces the measurement of corporate performance to a single, amoral metric and promotes unbalanced devotion to achieving a goal that can be easily gamed or manipulated by management.

Fifth, one of the startling omissions of the shareholder-centric model of the firm pointed out by Joseph Bower and Lynn Paine in a 2017 *Harvard Business Review* article is that public company shareholders are not held accountable in any way for the effects of whatever policies they encourage corporations to take. In their words, "shareholders have no legal duty to protect or serve the companies whose shares they own and are shielded by the doctrine of limited liability from legal responsibility for those companies' debts and misdeeds." Thus, by elevating the claims of shareholders over those of other important constituencies, "without establishing any corresponding responsibility or accountability on the part of shareholders who exercise those powers," managers inevitably succumb to increasing pressure "to deliver ever faster and more predictable returns and to curtail riskier investments aimed at meeting future needs and finding creative solutions to the problems facing people around the world."[8]

Sixth, the new theory of the firm is detached from evolving ideas about the legal status of shareholder claims on the public corporation. It is axiomatic in the world of capitalism that those who have placed risk capital into an enterprise through their shareholdings deserve a satisfactory return on that capital (the minimum return determined by the riskiness of the investment). It is less axiomatic but nevertheless supported by an array of legal scholars, organization theorists, business leaders, and members of the investment community that the interests of other constituencies comprising the firm need to be justly served as well (whatever justly means in case-specific situations) to ensure corporate stability and perpetuity.

Over the years, a variety of legal opinions and legislation have supported this view of corporate purpose. Today, corporate law does not impose on management an exclusive profit-maximizing duty, but merely links directors' and managers' fiduciary responsibilities to the corporation's and stockholders' long-term interests. While Delaware's corporate statute (directly relevant to the 60 percent of publicly traded corporations that are incorporated in the state of Delaware) is not totally precise on the matter of corporate purpose, the state's case law does convey a precise opinion on the matter. For example, after the court affirmed in *Revlon, Inc. v. MacAndrews & Forbes Holdings, Inc.* (1985) that corporate directors must put the interests of shareholders first in the case of takeovers and competitive takeovers bids (by accepting the highest price offered once they decided to put the company up for sale), it clearly left the door open for a more pluralistic conception of corporate purpose if doing so serves the interests of nonshareholders in a way that is rationally related to shareholder interests. This accommodation of plural interests is consistent with subsequent court opinions validating the idea that shareholder value does not need to be maximized in the short term in order to achieve corporate success in the long run, such as in the *Virtus Capital L.P. v. Eastman Chem. Co.* (2014) case. Indeed, what Delaware case law has revealed is a definite preference for corporations focusing on longevity rather than current shareholder wealth maximization.

It is pretty clear that members of the Supreme Court are largely in agreement with the Delaware court. As Justice Samuel Alito noted in *Burwell v. Hobby Lobby Stores, Inc.* (2014), "While it is certainly true that a central objective of for-profit corporations is to make money, modern corporate law does not require for-profit corporations to pursue profit at the expense of everything else, and many do not do so."

For all these pragmatic moral, economic, and legal reasons, one can argue that a more pluralistic vision of capitalism and corporate purpose has substantial merit—as long as managers and directors do not use "stakeholder" reasons to justify strategic decay due to underinvestment in the business and poor company performance. But can a more pluralistic vision of corporate purpose be judged as being more "just" and "efficient" than one rooted in shareholder value creation? Here is where the principle of reciprocity rooted in the insights of Aristotle come into play.

A Time for Reciprocity

In his book *Justice: What's the Right Thing to Do*, American political philosopher Michael Sandel observes that "it is hard to make sense of our moral lives without acknowledging the independent weight of reciprocity." Sandel's observation helps introduce how reciprocity (and Aristotle's theory of reciprocal justice) can serve as a sensible guiding principal for definitions of corporate purpose that are more attuned to the emerging collective social values of civil society than shareholder wealth maximization.

THE RECIPROCITY PRINCIPLE

According to Aristotle, reciprocity refers to an exemplary kind of social cooperation in a transactional setting. Reciprocity is a practice by which transacting parties preserve parity in the value or utility of the benefits exchanged over time. In Book V of *Ethics*, Aristotle proposes a theory of exchange between transacting parties that defines the exchange as primarily an ethical problem: the exchange of goods is the material content of social relations between people that can only be sustained as long as it represents an "exchange of equivalents," to use the words of philosopher Joseph Soudek in his 1952 essay on Aristotle's theory of exchange. At the societal level, Aristotle argues that in order for the economic basis of society to be secure—with that economic basis being defined by the division of labor and exchange of products of specialized labor—every exchange of goods also has to be an exchange of equivalent value between buyers and sellers. In other words, market exchanges cannot take place on a sustained basis unless the parties to such exchanges are assured that what they give away and what they receive is of equivalent value to each of them. For this to happen, some form of justice is required that holds people together, and that form is reciprocal justice, which involves the notion of equivalent or proportional returns between contracting parties.

What Aristotle means by this is that if a shoemaker and a housebuilder, to use his example, were to enter into an exchange, what makes such an exchange reciprocal is the value, or personal utility, of the work that is exchanged, not the specific cost of the individual units produced by the two parties. Accordingly, the more valuable a person's skill (say, the housebuilder) is to that of another person (say, the shoemaker), the greater will be the quantity of products that the first person can justly command from the second person.

For Aristotle, "wants" or needs for the traded good form the basis of exchange between parties and serve as a measure of the value of the goods exchanged. To meet the standard of reciprocal justice, the utility value of the goods exchanged must be proportional to each party's perceived needs and wants. If one party gets richer at the other's expense, there would not be reciprocal justice—because one party would have more than one's due share and the other would suffer the injustice of having less. Similarly, the value of each party's needs and wants can be accurately and fairly established only if the relevant exchange negotiations are free from the domination of one party over another. Where there is no voluntary exchange, there is no reciprocity.

(Money, of course, serves as a useful medium for expressing wants and thus the value of goods exchanged and facilitates exchange by transforming subjective, qualitative phenomena like wants and want satisfactions into objective, quantitative ones. This notion of value—the basis of Aristotle's concept of reciprocal justice—is utility-based, not cost-based. In this sense, Aristotle was an originator of the utility theory of value as well as the principle of reciprocity.)

Although Aristotle was preoccupied with exchanges between individuals and not with exchanges between many buyers and sellers competing with each other in markets of various degrees price transparency, his theory of exchange addresses a universal paradox that exists in all markets: namely, that exchanges of goods take place between nonequivalent parties who desire goods or skills that they do not possess; yet in order for the exchange to take place some sort of equivalency needs to be established. As explained by Soudek, the objective of this theory was to find a principle that could "equate" what appears to be "unequal" or inequivalent (by virtue of the different skills required to produce the desired goods).

How can we apply Aristotle's standard of freely negotiated equivalent and proportional returns between contracting parties if one of the parties—let's say shareholders—is seeking supernormal returns? What Aristotle would argue is that if shareholders and their designated decision agents (corporate officers) were to seek above-average corporate returns at the expense of hourly workers whose needs and wants are either unmet or underserved, then there could be no reciprocity. But if shareholders were to seek and achieve supernormal returns while at the same time being open to negotiate free of domination a new or exchange of equivalent utilities based on any related changes in the wants and needs of employees, then it could be possible to meet Aristotle's standard of reciprocity. In this way, exchanges meeting the standard of reciprocal justice are not subject to any cap on the utilities exchanged.

The fact that voluntary markets are competitively structured in a capitalist economy and thus are often adversarial in nature raises another important question: whether any market transaction can be expected to be truly reciprocal or, for that matter, fair. If "fairness" connotes absolute equality in the exchange of benefits, then the answer is no—for the simple reason that it is impossible to precisely estimate and guarantee absolute equality or equivalency in value of benefits exchanged. But if fairness is based on subjective, self-interested definitions of needs, wants, and value received from a transacting party, then the impossibility of fair, reciprocal transactions melts and the pursuit of individual self-interest can be consistent with just exchanges.

It should now be clear that an important feature of Aristotle's conception of reciprocal exchange is that such an exchange is the result of a bargain struck between parties making their own terms of exchange. The parties make their own estimates of the want satisfactions that they will derive from the goods or skills they get in exchange for their own goods or skills. In subsequent bargaining or negotiation, parties arrive at an exchange ratio that is an intermediate or mutually determined ratio between the two (pre-bargaining) estimations of want satisfactions. In the absence of domination of one party over another, this exchange ratio establishes each transacting party's "reserve price" for cooperation. And since the context of exchange relationships in business continually change, reciprocity is best understood as a procedural matter, based on dialogue and periodic renegotiations, where new agreements or contract can be forged and an "ex post settling up" (to use Eugene Fama's phrase) can take place if one party has been disadvantaged in the past.

ETHICAL RECIPROCITY

The principle of reciprocity is particularly relevant where exchange relationships extend over prolonged or uncertain time periods, and where unanticipated contingencies cannot be planned for. In contrast to situations where a business exchange takes place over a specified time period (as in spot markets) and contracts can easily state in advance the terms of exchange with specified services and returns, exchanges taking place over multiple time periods and involving conditions and terms that cannot be easily specified in advance call for another kind of reciprocity. Aristotle refers to the latter situation as requiring ethical reciprocity and the former as requiring only legal reciprocity.

The practice of ethical reciprocity requires a different conception of self-interest than that which has been become the bedrock of the economic theory of human behavior. The traditional economic conception of self-interest is "a commitment to one's interests without regard for how they affect others." This conception reflects a model of economic man (homo economicus) based on an assumption of infinite greed. It also reflects the assumption that in competitive markets, everyone behaves as if they were completely selfish and that there is little interest in "fair" outcomes. We can refer to this form of self-interest as competitive self-interest.

Competitive self-interest typically leads to conflicts in the business world where parties with nonidentical interests need to find a way of working together. In business life, the most common conflicts include those between shareholders and managers and between equity holders who have operational control of the company and creditors who have a first claim on company assets in the case of bankruptcy but little or no operational control. Competitive self-interest also leads to conflicts of interests with a firm's various constituencies in the pursuit of such winner-take-all strategies as hostile takeovers, aggressive pricing, labor lockouts, cornering commodity markets, and so on, all of which can seriously harm employment, a local community's economy, an industry's supplier base, or even the national interest.

An alternate conception of self-interest, one more consistent with the reciprocity principle, treats "the good of others as part of our own interests" and remains attuned to what others are giving up for the benefit of the community as a whole. Political philosopher Danielle Allen refers to this form of self-interest as ethical self-interest.

Ethical self-interest has direct applicability to the world of business. We rarely serve our best interests by pursuing and promoting our own interests to the exclusion of others' interests. We typically need others to help us achieve our goals, and the longer we are indifferent to the interests of others, the greater the chance that others will act in ways that hinder achievement of our goals. Similarly, our self-interest is often furthered by restraining ourselves from maximizing our own interests, knowing that taking into consideration the interests of others will make the social and political context of economic relationships more durable.

Put in other words, ethical reciprocity *always* requires, as Allen has argued, a certain amount of personal or institutional sacrifice. Sacrifice—namely, the surrender of something valued or desired for the sake of something regarded as having a higher or more pressing claim—is as central to the world of business as it is to the practice of democracy and democratic citizenship. With respect to democracy, sacrifice involves, for example, accepting defeat after a hard-fought election. In this way, sacrifice builds community and discourages violence. Sacrifice in the world of business involves not only completing mutually satisfying economic transactions between self-interested parties but also a willingness to defer personal and corporate gains to maintain the health of the economic system. Sacrifice in this broader context reflects a sense of responsibility by self-interested economic actors for the economic system as a whole and an understanding of what self-restraints are required so that system can better preserve itself.

Consider, for example, the case of an investment banker being invited to join representatives of major audit firms to discuss with the Financial Accounting Standards Board (FASB) accounting new rules pertaining to merger and acquisition transactions—with no other party present representing the general public present. In this case, as elaborated by Rebecca Henderson and Karthik Ramanna, the banker faces two choices: recommending rules that maximize the bank's current economic interests or deferring some private gains by acting as a steward for the system as a whole, in the absence of any public participants. Performing both roles is sometimes referred to as accepting dual agency, and dual agency is often required to manage competing responsibilities. In the FASB rulemaking case, ethical self-interest would require the adoption of a dual agency role by the banker and the possible deferral of something of value to bankers in order to advance the perceived legitimacy of the financial system and preserve the possibility of private gains over the long run.

ETHICAL RECIPROCITY AND ORGANIZATIONAL EFFICIENCY

Pursuing corporate purpose based on the principle of ethical reciprocity not only meets an Aristotelian standard of justice, but also brings with it access to a major source of organizational efficiency. The foundational writings of Chester Barnard on "cooperative systems" provide the link between the practice of ethical reciprocity and organizational efficiency in market economies.

Barnard spent a 40-year career at AT&T, including as president of New Jersey Bell Telephone company, and later served as president of the Rockefeller Foundation. His 1938 book *The Functions of the Executive* is one of the intellectual cornerstones of modern organizational theory. For Barnard, organizational survival and efficiency depend in large part on the distributive process embedded in cooperative systems.

According to Barnard, organizations are best conceived as systems of "cooperative human activities" whose primary functions are the creation, transformation, and exchange of utilities. These functions transcend and embrace such diverse "economies" as those encompassing the assembly of physical assets useful to the organization; the maintenance of relationships between the organization and other organizations and individuals not connected with the organization; and management of the changing balance between individual work and the material and social satisfactions received in exchange for this work.

In each of these economies, exchange relationships can either be reciprocal or exploitive, efficient or inefficient. Such relationships are efficient, according to Barnard, when the distributive process creates "a surplus of satisfaction" for each participant in the cooperative system and for the cooperative system as a whole. If each participant in a cooperative system gets back only what is put in and receives no surplus of satisfactions, then this cooperative system is inefficient because a balance between burdens and satisfactions does not exist. In other words, efficiency for both the participant and the system is that of satisfactory exchange.

An important precondition of efficient exchange is the generation of some kind of surplus or slack that can be put on the table and traded in a way that the eventual returns to all contracting parties are mutually satisfying. This may require some degree of sacrifice in order to achieve the surplus of satisfactions that can then be efficiently distributed. In the absence of such surplus to be traded away, there will be individual or group defections (including shirking of responsibilities) from the cooperative efforts, which in turn will threaten the continuance of that organization. While there can be no precise measurement of Barnard's efficient exchanges, the most telling indicator of the efficiency of an organization is in terms of its persistence or decline and failure.

Since cooperative systems need to be continually adaptive to changing conditions, a key executive function is to ensure that the bases of cooperation (exchanges) continually readjust as necessary to retain the structural integrity of the organization. This is very different perspective on executive leadership than shareholder wealth maximization. It is an essential executive function for firms pursuing ethical reciprocity as a guide to corporate purpose.

CAN ETHICAL RECIPROCITY SURVIVE SHAREHOLDER WEALTH-MAXIMIZING COMPETITION?

Can firms anchoring expressions of corporate purpose in the principle of reciprocal justice avoid being destroyed by aggressive wealth-maximizing competitors?

The answer to this question is yes, as long as a critical condition is satisfied. Ruthless wealth maximizers will always win, and reciprocity practitioners and society will always lose unless firms practicing reciprocity manage to sustain sufficient returns to attract and reinvest resources in the business at a rate comparable to that of wealth maximizers. This condition can only be satisfied when reciprocity practitioners continue to work for the creation of real long-term economic value while at the same time integrating the principles of ethical reciprocity into their business. This dual effort is a core commitment required to successfully rehabilitate corporate purpose and governance.

What does it take to make this happen? Part of the answer lies in what it has always taken to achieve competitive advantage: an ability to work smarter, faster, and harder than one's competitors in building sufficient product or service differentiation to command appealing prices in the marketplace and driving down costs at each stage of the value-added chain to ensure attractive operating margins and profit growth. As long as firms can earn their cost of capital and grow at or above the average growth rate of their competitors, they will be able to retain and attract sufficient capital to reinvest in the competitiveness of the business, while putting themselves in a strong position to generate a sufficient surplus of satisfactions for a firm's participants to cement their willingness to cooperate in the life of the enterprise (that is, to meet their reserve price for continued cooperation).

A second part of the answer lies in recognizing that achieving such economic performance through reciprocal exchanges rather than the extraction of value from other participants in the enterprise requires a solid understanding of the long-term economic value that voluntary reciprocal exchanges bring to the enterprise: how employment relationships based on reciprocity rather than the extraction of value benefit the enterprise over the long term (the rate of employee turnover can be a leading indicator of reciprocal employee relationships); how paying the full costs of environmental damage and repair improves the company's long-term strategic and financial position (unacknowledged and unfunded environmental liabilities can affect, for example, the availability of bank credit); and how attention to the full range of social issues facing a business can have a positive economic impact on the enterprise over time. Without such explicit understandings, it will be impossible to explain either internally or externally how a commitment to reciprocal exchange can improve long-term competitiveness and survivability.

There is of course nothing easy about meeting this test of survivorship. Rehabilitating corporate purpose and American-style capitalism is not for sluggards. There are embedded ideological barriers to cooperation that need to be overcome—such as managerial resistance to sharing decision rights with employees over the conditions of their employment or with the general public over how best to minimize environmental degradation and reverse damage to the environment that has already been done.

But, in contrast to popular understanding, there is also nothing in this approach suggesting that shareholders need to accept uneconomic returns in the pursuit of ethical reciprocity, as long as the sources of long-term competitiveness are in place and paid attention to. To the contrary: a review by McKinsey & Company of more than 2,000 empirical studies on the impact of corporate attention to ESG concerns on equity returns shows that such attention has an overwhelmingly positive effect on equity returns. Similarly, in a 2018 paper, George Serafeim reports that companies scoring better on environmental and social factors tracked by the Sustainability Accounting Standards Board (SASB) tend to trade at a premium relative to their more socially detached and uncommitted peers. What appears to be driving these early results is the combination of minimizing or eliminating future environmental and social liabilities and greater management discipline in driving revenue growth, reducing costs such as energy consumption, increasing productivity through greater employee motivation, and avoiding the trap of investing in "energy hungry" assets requiring premature write-downs. Echoing this academic research is a 2019 survey of 200 CEOs and CFOs of companies in the S&P 1500 Index by the Rock Center for Corporate Governance at Stanford University showing that "only 12 percent believe that addressing stakeholder interests requires a short-term cost in order to generate long-term value."

Fostering Change in Corporate Purpose

It would be a big step forward in the post-Covid world if CEOs and their boards of directors instantaneously saw the benefit of integrating ethical reciprocity into their expressions of corporate purpose and resulting corporate governance practices. But it took decades for shareholder wealth maximization to become the default purpose of most public corporations, and it will take years before there is a major course correction by public companies, one that embraces some version of ethical reciprocity as a principled guide to corporate purpose. Shifting management mindsets away from emphasizing domination of markets, competitors, suppliers, and employees in the quest for above-average returns toward the mutual interests of all constituencies comprising the firm is a huge break from established ideological and moral conceptions. Under our current version of market capitalism, it is reasonable to expect that public companies will hesitate to take the giant step of replacing the principle of shareholder wealth maximization with the principle of ethical reciprocity unless there are good business reasons for doing so.

In the case of distressed firms like US automakers responding to the intense competition from Japanese automakers in the 1970s and 1980s—

and others in the textile industry, clothing, semiconductors, telecommunications, and health care businesses, all of which also faced similar economic dislocations in the 1980s—ensuring survival creates strong incentives to forge more cooperative and less "maximizing" labor–management and business–government relationships.

For less economically troubled enterprises, however, the incentives and pressures to change will need to come from other sources. The most powerful sources of influence today are large asset holders and asset managers, who have enormous power and influence over the conduct of public companies. All told, large asset managers now own about 80 percent of US companies' stock through passive and actively managed investment funds. If encouraged and unleashed by their beneficiaries, the power of institutional investors to engage with current and prospective portfolio companies over their espoused purposes and resulting governance practices is incontestable.

There is evidence that the power source of large asset managers is beginning to be mobilized. Starting with the public letter from chairman Larry Fink of BlackRock (a global asset manager with over $7 trillion under management) to CEOs in January 2018 and followed by the highly publicized statement on corporate purpose by the Business Roundtable in August 2019, the message is out that large asset managers and CEOs of large US corporations are now recognizing that society is demanding that companies make a positive contribution to society as well as delivering financial performance. In the words of Larry Fink, "Companies must benefit all their stakeholders, including shareholders, employees, customers, and the communities in which they operate."

Although disparaged in some quarters for being a public relations exercise without any enforcement mechanisms, Fink's CEO letter and the Business Roundtable statement do not stand alone in calling for more attention to the social purposes and obligations of public corporations. They have lots of company from other asset managers who, reflecting the objectives of their clients, already take socially related issues into account in constructing their investment funds. For example, the Global Sustainable Investment Alliance found that in 2020, 36 percent of all professionally managed assets—or $35 trillion—were so-called sustainable assets, meaning that these assets were selected according to their environmental, social and governance performance. This is strong, suggestive evidence that many large asset managers in addition to BlackRock—such as Vanguard, State Street Global Investors, and Fidelity International, who collectively have another $10 trillion of assets under collective management—are assembling considerable market power aimed at influencing the goals and conduct of current and prospective portfolio companies.

If asset managers with tens of trillions of dollars under management continue to be encouraged by their clients to engage with portfolio companies on matters related to corporate purpose and environmental, social, and governance concerns, they will have at their disposal several ways of making their influence on operating companies manifest. One long-standing strategy is simply to walk away from "bad ESG companies" by selling shares, thereby punishing them with low share prices (and, conversely, rewarding good ESG companies with increasing share prices). This option, colloquially known as "the Wall Street Walk," is becoming less effective for many large asset managers with funds that choose to mimic market indices with index funds and other passive management funds. Since passive management funds—by far the fastest growing investment vehicles today accounting for 45 percent of all assets held by US stock-based funds—must own all the shares in the relevant market index, they have a built-in limit on their exit or walk-away options.

This leaves both passive and actively managed investment funds with four "voice" options for influencing the priorities and practices of portfolio companies: (a) submitting shareholder proposals to shareholders' meetings; (b) voting proxies; (c) screening companies for portfolio inclusion or exclusion according to ESG criteria; and (d) engaging face-to-face with companies in closed-door discussions and negotiations around material environmental, social, and governance matters.

The first two of these options have been available for many years. However, most shareholder proposals and proxy votes tend to focus on general issues of corporate governance—such as capital structure, takeover defenses, auditing, board composition, workplace practices, and the reporting of executive compensation and climate risk—rather than on detailed, firm-specific problems of environmental degradation (as in oil and chemicals) or employee safety (as in mining and minerals).

The next two options—the "screening" of companies according to ESG standards for potential inclusion and exclusion in investment portfolios and "active engagement" with portfolio companies on ESG matters—offer large asset managers a greater opportunity to move beyond generic governance issues and exert influence on company-specific matters. In practice, the level of influence exerted by asset managers pursuing these voice strategies depends on overcoming built-in information problems.

A 2019 study by Sakis Kotsantonis and George Serafeim shows that asset managers that screen potential investments for either exclusion or inclusion in their portfolios based on ESG performance data disclosed by companies can easily be misled by both large variations in reporting on ESG by operating companies (roughly 80 percent of S&P 500 companies currently discuss ESG issues in some way in their annual shareholder reports) and wildly divergent assessments of companies' performance by those producing ESG scores for sale to asset managers. In response to this problem, there has been a series of concerted efforts in recent years to pressure the Securities and Exchange Commission (SEC) to adopt mandatory disclosure requirements for certain ESG matters—the latest being a petition for rulemaking submitted in October 2018 by law professors Cynthia Williams of York University and Jill Fisch of the University of Pennsylvania, together with numerous institutional investors that collectively manage more than $5 trillion in assets. As of this writing, it is unclear whether or how the SEC will act on this petition, but the agency has sent letters to investment companies asking what they determine socially responsible investments to be.

A smaller group of asset managers have chosen to focus on active engagement through ongoing, face-to-face dialogue with corporate managements on stakeholder and ESG matters to help decide what companies to include and retain in their investment portfolios. A notable example of this active engagement approach is Fidelity International, Ltd. (FIL), which has invested heavily in training its own equity and fixed-income research staff to assess for themselves the ESG performance of each and every company in their portfolios (a total of 3,000 companies) and conduct detailed sustainability discussions with corporate managements on a recurring basis (in 16,000 meetings a year).

FIL has been willing to investment heavily in its own proprietary sustainability rating system and "active engagement" with portfolio companies on the belief that sustainable investing leads to higher investor returns. FIL's engagement strategy also reflects a desire to better align its fund management with the surging interest of their end investors on ESG matters. (Industrywide, financial assets under professional management are reportedly moving to ESG strategies at a 20 percent annual growth rate.)

There is emerging evidence that the investment thesis of FIL and other similarly committed asset managers has merit. I have already cited studies by George Serafeim and colleagues revealing that the adoption of "sustainability practices" requiring commitments to nonfinancial objectives and nonshareholding participants in an enterprise can be associated with superior financial performance. Morningstar and Fidelity's website also report that 54 percent of ESG funds were in the top two performance quartiles in 2017.

As a minimum, a 2015 Morgan Stanley study reports that the performance of institutionally-managed ESG funds in recent years have at least been on a par with traditional investment. Finally, using its own proprietary ratings, FIL carried out a performance comparison across more than 2,600 companies during the extreme bear market from February to March 2020. FIL found equity and fixed income securities issued by companies at the top of their ESG scale outperformed those with average and weaker ratings in this short period. On average, each of FIL's five ESG rating levels was worth 2.8 percentage points of stock performance during that short period of volatility.

Although it is still to be determined how much alpha (or returns in excess of overall market return or some other benchmark return) can be achieved over a longer time period by asset managers pursuing sustainable investment strategies, asset managers are definitely in a position to provide an ever-stronger impetus for public companies to embrace the principle of ethical reciprocity as a guideline for their espoused purpose and temper their extreme focus of portfolio companies on shareholder value maximization.

Preconditions for Durable Change

With tailwinds gathering behind the idea that corporations have some kind of direct obligation for their nonshareholding stakeholders, it is likely that corporate boards will be increasingly called on by large asset managers to integrate the reciprocal justice principle (or something akin to it) into their expressions of corporate purpose and management practices. For such declarations to be meaningful, certain preconditions for successful implementation need to be in place.

The first precondition is **unequivocal board commitment to fairness and reciprocity as governing principles**. Without such an unambiguous commitment in both internal and public communications, signaling a major shift from an ideology of shareholder self-maximization to collective value creation and fair exchanges of value, no change in corporate purpose and behavior is possible—not the least because the values underlying the measurement and reward of senior executives will remain unchanged, as will the choices they make.

This leads to the second precondition—the **elimination of perverse financial incentives** for senior executives emanating from the shareholder wealth maximization ideology. Financial incentives pegged principally to shareholder value metrics inevitably crowd out many other performance indicators. Without a decoupling or distancing of executive compensation from current measures of shareholder wealth, there can be no incentive to balance the conflicting interests of various groups participating, voluntarily or not, in the life of the enterprise. Indeed, incentives to claim value from these groups, rather than to exchange value, will remain intense, and executives will remain corseted in the economic straightjacket of absolute shareholder primacy. Asset managers will therefore look for evidence that firm-specific performance metrics beyond shareholder value have been integrated into a company's performance measurement system; that the time horizon of these performance measures have been stretched out beyond the annual financial reporting cycle; and that the holding period for all stock options and grants before they can be exercised or sold are similarly extended, reflecting the natural strategy cycle of the firm rather than quarterly or annual share price performance. Finally, asset managers will closely examine the extent to which directors and senior executives hold significant ownership stakes in their companies so that they will financially be liable for any costly breakdowns in corporate reciprocity and other foundational features of long-term sustainability.

A third precondition is **active monitoring of conformance with espoused principles of fairness and reciprocity**. Some asset managers have invested heavily in their own, proprietary methodologies for monitoring the sustainability of portfolio companies. But the most promising reciprocity practitioners will have also developed their own ways of monitoring and reporting on their espoused commitments to stakeholders. In an ethical reciprocity regime, many of the relevant performance measures will necessarily be qualitative (i.e., survey-based); some, however, may be amenable to quantitative reduction, based on indicators of time, costs, or value. In order to survive as a governance tool, whatever performance indicators emerge from this process will need to reflect an understanding of how reciprocity can be economically valuable for all parties. With respect to social and environmental performance metrics, two places to look for the latest thinking about measuring a company's social and environmental impacts include the SASB's Materiality Map (developed by the Sustainability Accounting Standards Board) and the work of professor George Serafeim and colleagues at the Harvard Business School on the Impact-Weighted Accounts Initiative, which aims to create financial accounts that reflect a company's financial, social, and environmental performance.

A fourth critical precondition is **enabling stakeholder voice**. This involves creating ways for key stakeholders and constituencies to voice their interests in corporate decisions that affect their separate (and overlapping) interests. In the post-pandemic world, this will be especially important with respect to employees whose economic insecurity and income inequality has been vividly exposed by the Covid-19 crisis. The precondition of employee voice is the most radical departure from a shareholder value maximization regime. In both the US and the UK, there is a revitalized political discussion about including employees on corporate boards of directors (even for unionized firms) as a way of guaranteeing employee voice in corporate matters. There are many reasons for questioning the practical implementation of these proposals, starting with the daunting task of re-legislating and perhaps re-litigating corporate governance regimes, which would tie up corporate governance for decades. Such a restructuring of board composition also runs the risk of narrowing a collective view of where the corporation should be heading and perpetuating a focus on short-term gains for nonshareholders rather than longer-term returns from risky investments in the business. This does not mean that there are not better ways to gain critical knowledge and decision input from employees. Indeed, the range of possible voice-participation and decision-influence is wide: in addition to reciprocal union–management dialogue and negotiation, where it exists, there are many examples of employee advisory committees (many universities), employee engagement committees (auto industry), and labor advisory committees (Office of the Trade Representative) to learn from and build on.

Increasing engagement between large asset managers and public companies over matters of corporate purpose—and derivative corporate governance practices—is a hugely important development. For this engagement to have the greatest chance of narrowing the gulf between what markets value and what people value, "sustainable investors" know that mere exhortations to balance shareholder interests against other parties' interests in defining and implementing corporate purpose is insufficient. What asset managers and corporate managers committed to sustainable investing are groping for, each in their own way, is a practical alternative to reliance on shareholder wealth maximization as the sole principle underpinning public corporations' expressions of corporate purpose. I suggest in this essay an alternate principle based on the age-old concept of reciprocal justice. In the absence of such moral principle, balancing the oft-conflicting interests of corporate stakeholders will likely continue to reflect personal preference, partiality, and improvisation untethered to any guiding principle at all, thereby perpetuating a pattern of unaccountable capitalism and an increasingly troublesome gulf between what markets value and what people value. This would be a politically and economically unsustainable outcome.

Notes

1. Mark Carney, "The World after Covid-19," *The Economist*, April 18, 2020.
2. "Corporate purpose" refers to how businesses organized as corporations define their primary obligations and responsibilities, in contrast to the goals and objectives involved in managing specific businesses on a day-to-day basis.
3. In addition to my rebuttal of this doctrine, other recent critiques include Joseph L. Bower, Herman B. Leonard, and Lynn S. Paine, *Capitalism At Risk: Rethinking the Role of Business* (HBS Press, 2011 and 2020); Lynn Stout, *The Shareholder Value Myth: How Putting Shareholders First Harms Investors, Corporations, and the Public Interest* (Berrett-Koehler, 2012); Joseph L. Bower and Lynn S. Paine, "The Error at the Heart of Corporate Leadership," *Harvard Business Review*, May–June 2017, 51–60; Colin Mayer, *Prosperity: Better Business Makes the Greater Good* (Oxford, 2018); Rebecca Henderson, *Reimagining Capitalism in a World on Fire* (Public Affairs, 2020).
4. As we will see, ethical reciprocity (and reciprocal exchange) is not to be confused with the concept of *shared value creation* (see Michael E. Porter and Mark R. Kramer, "Creating Shared Value," *Harvard Business Review*, January–February 2011, 62–77), which is rooted in the belief that corporations can meet social needs within a shareholder wealth maximization regime by focusing on the improvement of their competitive advantages through better serving existing markets or lowering costs or improving product quality through innovation. Economic value can certainly be shared after it has been created if approved by shareholders, and concessions to shareholder value can be avoided by highly competitive firms harvesting supernormal returns. But this is a very different process from that of practicing ethical reciprocity, which recognizes (a) that the interests of a firm's constituencies are not always mutual and, indeed, are rarely presented as such and (b) that these conflicting interests can be reconciled only by value exchanges honoring the reserve price of continued support and participation in the life of the firm. The practice of ethical reciprocity starts with a front-end bargain with constituencies; shared value creation is an after-the-fact distribution of benefits at the discretion of shareholders and their agents (comprising the board of directors).
5. Michael C. Jensen and William H. Meckling, "Theory of the Firm: Managerial Behavior, Agency Costs and Ownership Structure," *Journal of Financial Economics* 3, no. 4 (October 1976): 310–11.
6. Michael C. Jensen, "Value Maximization, Stakeholder Theory, and the Corporate Objective Function," *Business Ethics Quarterly* 12, no. 2 (April 2002): 237–38.
7. Elizabeth Anderson, "The Business Enterprise as an Ethical Agent," *Performance and Progress: Essays on Capitalism, Business, and Society* (Oxford Scholarship Online, September 2015), 189–190, 191.
8. Joseph L. Bower and Lynn S. Paine, "The Error at the Heart of Corporate Leadership," *Harvard Business Review*, May–June 2017, 52.

9 Corporate Engagement in the Political Process and Democratic Ideals

F. CHRISTOPHER EAGLIN

Introduction

This chapter takes up the question of whether and how large for-profit companies should engage in the political process from the perspective of democratic ideals. For the purpose of this analysis, the chapter takes as given many of the features of the contemporary landscape in the USA, one in which large for-profit business enterprises are heavily engaged in politics, their participation has had mixed outcomes, trust in government is declining, and government capacity at local, regional, and national levels is weakening.[1]

Management scholars have investigated how firms engage the political realm to improve financial performance, known as nonmarket strategy, but have given little consideration to the normative question of whether they should do so.[2] Some business ethicists have endeavored to address this normative question, but exactly *how* firms should engage in the political process remains critically underexamined.[3] This chapter seeks to help fill this lacuna by investigating whether our existing frameworks for corporate participation are appropriate both theoretically and practically.[4] Drawing on real-world cases, I argue that these frameworks are insufficient to provide guidance to firms and that if we want to continue to allow active corporate participation in the political sphere, we ought to rethink the corporate form.

To begin, I briefly summarize the ways in which firms can and do enter the political space. Firms justify their pursuit of "nonmarket strategies," despite any negative externalities they might create, by invoking the principle of shareholder value maximization.[5] I examine the standard neoclassical reasoning and argue that it fails to justify political participation of firms and therefore cannot provide guidance for appropriate firm behavior in the political sphere. Searching elsewhere for a more suitable framework, I investigate a collaborative approach most prominently advanced by Palazzo and Scherer that asks firms to fully participate in the deliberative democratic process. However, relying on the work of Hussain and Moriarty, I argue that the collaborative view is untenable because it assigns unaccountable and therefore inappropriate responsibilities to firms.

By examining the failure of the Boeing 737 Max, I argue that the restricted technical advisory role that Hussain and Moriarty seek as a remedy to the collaborative view of Palazzo and Scherer does not adequately safeguard against the sorts of concerns that one would imagine they seek to avoid. I put forward three shortcomings of the advisory view. First, the technical role they prescribe opens the door for temptation for corporate capture of regulators, which many firms leverage to their advantage. Second, even if firms had the best of intentions, the close relationship engendered by providing ongoing advice creates the opportunity for corporate capture through implicit bias. To overcome these first two challenges, I argue that we must consider revising the structure of the firm to make it more internally or externally democratic. The third shortcoming I advance, that we might in fact find a close relationship between public and private actors advantageous, requires a more thorough investigation beyond the scope of this chapter. I conclude by speculating on how future research could help us develop this line of inquiry.

Corporate Nonmarket Strategy

The nonmarket strategy literature[6] seeks to identify how firms undertake political and social activities and how those activities shape the institutional and social context of competition to their advantage.[7] Corporate political activity (CPA) is a category of nonmarket strategies that firms can pursue to manage political institutions or influence political actors in ways favorable to the firm.[8] Within CPA, firms can adopt two approaches. They can adopt "bridging" strategies, which are activities that support local institutions and expectations.[9] These strategies are meant to create a "bridge" with other stakeholder communities to increase legitimacy, which in turn improves performance.[10] Firms also can adopt "buffering" strategies that include lobbying, campaign contributions, public relations campaigns, and building strong ties to sociopolitical institutions and actors. Firms undertake these strategies to "buffer themselves from unwanted political interference and obtain access to and elicit support from political actors and institutions."[11]

Given the options available to firms, Stigler helpfully provides a taxonomy of the benefits firms might hope to receive from engaging in the political sphere.[12] According to Stigler, firms can seek direct subsidies for their industry, control entry of new rivals, encourage price fixing, and support complementary industries while suppressing competitive ones. To achieve these benefits, Stigler argues that companies provide direct resources such as campaign contributions and more indirect benefits such as employing workers from a political party. As larger firms have greater resources that can be deployed over a longer time horizon, they are able to shift the competitive landscape in their favor, often leading to increased profitability and returns to their shareholders.[13]

It is through these "buffering mechanisms" that firms primarily influence political actors and institutions. There are two buffering strategies in particular that are worth our attention: lobbying and campaign contributions. Drutman argues that over the last 40 years in the US, corporations have systematically increased their lobbying presence in order to gain outsize influence in the political process. As a result, oftentimes the influence of lobbyists determines the outcome of many legislative processes as they have extensive resources at their disposal to understand and communicate policy positions while legislative staff are overworked and underfunded in comparison.[14]

Beyond lobbying, firms have significantly increased their participation in the electoral process. Hsieh and Wu argue that this increase is due in large part to changing campaign finance laws such as Citizens United.[15] In 2010, the US Supreme Court "struck down prohibitions on two kinds of expenditures by corporate entities" in federal elections. These provisions are "independent expenditures," which constitute "spending that directly advocates for a specific candidate" but is not directly given to a campaign or party, and "electioneering communications," which consist of broadcast advertisements that did not "expressly advocate for or against specific candidates" or parties, although the candidate or party might be named.[16] Hsieh and Vu note the following:

> As both supporters and detractors perhaps expected, outside political spending increased dramatically in the years following Citizens United. According to the Center for Responsive Politics (CRP), a non-profit organization that tracks U.S. political spending, in 2010, independent political groups spent $309.8 million in federal elections, while in 2012, 2014, and 2016, they spent $1.039 billion, $562.7 million, and $1.436 billion respectively. This outside spending dwarfed the official political party committees' spending, which by comparison raised only $189.6 million, $255.4 million, $199.9 million, and $246.2 million in 2010, 2012, 2014, and 2016 respectively.[17]

As firms pursue nonmarket strategies at escalating rates, the state apparatus appears to have weakened. Welfare policies have been criticized for overreliance on outdated programs that are ill-fitted to the current needs of their citizenry.[18] Aging populations burden health and retirement budgets while restricting public income. Decreasing unionization has undermined the power of labor to negotiate equitable wages and weakened social ties.[19] Several governments have moved toward freezing or eroding the number of welfare benefits, changing the conditions for access or underinvesting in critical social and physical infrastructure.[20]

Concurrently, many scholars argue that large firms have been able to extract increasingly favorable terms from local, regional, and national governments to undertake large investments that bring jobs to areas often at the expense of generous social programs.[21] These concessions include tax breaks that last decades, the building of asset-specific infrastructure, relaxation of employment regulations, and direct subsidies, among other benefits.[22] Various firms also have moved operations from towns and cities in search of more profitable regulatory environments, leaving those communities bereft as they often depended on their presence as the primary economic engine.[23] Many researchers have argued that this absence leads to a host of negative social outcomes, including chronic unemployment, wage depression, skill displacement, and plummeting health metrics.[24] Coupled with the decline of unionization and other forms of social solidarity, some have argued that the cumulative effect of these business strategies helped to unravel the social fabric of many communities while at the same time draining governments of the funds to meaningfully address social dislocation.[25] As a result, there is a pervasive sense that firms have "rigged" the system in their favor, leaving the vast majority of the population at a severe disadvantage.[26]

Neoclassical View of Firm and Politics

My contention is that the argument commonly given in the defense of the nonmarket strategies described above fails on its own terms to accommodate corporate political behavior. This common argument is based on the principle of shareholder maximization, in which that the sole metric of success of a firm is the extent to which it enriches it owners. This is the firm's sole duty, it is argued, which at times requires difficult decisions about location, wages, and investments that privilege some and hurt others. Proponents of this view contend that the gains from efficiency and productivity should far outweigh the costs on the aggregate.[27] Michael Jensen provides a robust defense of this view. He argues that firms should pursue "long term value maximization as the firm's sole objective" and that rationality requires that managers have a clear mechanism to distinguish between viable alternatives to determine which choice is better or worse for the firm:[28]

> The intuition behind this criterion is simply that (social) value is created when a firm produces an output or set of outputs that are valued by its customers at more than the value of the inputs it consumes (as valued by their suppliers) in such production. Firm value is simply the long term market value of this stream of benefits. Maximizing the total market value of the firm . . . is one objective function that will resolve the tradeoff problem among multiple constituencies. It tells the firm to spend an additional dollar of resources to satisfy the desires of each constituency as long as that constituency values the result at more than a dollar.[29]

Jensen then contends that any negative externalities or natural monopolies should be addressed by the public bodies. Firms that endeavor to resolve externalities "will be eliminated by competition who chose not to be so civic minded or will survive only by consuming economic rents."[30] According to Jensen, creating multiple objectives for managers, which the stakeholder theory of the firm requires, provides significant opportunity for managers to justify almost any action as viable, whether helpful or harmful to the profitability of the firm, for it might satisfy one particular stakeholder.[31]

Jensen employs the analogy of the football team to justify the single objective of shareholder value maximization. He argues that in the game of football, there is one central objective and the entirety of the team strategy centers on this goal. Teams rightly adopt different strategies based on their resources and opponents but ultimately strive to win as many games as possible. Teams that are the most successful are those that focus on this single objective above all.

Jensen might not have anticipated how apt his example would be for our purposes. Rather than demonstrating the importance of an objective function, I argue that this example actually illustrates how entangled playing the game and rule setting actually can be. While on the surface Jensen's analogy is seems reasonable, he overlooks a host of underlying factors that impact "winning." Football teams play an active part in setting the rules of the game. They play in a league—in this case, the National Football League (NFL). It is a central organization they formed, fund, and control that determines how the game will be played down to the most granular minutiae. The NFL determines the number of games played per season, the length of the game, the time of day of play, and even more telling, how games will be refereed.

In fact, teams in the NFL are constantly creating, negotiating, and revising how the football game will be played while they are at the same time playing it. Even though rule setting and play of game happen on different time horizons, the process of determining the system of governance cannot be disentangled from the strategy that teams adopt to win. In addition, a small set of teams that form the NFL set the rules that college, high school, and amateur leagues seek to emulate.

I contend that firms behave in a similar manner. Firms, particularly large multinational ones, are at once maximizing shareholder value while at the same time determining the rules by which they can pursue this strategy. As the discussion of nonmarket strategy illustrates, firms are in constant conversation with the political and social sphere regarding what constraints and priorities they themselves will face.[32] In this way firms, particularly the largest and most well-resourced ones, determine how they will be governed. Given the available political tools, the focus on the single objective of shareholder value maximization has convinced many firms that they should bend the "rules of game" such that they might achieve even greater value.[33] In this light, it can be argued that it is rational for the largest firms to spend significant resources on political processes to ensure that they are the least encumbered by regulations and best able to pursue profit maximization, no matter the negative externalities.

To help further illustrate my objection to the neoclassical view, let us consider a current example in which a firm is both playing the game while seeking to shape the playing field. Uber is a mobile ride-sharing service that uses sophisticated GPS technology to match drivers with riders.[34] The price of the trip is determined by a complex algorithm that considers distance, journey time, traffic, availability of other drivers, vehicle type, among other factors.[35] Many economists are fascinated by Uber as it is one of the few examples of a firm actively capturing consumer surplus in a competitive market clearing environment.[36] Many have argued that riders are better off with this model as opposed to a traditional taxi service that has static pricing and a limited fleet. Uber has generated significant revenue by offering customers the benefit of affordable prices, constant availability, and high flexibility.[37] This is the economic strategy Uber employs.

At the same time, Uber employs a political strategy to ensure that it can enact its economic one, a strategy that Pollman and Barry call "regulatory entrepreneurship."[38] In many municipalities and states, taxi driving is a heavily regulated industry with mountains of legal statutes governing taxi usage. Pollman and Barry argue that Uber's political strategy is to dismiss, sidestep, or actively undermine these regulations. Knowing that their economic strategy relies on creating political space to operate, Uber employs an army of lawyers to lobby legislators, fight unions, and influence local governments. To achieve widespread adoption and commercial success, one could argue that Uber knowingly and actively works to shape the political sphere so that it might access new markets and remain in business.[39]

Interestingly, often when Uber enters a new market there are no regulations at all, given the relative novelty of the underlying technology and its rapid adoption.[40] One could argue that, in these liminal spaces, Uber influences how those regulations will be crafted. Gao and McDonald argue that in nascent industries, effectively navigating and shaping regulatory policies is crucial for firm survival.[41] Firms in nascent industries "cocreate" emerging regulation by actively anticipating, reacting to, and shaping the regulatory process. Governments often welcome this dynamic with firms as they require their technical assistance to determine the best regulatory approach balancing the priorities of the firm and that of society. The Uber case suggests that firms can simultaneously pursue an economic and political strategy with great success, undercutting Jensen's single objective function argument.

However, the pursuit of both an economic and political strategy that I have illustrated is a contradiction of a central assumption of the shareholder maximization theory. Milton Friedman, in his canonical argument, strenuously makes the case that firms and politics must remain separate and that managers of firms are only responsible for making as much money as possible for their owners.[42] Any social or political responsibility beyond this narrow remit is a failure of duty toward the owners. If managers were to dedicate resources for these purposes, he questions, how exactly should they determine how much to spend and on whom it should be spent. It requires the manager to assume political duties, as a legislator, executive, and jurist, which are clearly the province of the political process and elected officials. Asking managers to unilaterally make decisions on funding political priorities is a subversion of the appropriate separation of duties in a democratic system.[43]

If Friedman is to be believed, then one must see the strategy of Uber as far outside its shareholder maximization mandate. Here, Uber acts as legislators, writing and shaping new regulations that will govern how it can operate. However, as I have shown, Friedman's theory provides little guidance on how firms should behave other than put the proverbial genie back in the bottle. More troublingly, as the examples of Uber and football intimate, this view tacitly encourages firms to maximize shareholder value through political channels if it might support their central objective. If we accept the deep entanglement between business and politics and the weakening of the state apparatus, we must search for another approach to understand how firms should enter the public space.

Firms and Deliberative Democracy

The question remains whether and how firm participation in politics can be reconciled with democratic ideals. Palazzo and Scherer argue that firm participation can be justified through the framework of deliberative democracy. In their conceptualization, the current requirements placed on firms due to the withdrawal of the state apparatus merit their full inclusion in the deliberative process. Hussain and Moriarty argue instead that these principles suggest firms should play a more limited advisory role. Here, I explore the collaborative view proposed by Palazzo and Scherer, rely on the critique of Hussain and Moriarty to demonstrate its shortcomings, and then outline the advisory view of political participation for firms.

Palazzo and Scherer, drawing on the work of Habermas, argue that the central motivating feature of deliberative democracy is the requirement that social activity that affects important issues of public concern must be regulated by the free, unforced, and rational deliberation of citizens. Under ideal conditions, deliberation has a "discursive quality" and proceeds in argumentative form, where parties introduce proposals and offer various forms of information, reasoning, and argument in support of, or in opposition to, the proposal.[44] In this way an unforced consensus about what norms a society should adopt might emerge among members of a political community, which "will lead to more informed and rational results, will increase the acceptability of decisions, will broaden the horizon of the decision maker, will provide mutual respect and will make it easier to correct wrong decisions that have been made in the past."[45]

Having laid out the theory of deliberative democracy, Palazzo and Scherer turn to our current climate, emphasizing that firms have increasing responsibilities in the public sphere.[46] In this context, firms—particularly multinational corporations (MNCs)—incur "public duties," which if correct, undermines the Friedman and Jensen view of separation of economic and political responsibilities. If the state apparatus were strong, perhaps firms could be effectively regulated and sanctioned for socially unproductive practices. However, in a world in which the nation state is weakened:

> MNCs are in a position to effectively escape local jurisdictions by playing one legal system against the other by taking advantage of local systems ill-

adapted for effective corporate regulation and by moving production sites and steering financial investments to places where local laws are most hospitable to them.[47]

If this is the case, Palazzo and Scherer argue, we must move beyond the Friedman style scope of firm behavior and search for a model of social connectedness. Such a model should establish moral legitimacy for corporate behavior that would consist of "moral judgments about the corporation's output, procedures, structures, and leaders."[48] This legitimacy is to be built through the deliberative space and will allow society to interact with the "explicit considerations of the legitimacy of capitalist mechanisms and corporate activities by giving credit to the interests and arguments of a wide range of constituencies that are affected by the activities of (multinational) corporations."[49] Palazzo and Scherer conclude that firms ought to operate in political multistakeholder forums in two ways. First, they should operate with an enlarged sense of responsibility. Second, they must help solve political problems in collaboration with state and civil society actors.

Hussain and Moriarty have offered what I believe to be a thoughtful and thorough critique of Palazzo and Scherer's argument. They accept the premise that the changing role of firms creates a "democratic deficit" as firms take on multiple state-like functions but lack the accountability inherent in a representative process. They argue that the collaborative view encounters a fundamental problem as "it allows corporations to participate in governance arrangements in a policy-making capacity in much the same way as private citizens and political groups do."[50] The key misstep here centers around democratic accountability, which ensures "that people in positions of authority make decisions that are consistent with the voting state of deliberative reasoning in the public sphere" and "makes administrative officials answerable to citizens."[51] They note that the collaborative view does not require firms to alter their internal profit-maximizing procedures which would require "inward accountability." Instead, firms only accept an "outward accountability" as they do not invite stakeholders into their internal deliberations "but rather move themselves out into the political processes of public policy."[52] This unidimensional accountability places firms in the position of supervising authorities rather than just functionaries.

Palazzo and Scherer's view, according to Hussain and Moriarty, places firms in the position of both functionaries and supervising authorities as firms proactively participate in the deliberative process to determine policies while at the same time enacting those very policies. Hussain and Moriarty believe that this role as a supervising authority is inappropriate.[53] They argue that the only supervising authorities that can participate in the deliberative process are those individuals or organizations "that are possibly affected by the decisions of a community" and "have equal chances to enter and take part" in the process.[54] To help us understand why firms do not qualify, they define a class of institutions that can participate in the deliberative process, a politically representative organization (PRO). A PRO is an entity that has a social purpose to serve as a vehicle for citizens to present their political views in social deliberation and must satisfy the following conditions:

> [First], citizens must make decisions about joining, remaining in, or leaving the organization based in large part on the degree to which the organization's expressed objectives match up with their own social and political commitments. [Second], the formal and informal practices of democratic decision making in society must assign the organization a certain role to play in the overall political process.[55]

As profitability is their prime objective, firms do not fit this description and as such "cannot easily articulate and defend political viewpoints that may . . . lead to policies that would lower profits in the long run."[56] Given that their primary function is not political, firms often represent a heterogeneity of political interests between workers, managers, and shareholders. Therefore it is inappropriate for firms to participate in the deliberative process because they themselves are not members of the public, although their constituents might be. Hussain and Moriarty allow the inclusion of firms as technical advisers as they can provide valuable knowledge and skills critical to determining the most appropriate set of policies. However, they emphasize that firms may go no further, given their conflicting roles and interests.

Challenging the Advisory Role of Firms

Hussain and Moriarty's proposal that firms be included in the democratic process as technical advisers is inadequate as a guide for corporate action because it creates space for the sort of corporate malfeasance that one could reasonably assume they would seek to avoid. To understand why this might be so, I consider the case of the Boeing 737 Max to illuminate three difficulties with the Hussain and Moriarty argument. First, the technical adviser role opens the door for the temptation for corporate capture. Second, this role also creates a setting for implicit bias. To overcome the first two challenges, I contend that we ought to reconsider the appropriate corporate form. The third difficulty is more vexing. Suppose the state and society more broadly would welcome a more active role for firms in the deliberative process? If the Palazzo and Scherer argument is untenable on theoretical grounds, we are left to search for other solutions. I conclude this chapter speculating on what those solutions might involve, practically and theoretically.

Several tragic events surround the development of the Boeing 737 Max airplane. Over a six-month period, two 737 Max flights crashed, one operated by Lion Air and another by Ethiopia Airlines, causing the death of over 300 people. Technical investigations into these crashes led to the realization that a software program, the Maneuvering Characteristics Augmentation System (MCAS), malfunctioned, precipitating these calamities. A more thorough investigation uncovered that in fact this technical failure was a result of more complicated and troubling oversight on the part of Boeing and the government.[57]

The crashes notwithstanding, Boeing has built a sterling reputation as an aircraft manufacturer known for reliability, safety, and integrity.[58] In 2018, Boeing was recognized as the most powerful brand in the aerospace and defense industry, with its brand value estimated at $20 billion.[59] Despite its hard-earned and assiduously maintained reputation, like many large conglomerates, it responds aggressively to competitive pressure seeking to safeguard its market share and remain highly profitable.

The Boeing 737 Max was developed as a competitive response to the release of a new model by Boeing's primary competitor, Airbus. The Airbus A320neo was 15 percent more fuel efficient than other comparable Boeing aircraft in its class. As a result of its improved efficiency and other amenities, Airbus landed large contracts and significantly undercut Boeing business in this market segment.[60] In an effort to save a large contract with American Airlines, Boeing jettisoned a new model that would have taken an estimated decade to develop for a fast-tracked upgrade of the existing 737 aircraft.[61] In order to match the efficiency of the A320neo, Boeing refitted the 737 model with a larger engine but had to add the MCAS program to adjust for excessive lift at takeoff. Boeing added this program without informing pilots or including additional training in order to deliver the upgraded models on time. It did so with the consent of the US regulator, the Federal Aviation Administration (FAA). In fact, several journalists in the wake of the crashes contend that Boeing has helped shape FAA policy on wide-ranging matters including safety, technical requirements, and traffic patterns.[62] However, in this case, many believe that Boeing leaned on its relationship with the regulator to have the 737 Max expedited and brought to market early.[63] Multiple reports controversially suggest that the FAA shielded Boeing by deflecting criticism from pilots who raised concerns about MCAS before and after the crashes.[64]

Whatever the case, it was only when public outcry mounted internationally that the FAA finally grounded the 737 Max.[65]

In this context, let us consider the first difficulty that I argue might arise from the technical advisory role, which is a temptation for corporate capture. Hussain and Moriarty assume that firms in the technical advisory role would not be tempted to use that role to pursue their own end. As the discussion above demonstrates, this assumption might be unreasonable. The role of technical adviser allows firms to develop a deep and lasting relationship with government as providing technical advice in practice involves constant and dynamic contact. This constancy allows firms to shape policy in many cases. Within this context, it seems unreasonable to assume that firms, whose objective is to generate and sustain profits, will not use a technical advisory role to their advantage. This impetus is particularly forceful when firms face competitive pressure and view their political relationships as an asset to be utilized. This dynamic undoubtedly took place with the development of the 737 Max. After decades of developing a deep relationship with the FAA, Boeing leaned on the regulator to approve the new aircraft to ensure that it could capitalize on a large sales opportunity.

One would be particularly concerned about temptation for corporate capture in what Karthik Ramanna calls "thin political markets."[66] He argues that some of the most complex and essential policies that impact firm behavior and social well-being are determined in spaces where corporate managers are largely unopposed because of their own expertise and lack of public interest or awareness of the policy at hand. These process are shrouded in "technical secrecy" because the subject matter might be too complex for nonexpert sources to meaningfully address, such as accounting standards or white-collar crime. In this space, firms set policy that has far-ranging implications for social welfare.[67] In these thin political markets, the temptation for capture is overwhelming. As I have noted earlier, many firms would argue that it would be a failure of fiduciary duty to their shareholders not to influence the regulatory environment to help increase profitability. Therefore, if one wants to limit firm involvement to that of a technical adviser, one must also consider how the firm is structured so that its participation in an advisory capacity is limited not only by government but also by the firm's own internal processes.

One might object to my argument by asserting that we should work to strengthen enforcement. Perhaps in an ideal setting, where both firms and governments are clear on their respective roles, that might be the case.[68] However, here I argue that we need both theoretical and practical solutions. Given the current spending by firms, the deep entanglement between firms and politics, and the weakening of the state more broadly, it is difficult to imagine how this separation might be accomplished as one would need to strengthen not just government but multiple stakeholders in every single policy space, both currently existing and imagined. Even if one were to strengthen government significantly, as Gao and McDonald helpfully argue, government would still require the technical advice of firms in many settings, which would create the temptation and opportunity for corporate capture leading to long-lasting social, political, and economic consequences.

There is a second and even more subtle corollary to the temptation for corporate capture: implicit bias. I rely on the work of Max Bazerman to illustrate this concept. Bazerman and colleagues introduce the idea of implicit bias into the management literature by arguing that one might be well intentioned but ultimately could act unethically because of implicit stereotypes, conflicts of interest, in-group favoritism, and overclaiming credit.[69] I am most interested in the second and third ideas that they present. Conflicts of interest arise as professionals "routinely . . . can convince themselves that their product or service is the very best option for a client, even when, objectively, this is not the case."[70] Boeing advocated for the 737 Max both on the basis that doing so was good for the company and that it was good for government. It is reasonable to believe that it is highly unlikely that Boeing thought it created a substandard product. However, the firm leveraged its relationship with the FAA to ensure the project proceeded even though, in retrospect, it is clear that the 737 Boeing Max had fatal design flaws. In this way the technical advisory role opens up corporate capture as firms can believe the advice they give is unconflicted even if it unfairly benefits them. This conflict stems from their inability to fully separate their profit-motives from their ethics. Through the channel of implicit bias, firms in the role of technical advisers will tacitly tilt political processes in their direction, which could create tangible harm for society.

Bazerman and colleagues highlight that the potential for conflict of interest is particularly concerning in concert with in-group favoritism or "the tendency of people to give preferential treatment to members of groups to which they belong and consequently put outsiders at a disadvantage."[71] Here I am actually concerned with government. The technical advisory role allows firms to gain the trust and favor of government such that over time, government naturally gravitates to those firms that provide substantive guidance over others that remain more neutral. This dynamic is at work in the Boeing case as it is clear that the FAA wants Boeing to succeed over its European competitor Airbus. One could reasonably assume that the FAA knew that stalling or halting the development of the 737 Max would have allowed

Airbus to capitalize on the American Airlines contract. This "in-group favoritism" often occurs with existing industries versus new entrants to the market as government has built a long-term relationship with the incumbent firms even if the new entrants have superior product offerings that are better suited to the needs of the public.[72]

I argue that implicit bias works on both firms and the government through the technical advisory role. This channel could lead to clientelistic relationships at the expense of the public good, which Hussain and Moriarty might wish to avoid. One might respond to this concern that making firms and governments aware of this possibility would safeguard against the negative consequences. The challenge here, which research well documents, is that even if they are aware of implicit bias, individuals will not change behavior unless the terms of engagement or incentive structures themselves change.[73] Simply telling individuals to avoid implicit bias is rarely enough to meaningfully change the outcome positively.[74]

Given these two challenges, temptation and implicit bias, what friendly amendments might we make to the Hussain and Moriarty approach? As discussed previously, I believe that the most fruitful path is to reconsider the structure of the firm. In the spirit of pluralistic experimentation, I offer two amendments that might help resolve these challenges. The first pragmatic amendment to overcome both temptation and implicit bias could be to separate political decisions from the ongoing management of the firm.

A firm that intends to engage in the political space could form an external committee, called the political engagement committee (PEC), comprised of selected employees, board members, shareholders, and a broader set of stakeholders such as union leadership, related nonprofit directors, or other community leaders. The PEC would meet regularly to consider, recommend, revise, and direct any political activity that the firm undertakes. The primary remit of the PEC would be to direct and monitor activities such as lobbying, campaign contributions, and interactions with regulators. These political activities are clear, discrete, and easily monitored.

Secondarily, the PEC also could consider how firm processes, products, and services might generate political and social consequences, in turn providing guidance to the firm on how best to mitigate these risks. On a regular basis, the PEC would disclose to the public its membership, decision process, and any political participation. Most important, the PEC would have veto power over the defined set of political activities within its remit and would be incentivized to both consider the public good and the longevity of the firm. This structure would satisfy the concern for both inward and outward accountability that Hussain and Moriarty argue is critical.

One might note that governance committees on corporate boards and regulatory affairs departments already exist, particularly in large firms.[75] While this is certainly the case, the key difference of the proposed PEC is the inclusion of external voices on a semi-independent body. The PEC has no fiduciary responsibility other than to ensure that its related firm engages with the public sphere responsibly and ethically as opposed to the board of the firm or any internal department. The external presence, I argue, will create a more contested, thoughtful, and dynamic decision-making process.[76]

One can see how such a committee might have helped to avoid the Boeing 737 Max tragedy. By externalizing political activity, Boeing would have undergone a much more rigorous scrutiny of the new aircraft and would have been less able to lean on the regulator to expedite the process. There is reason to believe that the multistakeholder committee could have potentially delayed the development process, which would have either prompted further design changes or perhaps a restructuring of the deal with American Airlines altogether. Furthermore, employees and pilots wary of the new aircraft could have voiced their concerns to an independent body overseeing the political implications of business decisions as opposed to the current system in which those concerns could have been dismissed in favor of profitability.

In this way, the committee proposal might help firms become more like PROs through the PEC. The political decision-making process would be clear and independent, allowing employees to make decisions about joining, remaining, or leaving the firm based on whether their own individual commitments align with firm behavior, a criteria Hussain and Moriarty set forth.

The recommendation of an external body to govern political engagement is neither small nor insignificant. The establishment of a PEC invites questions of the allocation of fiduciary responsibilities between shareholders and stakeholders. Empowering the PEC to direct the political strategy of a firm allows external stakeholders to have a meaningful say in the profitability of a company, which at the present moment is reserved for shareholders.[77] Consider the Uber example. As constructed here, the PEC would have enormous sway over Uber's ability to operate and generate revenue as Uber employs both an economic and political strategy. The PEC would govern Uber's political strategy, which has opened and shaped a number of markets for its product offerings. Most likely an Uber PEC would heavily curtail its "regulatory entrepreneurship," which would come in conflict with its current shareholders. Given this scope of powers, the implementation of a PEC would mostly likely require a new legal framework that would formalize the powers described herein and assign liability responsibilities.[78]

Another approach to solving the corporate capture problem might be to consider changing the composition of the shareholders rather than changing the decision-making powers at the level of governance. Therefore, the second amendment I suggest to overcome temptation and bias would be to consider democratizing the firm. By democratization, I mean adopting a model in which the firm is both run and owned by its employees. This structure provides a number of benefits that would assist our concerns. I rely on famed political and economic philosopher Joshua Cohen to provide a useful roadmap to understand the appropriate dynamic between capital and what he terms a deliberative democratic order.[79] Cohen argues that a truly democratic society requires a socialist organization of capital. He does not refer to the communist schemes of the twentieth century in which social ownership of the means of production is rationalized based on the search for the optimal development of productive forces. Rather, he argues that the deliberative view of democracy requires a commitment to socialism "where democracy is understood to be an association that realizes the ideal of free deliberation among equal citizens."[80] He lays out four arguments for the socialization of capital to provide what he calls "an unifying structure for a family of considerations" that leads from a commitment to democratic association to a commitment to a form of socialism.[81] I will use these arguments to shed light on how internal democratization might overcome corporate capture and implicit bias.

The first argument he calls the "parallel case." Here the argument for worker self-management stems from the same principles that justify democratic governance. Workers are in cooperative economic activities, and, like their political counterparts, they should be governed by rules that they have the capacity to assess and change based on their ability to deliver mutual advantage for the participants.[82] The second argument, the psychological argument, borrowing from John Stuart Mill, states that the principle of self-government develops character and a sense of the common good, which democratic work would also do. Social arrangements are malleable and their improvement is subject to the efforts of individuals. Working toward their improvement "builds an active character."[83] This effort develops a "capacity to judge in terms of the common good and a desire to act on such judgements."[84] The two arguments here justify democratic governance of the workplace based on individual improvement, or more colloquially, they advocate for "making better people."

The next two arguments consider the relationship of the firm to the broader society. The structural constraints argument contends that "the private control of investment importantly limits the democratic character of the state by subordinating the decisions and actions of the state to the investment decisions of capitalists."[85] Investment decisions impose "constraints on the collective choices of citizens," therefore public control of investment is the appropriate remedy.[86] The resource constraint argument posits that an unequal distribution of wealth within capitalism "limits the democratic character of politics undermining the equal access of citizens to the political arena and their equal capacity to influence outcomes in that arena."[87] Individuals and organizations with significant economic resources can unfairly impose their political will on the broader populace as economically deficient individuals and organizations are severely disadvantaged in these negotiations. The structure and resource constraints argument presents a compelling narrative for the socialization of capital in that inequality severely hampers the ability of a democracy to attend to the needs of all and instead focuses on the projects of the very few.

Having made these arguments, Cohen reminds us that a deliberative democracy is rooted in the ideal of a social order constructed by public argument among equal citizens. If we take this ideal seriously, a society in which equals set the agenda, propose alternative solutions to problems, support those solutions with discernible reasons, and conclude by selecting some alternative, then only a socialist firm structure will provide such a society with worker arrangements that can satisfy the deliberative requirements.[88] He argues that a socialist realization would require "public control of investment in which public owned means of production are operated by worker managed firms."[89]

Cohen's argument nicely illustrates how democratic-run firms would materially contribute to strengthening the deliberative process and, in our case, would limit temptation and bias. I argue that Cohen's parallel case and psychological arguments, which focus on the internal environment, could help overcome overt temptation. The psychological argument would work to improve the character of firm managers who in turn would be able to more readily recognize instances of corporate capture and, critically, restrain themselves from undermining public priorities. The parallel case argument aids managers in understanding the process of government and therefore tacitly encourages them to accept its goals, directives, and constraints.[90]

I contend that the resource and structural constraints arguments, which focus on the external environment, more directly assist in overcoming implicit bias as they address systemic concerns for firms. The structural argument aligns the incentives of the firm and the state, thereby limiting the temptation and opportunity to tilt the playing field toward the interests of firms over the state. The resource argument goes deeper by rectifying broader inequality, which in turn will disincentivize firms seeking to capture additional rents for managers and shareholders at the expense of the general public. The recommendation to democratize the firm might seem more radical than the first option, the PEC, but one could argue that it would be a more long-lasting and durable fix to temptation and implicit bias.

There are two primary objections commonly voiced against democratization of firms. First, many scholars wonder if the proposal for firm democratization would adequately address the difficulties it seeks to remedy. While it is unclear if this proposal is sufficient to overcome the enormity of the concerns I have outlined above, it is presented as a robust one among many that might address these difficult social, political, and economic challenges in concert and conversation with other proposals put forward within this book.[91] It is the search for viable alternatives that is critical to overcome our current predicament, and this proposal is manifestly one of them.

The second objection that many raise, in particular many economists and business practitioners, centers on potential enormous efficiency losses. The objection is that given the potential upheaval to the current system that such a proposal would have, how much economic efficiency would we lose by encouraging widespread firm democratization. There are three primary difficulties with the efficiency concern. First, there are a number of alternative proposals for resolving the challenges of corporate capture and implicit bias, yet they all require an oligarchic top-down coordinated effort rather than a grassroots democratic one.[92] As I have argued above, if one believes the deliberative democratic framing, then the solution should seek to increase equality, not diminish it. Second, the question of whether the democratization of the firm would create efficiency losses is in large part an unanswered empirical query. Further experimentation and comparative analysis is required to determine if there would be large-scale efficiency losses, in which economic spheres, and over what time horizon. It is plausible that this form might be most effective for companies of particular scope and size. Such rigorous exploration would then inform how society might mandate democratization and under what conditions. Third, it is worthwhile considering that by adopting internal firm democratization the polity might gain on a number of dimensions, even if there were significant efficiency losses as the arguments put forward by Cohen suggest. Surely the need for economic growth and firm optimization should be balanced against the maintenance of rights, creation of space for individual and community flourishing, and general social stability.

Returning to the advisory view of corporate engagement, there is a third and more intractable difficulty with the Hussain and Moriarty perspective. How should we consider the fact that the FAA has a legitimate reason to develop a deep and lasting partnership with Boeing? Boeing is a major economic contributor to the US economy and has assisted in developing many technologies with the support of government that have been transformational for our society. Asking socially and economically productive firms such as Boeing to disengage from this deeper collaborative process robs society of tangible benefits. Palazzo and Scherer attempt to construct a theory of engagement that takes this dynamic into account, but their proposal ultimately falls short, as Hussain and Moriarty cogently argue.

Another line of inquiry might be to consider the role of the economy in a just society. Robust deliberative systems need effective and productive economies to function. If we hope to achieve an egalitarian ideal, individuals need the space to pursue their independent projects, which oftentimes firms provide. Additionally, social welfare programs provide a baseline of support that comes through large tax transfers funded in large part by firms and their shareholders and senior managers. Given the deep reliance on firms and their economic resources, one wonders if it could be reasonable to seek their consent and even active participation in the deliberative process.

Rebecca Henderson outlines a compelling argument that we might need this collaboration to achieve lasting peace.[93] She cites three historical examples: Denmark at the turn of the twentieth century, Germany in the post–World War II years, and Mauritius post-independence in the 1960s. The examples suggest political and business elites arrived at a mutually agreeable, deliberative-style arrangement ensuring prosperity for their prospective countries. They did so to avoid further unrest and bloodshed. In each case, firms retained autonomy but also agreed to generous tax transfers and worker protections. It is my suspicion that this underlying agreement between those representing political and economic power is in fact what enables the deliberative process to move forward. If one considers the concerns of Hussain and Moriarty, they perhaps are arguing that we must restrict firm behavior in part because we cannot trust firms to participate meaningfully and equitably in the deliberative process, which given our current climate is imminently reasonable.

However, another way to approach this lack of trust might be to consider exploring how those who hold the majority of economic resources would and should consent to the deliberative process, given their integral role in its development and perpetuation. Therefore, a fruitful avenue for future research would be to explore how these two parties develop a binding social contract. One perhaps could argue that the unraveling of state power, the overreach of firms, and populist discontent in the US at the present moment is in part a result of a failure to maintain a viable social contract between economic and political elites. To my understanding, political philosophy and business ethics have few theoretical tools to assist us in investigating this line of inquiry. I recommend that new research focus on how we might understand this dynamic and its importance in supporting a deliberative economic system. Furthermore, as we develop and revise our philosophical tools to investigate this space, we also should consider the implications for firm behavior: How should they interact with the state, for what might they advocate, and what do they owe their employees and the body public more generally?

Conclusion

In this chapter, I have examined three theories for how firms can engage in the political process from the perspective of democratic ideals. The neoclassical view advocates for the complete separation of firms and the political process. The collaborative view proposes complete integration between firms and politics. The advisory view asks firms only to participate in the deliberative democratic process as technical advisers. The last theory, forwarded by Hussain and Moriarty, is the most satisfying yet remains inadequate given the potential for corporate capture through temptation and implicit bias. I have proposed two potential amendments to the corporate form to assist in overcoming these challenges. The first is an external fix through the establishment of an independent committee that will oversee a firm's political actions. The second is an internal fix, the complete democratization of the firm. There is also a deeper challenge to the advisory view to speculate about—namely, that to investigate how firms can have a deeper relationship with the deliberative process we ought to theoretically investigate the way in which we understand how social contracts between economic and political elites are formed and sustained over time. I contend that it is only through this final investigation that we might find a truly satisfying answer to how firms should engage in the political process and understand their commitments more broadly to deliberative democracy.

Notes

I thank Nien-he Hsieh, J. Peter Scoblic, Sophus Reinhert, Matthew Weinzerl, Kriston McIntosh, and the organizers and participants of the Political Economy and Justice workshop for very useful feedback on previous drafts.

1.   Many scholars have addressed this topic. For the business ethics perspective, see for, example, Sandrine Blanc and Ismael Al-Amoudi, "Corporate Institu-

tions in a Weakened Welfare State: A Rawlsian Perspective," *Business Ethics Quarterly* 23, no. 4 (2013): 497–525; and Guido Palazzo and Andreas Georg Scherer, "Corporate Legitimacy as Deliberation: A Communicative Framework," *Journal of Business Ethics* 66, no. 1 (2006): 71–88.

2.   For a review of nonmarket strategy, see Kamel Mellahi, Jdrzej George Frynas, Pei Sun, and Donald Siegel, "A Review of the Nonmarket Strategy Literature: Toward a Multi-Theoretical Integration," *Journal of Management* 42, no. 1 (2016): 143–73; and Felix Oberholzer-Gee and Dennis A. Yao, "Integrated Strategy: Residual Market and Exchange Imperfections as the Foundation of Sustainable Competitive Advantage," *Strategy Science* 3, no. 2 (2018): 463–80.

3.   I rely primarily on the following for the discussion in this chapter: Andreas Georg Scherer and Guido Palazzo, "Toward a Political Conception of Corporate Responsibility: Business and Society Seen from a Habermasian Perspective," *Academy of Management Review* 32, no. 4 (2007): 1096–120; and Waheed Hussain and Jeffrey Moriarty, "Accountable to Whom? Rethinking the Role of Corporations in Political CSR," *Journal of Business Ethics* 149, no. 3 (2018): 519–34.

4.   This chapter adopts the pluralistic experimental approach to reforming the political economy rather than proposing radical or foundational change. This approach follows other contributions in this book, including the chapters by Deva Woodley, Rebecca Henderson, and Dani Rodrik and Charles Sabel, which will be referenced later.

5.   There has been increasing acknowledgment among scholars in recent years that there has been considerable "scope creep" for firms in pursuit of shareholder value maximization. For an overview see Lynn A. Stout, *The Shareholder Value Myth: How Putting Shareholders First Harms Investors, Corporations, and the Public* (Berrett-Koehler Publishers, 2012).

6.   There is a large literature within economics and management that examines corruption and political engagement of firms. This literature primarily focuses on the valuation of particular connections rather than exploring types of political activity and why firms might adopt them. For a good analysis for the economic reasons for corruption, see, for example, Pranab Bardhan, "Corruption and Development: A Review of Issues," *Journal of Economic Literature* 35, no. 3 (1997): 1320–46. For an estimation of the value of political connections, see, for example, Raymond Fisman, "Estimating the Value of Political Connections," *American Economic Review* 91, no. 4 (2001): 1095–102; Asim Ijaz Khwaja and Atif Mian, "Do Lenders Favor Politically Connected Firms? Rent Provision in an Emerging Financial Market," *Quarterly Journal of Economics* (2005): 1371–411.

7.   Mellahi et al., "A Review of Nonmarket Strategy Literature," 144.

8.   Mellahi et al., 146.

9.   Mellahi et al., 150.

10.   Bridging strategies are almost often referred to as corporate social responsibility (CSR). For an ethical overview of CSR, see Elisabet Garriga and

Domènec Melé. "Corporate Social Responsibility Theories: Mapping the Territory," *Journal of Business Ethics* 53, no. 1–2 (2004): 51–71. For a review of the impact of CSR on firm performance, see Michael E. Porter and Mark R. Kramer, "The Link between Competitive Advantage and Corporate Social Responsibility," *Harvard Business Review* 84, no. 12 (2006): 78–92.

11. Mellahi et al., "A Review of Nonmarket Strategy Literature," 151–52.

12. George Stigler, "The Theory of Economic Regulation," *Bell Journal of Economics and Management Science* 2, no. 1 (1971): 3–21.

13. Stigler, "The Theory of Economic Regulation," 5–7.

14. Lee Drutman, *The Business of America Is Lobbying: How Corporations Became Politicized and Politics Became More Corporate* (Oxford University Press, 2015).

15. Nien-hê Hsieh and Victor Wu, "Making Target the Target," Harvard Business School No. 9-317-113 (2017): 4.

16. Hsieh and Wu, "Making Target the Target," 4.

17. Hsieh and Wu, 6.

18. Blanc and Al-Moudi, "Corporate Institutions in a Weakened Welfare State," 498–500.

19. Ryan Nunn, Jimmy O'Donnell, and Jay Shambaugh, "The Shift in Private Sector Union Participation: Explanation and Effects," *Brookings*, August 22, 2019.

20. Blanc and Al-Moudi, "Corporate Institutions in a Weakened Welfare State," 501.

21. Scherer and Palazzo, "Toward a Political Conception of Corporate Responsibility," 1097–100.

22. See, for example, Florian Wettstein, *Multinational Corporations and Global Justice: Human Rights Obligations of a Quasi-Governmental Institution* (Stanford University Press, 2009).

23. For an overview, see, for example, Margaret Cowell, *Dealing with Deindustrialization: Adaptive Resilience in American Midwestern Regions* (Routledge, 2014).

24. For this dynamic in urban settings, see William Julius Wilson, *When Work Disappears: The World of the New Urban Poor* (Vintage, 2011).

25. For a compelling analysis of business tax incentives on US state economic development, see Soledad Artiz Prillaman and Kenneth J. Meier, "Taxes, Incentives, and Economic Growth: Assessing the Impact of Pro-Business Taxes on US State Economies," *Journal of Politics* 76, no. 2 (2014): 364–79.

26. For an analysis on the rise of economic and cultural populism in the US, see Ronald F. Inglehart and Pippa Norris, "Trump, Brexit, and the Rise of Populism: Economic Have-Nots and Cultural Backlash," Harvard Kennedy School Working Paper No. RWP16-026 (August 2016).

27. Stephen M. Bainbridge, "Corporate Purpose in a Populist Era," UCLA School of Law, Law-Econ Research Paper 18-09 (2018).

28. Michael C. Jensen, "Value Maximization, Stakeholder Theory, and the Corporate Objective Function," *Business Ethics Quarterly* (2002): 235–256.

29. Jensen, "Value Maximization," 240.

30. Jensen, 241.

31. For a seminal discussion on stakeholder theory, see Thomas Donaldson and Lee E. Preston. "The Stakeholder Theory of the Corporation: Concepts, Evidence, and Implications," *Academy of Management Review* 20, no. 1 (1995): 65–91.

32. In this book, in their chapter on "Building a Good Jobs Economy," Rodrik and Sabel present a compelling positive argument that encourages the cocreation of regulation. I very much agree with the need for firms and government to dynamically coevolve to tackle difficult private and policy issues. However, I caution about the danger of corporate capture (as discussed later in this chapter).

33. Many have commented upon the social costs of shareholder value maximization theory. See for example Lynn A. Stout, *The Shareholder Value Myth: How Putting Shareholders First Harms Investors, Corporations, and the Public* (Berrett-Koehler Publishers, 2012).

34. For an in-depth look at Uber pricing and strategy, see Le Chen, Alan Mislove, and Christo Wilson, "Peeking Beneath the Hood of Uber," in *Proceedings of the 2015 Internet Measurement Conference* (ACM, 2015), 495–508.

35. For a review of early regulation of Uber, see Geoffrey Dudley, David Banister, and Tim Schwanen, "The Rise of Uber and Regulating the Disruptive Innovator," *Political Quarterly* 88, no. 3 (2017): 492–99.

36. For an investigation of the consumer surplus captured by Uber, see Peter Cohen, Robert Hahn, Jonathan Hall, Steven Levitt, and Robert Metcalfe, "Using Big Data to Estimate Consumer Surplus: The Case of Uber," National Bureau of Economic Research, NBER Working Paper No. 22627 (2016).

37. Cohen et al., "Using Big Data to Estimate Consumer Surplus," 3.

38. Uber is not alone in shaping its regulatory environment. Other major technology firms such as Airbnb, Tesla, and others are engaging in this practice with varied results. For an overview, see Elizabeth Pollman and Jordan M. Barry, "Regulatory Entrepreneurship," *Southern California Law Review* 90 (2016): 383–448.

39. Pollman and Barry, "Regulatory Entrepreneurship," 385–400.

40. Brishen Rogers, "The Social Costs of Uber," *University of Chicago Law Review Dialogue* 82 (2015): 85.

41. See Cheng Gao and Rory McDonald, "Shaping Nascent Industries: Innovation Strategy and Regulatory Uncertainty in Personal Genomics," working paper (2019). It should be noted that this line of inquiry is also explored heavily in Rodrik and Sabel in "Building a Good Jobs Economy" in this book.

42. Milton Friedman, "The Social Responsibility of Business Is to Increase Its Profits," in *Corporate Ethics and Corporate Governance*, ed. Walther C. Zimmerli, Markus Holzinger, and Klaus Richter (Springer, 2007), 173–78.

43. Friedman, "The Social Responsibility of Business Is to Increase Its Profits," 178.

44. Scherer and Palazzo, "Toward a Political Conception of Corporate Responsibility," 1107.

45. Scherer and Palazzo, 1107

46. Scherer and Palazzo, 1110.

47. Scherer and Palazzo, 1111.

48. Scherer and Palazzo, 1112.

49. Scherer and Palazzo, 1112.

50. Hussain and Moriarty, "Accountable to Whom?," 521.

51. Hussain and Moriarty, 522.

52. Hussain and Moriarty, 525.

53. This argument poses a more fundamental challenge to the work of Henderson and of Rodrik and Sabel in this book. Does the participation of firms in the cocreation of regulation or the political order more generally create an insurmountable democracy deficit? As I will argue later, we need to develop new tools to consider how to resolve the desire for cooperation but with the need for robust accountability.

54. Hussain and Moriarty, "Accountable to Whom?," 526.

55. Hussain and Moriarty, 527.

56. Hussain and Moriarty, 530.

57. For a compelling overview of the events leading up to the crash, see Alvin Chang, Dion Lee, and Kimberly Mas, "The Real Reason Boeing's Plane Crashed Twice," *Vox*, April 15, 2019, https://www.vox.com/videos/2019/4/15/18306644/boeing-737-max-crash-video.

58. There is a great deal of research that links the creation of a strong positive brand and financial performance. For a thoughtful empirical investigation, see Robert A. Peterson and Jaeseok Jeong, "Exploring the Impact of Advertising and R&D Expenditures on Corporate Brand Value and Firm Level Financial Performance," *Journal of the Academy of Marketing Science* (2010): 677–90.

59. Brand Finance, *Aerospace and Defence 25* (London, 2018).

60. David Gelles, Natalie Kitroeff, Jack Nicas, and Rebecca R. Ruiz, "Boeing Was 'Go, Go, Go' to Beat Airbus with the 737 Max," *New York Times*, March 23, 2019.

61. Gelles et al., "Boeing Was 'Go, Go, Go' to Beat Airbus."

62. See, for example, Stephen Mihm, "The FAA Has Always Played Cozy with the Aviation Industry," *Bloomberg*, March 21, 2019.

63. D. Saint Germain, "The Boeing Debacle Is the Latest Example of Regulatory Capture," *Medium*, March 15, 2019.

64. Associated Press, "Lawmakers Grill FAA Chief about Boeing 737 Max Safety Concerns," May 15, 2019.

65. Thomas Kaplan, Ian Austen, and Selam Gebrekidan, "Boeing Planes Are Grounded in US after Days of Pressure," *New York Times*, March 13, 2019.

66. Karthik Ramanna, "Thin Political Markets: The Soft Underbelly of Capitalism," *California Management Review* 57, no. 2 (2015): 5–19.

67. Ramanna, "Thin Political Markets," 6.

68. As the neoclassical view would argue, the appropriate scope of government is to provide oversight. However, a great deal of firm lobbying is targeted to undermine this very capacity, therefore an alternative formulation is required. See, for example, Zhiyan Cao, Guy D. Fernando, Arindam Tripathy, and Arun Upadhyay, "The Economics of Corporate Lobbying," *Journal of Corporate Finance* 49 (2018): 54–80.

69. Max H. Bazerman, Dolly Chugh, and Maharzin R. Banaji, "When Good People (Seem to) Negotiate in Bad Faith," *Negotiation* 8, no. 10 (2005): 3–5.

70. Bazerman, Chugh, and Banaji, "When Good People (Seem to) Negotiate in Bad Faith," 4.

71. Bazerman, Chugh, and Banaji, 5.

72. Bazerman, Chugh, and Banaji, 4.

73. Marianne Bertrand, Dolly Chugh, and Sendhil Mullainathan, "Implicit Discrimination," *American Economic Review* 95, no. 2 (2005): 94–98.

74. Bazerman, Chugh, and Banaji, "When Good People (Seem to) Negotiate in Bad Faith," 5.

75. Corporate governance committees as currently constituted have mixed results in curbing political activity of the corporation. For an argument that CEO political ideology overrides board influence, see Omer Unsal, M. Kabir Hassan, and Duygu Zirek, "Corporate Lobbying, CEO Political Ideology and Firm Performance," *Journal of Corporate Finance* 38 (2016): 126–49. For ethical challenges that face corporate boards in engaging in political activity, see Nicolas M. Dahan, Michael Hadani, and Douglas A. Schuler, "The Governance Challenges of Corporate Political Activity," *Business & Society* 52, no. 3 (2013): 365–87.

76. Thank you to the editors for pointing out this concern.

77. This is true for both reforms to corporate governance such as benefit corporations and employee-owned firms, as discussed below. B corps expand the scope of responsibilities for managers and directors but do not externalize responsibilities. See, for example, Suntae Kim, Matthew J. Karlesky, Christopher G. Myers, and Todd Schifeling, "Why Companies Are Becoming B Corporations," *Harvard Business Review* 17 (2016).

78. This is an ongoing debate with the legal literature as to whether stakeholders should be granted fiduciary responsibilities. For a current investigation of incorporating different voices in corporate governance, see Andrew Keay, "Shareholder Primacy in Corporate Law: Can It Survive? Should It Survive?," *European Company and Financial Law Review* 7, no. 3 (2010): 369–413. For a classical argument against this approach, see Mark E. Van der Weide, "Against Fiduciary Duties to Corporate Stakeholders." *Delaware Journal of Corporate Law* 21 (1996): 27.

79. Joshua Cohen, "The Economic Basis of Deliberative Democracy," *Social Philosophy and Policy* 6, no. 2 (1989): 25–50.

80. Cohen, "The Economic Basis of Deliberative Democracy," 26.

81. Cohen, 26.

82.   Cohen, 27.

83.   Cohen, 29.

84.   Cohen, 29.

85.   Cohen, 28.

86.   Cohen, 28.

87.   Cohen, 29.

88.   Cohen, 32.

89.   Cohen, 40–42.

90.   For a full articulation of these arguments and their connection to labor, see Nien-he Hsieh, "Justice in Production," *Journal of Political Philosophy* 16, no. 1 (2008): 72–100.

91.   This approach tracks other contributions in this book in offering suggestions for experimentation that might be refined and enhanced over time. See, for example, the chapters on "Polypolitanism" and "Building a Good Jobs Economy."

92.   While recent statements by large investment funds are encouraging, having these deeply wealthy and elite entities lead the charge on addressing corporate malfeasance without democratic accountability raises many concerns. For early popular research on this front, see Kelsey Piper, "'Impact Investment' Funds Advertise Great Returns and Social Impacts. They Aren't Delivering," *Vox*, December 19, 2018, https://www.vox.com/future-perfect/2018/12/18/18136214/impact-investing-socially-responsible-sri-report.

93.   Rebecca Henderson, *Reimagining Capitalism in a World on Fire* (Public Affairs, 2020).

10 *The Just and Democratic Platform? Possibilities of Platform Cooperativism*

JULIET B. SCHOR AND SAMANTHA EDDY

Introduction

The Great Recession shone a bright light on structural problems that had been accumulating in the global economy for years: the acceleration of extreme inequality in the household distributions of income and wealth, weak demand, hidden unemployment, unsustainable consumer debt, and growing imbalances between rural and urban areas. At the same time, the climate crisis intensified as the international community proved unable to control emissions and engineer the turnaround required to avoid runaway climate chaos. The failure of national governments to solve these economic and ecological challenges, coupled with a decades-long right-wing attack on the state, resulted in widespread pessimism about the possibility and efficacy of political action, particularly in the United States. This proved to be fertile ground for optimism about a variety of market-based solutions. One of those solutions came to be known as the "sharing economy." It emerged with the Great Recession and promised a new way of organizing economic activity. It would be smaller-scale, more personal, and much more efficient. Power would not be concentrated in the hands of a few. It represented a way to deploy new technology in the service of human needs. Indeed, founders and ordinary participants claimed it could be the solution to multiple problems facing capitalist societies: inequality and exclusion, stagnant incomes, climate chaos, and social disconnection (Schor 2014, 2020). The central vehicle for realizing these goals was online person-to-person exchange made newly feasible by innovations in digital technology (Benkler 2006).

The core idea is that small-scale, personal economic activity becomes viable as a result of digital tools, matching algorithms, and crowdsourced reputational data. These features overcome the long-standing drawbacks of peer-to-peer or person-to-person markets, such as costly search and risky exchanges.

Consumers reap benefits and individual providers can control their work lives in new and empowering ways (Castillo, Knoepfle, and Weyl 2018; Einav, Farronato, and Levin 2016; Horton and Zeckhauser 2016; Schor 2020; Sundararajan 2016). In particular, the "sharing economy" offered the possibility of giving workers control over their schedules, total hours of work, and the labor process itself. The promise is that individuals can do it themselves by participating in this emergent, humane market (Fitzmaurice et al 2020).

Not everyone believed in the promise of the "sharing economy." There has been widespread skepticism about some platform companies, particularly Uber, which has the largest labor force by a big margin. Some argued that the sharing sector represented the emergence of a hyper-predatory regime of labor control (Hill 2015; Rosenblat 2018; Scholz 2016b). Others foresaw a new frontier in the commodification and corporatization of everyday life and the destruction of urban quality of life (Morozov 2013; Slee 2015; see also the chapter by Stears in this book). A decade after its founding, many in the US have written off the sharing economy as a malignant force degrading workers and neighborhoods. Others still see potential in the technologies and peer-to-peer structure. The experiences of some European countries, which have subjected platforms to more stringent regulation, suggest that policies and impacts are not predetermined by economics or technology (Rahman and Thelen 2019; Söderqvist 2017; Thelen 2018). Since 2018, regulatory activity protecting residents and workers has increased in the US, particularly in ride-hailing and accommodation. And after years of unsuccessful legal efforts to reclassify platform workers from independent contractors to employees (Collier, Dubal, and Carter 2017), pioneering legislation to convert providers to employees has been enacted, although this fight is ongoing. It is possible that after a decade of regulatory arbitrage and nullification by the firms (Acevedo 2016; Calo and Rosenblat 2017; Collier, Dubal, and Carter 2018; Rahman 2016), the power of platforms is being reined in. If so, workers and urban residents will likely benefit.

But this familiar turn to regulation, welcome as it will be, may not exploit the more transformative possibilities of the new technologies used by platforms in the sharing economy (Benkler 2004, 2006, 2013; Schor 2010). That may require a less traditional approach. In particular, the peer-to-peer (P2P) structure enabled by technology may not only make transactions more efficient, it may also do the same for democratic governance. This is the contention of a small but growing movement for platform cooperativism (Scholz 2014, 2016a; Scholz and Schneider 2016). Platform cooperatives borrow some of the features of worker cooperatives, in particular worker ownership and governance. But because platforms typically operate differently than conventional firms, they also offer new opportunities and challenges. Platform co-ops raise the possibility that P2P marketplaces can support a new enterprise form that is capable of achieving greater economic justice and democracy than conventional firms.

Platform cooperatives are best understood as one type of firm within a larger, more pluralist economy. This vision counters the conceit of twentieth-century economic theory that the capitalist firm is optimal and that econo-mies should evolve toward a singular business form. Rather, it sees platform cooperatives as one type in a diverse ecosystem of ownership and governance arrangements that include small and large-scale commons, trusts, varied fi-nancial arrangements (public banks, crowdsourcing, credit cooperatives), small and owner-run businesses, nonprofits, networked enterprises, and oth-ers (Alperovitz 2011; Benkler 2006; Ostrom 1990; Piore and Sabel 2000).

This chapter draws on findings from our research on the sharing economy conducted in the sociology department of Boston College from 2011 to 2018. The research covered 12 cases of for-profit and nonprofit entities, including the first academic study of a platform cooperative. Our cases are Airbnb, Turo, TaskRabbit, Lyft and Uber, Postmates and Favor, a timebank, a food swap, a makerspace, Stocksy (the platform co-op), and an open education case. We did interviews, hundreds of hours of ethnography, web scraping, and quantitative analysis. Our database contains roughly 325 interviews. De-tails on our methods and findings are available on our project website,[1] and a summary of our work is contained in Schor (2020). This chapter begins with a short history of the sharing economy, discusses the labor outcomes on for-profit platforms, and then turns to a discussion of the not-for-profit cases, as they are relevant for platform cooperatives, and our research on Stocksy, one of the earliest and most well-established platform cooperatives.

"Sharing Economy" Practices: Goods, Space, and Labor Services

There are three main subsegments within the sharing economy: goods, space, and gig labor services, although this division is somewhat arbitrary, given that all exchanges take place in space and require both labor and capital.[2] The precursors of today's sharing economy are eBay and Craigslist, two peer-to-peer markets that were established in 1995 and familiarized users with the P2P structure (Schor and Fitzmaurice 2015). In addition, eBay pioneered the use of a crowdsourced ratings and reputation system, a feature integral to nearly all the commercial platforms and that many of its former employees went on to employ as founders of sharing economy sites (Stein 2015). The pairing of the for-profit eBay with the not-for-profit Craigslist is also notable, as it mirrors the mixed composition of the sector in its original incarnation. Both also began as marketplaces for used goods, responding to the surfeit of imported consumer items available at historically low prices (Schor 2010). By creating online markets for used mass-market goods, these platforms transformed used-goods exchanges, which had previously operated as informal, low-value markets. Digital technology made these trades more convenient, and the reputation system helped build trust among transactors, a key factor that has historically limited secondhand markets. The size of this market is difficult to estimate. However, in terms of participation on the provider side, it is the largest of the three subsections of the sharing sector. In 2016, an estimated 18 percent of Americans earned money by online selling (and 14 percent of those sold used goods), in comparison to 8 percent who earned income from gig labor tasks, such as digital work, ride-hailing, and cleaning (Pew Research Center 2016). There are now many sites organizing P2P exchange, particularly in the apparel sector, where the development of fast fashion resulted in the acceleration of the cycle of acquisition and discard. General exchange sites have also proliferated, employing a range of exchange practices. The largest, Freecycle, uses a gift model and stresses reciprocal giving (Aptekar 2016). Other sites, such as Freegle (a Freecycle offshoot), do not discourage income-based asymmetry with affluent donors and low-income receivers (Martin, Upham, and Budd 2015). Some platforms organize P2P short-term rental of durable goods, such as cars, camping gear, photography equipment, tools, apparel, and household items that are used intermittently. These platforms also operate with a range of exchange practices, from the purely commercial to nonmonetized forms such as tool and toy libraries.

The second category is space-sharing. Here the originator is Couchsurfing, which was started in 1999 and uses a gift exchange model for hosting travelers. Like successor sites such as Airbnb, Couchsurfing uses crowdsourced reputational data to build trust among potential hosts and guests. It has a mission to build connection among people across the world, and research shows that has been successful building friendships, although the strength of induced social ties declines with frequency of use (Parigi and State 2014; Parigi et al. 2013). Airbnb, a rental model that grew explosively, came to dominate this subsegment. Other space-sharing sites offer storage, parking, offices, kitchens, and land. These are frequently termed *capital platforms* (Farrell and Greig 2016) because the bulk of income earned in this sector is from a capital "good" (i.e., the space). Makerspaces, a rapidly growing offering in both for- and not-for-profit versions, combine space and tools. Airbnb is a salient example of a broader trend seen on some of the commercial capital platforms—it began with a P2P structure but evolved toward business-to-consumer (B2C) transactions (i.e., commercial operators renting multiple units). Recent regulatory actions and enforcement may now be reversing this trend, although there is uncertainty about whether these measures will be successful (Schor 2020).

The third subsegment is labor services, also known as the gig or on-demand economy. This is a diverse segment, including ride-hailing and delivery, caring labor, housecleaning, and errands or "handyperson" odd jobs.[3] Uber reports an estimated 3.9 drivers globally, with perhaps one million in the United States. Care.com, the largest platform for caring labor, reports 13.9 million caregivers as of March 2019.[4] There are also not-for-profits in this segment. Timebanks organize multilateral barter exchange on the principle that each provider's time is equally valued. Other examples include repair cafes and food exchanges (swaps, surplus redistribution, food preparation).

The diversity of business organization, exchange model, user type and structure, and mix of capital and labor has contributed to terminological and analytic ambiguity and controversy (Frenken and Schor 2017; Schor and Attwood-Charles 2017). Figures 10.1 and 10.2 categorize entities according to their profit-status, user structure (P2P versus B2C), skill level, and mix of capital and labor. Other relevant dimensions include the form of exchange (monetary, barter, gift, loan), medium of exchange (some sites create their own currencies), whether the work is done offline or online, and whether the customers are individuals or businesses.

The earliest term for the sector was "collaborative consumption" (Botsman and Rogers 2010), which focused on arrangements that increased the utilization of existing assets and included sharing space (e.g., accommodations and

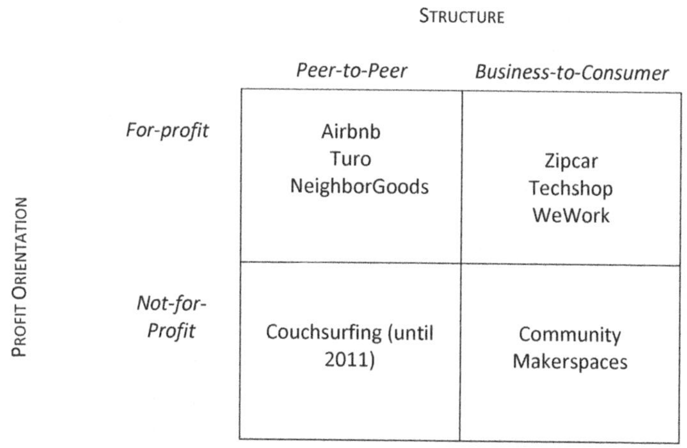

STRUCTURE

	Peer-to-Peer	Business-to-Consumer
For-profit	Airbnb Turo NeighborGoods	Zipcar Techshop WeWork
Not-for-Profit	Couchsurfing (until 2011)	Community Makerspaces

PROFIT ORIENTATION

Figure 10.1. Capital platforms.

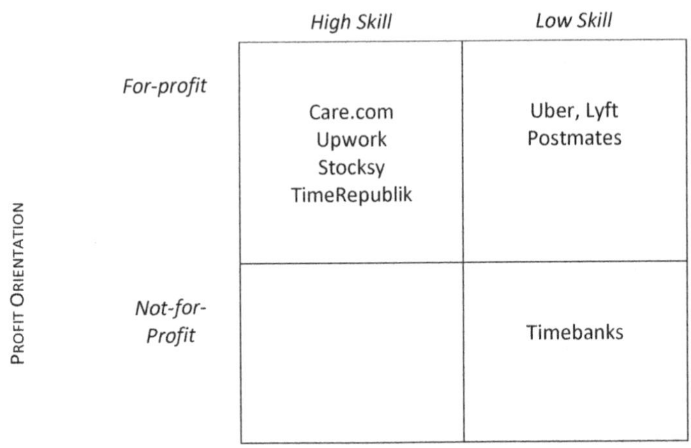

	High Skill	Low Skill
For-profit	Care.com Upwork Stocksy TimeRepublik	Uber, Lyft Postmates
Not-for-Profit		Timebanks

PROFIT ORIENTATION

Figure 10.2. Labor platforms.

offices) and goods (e.g., car rentals, household items). Some analysts reserve the term "sharing economy" for this type of exchange, whether monetized or not, because it involves shared use of the asset across time (Frenken and Schor 2017). However, others argue that if a rental fee is charged, the practice is not sharing because it is done for monetary gain (Belk 2007). In practice, the term has been used indiscriminately and incoherently to encompass nearly all platforms that use matching algorithms (Schor and Attwood-Charles 2017). As some platforms became increasingly predatory toward their workers, the use of the word "sharing" became less defensible and declined in favor of terms such as the gig and on-demand economy, for labor platforms, and the platform economy (Kenney and Zysman 2016) for the entire sector. However, those terms are both broader (including B2B and digital labor, as well as social media and retail sites) and narrower (excluding nonprofits). The term "sharing economy" has traditionally been used to refer to both for-profit and not-for-profit consumer-oriented P2P entities of the three types discussed above (goods, space, and labor). Because that is the segment that we have focused on in our research, that is the term employed here. However, it is important to note that describing commercial entities such as Airbnb or Uber as "sharing" companies can serve to obscure their antisocial practices.

A Disruptive Innovation

Platform technology has been hailed as a disruptive innovation that will yield welfare for producers and consumers in these multisided markets (Rochet and Tirole 2003), as well as additional common good claims.[5] There is widespread agreement that these firms have been disruptive, but observers differ in their analysis of why. Some argue that political economy factors account for the success of the major platforms, in particular the ability to ignore regulations and to misclassify workers as independent contractors and other factors related to market and political power (Calo and Rosenblat 2017; Collier, Dubal, and Carter 2017; Dubal 2017; Rahman and Thelen 2019; Vallas 2019; van Doorn 2017). However, the viability of platforms in countries where they have conformed to regulations suggests that this is not the whole story (Rahman and Thelen 2019; Söderqvist 2017; Thelen 2018).

The alternate approach focuses on the novel technological features of platforms. Most important is that these technologies render peer-to-peer markets more efficient and therefore more feasible. Three aspects of the technology are salient. First, platforms reduce the transaction costs associated with exchanges by organizing electronic payments and insurance, mobilizing GPS technology, and facilitating easy entry and exit of suppliers. This reduces setup and financial outlays for sellers to engage in income-generating activity. Second, algorithms make efficient matches between buyers and sellers and reduce search, a previously costly activity in P2P markets on account of the heterogeneity of sellers. And third, the platforms gather crowdsourced reputational information to create trust among strangers, which enables a key feature of multisided markets—namely, that they enable "stranger sharing" (Schor 2014). (The classic contribution on new forms of sharing is Benkler [2004], who uses the term social sharing.) Historically, stranger sharing has been limited on account of the risks of transacting with unknown others. The presence of both brokers and other intermediaries and trusted brands can be understood partly as ways to mitigate the risks associated with exchanges among unknowns. Crowdsourced reputational data has the potential to perform a similar function and increases willingness to transact with strangers.[6] The combination of these three factors results in lower barriers to entry and enhanced viability for single-person producers, as simple economic analysis can show (Einav, Farronato, and Levin 2016). Some economists have even gone as far as to predict that it heralds the "end of employment" (Sundararajan 2016) although that seems unlikely given that the efficiencies of the technology are less relevant for complex production processes that require extensive coordination. However, platform technology is well suited to services, which currently employ a majority of the US labor force. Thus, the question arises: Can these digital innovations be an enabling factor for a substantial sector of the economy to be organized as independent entities with substantive control over their conditions of production?

The hope that platform technology will result in viable, nonpredatory peer-to-peer markets runs counter to the view that technology markets have a tendency toward monopoly (Dube et al. 2018; Kahn 2017). Dominant firms such as Google, Facebook, and Amazon are considered to be beneficiaries of network effects (i.e., a cost structure that declines with additional users). In a monopolistic market, the platform can engage in predation and manipulation of users, thereby undermining the possibility for viable independent production (Calo and Rosenblat 2017; Rahman 2016). This is less of an issue in the sharing sector than in online tech markets. There are some genuine network effects—for example, on lodging sites. However, many of the services on offer (ride-hail, delivery, caring labor) are local (Horan 2016), which curtails network effects. Furthermore, these markets differ from Facebook and Google because those firms are selling their own products. Sharing platforms are intermediaries among independent producers and consumers. (Amazon is a hybrid in this respect.) Even if the platform is large, if it can facilitate an ecosystem of small or independent producers and if it is democratically owned and/or governed, it can serve their needs.

Labor Outcomes on For-Profit Platforms

One decade in, have platforms met the promises of the sharing economy discourse? For consumers, there has been clear benefit, especially in ride-hail, lodging, and delivery, through lower prices and increased supply. For workers, the picture is mixed, although it is difficult to quantify outcomes because of a lack of data from the platforms and the casualness of this type of employment. The literature is plagued by Uber-centricity, and while ride-hail does comprise a large segment, it is unique in a number of ways (Schor et al. 2020; Ticona and Mateescu 2018). The research is especially limited on higher-skilled providers and caring labor, despite the latter being the largest category of earners in the sector (Ticona, Mateescu, and Rosenblat 2018). Furthermore, conditions in this sector change rapidly, as platforms can easily alter compensation, incentives, rules, and terms of service, and many do so frequently. However, some conclusions are possible. We address three main areas: wages and compensation, autonomy and labor process, and governance/voice in the firm.

With respect to wages and compensation, the picture is mixed, with marked differences across skill level and between capital and labor platforms. In general, the relatively high wages of the early years have been reduced as more providers join platforms. However, on a number of platforms, earnings are comparatively good. For example, on TaskRabbit, the platform we have studied, hourly wages remain high and workers are generally satisfied (Schor et al. 2020). Similarly, we have found that earners on "capital" platforms such as Airbnb are earning substantial sums and express high levels of satisfaction; see also Farrell, Greig, and Hamoudi (2018). By contrast, in ride-hail there is accumulating evidence of a race to the bottom, as the dominant platforms squeeze drivers' earnings (Horan 2016) and exert more control (Rosenblat 2018). Studies of some of the nation's largest cities reveal that full-time ride-hail work is common, and earnings after expenses are often below the hourly minimum wage (Parrott and Reich 2018; UCLA Institute for Research on Labor and Employment 2018). Bank account data reveals a 53 percent collapse in monthly driver earnings between 2014 and 2018 (Farrell, Greig, and Hamoudi 2018). Journalistic accounts and qualitative research have documented deteriorating conditions, with drivers sleeping in their cars, going deeper into debt, and expressing tremendous frustration with the growing share of revenue being extracted by the platforms (Robinson 2017; Streitfeld 2019). Delivery work appears to be on a similar trajectory, with declining income for workers and growing evidence of discontent. We have found that platform outcomes are much better for supplemental earners than for those attempting to make full-time livelihoods (Schor et al. 2020). Across platforms, supplemental earners have safer conditions, greater job satisfaction, and often higher hourly wages than those who are dependent on their platform earnings to pay their basic expenses.

On questions of autonomy, control over schedules, and conditions of work, there is also mixed evidence. The opportunity to work without a boss and with control over one's own schedule and conditions of work has been a major attraction for many platform earners. For supplemental earners, those aspects of the experience are mostly realized and highly appreciated. On the other hand, dependent workers lose flexibility, and while they continue to appreciate the lack of a "boss," in the most predatory sectors (e.g., ride-hail and delivery), they are more subject to "algorithmic control" (Rosenblat and Stark 2016) and the discipline of the market (Schor et al. 2020). Dependent workers are more compelled to conform to demand-based schedules that maximize their earnings, and on the lower-wage platforms they must work very long hours. Thus, they lose a good deal of the flexibility of short and personalized hours. However, except among the most exploited dependent earners, autonomy remains a positive feature of platform work. There are additional downsides to dependent work such as a higher likelihood of accepting jobs that pose risk, either to personal safety or in terms of the financial payoff (Ladegaard, Ravenelle, and Schor 2022; Ravenelle 2019; Rosenblat 2018). We find that supplemental earners are more likely to disregard ratings and flout company rules in order to ensure their safety or do the work as they prefer. Dependent workers describe more desperation and precarity, even if they prefer platform work to other options.

Finally, on the question of governance and voice, we also find variation over time and across platforms. In the early years, and especially outside of ride-hail, many earners felt heard and part of a community. That has changed as platforms have attempted to grow and increase revenue. On larger platforms that provide little "customer service" for earners (such as Uber), workers have voiced strong frustration with the lack of support and the absence of voice. Indeed, some platforms have become notorious for failing to consider earners' situations and experiences. For example, a three-day strike by Instacart delivery workers in the fall of 2019 was quickly met by the company with a pay cut. While some platforms articulate a discourse of "partnership" with earners, there are almost no formal mechanisms in the sector for effective voice. This is central to what platform cooperatives can offer, as we discuss below.

Race and Class Inequality

The discourse of disruption associated with the emergence of the sector suggested that sharing platforms would undermine long-standing inequalities of race and class by providing open access with low barriers to entry. Economists Samuel Fraiberger and Arun Sundararajan (2017) argued that low-income households would benefit disproportionately from the opportunity to rent out assets. However, a growing body of research suggests that racial and class inequality is reproduced on platforms (Ticona and Mateescu 2018; van Doorn 2017). While there is some evidence of reduced barriers (e.g., there are more women ride-hail drivers than taxi operators), most studies find discriminatory behavior by race. We find that the platform sector is reproducing a hierarchy of outcomes based on skill and capital that parallels the legacy labor market. A study of TaskRabbit found that the algorithm is less likely to recommend Black Taskers (Hannák et al. 2017), perhaps because they receive lower ratings. Another study of TaskRabbit in Chicago found that low-income residents were disproportionately unlikely to be earning on the platform and that Blacks, and especially Black men, received lower ratings (Thebault-Spieker, Terveen, and Hecht 2015). In our analysis of outcomes on Airbnb across 10 US markets, we find that while residents of neighborhoods with more non-white households are more likely to list their properties, their outcomes are worse on nearly all dimensions than counterparts in areas with higher white populations. Hosts get lower prices for their listings, book less frequently, and receive lower ratings (Cansoy 2018; Cansoy and Schor 2019).

The platforms have also been characterized by "opportunity hoarding" with respect to education and employment status (Schor 2017). From the beginning they have attracted earners with high education levels. Because the kinds of activities done on sharing platforms (driving, cleaning, handyperson, errands) have traditionally been done by people without college educations, this represents a crowding-out effect by educational credential. While there has also been an expansion of demand for these services, in ridehail and lodging traditional taxi drivers and hotel cleaners seem to have lost out (Dubal 2017; Zervas, Proserpio, and Byers 2014). Hoarding by employment status occurs because of the prevalence of platform earners who hold other full-time jobs (Schor et al. 2020).

While the dystopian fears of some critics are likely overblown, the optimistic accounts of the early days are also inaccurate. The track record of platforms on issues of work and income suggests that while they have been vital for some participants to earn extra money, they are failing as a new source of full-time livelihood. The question of whether the downward trajectory experienced by ride-hail drivers will be replicated on other platforms is also still unanswered. It is also worth noting that platforms have taken advantage of their political clout both to evade existing regulations and restructure the regulatory environments in which they operate (Calo and Rosenblat 2017; Collier, Dubal, and Carter 2018; Rahman 2016; Stemler, Perry, and Haugh 2019; Thelen 2018). While the bulk of the regulatory change has benefited the platforms at the expense of legacy industries and worker protections, more recently that has been changing, with the institution of minimum wage guarantees (in the case of New York City ride-hail drivers), data-sharing requirements, and stricter enforcement of limitations on short-term rentals. However, while regulatory action is to be welcomed, it is unlikely to fundamental change the political economy of the sector. Large platforms will remain dominant and will mainly operate in their own interests. A deeper transformation of power will require new enterprise structures. In the early days of the sharing economy, there was considerable enthusiasm and hope that nonprofits were a dynamic form with a compelling economic model and the ability to scale rapidly. Let us turn now to those experiences.

Are Nonprofits the Alternative?

In each of the three subsegments of the "sharing economy," there are noncommercial entities engaged in similar activities to the commercial companies.[7] The nonprofits also promised many of the benefits that were expected to flow from platform technology: the expansion of P2P exchange, putting idle capacity to use, safe stranger exchange, and meeting needs the market was failing to address. While the activities of the nonprofit segment have not resulted in the negative externalities (e.g., congestion, rising rents) associated with a number of the for-profit companies, in the United States they have largely failed to scale and many have failed altogether.[8] Given that many of these sites used similar technology to their commercialized comparators, albeit in simpler, lower-cost versions, this divergence in trajectory needs explanation. In our research we have identified two factors to account for the slow development of this sector: a lack of instrumental value for users, and practices of social exclusion (Attwood-Charles and Schor 2019; Fitzmaurice and Schor 2018; Fitzmaurice et al. 2020; Schor et al. 2016).

All the nonprofit sites were founded to promote social benefits. These include reducing inequality and bridging social class (timebanks, surplus food redistribution, goods gifting), lower carbon and eco-footprints (used-goods loaning and exchange sites, repair efforts, most food-related efforts), and building community (nearly all). Yet many have failed or grown slowly despite their appealing missions.[9] Among our cases, the swap failed altogether (Fitzmaurice and Schor 2018), the timebank had limited trading volume (Dubois, Schor, and Carfagna 2014), and the makerspace was successful but highly socially and culturally exclusionary (Attwood-Charles 2017; Attwood-Charles and Schor 2019). In the first two cases, many participants joined because of ideological commitment to mission and values, but they were not motivated to make trades because they had no need for the goods and services on offer. Some timebank members treated it like a charity activity, accumulating hours for services they performed with no desire to spend them. Food-swap participants left events with their own offerings. The lack of instrumental value for users has also been found in case studies of other nonprofits. Bellotti and colleagues explained low trading volume in a California timebank by a mismatch between ideologically and instrumentally oriented participants (Bellotti et al. 2015, 2014). A study of a Finnish goods and service exchange site for university students found that while they appreciated the goals of the site it offered limited utility (Suhonen et al. 2010). A study of neighborhood initiatives in the UK designed to create innovative, nonmonetized markets had similar findings (Light and Miskelly 2015).[10] A US national survey of sharing practices found that fewer than one-third of respondents indicated they were interested in engaging in higher levels of sharing of tools and household items.[11] This is likely due in part to the low cost of durable goods in the US (Schor 2010, ch. 2) in comparison to the time and inconvenience of P2P trading.

In some cases, the structure of the market is responsible for low activity.

This was especially the case in the timebank. A key principle of timebanks is that every person's time is valued equally. While this is an ideologically appealing attraction that members frequently referenced as a motive for joining, in practice they are reluctant to price their own specialized skills at the wage level associated with generalized skills such as driving, child care, or household help. Furthermore, many members failed to offer the valuable skills they had (legal advice, coding) in preference to their amateur avocations. These practices reduced trading volume and the objective of bridging social class.

Socially exclusionary practices in these sites also contributed to the absence of instrumental value. One example is that critiques of capitalism, which were common, included a critical attitude toward money itself. Exchanges in gift, barter, or alternative currencies were sacralized, in contrast to the profanity of trades in legal tender.[12] Some members of the timebank we studied aimed to live in what one termed a "de-monied" state. At the makerspace we found that trades (for help) took place using both money and beer. The former was used for "profane" trades between high-status makers and ordinary participants; the latter was the "sacred" medium of choice among an exclusionary elite of highly-skilled makers (Attwood-Charles and Schor 2019). More generally, the critique of money is evidence of the class privilege of participants on these sites, as their comfortable lifestyles made this rejection possible (Bourdieu 1984). By conflating the medium of exchange with the social relations of exchange, many nonprofit sites failed to attract participants who had urgent needs for income, in contrast to the for-profit platforms that offered easy opportunities for earning.

We also found evidence of widespread practices of social exclusion across our sites, which were highly skewed by class and race. The sites were all racially segregated, with very few or zero African Americans and Latinx participants. There was also strong gender segregation across and, in the case of the makerspace, within the site. Education levels were not merely high but stratospheric. The most extreme case was the timebank where all respondents had a BA degree, more than half had a master's level degree, and more than half had at least one parent with a graduate degree. The high cultural capital of participants led to a variety of snobbish and distinguishing practices, such as the rejection of trading partners on account of bad grammar or unprofessional profiles, or in the food swap for failure to adhere to new foodie tastes (Carfagna et al. 2014; Johnston and Baumann 2007; Fitzmaurice and Schor 2018). At the makerspace, cultural capital took the form of extreme "distancing from necessity," with exotic, impractical, and idiosyncratic creations. Functional making and repair (valuable to income-constrained households) was largely invisible and clearly devalued (Attwood-Charles and Schor 2019).

While the relative lack of instrumental value has inhibited the growth of the nonprofits, they do have a strong asset that a number of the for-profit platforms have largely forfeited—credible claims to deliver multiple common good benefits. The desire for fair economic outcomes, sustainable ecological impact, and more social connection is widespread among the population, especially among younger generations. We found this was not only the case with respondents in our nonprofit sites, but participants on commercialized platforms expressed the hope that their activities would contribute to these goals (Fitzmaurice et al. 2020). Despite their "hostile worlds" (Zelizer 2000) view of the relation between the market and nonmarket society, they were optimistic that sharing platforms were capable of constructing an alternative, more humane, and sustainable market. This suggests the possibilities of hybrid models, which have genuine commitments to the common good outcomes but which also offer instrumental value to users. Potential examples include TimeRepublik, a for-profit online timebank with its own (time) currency that has been able to attract large numbers of users,[13] and the first decade-plus of Etsy, an online marketplace for handmade goods that operated as a B corporation with a small fee and a commitment to social benefit.[14] The lesson of these examples, however, is that in both instances, the need to meet investors' profit expectations led to a reorientation toward financial goals. That tension had led to a movement for a new digital form, the platform cooperative, which operates in the interest of its user-owners rather than investors.

Platform Cooperativism

The failures of the for-profit platforms to deliver good outcomes to workers on the three dimensions we identified above (compensation, autonomy, and voice), in combination with the lack of growth in the nonprofit sector, have resulted in the emergence of a movement for platform cooperatives. They are a subset of the larger class of worker cooperatives that date from the early nineteenth century in England. While this is still a new form, the innovations associated with platform technology may help to solve long-standing questions about cooperatives.

In the literature there are two broad classes of questions and research about the cooperative form—economic performance and democratic governance. Key economic questions are the cooperative's relative performance on productivity, employment, and wages in comparison to conventionally managed firms. There is now quite a bit of evidence to conclude that employee-owned and governed firms are economically sustainable and that they return more economic value to workers, reduce turnover, and motivate work effort (Blasi, Freeman, and Kruse 2017; Cheney et al. 2014; Pencavel 2013). While there may be differences between conventional and cooperative firms in terms of rates of innovation, how employment responds to reduced demand, and other economic outcomes, the cooperative form is clearly viable. The biggest economic challenge to the scaling of this model remains one that was identified decades ago: access to capital (Gintis 1989). If this problem were solved, it is likely that the cooperative sector could grow and prosper. Indeed, that seems to be occurring in many places in the world (Cheney et al. 2014). One challenge is what researchers have termed "degeneration," or the decline of worker ownership and devolution to a conventional setup in which owners hire workers (Cheney et al. 2014; Pencavel 2013). One explanation is the "iron law of oligarchy," in which an owner-elite comes to dominate.

A related set of questions involves the extent of democratic participation. There is less literature on this issue, although ensuring robust participation by workers and maintaining democratic control over elected management are ongoing challenges. One argument is that robust democracy is difficult when participatory firms are embedded in larger societies that have few democratic structures (Varman and Chakrabarti 2004). A second issue is a potential trade-off between democracy and efficiency, which has been noted in some cooperatives (Ng and Ng 2009). However, there is also evidence in the literature of "regeneration," when enterprises revitalize their governance mechanisms and practice (Cheney et al. 2014). How might platform cooperatives fare on these issues?

The platform cooperative is an online enterprise that is owned and governed by those who work on it (Scholz 2014, 2016a; Schneider 2018; Chase 2015).[15] This form harnesses the benefits of the technology with a structure that is oriented to fair treatment and self-determination for producers. If governance is robust, it can also create social ties and even solidarity. Platform cooperatives have the potential to overcome some of the weaknesses of both the for-profit and nonprofit forms as discussed earlier. With respect to the former, they deliver a larger fraction of the revenue to the workers and are more likely to institute rules and policies that a majority of workers consider fair and equitable. For example, algorithmic management is less problematic if workers help develop the algorithms and the software remains accountable to worker-owners. Democratic governance also allows members to reject clients or projects they are ethically opposed to, an issue that has become a particular flashpoint at tech companies (Fang 2019; Shaban 2018).

At the same time, if the cooperative is successful it can deliver valuable instrumental benefits to members.

In conventional economic theory, the ownership and governance of the platform should be largely irrelevant. Capital receives only the reward that it earns through its contribution to the value of the product. Labor earns the same. Optimal policies are generally assumed to be attributable primarily by the requirements of technology.[16] Of course, the conventional economic perspective is obviated in cases where markets are not perfectly competitive and capital can extract more than its marginal product, which is true of many segments of the sharing economy. Indeed, most advocates of platform cooperatives depart from the conventional economic wisdom and believe that the owners of capital typically have power that they exert over workers. If so, worker ownership should result in meaningful differences in outcomes. Of particular importance is the fact that algorithms and crowdsourced reputational information can take over management functions such as vetting and ensuring the quality and character of providers, and some of the value from these tasks can be retained by worker-owners. This is particularly important in care work, cleaning, and other personal services with high-risk potential so that agencies are able to capture a large fraction of the product. These occupations are ideal for the platform cooperative form (Schor 2014).

To date, there are relatively few platform cooperatives in operation, particularly in the US.[17] Large international examples include SMart, a freelancers co-op in Europe with 35,000 members,[18] and Fairmondo, a German retail cooperative selling ethical and sustainable products, which has 2000 members.[19] In the United States, there are small sharing economy cooperatives of taxi drivers and housecleaners currently operating, with health care cooperatives in formation.[20] The literature on platform cooperatives is small (Benkler 2016; Fedosov et al. 2019; Jackson and Kuehn 2016; Lampinen, Huotari, and Cheshire 2015; Schneider 2018; Scholz and Schneider 2016). Our team did what we believe to be the first case study of a platform cooperative—a stock photography company called Stocksy United (Sulakshana, Eddy, and Schor 2018). At 1000 members, it is the largest and most well-established North American producer-owned platform cooperative currently in operation. (In contrast to our other cases, it is not a "sharing economy" company because its customers are mainly businesses. One difference is that they do not use a public reputation system and there is no direct contact between the artists and the customers. However, at the time we were undertaking our research, there were no other viable options to study.)

Stocksy was founded by Bruce Livingstone and Brianna Wettlaufer, two owners of a stock photo platform that they sold to Getty, the industry leader.

The acquisition resulted in artists' dissatisfaction with pay and policies under the new regime. The former owners then decided to organize a new cooperative to foster creativity, provide higher returns to artists, and enable democratic governance. Founded in 2012, Stocksy is a multistakeholder[21] co-op in which the staff and a governing board[22] also hold shares. The biggest obstacle to establishing cooperatives, financing, was not relevant, as the founders offered a $1.3 million loan from the proceeds of the original sale. Stocksy also began with high levels of industry-specific knowledge and expertise and a proven track record. While it is impossible to know how much that mattered, it seems obvious that it did.

By most metrics, Stocksy has been extremely successful. It has robust revenues and was able to repay its loan and begin profit-sharing in its second year. It has carved out a lucrative market niche with a unique positioning in the industry—as a boutique shop with a distinctive aesthetic style. We found that members report high levels of satisfaction. The cooperative structure attracted highly talented and successful artists who ordinarily will not sell in the low-prestige stock portion of the industry. Members did not complain about exploitation or unfair treatment. Artists receive 50 percent of one-time sales, in comparison to the 15 percent industry standard, and 75 percent for extended licenses (versus 45 percent). Some take advantage of the community aspects of the site, getting support from the online forum and, in some cases, meeting up with other Stocksy members.

Stocksy differs from most platforms because membership is by application and has been subject to limits. It has been extremely competitive to join, with a 6 percent initial acceptance rate, which rose to 10 percent. Demand to participate is a good metric for how well the cooperative is serving its members' interests. Total membership was capped at 1000 and expansion has been controversial. However, management would like to grow, and after a few proposals to add artists were rejected by members, they found a compromise that is enabling modest annual growth, with accountability to membership. More generally, balancing provider supply and consumer demand is a key question for platform cooperatives. Capping membership may reduce the flexibility to choose hours and schedules, but it also allows the cooperative to maintain a good balance between supply and demand. By contrast, freelancer cooperatives such as SMart do not maintain membership limits.

In our research we found that members were mostly satisfied with governance. Communication occurs in an online forum, which is also the mechanism for taking decisions. Approximately 200 to 300 of the 1000 members participate. Members come from 65 countries (spanning many time zones) and speak different languages, therefore it is not possible to hold conventional real-time meetings and decisions must be made by nonsynchronous participation. It is our impression that nonparticipation does not stem from dissatisfaction, but either low overall involvement with the platform and a general satisfaction with decisions and operational practices.

The success of Stocksy is especially impressive in view of a dynamic that we find endemic to most platforms in the sharing space: diversity of participant orientations. As we found in our other case studies, there is variation in the extent to which earners rely on platforms for income, with the coexistence of supplemental and dependent earners. This range is found on the labor and capital platforms we studied and has been found on marketplaces such as Etsy (2013) and digital platforms Upwork and Amazon Mechanical Turk (Caraway 2010; Gray and Suri 2019; Popiel 2017). In Stocksy, the distinction manifests itself between professionals and what are called hobbyists (or more derogatorily by the former, "mom-tographers"). The high quality of smartphone cameras has allowed participation with low investment in equipment—an example of the low barriers to entry that characterize many sharing platforms. On Stocksy, a second axis of differentiation is between those with an artistic versus a commercial orientation, which does not overlap fully with the professional/hobbyist divide. In our research, we found some low-level tension among these groups.

Another issue, also common to the platforms noted above, is that Stocksy is a winner-take-all market. In 2016, 87 of the 1000 members earned 66.2 percent of the total royalties. Among those 87, the top nine contributors earned 26.5 percent.[23] Stocksy's perhaps uniquely extreme concentration is due to a number of factors. One is the presence of highly talented artists, who are attracted by the cooperative setup. The second is the diversity noted previously, and specifically the presence of a small number of highly commercially oriented producers who invest considerable sums on shoots (up to $20,000 for one shoot) and submit large portfolios alongside hobbyists who rarely submit. This "challenge of individual contribution" is especially an issue with online co-ops because conventional worker co-ops are more likely to make collaborative products. Online, individual contribution is the norm, members are competing against each other, and scarce skills can earn rents. Where the skill distribution is more equal, such as in driving, delivery, care, and homework, earnings distributions are more equal, driven more by hours worked than hourly remuneration. Those cooperatives may also set fixed rates or narrow hourly wage ranges. For Stocksy, the replicability of each photograph means a few very popular images can yield high earnings.

Stocksy is an instructive example for advocates of the platform cooperatives, however, it is also in many ways a best case. Its founders had deep experience in the industry and ample financing. It also carved out an upscale, profitable niche in a competitive market. Cheney and colleagues (2014) note that to be successful in global markets, cooperatives may now need to not merely respond to markets, but may have to create and lead them. Stocksy is a successful example of doing just this.

Furthermore, it did not face issues that are central for consumer-oriented service labor cooperatives (e.g., ride-hail, cleaning, and caring labor), such the "tyranny of the market," when consumers are not willing to pay living wages or there is a sharp trade-off between prices and demand. For a discussion of this kinds of dilemmas, see Sandoval (2019). Stocksy artists were generally insulated from these economic dilemmas.[24]

Envisioning a Pluralist Economy

It is too early to know whether cooperatives will become widespread. However, if they do, they may prove to be an important innovation in the platform ecosystem that can protect workers against exploitative employers and provide the opportunity for self-determination. The costs of the basic technology are in decline, and there are efforts underway to create open-source toolkits that will make establishing a platform cooperative relatively easy. For providers, platform cooperatives are likely better than monopolistic companies. However, they are not a panacea. Their ability to shape the larger labor market in which they operate is limited except in the case of substantial monopsonist power or cross-industry collaboration among cooperatives. However, that type of price setting is likely illegal. This suggests that platform cooperativism, even in its most successful incarnation, can only be one component of a system-wide restructuring that is capable of producing economic democracy and justice. Furthermore, platform cooperatives have little inherent advantage over for-profits on issues of ecological and carbon sustainability. To deliver those outcomes, this enterprise structure must be paired with a robust regulatory regime that internalizes key externalities and an expanding culture of solidarity and ecological responsibility.

In our view, platform cooperatives should be seen as one, albeit important, type of enterprise form in a hybrid or pluralist economy (Alperovitz 2011; Benkler 2006; see also Rodrik and Sabel's chapter in this book). Cooperatives, both offline and online, address working conditions and help to create democratic workplaces. But other forms of economic organization are also feasible and desirable. Municipally-owned platforms are a close cousin that may be well suited to certain kinds of services. More conventional options include small businesses and self-employment. Resources held in common by local and regional communities are another important form that has become increasingly popular. Some of these may function as not-for-profits. Land and housing trusts are another building block of a new hybridized economic ecosystem. The global community must also find a structure for managing the atmospheric commons sustainably. We do not yet know what that will be. What we do know is that there is now growing excitement and energy around various alternative forms of economic organization. If these forms expand, they hold the possibility for creating a more democratic and just economy.

Notes

This chapter was prepared for the workshop on Political Economy and Justice, Edmond J. Safra Center for Ethics, Harvard University, June 24–26, 2019. We would like to thank the members of our research team—William Attwood-Charles, Mehmet Cansoy, Luka Carfagna, Connor Fitzmaurice, Isak Ladegaard, and Robert Wengronowitz—for collaboration on the research discussed in this chapter. We are also indebted to colleagues in the MacArthur Research Network on Digital Media and Learning and members of the Political Economy and Justice Working Group, who provided very useful feedback and inspiration. Thanks are especially due to the organizers, Danielle Allen, Yochai Benkler, and Rebecca Henderson. Generous funding for this research was provided by the MacArthur Foundation.

1. Connected Consumption and Connected Economy (https://www.bc.edu/bc -web/schools/mcas/departments/sociology/connected.html).
2. For example, ride-hailing services require a car, used-goods exchange re-quires cleaning and shipping materials, and accommodation rentals require the labor of cleaning and hosting. However, the mix of capital and labor across these three segments varies considerably.
3. Another segment of the gig economy is online, digital labor contracted through platforms such as Amazon Mechanical Turk. This type of work is typically not included in the "sharing economy," although it is considered gig or platform work (Gray and Suri 2019; Irani 2015).
4. Statistic on Uber drivers at https://www.uber.com/newsroom/company -info/. For more information on Care.com, see "Company Overview," https:// www.care.com/company-overview.
5. The discourse associated with the sector also focused on two other types of claims: social and ecological. The social claim linked the P2P structure to the creation of ties among transactors and to a widely perceived sense of disconnection within society. The ecological claim argued that the develop-ment of used-goods markets and the more intensive use of "capacity" would reduce the demand for new goods, thereby lowering ecological and carbon footprints. The ecological claim is particularly dubious given that sharing

services reduced prices considerably and the two largest platforms are in transport and travel (Schor 2020).

6. This is a potential result in part because public reputation systems suffer from ratings bias and may not be very effective in excluding malfeasants (Cansoy 2018). It seems likely that the small number of problematic exchanges in the early days of the sector was less a function of a robust rating system than the absence of ill-intentioned actors on the sites. Over time, the largest platforms seem to have attracted more problematic actors.

7. In the used-goods sector, Freecycle, Yerdle, and other sites were organized using practices other than conventional cash trading (e.g., gift, platform-specific currency). The counterparts to monetized rental platforms are tool and toy libraries that have free loans. In space-sharing, examples include Couchsurfing, Landshare, and co-working offices. In the labor services segment, timebanks and child care co-ops are alternatives to TaskRabbit and similar sites.

8. Efforts to establish cooperative, commons, and collaborative initiatives seem to have been more successful in Europe, particularly in those areas with a long tradition of this type of activity (Bauwens and Onzia 2017; Morell 2018).

9. For example, the Repair Café movement (https://repaircafe.org/en/visit/), which is supported by a European Foundation and offers a replicable model, has only about 100 listed sites in the US in comparison to more than 1500 in Europe.

10. Another factor undermining instrumental value is that some of the new sharing entities attempted to create networks of reciprocity in areas where informal economies were already operating, but which were invisible because the innovators were not members of the relevant communities (Light and Miskelly 2015).

11. Survey results are available at "New American Dream Poll 2014," *New Dream*, https://newdream.org/resources/poll-2014.

12. Many participants and organizations held a "hostile worlds" (Zelizer 2000) view of the relationship between market and nonmarket activity. This antimonetary stance is also found in anarchist and left initiatives.

13. On TimeRepublik, see https://timerepublik.com/. In 2017 the company pivoted toward a B2B orientation: https://www.startupticker.ch/en/news/january-2017/the-leading-banking-group-in-italy-to-test-the-b2b-timerepublik-platform

14. David Gelles, "Inside the Revolution at Etsy," *New York Times*, November 25, 2017, https://www.nytimes.com/2017/11/25/business/etsy-josh-silverman.html.

15. Benkler's contributions (Benkler 2004, 2006) were formative.

16. Worker preferences can also play a role in policies such as working hours or worker autonomy. Standard theory suggests that if there are significant differences in preferences, workers will sort into firms that reflect those differences.

17.   Schneider (2018) maintains a list of platform cooperatives at his site entitled Internet of Ownership (http://ioo.coop/); a Google sheet is available at https://docs.google.com/spreadsheets/d/1RQTMhPJVVdmE7 YeopliwYhvj46kgvVJQnn1lEPGwzeY/edit#gid=674927682. See also the Platform Cooperativism Consortium: https://platform.coop/.

18.   See Smartcoop in Europe (https://smart.coop/). A hybrid cooperative that has its own currency is the Brazilian Fora do Eixo (http://foradoeixo.org .br/), which is a network of musicians, artists, producers, and venues with 200 collectives and 2000 employees.

19.   See Fairmondo (https://www.fairmondo.de/).

20.   Co-ops have already formed: see Up & Go (https://www.upandgo.coop/), Green Taxi Cooperative (http://greentaxico-op.com/), and Shift (https://www.shift.coop). NursesCan Cooperative is discussed in Nithin Coca, "Nurses Join Forces with Labor Union to Launch Health Care Platform Cooperative," *Truthout*, September 4, 2017, https://truthout.org/articles/nurses -join-forces-with-labor-union-to-launch-health-care-platform-cooperative/.

21.   Some cooperatives are structured so that multiple stakeholders have ownership and voting rights. See Chase (2015) for an argument for this form.

22.   The board also has the possibility of vetoing proposals that have passed the membership.

23.   Management not only gave us these numbers, they also permitted us to publicize them. The contrast with for-profit platforms is striking.

24.   They did face cultural tyrannies, in the form of customers' biases. Buyers hold a "neo-imperialist aesthetic," with preferences for pictures of affluent, white Westerners. Artists felt they needed to comply in order to be successful.

References

Acevedo, Deepa Das. 2016. "Regulating Employment Relationships in the Sharing Economy." *Employment Rights and Employment Policy Journal* 20:1–35.

Alperovitz, Gar. 2011. *America beyond Capitalism: Reclaiming Our Wealth, Our Liberty, and Our Democracy*. Boston: Democracy Collaborative Press/Dollars and Sense.

Aptekar, Sofya. 2016. "Gifts among Strangers: The Social Organization of Freecycle Giving." *Social Problems* 63, no. 2 (May): 266–83.

Attwood-Charles, William. 2017. "Work in Post-Bureaucratic Environments." Unpublished paper, Boston College.

Attwood-Charles, William, and Juliet B. Schor. 2019. "Distinction at Work: Status Practices in a Community Production Environment." Unpublished paper, Boston College.

Bauwens, Michael, and Yurek Onzia. 2017. "A Commons Transition Plan for the City of Ghent." *Commons Transition*, September 8.

Belk, Russell. 2007. "Why Not Share Rather than Own?" *The ANNALS of the American Academy of Political and Social Science* 611, no. 1 (May): 126–40.

Bellotti, Victoria, Alexander Ambard, Daniel Turner, Christina Gossmann, Kamila Demkova, and John M. Carroll. 2015. "A Muddle of Models of Motivation for Using Peer-to-Peer Economy Systems." In *Proceedings of the 33rd Annual ACM Conference on Human Factors in Computing Systems—CHI '15*, 1085–94. Seoul: ACM Press.

Bellotti, Victoria M. E., Sara Cambridge, Karen Hoy, Patrick C. Shih, Lisa Renery Handalian, Kyungsik Han, and John M. Carroll. 2014. "Towards Community-Centered Support for Peer-to-Peer Service Exchange: Rethinking the Time-banking Metaphor." In *Proceedings of the SIGCHI Conference on Human Factors in Computing Systems—CHI '14*, 2975–84. New York: ACM Press.

Benkler, Yochai. 2004. "Sharing Nicely: On Shareable Goods and the Emergence of Sharing as a Modality of Economic Production." *Yale Law Journal* 114, no. 2 (November): 273–358.

———. 2006. *The Wealth of Networks: How Social Production Transforms Markets and Freedom.* New Haven, CT: Yale University Press.

———. 2013. "Practical Anarchism Peer Mutualism, Market Power, and the Fallible State." *Politics & Society* 41:213–51.

———. 2016. "The Realism of Cooperativism." In *Ours to Hack and to Own: The Rise of Platform Cooperativism, a New Vision for the Future of Work and A Fairer Internet*, edited by T. Scholz and N. Schneider, 91–95. New York: OR Books.

Blasi, Joseph R., Richard B. Freeman, and Douglas L. Kruse. 2017. "Evidence: What the US Research Shows about Worker Ownership." In *Oxford University Press Handbook of Mutual, Co-Operative and Co-Owned Business*, edited by J. Michie, J. R. Blasi, and C. Borzaga, 211–26. Oxford: Oxford University Press.

Botsman, Rachel, and Roo Rogers. 2010. *What's Mine Is Yours: The Rise of Collaborative Consumption.* New York: Harper Business.

Bourdieu, Pierre. 1984. *Distinction: A Social Critique of the Judgement of Taste.* Cambridge, MA: Harvard University Press.

Calo, Ryan, and Alex Rosenblat. 2017. "The Taking Economy: Uber, Information, and Power." *Columbia Law Review* 117:1623–90.

Cansoy, Mehmet. 2018. "'Sharing' in Unequal Spaces: Short-Term Rentals and the Reproduction of Urban Inequalities." PhD diss., Boston College.

Cansoy, Mehmet, and Juliet B. Schor. 2019. "Who Gets to Share in the 'Sharing Economy': Understanding the Patterns of Participation and Exchange in Airbnb." Unpublished paper, Boston College.

Caraway, Brett. 2010. "Online Labour Markets: An Inquiry into oDesk Providers." *Work Organisation, Labour & Globalisation* 4, no. 2 (Autumn): 111–25.

Carfagna, L. B., E. A. Dubois, C. Fitzmaurice, M. Y. Ouimette, Juliet B. Schor, M. Willis, and T. Laidley. 2014. "An Emerging Eco-Habitus: The Reconfiguration of High Cultural Capital Practices among Ethical Consumers." *Journal of Consumer Culture* 14, no. 2 (July): 158–78.

Castillo, Juan Camilo, Dan Knoepfle, and E. Glen Weyl. 2018. "Surge Pricing Solves the Wild Goose Chase." https://papers.ssrn.com/sol3/papers.cfm?abstract_id= 2890666.

Chase, Robin. 2015. *Peers Inc: How People and Platforms Are Inventing the Collaborative Economy and Reinventing Capitalism*. New York: Headline/PublicAffairs.

Cheney, George, Iñaki Santa Cruz, Ana Maria Peredo, and Elías Nazareno. 2014. "Worker Cooperatives as an Organizational Alternative: Challenges, Achievements and Promise in Business Governance and Ownership." *Organization* 21, no. 5 (September): 591–603.

Collier, Ruth Berins, V. B. Dubal, and Christopher Carter. 2017. "Labor Platforms and Gig Work: The Failure to Regulate." Institute for Research on Labor and Employment (IRLE) Working Paper 106-17.

Collier, Ruth Berins, V. B. Dubal, and Christopher L. Carter. 2018. "Disrupting Regulation, Regulating Disruption: The Politics of Uber in the United States." *Perspectives on Politics* 16, no. 4 (December): 919–37.

Dubal, V. B. 2017. "The Drive to Precarity: A Political History of Work, Regulation, and Labor Advocacy in San Francisco's Taxi and Uber Economies." *Berkeley Journal of Employment and Labor Law* 38:73–135.

Dube, Arindrajit, Jeff Jacobs, Suresh Naidu, and Siddharth Suri. 2018. *Monopsony in Online Labor Markets*. NBER Working Paper 24416.

Dubois, Emilie, Juliet B. Schor, and Lindsey Carfagna. 2014. "New Cultures of Connection in a Boston Time Bank." In *Sustainable Lifestyles and the Quest for Plentitude: Case Studies of the New Economy*, edited by J. B. Schor and C. J. Thompson, 95–124. New Haven, CT: Yale University Press.

Einav, Liran, Chiara Farronato, and Jonathan Levin. 2016. "Peer-to-Peer Markets." *Annual Review of Economics* 8:615–35.

Etsy. 2013. *Redefining Entrepreneurship: Etsy Sellers' Economic Impact*. New York: Etsy.

Fang, Lee. 2019. "Google Hired Gig Economy Workers to Improve Artificial Intelligence in Controversial Drone-Targeting Project." *The Intercept*, February 4.

Farrell, Diana, and Fiona Greig. 2016. *Paychecks, Paydays, and the Online Platform Economy: Big Data on Income Volatility*. JPMorgan Chase & Co. Institute.

Farrell, Diana, Fiona Greig, and Amar Hamoudi. 2018. *The Online Platform Economy in 2018: Drivers, Workers, Sellers, and Lessors*. JPMorgan Chase & Co. Institute.

Fedosov, Anton, Airi Lampinen, Tawanna R. Dillahunt, Ann Light, and Coye Cheshire. 2019. "Cooperativism and Human-Computer Interaction." In *Extended Abstracts of the 2019 CHI Conference on Human Factors in Computing Systems—CHI '19*, 1–4. Glasgow: ACM Press.

Fitzmaurice, Connor, Isak Ladegaard, William Attwood-Charles, Mehmet Cansoy, Lindsey B. Carfagna, Juliet B. Schor, and Robert Wengronowitz. 2020 "Domesticating the Market: Moral Exchange and the Sharing Economy." *Socio-Economic Review* 18(1): 81–102.

Fitzmaurice, Connor, and Juliet B. Schor. 2018. "Homemade Matters: Logics of Exclusion in a Failed Food Swap." *Social Problems* 66:144–61.

Fraiberger, Samuel P., and Arun Sundararajan. 2017. "Peer-to-Peer Rental Markets in the Sharing Economy." NYU Stern School of Business Research Paper.

Frenken, Koen, and Juliet B. Schor. 2017. "Putting the Sharing Economy into Perspective." *Environmental Innovation and Societal Transitions* 23 (June): 3–10.

Gintis, Herbert. 1989. "Financial Markets and the Political Structure of the Enterprise." *Journal of Economic Behavior & Organization* 11, no. 3 (May): 311–22.

Gray, Mary L., and Siddharth Suri. 2019. *Ghost Work: How to Stop Silicon Valley from Building a New Global Underclass*. Boston: Houghton Mifflin.

Hannák, Anikó, Claudia Wagner, David Garcia, Alan Mislove, Markus Strohmaier, and Christo Wilson. 2017. "Bias in Online Freelance Marketplaces: Evidence from TaskRabbit and Fiverr." In *Proceedings of the 2017 ACM Conference on Computer Supported Cooperative Work and Social Computing—CSCW '17*, 1914–33. New York: ACM Press.

Hill, Steven. 2015. *Raw Deal: How the "Uber Economy" and Runaway Capitalism Are Screwing American Workers*. New York: St. Martin's Press.

Horan, Hubert. 2016. "Can Uber Ever Deliver? Part One." *Naked Capitalism*, November 30. https://www.nakedcapitalism.com/2016/11/can-uber-ever-deliver-part-one-understanding-ubers-bleak-operating-economics.html.

Horton, John J., and Richard J. Zeckhauser. 2016. "Owning, Using and Renting: Some Simple Economics of the 'Sharing Economy.'" NBER Working Paper 22029.

Irani, Lilly. 2015. "The Cultural Work of Microwork." *New Media & Society* 17:720–739.

Jackson, Sam K., and Kathleen M. Kuehn. 2016. "Open Source, Social Activism and 'Necessary Trade-Offs' in the Digital Enclosure: A Case Study of Platform Co-Operative, Loomio.Org." *TripleC: Communication, Capitalism & Critique. Open Access Journal for a Global Sustainable Information Society* 14, no. 2.

Johnston, Josée, and Shyon Baumann. 2007. "Democracy versus Distinction: A Study of Omnivorousness in Gourmet Food Writing." *American Journal of Sociology* 113, no. 1 (July): 165–204.

Kahn, Lina M. 2017. "Amazon's Antitrust Paradox." *Yale Law Journal* 126, no. 3 (January): 710–805.

Kenney, Martin, and John Zysman. 2016. "The Rise of the Platform Economy." *Issues in Science and Technology* 32, no. 3 (Spring): 61–69.

Ladegaard, Isak, Alexandrea Ravenelle, and Juliet B. Schor. 2022. "'God is Protecting Me . . . and I Have Mace': Defensive Labor in Precarious Workplaces." *British Journal of Criminology*, forthcoming.

Lampinen, Airi, Kai Huotari, and Coye Cheshire. 2015. "Challenges to Participation in the Sharing Economy: The Case of Local Online Peer-to-Peer Exchange in a Single Parents' Network." *Interaction Design and Architecture(s): Special Issue on Peer-to-Peer Exchange and the Sharing Economy* 24:16–32.

Light, Ann, and Clodagh Miskelly. 2015. "Sharing Economy vs. Sharing Cultures? Designing for Social, Economic and Environmental Good." *Interaction Design and Architecture(s): Special Issue on Peer-to-Peer Exchange and the Sharing Economy* 24:49–62.

Martin, Chris J., Paul Upham, and Leslie Budd. 2015. "Commercial Orientation in Grassroots Social Innovation: Insights from the Sharing Economy." *Ecological Economics* 118:240–51.

Morell, Mayo Fuster, ed. 2018. *Sharing Cities: A Worldwide Cities Overview on Platform*

Economy Policies with a Focus on Barcelona. Barcelona: Universitat Oberta de Catalunya.

Morozov, Evgeny. 2013. "The 'Sharing Economy' Undermines Workers' Rights." *Financial Times*, October 14.

Ng, Catherine W., and Evelyn Ng. 2009. "Balancing the Democracy Dilemmas: Experiences of Three Women Workers' Cooperatives in Hong Kong." *Economic and Industrial Democracy* 30, no. 2 (May): 182–206.

Ostrom, Elinor. 1990. *Governing the Commons: The Evolution of Institutions for Collective Action*. Cambridge: Cambridge University Press.

Parigi, Paolo, and Bogdan State. 2014. "Disenchanting the World: The Impact of Technology on Relationships." *Social Informatics* 8851:166–82.

Parigi, Paolo, Bogdan State, Diana Dakhlallah, Rense Corten, and Karen Cook. 2013. "A Community of Strangers: The Dis-Embedding of Social Ties." *PLoS ONE* 8, no. 7 (July): e67388.

Parrott, James A., and Michael Reich. 2018. *An Earnings Standard for New York City's App-Based Drivers*. New York: The New School, Center for New York City Affairs.

Pencavel, John. 2013. "Worker Cooperatives and Democratic Governance." In *Handbook of Economic Organization: Integrating Economic and Organization Theory*, edited by A. Grandori, 462–80. Cheltenham, UK: Edward Elgar.

Pew Research Center. 2016. *Gig Work, Online Selling and Home Sharing*.

Piore, Michael J., and Charles F. Sabel. 2000. *The Second Industrial Divide: Possibilities for Prosperity*. New York: Basic Books.

Popiel, Pawel. 2017. "'Boundaryless' in the Creative Economy: Assessing Freelancing on Upwork." *Critical Studies in Media Communication* 34, no. 3:1–14.

Rahman, K. Sabeel. 2016. "The Shape of Things to Come: The On-Demand Economy and the Normative Stakes of Regulating 21st-Century Capitalism." *European Journal of Risk Regulation* 7, no. 4 (January): 652–63.

Rahman, K. Sabeel, and Kathleen Thelen. 2019. "The Rise of the Platform Business Model and the Transformation of Twenty-First-Century Capitalism." *Politics & Society*: 177–204.

Ravenelle, Alexandrea J. 2019. *Hustle and Gig: Struggling and Surviving in the Sharing Economy*. Berkeley: University of California Press.

Robinson, H. C. 2017. "Making a Digital Working Class: Uber Drivers in Boston, 2016–2017." PhD diss., MIT.

Rochet, Jean-Charles, and Jean Tirole. 2003. "Platform Competition in Two-Sided Markets." *Journal of the European Economic Association* 1, no. 4 (June): 990–1029.

Rosenblat, Alex. 2018. *Uberland: How Algorithms Are Re-Writing the Rules of Work*. Berkeley: University of California Press.

Rosenblat, Alex, and Luke Stark. 2016. "Algorithmic Labor and Information Asymmetries: A Case Study of Uber's Drivers." *International Journal of Communication* 10:3758–84.

Sandoval, Marisol. 2019. "Entrepreneurial Activism? Platform Cooperativism between Subversion and Co-Optation." *Critical Sociology* 46:801–17.

Schneider, Nathan. 2018. An Internet of Ownership: Democratic Design for the On-line Economy." *Sociological Review* 66:320–40.

Scholz, Trebor. 2014. "Platform Cooperativism vs. the Sharing Economy." *Medium,* December 5. https://medium.com/@trebors/platform-cooperativism-vs-the -sharing-economy-2ea737f1b5ad.

———. 2016a. *Platform Cooperativism: Challenging the Corporate Sharing Economy.* New York: Rosa Luxemburg Stiftung.

———. 2016b. *Uberworked and Underpaid: How Workers Are Disrupting the Digital Economy.* Cambridge: Polity Press.

Scholz, Trebor, and Nathan Schneider, eds. 2016. *Ours to Hack and to Own: The Rise of Platform Cooperativism, a New Vision for the Future of Work and a Fairer Internet.* New York: OR Books.

Schor, Juliet B. 2010. *Plenitude: The New Economics of True Wealth.* New York: Penguin Press.

———. 2014. "Debating the Sharing Economy." *Great Transition Initiative,* October.

———. 2017. "Does the Sharing Economy Increase Inequality within the Eighty Percent?: Findings from a Qualitative Study of Platform Providers." *Cambridge Journal of Regions, Economy and Society* 10:263–79.

———. 2020. *After the Gig: How the Sharing Economy Got Hijacked and How to Win It Back.* Berkeley: University of California Press.

Schor, Juliet B., and William Attwood-Charles. 2017. "The Sharing Economy: Labor, Inequality and Sociability on for-Profit Platforms." *Sociology Compass* 11:1–16.

Schor, Juliet B., William Attwood-Charles, Mehmet Cansoy, Isak Ladegaard, and Robert Wengronowitz. 2020. "Dependence and Precarity in the Platform Economy." *Theory and Society* 49:833–61.

Schor, Juliet B., and Connor J. Fitzmaurice. 2015. "Collaborating and Connecting: The Emergence of the Sharing Economy." In *Handbook of Research on Sustainable Consumption,* edited by L. A. Reisch and J. Thogersen, 410–25. Cheltenham, UK: Edward Elgar.

Schor, Juliet B., Connor Fitzmaurice, William Attwood-Charles, Lindsey B. Carfagna, and Emilie Dubois Poteat. 2016. "Paradoxes of Openness and Distinction in the Sharing Economy." *Poetics* 54:66–81.

Shaban, Hamza. 2018. "Amazon Employees Demand Company Cut Ties with ICE." *Washington Post,* June 22.

Slee, Tom. 2015. *What's Yours Is Mine: Against the Sharing Economy.* New York: OR Books.

Söderqvist, Fredrik. 2017. "A Nordic Approach to Regulating Intermediary Online Labour Platforms." *Transfer: European Review of Labour and Research* 23:349–52.

Stein, Joel. 2015. "Baby, You Can Drive My Car, and Do My Errands, and Rent My Stuff . . . ," *Time,* January 29.

Stemler, Abbey, Joshua E. Perry, and Todd Haugh. 2019. "The Code of the Platform." *Georgia Law Review* 54, no. 2 (March 2020):1–55.

Streitfeld, David. 2019. "He Has Driven for Uber since 2012. He Makes about $40,000 a Year." *New York Times*, April 12.

Suhonen, Emmi, Airi Lampinen, Coye Cheshire, and Judd Antin. 2010. "Everyday Favors: A Case Study of a Local Online Gift Exchange System." In *Proceedings of the 16th ACM International Conference on Supporting Group Work*, 11–20. New York: ACM Press.

Sulakshana, Elana, Samantha Eddy, and Juliet B. Schor. 2018. "Democratic Governance in the Sharing Economy: A Case Study of a Platform Cooperative, Stocksy United." Unpublished paper, Boston College.

Sundararajan, Arun. 2016. *The Sharing Economy: The End of Employment and the Rise of Crowd-Based Capitalism*. Cambridge, MA: MIT Press.

Thebault-Spieker, Jacob, Loren G. Terveen, and Brent Hecht. 2015. "Avoiding the South Side and the Suburbs: The Geography of Mobile Crowdsourcing Markets." In *Proceedings of the 18th ACM Conference on Computer Supported Cooperative Work and Social Computing— CSCW '15*, 265–75. New York: ACM Press.

Thelen, Kathleen. 2018. "Regulating Uber: The Politics of the Platform Economy in Europe and the United States." *Perspectives on Politics* 16, no. 4 (November): 938–53.

Ticona, Julia, and Alexandra Mateescu. 2018. "Trusted Strangers: Carework Platforms' Cultural Entrepreneurship in the On-Demand Economy." *New Media & Society* 20, no. 11 (November): 4384–404.

Ticona, Julia, Alexandra Mateescu, and Alex Rosenblat. 2018. "Beyond Disruption: How Tech Shapes Labor across Domestic Work and Ride-Hailing." *Data & Society*, June 27.

UCLA Institute for Research on Labor and Employment. 2018. *More than a Gig: A Survey of Ridehailing Drivers in Los Angeles*. Los Angeles: UCLA.

Vallas, Stephen P. 2019. "Platform Capitalism: What's at Stake for Workers?" *New Labor Forum* 28, no. 1 (January): 48–59.

Van Doorn, Niels. 2017. "Platform Labor: On the Gendered and Racialized Exploitation of Low-Income Service Work in the 'On-Demand' Economy." *Information, Communication & Society* 20:898–914.

Varman, Rahul, and Manali Chakrabarti. 2004. "Contradictions of Democracy in a Workers' Cooperative." *Organization Studies* 25, no. 2 (February):183–208.

Zelizer, Viviana A. 2000. "The Purchase of Intimacy." *Law & Social Inquiry* 25, no. 3 (Summer): 817–48.

Zervas, Georgios, Davide Proserpio, and John Byers. 2014. "The Rise of the Sharing Economy: Estimating the Impact of Airbnb on the Hotel Industry." Boston University School of Management Research Paper No. 2013-16. https://papers .ssrn.com/sol3/papers.cfm?abstract_id=2366898#.

Part 3

THE ROLE OF DEMOCRATIC ASSOCIATIONS,
INSTITUTIONS, AND GOVERNANCE
IN A JUST ECONOMY

11 *New Rules for Revolutionaries: Reflections on the Democratic Theory of Economic System Change*

MARC STEARS

In January 2016, I took over the running of a large, left-leaning British think tank, the New Economics Foundation (NEF). On the first day, I gathered the staff together, around 50 mainly twentysomethings, to find out what it was they wanted to achieve in the time that we were working together. "It is simple: we're going to change the whole economic system," one of them announced. The others nodded vigorously. It was not what I had been expecting. I had just emerged from a bruising general election campaign working for the British Labour Party, which we had lost to the incumbent Conservatives. The orthodoxy among political scientists and commentators was that our defeat was due to a platform of mild tax increases, corporate governance reform, and increased public spending in key services, all of which had been too radical for "middle England." [1] In other words, one moment I was being told the only route for a progressive to return to power was not to rock the boat and the next I was confronted, loud and proud, with the demand to go far further still. To a jaded political operative, it did not make much sense. [2]

I rationalized it all at the time as the enthusiasm of youth, and I thought that it would die away fast enough. But now, six years later, the explicit, if still ambiguous, demand for a "new economic system" has gone global. From campuses to Capitol Hill, it is a commonplace to hear that we live in the end times for neoliberalism, possibly even capitalism itself. For the first time in generations, political candidates have designed bold and potentially transformative programs, from the Green New Deal of the USA's Justice Democrats to the on-the-ground transformations in cities like Barcelona. [3] Within broader public debate, too, the shift is unmistakable. Where there were thin pickings only years ago, there are now airport best sellers on the end of capitalism and a host of new journals and websites committed to "new economy" thinking and action, including *Jacobin* and *Tribune*. [4] Even within the mainstream press, perspectives almost entirely unheard for a generation now enjoy regular columns in established newspapers.[5]

The demand for system change reaches into the most surprising of places. Much of the World Economic Forum's debate at Davos in 2019 centered on the question of whether the current economic order was being up-ended, either by a technological fourth industrial revolution or by new political forces.[6] And similar debates are almost ever-present across the globe, wherever business school experts gather or corporations hold their strategic retreats. Some even offer eager support. A few years ago, a handful of multimillion-dollar philanthropic foundations teamed together to create Partners for a New Economy, "an international donor collaborative" that funds researchers and campaigners committed to shaping "a new economy," one "that enables communities, people and nature to thrive."[7]

For all of us committed to justice in political economy, there is much that is exciting in this new trend. Climate emergency, rampant economic inequality, and the rise of far-right populist politics each demand an urgent and far-reaching response—a response that conventional social democracy has signally failed to provide. Seen this way, we are witnessing the creation of a vital force capable of generating the energy that our moment demands. This is in part political—with the arrival of new candidates and movements reinventing old parties and upturning old ones, reinvigorating the democratic process across the world (with the notable exception of Australia, from where I am writing)—and in part intellectual, with a refashioning occurring in departments of economics and political economy around the world, which could surely not have come soon enough.

And yet the doubts that I had on that January day in 2016 at NEF stubbornly refuse to die away. With Donald Trump in the White House and the reactionary right rampant across Europe, is this really the time to turn our intellectual and campaigning attention to the crafting of a wholly new economic system? What would doing so really mean? Is it even possible? More worryingly, we know that in the past the combined language of "system change" and "emergency" has led to an unbearable harshness in politics, an unwillingness to build consensus or to consider compromise, which in turn can lead either to political failure, as coalitions fracture and purism leads to the splintering of movements or, far worse, to repression. Could any of that be the case this time? What does the practical, democratic politics of economic system change really look like?

In public commentary, this sort of debate swirls almost exclusively around the sharply pragmatic question of electoral politics. Will more radical candidates, those committed to upending the system, perform better than more moderate candidates? Or, in other words, is system-change politics the new route to power or, to use Bret Stephens's phrase, a "recipe for nonstop political defeat leavened only by a sensation of moral superiority"?[8] This all too often collapses into the debate between backing one candidate for president over another—we have seen Bernie Sanders *versus* Joe Biden, Elizabeth Warren *versus* Pete Buttigieg—or takes the form of one of those aggressive Twitter spats about the electoral merits of particular policy proposals that such candidates make (e.g., Medicare for all *versus* Medicare for those who want it).

Important though these electoral elements are, they do not provide my focus here. Instead, I want to take one step back and examine the issue at a more fundamental level. What follows is, to paraphrase T. S. Eliot, a prolegomena to political recommendation rather than a political recommendation in itself.[9] In what is to come, therefore, I ask: If we are going to try to shape what I will call *a democratic politics of economic system change*, what should its essential parameters be? What kind of constraints should structure its campaigning style? How should its activists consider themselves and how should they think about their relationships to their opponents? From what democratic traditions should they draw? What moral mistakes are they most likely to make and how can they best avoid them?

I do not expect to answer all of those issues fully here, of course; in fact, I just want to make one major argument. But it is important to acknowledge too that as the movement is growing so fast, the large array of questions possess an urgency of their own. If we do not reflect openly and critically on the democratic politics of changing the economic system and reach some even tentative conclusions soon, then events will take their own course. And that is not a recipe for a desirable democratic outcome.

Essential Parameters of Democratic System Change

The emergent system-change movement has three parts, which I will call the *intellectual*, the *practical*, and the *political*. Some individuals and groups participate in all three, some in two, and others only in one. The movement discussed here is a loose one, and I do not expect that everyone categorized as belonging to it (or not) will be immediately satisfied with their assigned role. Nonetheless, the family resemblances between the different sections are strong and some fairly distinct patterns do emerge.

First, there is the intellectual labor, which chiefly involves economic analysis. This work is broad and largely, but not entirely, takes place within the academy. It involves, at the very least, the questioning of fundamental neoclassical and neoliberal economic assumptions; the refashioning of economic analysis so as to include a greater reference to empirical phenomenon; the development of new macroeconomic models; and at least the initial stages of policy design. Participants range from those who are open about their ambitions to playing a part in the shaping of large-scale change—including the Next System Project, the heterodox economists' group Rethinking Economics, and the Institute for Innovation and Public Purpose in London—to those who are more open-ended in their stated ambitions but whose work nonetheless has a potentially enormously powerful and disruptive effect on orthodoxies within the discipline—including the pathbreaking CORE program for reshaping economics curricula around the world.[10]

Second, there is the establishment of practical pilot projects designed to establish and to test ideas for "the new system." Such projects have been an element of movements for system-wide economic change since at least the nineteenth century, with Robert Owen's ill-fated cooperative communities in the United States, Britain, and Australia continuing to provide an inspiration to contemporaries. Current examples are, of course, significantly less ambitious than Owen's, but there is nonetheless a vast array of pilots, and they are gathering momentum internationally. The most notable examples include initiatives to establish "community wealth-building" in large cities through the development of public banks, land trusts and cooperatives; to utilize the procurement powers of local councils to reward enterprises that pay living wages, promote environmental sustainability, or endorse other "new economy" principles; to facilitate unionization in industries with traditionally low union density, such as among the self-employed and "gig" economy workers; to develop local currencies in a host of cities; and to create "transition towns" that help move particular geographical districts to negative net carbon emissions.[11] Some superb examples along these lines feature in the chapters in this book by Yochai Benkler, Dani Rodrik and Charles Sabel, and Glen Weyl.

The third part is the one that most concerns me here. It is the political, campaigning element of the demand for system change. Emerging out of the ashes of the Occupy Wall Street movement, this has taken the mainstream political world almost wholly off guard over the course of the past decade. The approach is best captured in prose in Becky Bond and Zack Exley's *Rules for Revolutionaries: How Big Organizing Can Change Everything* (where the title pretty much gives the whole argument away) and in Chantal Mouffe's *For a Left Populism*.[12] But its practical reach is far more impressive than either of these books allow. It gained huge energy from Bernie Sanders's primary campaign against Hillary Clinton in the USA; the anti-austerity campaign in the United Kingdom, which led in turn to the election of Jeremy Corbyn as leader of the Labour Party; the creation of Podemos party in Spain and Syriza in Greece; and the municipalist movements that gained power in Barcelona.

The centrality of this brand of political campaigning to the overall system-change movement should not be underestimated. Within the international philanthropic community, for example, funding for training and development in "system-change campaigning and organizing" is at least as great a concern as support for academic research and pilot projects. When I was running NEF, the largest injection of cash we received was for close to $1.5 million from the Swiss-based Oak Foundation for a project on European "movement building for a new economy," which in turn helped underpin Britain's New Economy Organizers Network (NEON), a powerful political force behind the rise of Jeremy Corbyn.[13] In fact, it is hard even for university researchers in this context to be awarded financial support without a commitment to also training advocates and leading campaigns.

The campaigning approaches advanced by these international system-change groups have many features in common, but two are of particular importance here. First, they are committed to "going big" and "going fast." "You won't get a revolution if you don't ask for one," Bond and Exley explain.[14] Instead of a focus on individual policy asks or particular injustices, therefore, Bond and Exley argue that public rhetoric should proceed straight to the large-scale and make immediate, urgent demands for systemic transformation. "People are waiting for you to ask them to do something big," they explain. "Movements require clear demands for solutions as radical as our problems." In order to "unleash the makings of a real political revolution," you have to "ask for one," they write, outlining "the radical solutions our moments call for, not the tepid incrementalist compromises that most politicians think are all that is feasible."[15] It is crucial, the case continues, to emphasize the "life-or-death stakes of the most urgent issues of the day, from income inequality to immigration reform to climate change."[16]

One consequence of this commitment is that system-change groups not only reject the standard social democratic policymaking of established political parties. They have no time either for the slow, community-oriented approach to political organizing associated with Saul Alinsky and the Industrial Areas Foundation (IAF). The IAF's approach has, after all, long been skeptical of big, programmatic, and ideologically derived demands and has insisted that, because it takes time to build the trust required for sustained political work, relationship building should precede the taking of action. Within the system-change groups, this style of organizing is dismissed as "folk politics," incapable of responding to the scale of the challenge our societies currently face.[17] Sometimes indeed, the charge goes further. Seeking to

provoke as always, Bond and Exley describe advocates of Alinsky-style organizing as "counterrevolutionaries" whose work can suck the energy, passion,
and confidence out of a necessarily bold political moment. "Take note of the
counterrevolutionaries when they reveal themselves. They're definitely not
allies, and sometimes they even become enemies." [18]

The second characteristic of these political movements emerges out of
the first. They possess a far greater willingness than is conventional in recent
progressive movements to call out an explicit "enemy." The system-change
groups described here are wholly uninfluenced by the deliberative approach
to politics that was dominant on the left only a decade ago. Not for them,
the anxiety about making arguments that are grounded in public reason or
for which they might expect broad support that crosses the boundaries of
different sections of society with their own comprehensive conceptions of
the good. [19] They are equally unpersuaded by pragmatic arguments that recommend building alliances with established power groupings, believing that
such efforts are always bound to lead to a watering down of fundamental
goals and also to wither away support, especially among the young. Instead,
there is a repeated desire to build tension, sharpen cleavages, and mobilize
support through an intensification of hostilities. Occupy Wall Street, of
course, began this process with its willingness to name the "one percent"
as the enemy of the people, but the tendency now goes much deeper and
further, with clear enemies being regularly identified within even previously
progressive alliances.

In practical terms, this commitment to heightening tension through the
invocation of clear sides in political debate manifests in multiple ways. At
the most straightforward, it leads to the kind of slogan-writing that is characteristic of the British Labour Party under Jeremy Corbyn: "for the many *not*
the few," replacing the far more timid "for the many, not *just* the few," that
was occasionally deployed by his predecessor Ed Miliband. But more important, it encourages activists to take dramatic stands against social groups and
institutions often previously seen as allies, neutral bystanders, or as simple
annoyances rather than enemies. The repertoire of system-change political
movements now commonly includes rhetorical and campaigning attacks on
the "mainstream media," including public broadcasters like the BBC; on cultural institutions like national museums that have collections derived from
historic colonial adventures; established universities that accept corporate
donations from the fossil fuel industry; and on the established NGO sector,
which is often dismissed as being intent on ameliorating social injustice
rather than being interested in challenging underpinning structural forms.

The training provided by groups such as NEON and funded by Partners for a New Economy focuses on just such elements, as does the Sunrise Fellowship, offered by the Sunrise Movement, the driving force behind the USA's Green New Deal. As with all forms of organizing, the most important element of the action is often said to be "in the reaction." A high-profile case in an unexpected domain can both capture attention and sharply divide conventional opinion, drawing enemies to the surface and revealing once hidden friends. The intense public argument that the initial intervention provokes leads people to be more willing than previously to rally to the broader cause or at least to take sides. That way, the movement grows, and the end of economic system change—apparently—comes closer into view. By redefining the terms of political debate and shifting the boundary between the permissible and the impermissible, this tactic is often combined with the demand for radical policy solutions, especially those previously thought impossible because of entrenched opposition. This is said to broaden the range of potential political outcomes, a process system-change activists call "moving the Overton window." [20]

In political theory terminology, the overall approach combines elements of political realism, agonism, and populism. As Chantal Mouffe has said, the emerging system-change movement "sees the public sphere as the battlefield on which hegemonic projects confront one another with no possibility of a final reconciliation" and that determines the ways in which they work.[21] It is acutely conscious of the dominant role of power hierarchies in shaping political outcomes, enthusiastic about the place of the emotions and the passions in political argument, and determined to draw energy from dividing lines between those who are "in" and those who are "out."

Constraints on Campaigning Style

Whenever the question of system-change politics comes into view, my mind goes to George Orwell. No one captures my own paradoxical reaction to the movement as well as Orwell. For all of his adult life, Orwell was committed to the end of capitalism. It was, he argued, an economic order that had entirely failed. It was responsible for trashing millions of lives, despoiling the environment, and provoking military conflicts on an unprecedented scale. At the same time, however, he was entirely unconvinced that anyone had yet found a desirable way in which politically to campaign against it. The revolutionary politics of the 1930s and 1940s terrified him. Serving in the Spanish Civil War, he had seen the grand ambitions of communists used to justify horrific acts of political violence. But even before that he found the tendency of radical activists to discuss complex, concrete political issues in grand, vague abstractions deeply off-putting. Such language obscured more than it enlightened, he insisted, and almost always resulted in empowering elites who were able to give their own very practical meanings to the generalized aspirations that they shared with others. He was also unpersuaded by the materialist foundations of Marxist and quasi-Marxist thinking and by their unwillingness to acknowledge that the future is, in many profound ways, essentially unknowable. He was, as such, probably the only serious anti-capitalist to write a positive review of F. A. Hayek's, *The Road to Serfdom* on its release.[22]

These concerns are well recognized in the voluminous academic literature on Orwell. But the very heart of Orwell's objection to anti-capitalist politics is actually far more often overlooked. That was the belief, first fully advanced in his novel *Coming Up for Air* but from then on ever-present in his work, that there is something in the everyday life of ordinary people that contains the source of great hope yet is wholly missed by both conventional capitalist and revolutionary anti-capitalist politics.[23] Even within capitalism, Orwell insisted, ordinary lives contain a fulfilling richness and a texture that matter enormously to the people living them, including a sense of belonging to place, a feeling of community, a dedication to preserving the best of memory and past. Capitalism always threatens to erode these features with the pressures it places on ordinary life or to destroy them by seeking to commodify them.[24] But it has never managed to extinguish them. These aspects of life are small, not grand. They grow in parochial spaces and the familial. They are best described with texture and detail, not in the booming or the abstract. For Orwell, politics—whether of the left or the right—is destructive and dangerous when it does not realize all of this. It can be inspiring and fulfilling when it does. Both extreme market-fundamentalism *and* revolutionary, anti-capitalist mobilization, with its obsession with changing the system come-what-may, have a tendency to be unaware of these features of life, often even dismissing them as the products of false consciousness. But without these elements, life is not worth living.[25]

This fundamental idea has recently begun to surface once again in response to our current political malaise. One of the most striking of these examples is the work of the British psychotherapist Adam Phillips. Phillips draws attention to what he calls the fundamental difference between "forbidden" and "unforbidden" pleasures in the human *psyche*.[26] Although the terminology might be unusual, Phillips's description of it is profoundly helpful one. The forbidden pleasures, he says, are those that get all of the attention in public life. These are the boundary issues: the "what is permitted" and the "what is not permitted." In the market, these issues reflect the major decisions of global corporations. In politics, they include issues like sovereignty and nationhood, the constitutional rules governing decision-making, and questions of economic control, social justice, and the place of state and market in our lives. It is precisely the realm, in other words, of what Bond and Exley call "bigness." Thinking about and acting on commitments surrounding these concerns emotionally provides a sense of importance and consequence, the feeling of dedicating one's life to a mighty cause, like creating a better or fairer or greater world or preventing some grave evil. Rationally, it speaks to people's cognitive desire to create a blueprint for the future.

In contrast, what Phillips calls the "unforbidden pleasures" involve the bulk of what goes on in the everyday. Unforbidden pleasures are found in events like preparing and eating a regular family meal, meeting the kids at the school gate, having a chat with someone on the bus, walking in the park, checking in on an elderly friend or relative after work, going to the shops, planning a weekend away with friends. These pleasures matter to everyone enormously. They are the content of most of our lives and most of us are pleased that they are. When we look through our memories, whether captured in photos, letters, diaries, or just at the backs of our minds, it is usually these unforbidden moments that loom the largest for all of us. They are the cause of the most intense enjoyment and sense of satisfaction. They reflect the connections and experiences that give meaning to our lives.[27] Even when we remember the "big events" of our lifetimes—the shooting of JFK, the fall of the Berlin Wall, or for a Brit, the 2012 Olympics—we do so through the prism of our own everyday experiences. That is why the saying goes, "I remember where I was when. . . ."

There are times when individual elements within the forbidden and the unforbidden switch. When governments attempt to prohibit everyday acts that have previously been taken for granted, then the unforbidden can become the forbidden. This was the cause of Orwell's deepest terror in *Nineteen Eighty-Four*. What would society be like, he asked, if basic, unremarkable, entirely everyday pleasures, like beginning a romance, telling stories to your children, buying a present for a friend, were suddenly prohibited by the government, with your every effort to engage in them monitored and repressed? How intensely would we suffer? How could we plausibly resist? Likewise, there are also occasionally moments when the reverse occurs, when previously deeply controversial practices cease to be controversial and forbidden pleasures becomes unforbidden one. Changing attitudes and legislative practices about gay and lesbian relationships in many places across the world right now are an example of a once strictly forbidden pleasure now entering the realm of the unforbidden.

Even if the precise content of the categories can change over time, though,

Phillips insists that the distinction itself remains crucial. And that is because when it comes to politics, almost all of the energy and time tends to
be sucked up in concern with the forbidden—the big—and overlooks the
unforbidden—the small. But this is not without consequences. When human beings spend their time thinking about the forbidden—what should
and should not be permitted in society—they can become harsher, more determined, more narrow-minded people, more likely to see the world in "us"
and "them" than when their attention is on the unforbidden. Phillips does
not think the forbidden unimportant (turning one's attention there may be
required from time to time), but it comes at a high psychological cost.

Moreover, if the focus on the forbidden can result in an increase in hostility and conflict, it also has a tendency to draw attention like a magnet, de-
priving people of the emotional and cognitive space to attend to other, more
mundane, elements of their lives. "When it comes to the forbidden," Phillips
writes, "we are not supposed to let our minds wander; we are supposed to be
utterly gripped, and in the grip of the law."[28] The result is both that people's
lives are impoverished—they are drawn away from everyday fulfillments that
are just there waiting to be achieved—and, paradoxically, that they are not
even able to function effectively in the realm of the forbidden, emotionally
exhausted as they are from the constant pressure to be "on top" of what con-
fronts them with no sustaining internal resource on which to draw.

Phillips, then, longs for an alternative. He wants people to find far greater
space in their lives, including in their political lives, for the unforbidden pleasures. He wants us to step back from the immediacy and urgency of the big
arguments and to take time to revel in and experiment with the small and
otherwise unremarkable aspects of our life. "Promoting unforbidden pleasures means finding new kinds of heroes and heroines or dispensing with
them altogether," he says, and it "privileges the more ordinary at the cost of
whatever we take to be the alternatives to the ordinary." [29] For Phillips, this
begins with the power of everyday relationships. We should "start with the
simple acknowledgment that it is extraordinary how much pleasure we can
get from each other's company, most of which is unforbidden," he says.[30]

The idea of the unforbidden can also prompt system-change activists to
look again at their own place in the shaping of a new order. Those who think
mostly on the forbidden, rather than the unforbidden, often do so because
they believe those are the things that really matter—they are the factors that
will determine the lives we can all live in the future. At least occasionally,
dwelling in the ordinary and the everyday, the small rather than the big, can
deprive us of a sense that we can be a personal agent of great change. Some
of us, especially those of us drawn to system-change politics, can find that an

enormous psychological challenge. How can we give up the sense that we are personally responsible—at least in part—for the creation of a better future? The answer lies in an ability to extend what we are able to do, think, and feel in the present as opposed to in the future. Seeing the world through the lens of the unforbidden places the present far closer to the center of our concern. As the American sociologist Andrew Abbott puts it, seen this way the challenge for our lives ceases primarily to be how each of us can play a part in improving an imaginary future state and instead becomes how we can learn to avail ourselves of every means necessary to extend our experience in the here and now and in the repeated nows to come.[31]

This is not best understood in a narrowly selfish or individualistic way. Instead, it is a call on us to develop an ability to enrich both our experience and the experience of others in the here and now. Andrew Abbott believes that we best do that by cultivating a tenderness and curiosity that can expand our sense of the world and people around us. If, he explains, we cultivate "the habit of looking for new meanings, of seeking out new connections, of investing experience with complexity or extension," then we can make that experience feel both "richer and longer, even though it remains anchored in some local bit of both social space and social time."[32]

What it does mean, however, is letting go of the hubristic idea that our personal role in developing our most desired future outcome *determines* the likelihood of that outcome and thus our future pleasures and the pleasures of others. Such a view overstates our own personal importance, the likelihood of our success, and the chance that even if we got where we wanted it would prove as worthwhile as we think. Moreover, by using the very idea of a singular point-in-time "outcome," it presumes that there is some moment in the future more important than the present when everything will somehow stop. But that is clearly false. Even the future will be the present once we actually arrive at it. There are no outcomes in human lives beyond death. Our task, then, at least in part, must be to know how to experience something meaningful and worthwhile now and in that "future present," for ourselves and for those around us.

From a Focus on the Ordinary to Big Change

On the surface, this talk of the unforbidden can look like an abandonment not only of the populist drama of system-change politics but of the desire to change the system at all. Its celebration of smallness can look like a rejection of bigness. It can seem conservative, rather than radical, committed to seeing change, at worst, as something to be regretted or, at best, as something that is shaped only by forces larger than ourselves. It can also seem woefully smug. It is all too easy, after all, for those who do reasonably well in the present social, economic, and political order to tell everyone else to sit back and enjoy the moment, rather than to join a struggle for change.

But this, I believe, is a mistake. A focus on the fundamental importance of the unforbidden does not preclude us from campaigning for wholesale economic change. Quite the opposite. The prevailing neoliberal economic and political order, after all, poses an enormous challenge to millions of people trying to prioritize the unforbidden pleasures in their lives. Neoliberalism has wrenched millions away from having the opportunity to do just that, because it denies people the space and the time they need if they are to settle into the local, the familial, or the personal. The lives we are able to lead in the current economic system are lives of overwork and underpay, of precarious family budgets, and of a decaying public realm.[33]

There is, therefore, expansive potential common ground between those who are concerned about enabling people to enjoy the unforbidden pleasures and those concerned to see far-reaching social and economic change. To take a clear example, anyone concerned with promoting the unforbidden pleasures will surely agree that the increasing social segregation of communities along lines of class and wealth, the shrinking of open-to-access public space, the increasing number of people unable to spend time with families and friends because of the demands of paid work, and the burdens of cutthroat competition in the workplace all provide serious and growing obstacles to their goal. As Eric Klinenberg has shown, a concern for enhancing the opportunities for fulfillment in the everyday requires us to build real "social infrastructure," including publicly provided, free-to-use spaces for people to meet and socialize safely and without fear. That means easy access to the beauty of the natural environment, be it in the form of urban parks or the expanses of the countryside. It also means schools that teach people more than just how to pass exams but also how to live well together. It means too doing what we can to reform as many workplaces as possible, so they are not alienating and hierarchical experiences that suck the life and soul out of us, but are places where we feel we can share a sense of purpose with others, learn and develop new ways of looking at the world, as well as making ends meet.[34] All of that requires real economic system change.

But if an emphasis on unforbidden pleasures does not tell us to stop seeking economic system change, it assuredly does tell us how we should proceed to do so. System-change political campaigning should at the very least be conducted in a way that does not undermine the crucial features of the everyday. This form of politics must not further endanger citizen qualities like social friendship, care, and a sense of belonging to community, but it should seek to enhance them. Moreover, system-change political action itself might in fact most effectively begin in the everyday—be rooted in the realm of the unforbidden—and then move to the bigger realm. System-change campaigning might, that is, actually become stronger and more effective on its own terms as a result of beginning in the realm of the unforbidden. This is the notion at the heart of the IAF-style community organizing dismissed by Bond and Exley. IAF organizing prioritizes the building of connections between citizens in everyday settings over taking immediate political action like electoral campaigning, not because IAF thinks that campaigning is unimportant but because it believes it cannot be conducted effectively unless it is rooted in the everyday settings of people's lives. Relationship *precedes* action, in the IAF mantra, it does not *replace* it.[35] Beginning our politics in the unforbidden allows us to make meaningful contributions to debates in the forbidden.

System-change politics as currently constituted in most of the developed world has a strikingly poor record in this regard. The desire for speed, for bigness, and the willingness to denounce enemies that is characteristic of many campaigning groups frequently leads them to denounce a host of everyday activities as, at best, irrelevant to the larger struggle or, at worst, a contribution to the very injustices that should be fought. When I was at NEF, for example, the most ideologically committed regularly hosted all-staff meetings that they called "living our values." Despite the uplifting name, these gatherings too often descended into the voluble denouncing of those among them who continued to live their lives in a host of other very ordinary ways, such as buying their lunch at one of the major supermarkets rather than at the organic deli. The unforbidden was morphed into the forbidden. Such practices will be well known to anyone who has spent time in an activist community of late; they are precisely what makes so many ordinary people so hostile to the woke.

All of this has to stop for a democratic politics of economic system change to take hold. The cynicism and contempt for people that are at its core are just too transparent. As the socialist literary critic Raymond Williams once argued, to find resonance in the world, political activists have to avoid making "the extraordinary error of believing that most people only become interesting when they begin to engage with political . . . actions of a previously recognized kind." Instead, "if we are serious about even political life, we have to enter that world in which people live as they can as themselves . . . within a whole complex of work and love and illness and natural beauty."[36]

But despite the poor record, system-change political movements could take a lead in this regard. For decades now, the professionalization of political parties and the bureaucratization of government have also generated a cult of expertise and detachment, a sense that ordinary people do not understand their own lives, that the fundamental aspects of their affairs are better run for them from on high either by the officials of the state or the giants of the market.[37] If even a handful of campaigning groups made a genuine commitment to working against that trend, by working with the grain of the everyday rather than against it, they would surely see rewards. If they made conscious efforts not to criticize endlessly and condemn the ordinary lives of ordinary people, then positive change would be more likely to result. Bold change, in other words, is more likely to come about when actual power is shared and when the voices of everyday people play a larger role in shaping the circumstances of their everyday lives.[38]

This would not mean, of course, that such groups need take a vow of silence on everyday practices that they find deeply challenging. No one is suggesting that anti-racism groups should fail to respond to everyday racism or that gender equality groups should reserve judgment in the face of everyday sexism. Nor should it mean groups shy away from controversy, from picking a fight where fights are needed or by laying out arguments that radically break from the status quo. But it should mean that when groups do these things, they interrogate themselves in each instance and resist defaulting to destructive hubris and aggression simply because it is the standard mode of the conventionally political. Moreover, it could also involve a striking change of pace. As Sheldon Wolin once told us, within contemporary political life, the "mind is not given much to reflection or contemplation and does not easily give itself over to mental rhythms suggestive of calm and serenity." [39] But it is out of these moments of calmness, out of these reflections on the ordinary world around us, that can come the most humane of personal attachments and the most profound of political lessons.

A New Political Strategy for System Change

This an agenda for a democratic politics of economic system change derived from the belief that there is enormous untapped strength in the everyday. It is an agenda that shows how the style, policy content, institutions, and campaigning that make up our political lives need to be adapted better to reflect the importance of the unforbidden pleasures in the rest of our lives. It is undeniably hard. But it is also happening already.

At the outset of the chapter, I described the broader system-change movement as consisting of three parts: the intellectual, the practical, and the political. Within the second of those parts—the practical—real efforts are already being made that successfully capture the best of the pursuit of the unforbidden with the best of the pursuit of a new system. In Britain alone, the last few years have witnessed an explosion in practical efforts to work in just this way. One of the largest of these efforts is the Every One, Every Day initiative run by the Participatory City Foundation, masterminded by the social entrepreneur Tessy Britton, in the East London Borough of Barking and Dagenham. Founded on the idea that "what people do together every day matters," Every One, Every Day fosters and facilitates "widespread networks of cooperation and friendship" in one of the most economically deprived and ethnically diverse communities in the whole of the UK. It does so in a host of projects, each and every one of which is codesigned and coproduced by ordinary residents themselves.

In its first year alone, funded both by the local council and a host of major philanthropic foundations, Every One, Every Day has seen at least 2,000 people involved in 40 different ongoing projects, including taking over shops on the high street and turning them into welcoming spaces for people to meet and socialize, cultivating disused public land as community gardens where people can grow food to eat, providing spaces and equipment for families from different backgrounds to cook together and to entertain their children, and opening a warehouse equipped with free-to-use tools, IT equipment, sewing machines, laser cutters, coworking space, financial advice, and a cooperatively run child care facility to help foster new community businesses. The ambition is enormous. "This is hope at last," one participant told *Guardian* reporter George Monbiot when he visited. "Hope for my generation. Hope for my grandchildren." [40]

That hope does not just lie with Every One, Every Day. There is a similar initiative in Wigan, in the North of England, where the local council has worked to create what it calls "The Deal," which it describes as an "informal agreement between the council and everyone who lives or works here to work together to create a better borough." Deal projects include programs for supporting community businesses and for enabling children and young people to exercise their own influence in shaping education and social services; another program is a wholly new way of providing social care to the elderly, developed on the principle that residents should never be approached as "a collection of needs and problems" but rather as "unique individuals, who have strengths, assets, gifts, and talents." [41]

The same principle motivates the "People in the Lead" strategy adopted in 2015 by the Big Lottery Fund (now called the National Lottery Community Fund), the largest community grant-giving foundation in the UK. "We want to start with what people bring to the table, not what they don't have, and from the belief that people and communities are best placed to solve their problems, take advantage of opportunities, and rise to challenges," the Big Lottery's CEO Dawn Austwick insists. "From this everything else follows." Similar declarations have followed from other multimillion-dollar philanthropic trusts and foundations, including the Paul Hamlyn Foundation and the Esmée Fairbairn Foundation, as well as from think tanks and pressure groups, including Participle, whose founder Hilary Cottam has literally written the textbook on this new approach in her masterful *Radical Help*, and the New Local Government Network, whose new "community paradigm" is a long list of practical instructions to local authorities and service providers that has at its core just "one shared feature: handing power over to communities." [42]

This is profoundly important work, connecting elements of the everyday to the deep business of system change. It is too early to evaluate the impact of each individual effort fully, of course. That will come sure enough. But at least it offers a new sense of direction. Despite all of this, it goes almost wholly unnoticed in the world of politics in general, including system-change politics. No current political leader speaks of it. No one includes it in their manifestos.[43] Perhaps in the UK they are put off in part by the sense that it is too close to David Cameron's ill-fated "Big Society," a much less forthright ambition with similar rhetoric. But the explanation also lies, as Adam Phillips tells us, in campaigners' psychological inability to take our eyes off the forbidden when we should be looking at the potential of the unforbidden. As David Brooks has perceptively explained, professional journalists "barely cover" the efforts of these "social change agents" because they are dismissed as "goody-goody." But, he continues, "these people are not goody-goody. They are raw, honest and sometimes rude. How do we in our business get in that spot where we spend 90 percent of our coverage on the 10 percent of our lives influenced by politics and 10 percent of our coverage on the 90 percent of our lives influenced by relationship, community and the places we live every day?"[44] The conservatively inclined Brooks still gets things a bit wrong, though. For this kind of grounded changemaking, with its roots firmly planted in community and the everyday, is not best seen as an *alternative* to politics. It should, instead, be understood as the beginning of a new political strategy. If it was seen that way, it could be one of the biggest sources of hope in a profoundly dark time.

Conclusion

Hope it might be. But what if it is too little and what if it is too late? What if the times are too dark for whatever light this kind of politics might bring? There is no doubt that we live in an era of enormous democratic disruption. A time when populist forces, of both the right and the left, are ripping through the orthodox institutions, calling for the abolition of public broadcasting, the destruction of centuries-old legal conventions, and the abolition of crucial human rights. It is a time of deepening climate emergency, spiraling economic inequality, and rapid and disorientating technological change; a time when millions of young British people believe that they face a future without affordable housing, stable employment, or a secure safety net from the welfare state. And it is a time when politics seems incapable of responding. It is a moment of Twitter wars and dark social media arts, of fake news on Facebook, of deep distrust of the new and the unseen, alongside rampant foreign interference in national democratic practices.

In an age like this, the demand that system-change politics should embrace the mundane and the parochial, the ordinary and the everyday, can seem puny at best and indulgent at worst. Shouldn't we be trying, as my old boss Ed Miliband has argued, to get people on a "war footing" in response to these ills? Or, as Greta Thunberg even more evocatively suggests: Isn't the best response just to panic?[45]

Such responses are wholly understandable—we really do live in frightening times—but they also miss the point. For, as George Orwell knew, the quest to overcome our current ills and the effort to draw politics and the everyday closer together are intricately related. Our current age of despair is, after all, a direct consequence of the rupture of politics from everyday life in the neoliberal era. If political parties, public-service providers, and campaigners had attended more to the unforbidden pleasures and ordinary rhythms of life in the last few decades, our nations would be less unequal, our communities would cohere more strongly, and trust in our institutions would be higher. The current system is falling apart precisely because we have failed to attend to its impact on real, everyday lives. It may turn out to be too late for this generation to change that—the climate emergency might determine that if the coronavirus does not—but it is certainly our duty to try.

Notes

I thank Will Brett, Rom Coles, Bonnie Honig, Amanda Tattersall, and all of the participants in the Political Economy and Justice workshop for extremely helpful comments on earlier drafts of this chapter. Particular thanks are due to Danielle Allen, both for inviting me to be part of the project and for her generous and insightful comments each step of the way.

1.   See Philip Cowley and Dennis Kavanagh, *The British General Election of 2015* (London: Palgrave, 2016).

2.   I should not have been quite as surprised, as my predecessor as CEO at NEF, Stewart Wallis, had explicitly committed the organization to "systemic social, economic, and environmental transformation" and to building "the economic system we need" through a funded program called the "Great Transition." See Stewart Wallis, "An Economic System That Supports People and Planet Is Still Possible," *The Guardian*, November 4, 2014.

3.   For examples, see the website of the Justice Democrats (https://www.justicedemocrats.com/home/); see also Masha Gessen, "Barcelona's Experiment in Radical Democracy," *New Yorker*, August 6, 2018, https://www.newyorker.com/news/our-columnists/barcelonas-experiment-in-radical-democracy.

4.   For examples of varying quality, see Aaron Bastani, *Fully Automated Luxury Communism* (London: Verso, 2018); Naomi Klein, *The Changes Everything: Capitalism and the Climate* (New York: Simon and Schuster, 2014); Paul Mason, *Postcapitalism: A Guide to Our Future* (London: Allen Lane, 2015); Nick Srnicek and Alex Williams, *Inventing the Future: Postcapitalism and a World without Work* (London: Verso, 2017); Wolfgang Streeck, *How Will Capitalism End? Essays on a Failing System* (London: Verso. 2017); Yanis Varoufakis, *Talking to My Daughter about the Economy* (London: Penguin, 2017).

5.   See, for example, the columns of London School of Economics academic Lea Ypi in *The New Statesman* and *The Independent*.

6.   See World Economic Forum, "Fourth Industrial Revolution," accessed July 9, 2021, https://www.weforum.org/focus/fourth-industrial-revolution.

7.   See Partners for a New Economy, "Who We Are," accessed May 2019, https://p4ne.org.

8.   Bret Stephens, "How Trump Wins Next Year," *New York Times*, May 24, 2019, https://www.nytimes.com/2019/05/24/opinion/trump-elections-india-australia.html.

9.   T. S. Eliot, "Preface" to Simone Weil, *The Need for Roots: Prelude to a Declaration of Duties towards Mankind* (London: Routledge, 1995), xi.

10.   See the websites of the Next System Project (https://thenextsystem.org), Rethinking Economics (https://www.rethinkeconomics.org), and the University College London (UCL) Institute for Innovation and Public Purpose (https://www.ucl.ac.uk/bartlett/public-purpose/).

11.   For a good survey, see Joe Guinan and Martin O'Neill, "From Community Wealth-Building to System Change," *Progressive Review*, Spring 2019, 382–92.

12.   Becky Bond and Zack Exley, *Rules for Revolutionaries: How Big Organizing Can Change Everything* (White River Junction, VT: Chelsea Green, 2016) and Chantal Mouffe, *For a Left Populism* (London: Verso, 2018).

13.   NEON, "What We Do," accessed July 9, 2021, https://neweconomyorganisers.org.

14.   Bond and Exley, *Rules for Revolutionaries*, 11.

15.   Bond and Exley, 11.

16.   Bond and Exley, 116.

17.   See Srnicek and Williams, *Inventing the Future.*

18.   Bond and Exley, *Rules for Revolutionaries*, 164.

19.   Contrast with, for example, Archon Fung, "Deliberation before the Revolution," *Political Theory* 33 (2005): 397–419.

20.   See Maggie Astor, "How the Politically Unthinkable Can Become Mainstream," *New York Times*, February 26, 2019.

21.   Mouffe, *For a Left Populism*, 93.

22.   For examples, see George Orwell, "Can Socialists Be Happy?" available at the Literature Network (http://www.online-literature.com/orwell/895/) and George Orwell, "Politics and the English Language" reprinted in George Orwell, *Why I Write* (London: Penguin, 2016).

23.   George Orwell, *Coming Up for Air* (London: Penguin, 1990).

24.   See George Orwell, "The Lion and the Unicorn: Socialism and the English Genius," reprinted in Orwell, *Why I Write.*

25.   I develop these arguments in my own work; see Marc Stears, *Out of the Ordinary: How Everyday Life Once Inspired a Nation and How it Can Again* (Cambridge, MA: Harvard University Press, 2020).

26.   See Adam Phillips, *Unforbidden Pleasures* (London: Hamish Hamilton, 2016).

27.   The essays from Julie Rose and Deva Woodly in this book also point to the centrality of these experiences in their accounts of human flourishing.

28.   Phillips, *Unforbidden Pleasures*, 126.

29.   Phillips, 162.

30.   Phillips, 195.

31.   Andrew Abbott, "Aims of Education: Address," University of Chicago, 2002, https://college.uchicago.edu/student-life/aims-education-address-2002 -andrew-abbott.

32.   Abbott, "Aims of Education." See, too, Jenny Odell, *How to Do Nothing: Resisting the Attention Economy* (Brooklyn, NY: Black Inc., 2019).

33.   See Benjamin H. Snyder, *The Disrupted Workplace: Time and the Moral Order of Flexible Capitalism* (Oxford: Oxford University Press, 2016).

34.   See Eric Klinenberg, *Palaces for the People: How to Build a More Equal and United Society* (London: Penguin, 2018).

35.   On IAF organizing, see Rom Coles, *Beyond Gated Politics: Reflections for the Possibility of Democracy* (Minneapolis: University of Minnesota Press, 2005) and Jeffrey Stout, *Blessed and the Organized: Grassroots Democracy in America* (Princeton, NJ: Princeton University Press, 2010).

36.   Raymond Williams, *Politics of Modernism: Against the New Conformists* (London: Verso, 2007), 116.

37.   See Peter Mair, *Ruling the Void: The Hollowing of Western Democracy* (London: Verso, 2013).

38.   See Danielle Allen, "Toward a Connected Society," in *Our Compelling Interests: The Value of Diversity for Democracy and a Prosperous Society*, edited by E. Lewis and N. Cantor (Princeton, NJ: Princeton University Press, 2016).

39. Sheldon Wolin, "The Ordinance of Time," in *Fugitive Democracy and Other Essays* (Princeton, NJ: Princeton University Press, 2016), 258.

40. See George Monbiot, "Could This Local Experiment Be the Start of a National Transformation?" *The Guardian*, January 24, 2019.

41. See Wigan Council, "What Is the Deal?" accessed July 9, 2021, https://www.wigan.gov.uk/council/the-deal/the-deal.aspx.

42. See Big Lottery Fund, "Putting People in the Lead," March 24, 2015, https://bigblog.org.uk/2015/03/24/people-in-the-lead/; Hilary Cottam, *Radical Help: How We Can Remake the Relationships between Us and Revolutionise the Welfare State* (London: Virago, 2019): and Adam Lent and Jessica Studdert, "The Community Paradigm: Why Public Services Need Radical Change and How It Can Be Achieved," *New Local*, March 4, 2021, http://www.nlgn.org.uk/public/2019/the-community-paradigm-why-public-services-need-radical-change-and-how-it-can-be-achieved/.

43. See John Harris, "For Real Change Labour Should Ditch Its Top-Down Thinking," *The Guardian*, November 18, 2019.

44. David Brooks, "The Big Story You Don't Read About," *New York Times*, May 16, 2019.

45. See Rob Merrick, "UK Must Fight Climate Change on 'War Footing' Like Defeat of Nazis, Theresa May Told," *Independent*, April 29, 2019; and Greta Thunberg, "Our House Is on Fire," *The Guardian*, January 26, 2019.

12 Structural Justice and the Infrastructure of Inclusion

K. SABEEL RAHMAN

Introduction

In August 2019, educators in Flint, Michigan, saw a dramatic spike in the number of schoolchildren needing special care—following years of a crisis of lead poisoning afflicting the city's water supply with devastating consequences for the long-term health and well-being of the community, particularly its children.[1] The experience of Flint is tragically common: from Detroit to Baltimore to Newark to Washington, D.C., there is an ongoing crisis over the access of communities, especially communities of color, to that most basic human necessity of water. Many of these cities struggle with excessive levels of lead and other contaminants in the water, even as growing utility costs also are creating a crisis of water affordability that puts homeowners at risk of tax liens and even foreclosure.[2]

But the water crisis in American cities is not just about the failures of water utility officials to treat water supplies adequately for contaminants. The crisis is in part a product of deeper systemic rules: failures of governmental agencies to monitor environmental conditions, failures of water utility boards to ensure safe and cheap access; the deeper conditions of municipal austerity and budget cuts that have placed further strain on water infrastructure; the increasing privatization of those utilities such that many of them are now owned by profit-maximizing private equity funds; and historical patterns of racial segregation in urban planning and zoning that have concentrated poverty and environmental toxins particularly among communities of color.[3]

The water crisis exemplifies a broader pattern in our twenty-first-century political economy. We are living in a period of devastating inequality—an inequality that is the product of background economic and political-institutional rules. From scholars to policymakers to social movements, there is a growing focus on not just conventional forms of inequality but on deeper structural roots of inequality and injustice.[4] Injustice, in this structural lens, is understood as a product, not as a naturally occurring phenomenon, nor as the result merely of individual malfeasance, but rather as a product of deep background systems that combine to produce the lived reality of subordination, domination, and exclusion. These systems are themselves the products of deliberate legal and policy choices, the product of human agency. And those choices often arise because they serve a configuration of political, economic, and social interests, whether in the form of corporate actors seeking greater economic returns, social resentments seeking to reassert prior modes of racial and gender hierarchy, or efforts at concentrating political power and control.

This chapter focuses on two key arguments. First, the project of advancing structural *justice*—of realizing an inclusive democracy and economy that overcomes these systemic forms of exclusion and inequity—requires construction of new forms of public, democratic power capable of remaking background rules of our economy and society. It is virtually impossible to redress and prevent structural injustices like the concentration of poverty and environmental harm on communities of color and arising from the way cities are zoned and built without institutions that have the ability and the power to monitor such systemic patterns and remake background rules of urban planning, energy production, and market inequities to remedy these harms. The project of structural justice, then, is also closely tied to the project of *democracy*—of constructing new institutions through which we the people engage in collective action to govern ourselves and our larger political economy.

Second, the political fights over these political institutions—the instrumentalities of inclusion—represent a critical battleground where ideas of democracy, freedom, domination, and neoliberalism have real purchase. Neoliberal thought operates on both the economic and the political front and is deployed strategically by political actors. As a political-institutional regime, neoliberalism operates through the *erasure and manipulation of public power*—through policy levers like deregulation, privatization, and through the manipulation of administrative regimes governing access to basic goods and economic protections. This political project of neoliberal thought is often overlooked but is a key driver of the current crises of inequality and exclusion.

The implication, then, is that the project of advancing a vision of twenty-first-century democracy requires both a moral and institutional project of building new public institutions charged with advancing and enforcing values of equity and inclusion and overcoming the legal and institutional strategies for dismantling these public institutions. There are many barriers to advancing a vision of justice, and one of those barriers is the role of government in particular. The administrative apparatus—encompassing state actors like departments of labor, environmental justice, or civil rights enforcement—represent one of the key underlying political infrastructures needed to realize justice. But, crucially, this chapter argues that the goal for a project of justice must be more than simply "restoring" or "defending" the idea of good government; it must be instead to build a specifically *democratic* conception of government in which structural roots of injustice are made visible and changeable through state action, *and* where that state action is itself democratically constituted. In other words, we must both build governmental power capable of dismantling the root drivers of injustice *and* at the same time construct these instruments of state power in democratically accountable ways.

I begin with a conceptual foundation for the argument, suggesting that today's inequality crisis should be understood as a problem of *domination*— the concentration of arbitrary, unaccountable power. The moral aspiration for reform, then, should be more than simply improving democracy or increasing economic welfare; rather, it should be a deeper and more ambitious goal of *emancipation*, of freedom from structural economic, racial, and gender inequities, and the freedom for communities to thrive and flourish. Viewed from the standpoint of domination and emancipation, the challenge for building a more inclusive political economy lies in transforming both the background institutional rules of our political economy and in remaking the ideas that animate that political economy. In particular, it means overcoming a set of *neoliberal* ideas and institutional structures. Neoliberalism, in this analysis, emerges as a key conceptual approach that serves to validate various forms of domination by appealing to ideas of unfettered markets and a hostility toward government. Neoliberalism also operates as an actual political and institutional project, as key constituencies have used the ideas of neoliberal political economy to advance a policy agenda premised on the dismantling of public institutions charged with advancing economic, racial, and gender equity.

Next, I take a more in-depth look at the political economy of neoliberalism, focusing in particular on the political-institutional dimensions of this project: how neoliberal ideas and interests have driven American institutional change, specifically to dismantle those constitutional, administrative, and local regimes at the heart of efforts to promote greater economic inclusion and democracy. I then bring attention to the affirmative project implied by this analysis: the reconstruction of administrative institutions that will be critical to realizing in practice values of inclusive economic freedom and democracy.

Domination, Neoliberalism, and the Problem of Governance

FROM DOMINATION TO EMANCIPATION

Before we can understand what kinds of democratic, political institutions are needed to realize a more equitable political economy, we first need to understand the nature of the inequities we are looking to dismantle and overcome. The inequities experienced by subordinated groups encompass more than the directly visible and tangible forms of discrimination, exploitation, or exclusion. Often, conditions of subordination are a product not of an individual malefactor but rather of a larger system of economic and political-institutional arrangements that combine to produce disparities of power, wealth, opportunity, and position. But a key challenge for justice and ultimately freedom is the degree to which these structural roots of inequity are often experienced by individuals as exogenous, "natural," and beyond the scope of individual responsibility, will, or reform.[5] One way to bring into relief, to conceptualize and diagnose, these structural inequities is through the lens of *domination*: the concentration of arbitrary, unchecked power and control. At its core, domination is about power and the ways in which inequitable distributions of power preclude freedom and flourishing—even if that power lies dormant or is at times used benevolently.

Consider, for example, the kinds of inhibitions on freedom and moral standing that arise in context of the unchecked "private government" of the workplace, where labor is at the mercy of corporate owners and managers, unrestrained by checks and balances.[6] Or the ways in which monopolies and finance can, by virtue of their market power and control over firms and industries, set unfair and rent-extractive terms for consumers and workers alike. Even if these forms of control—in the firm or by corporate titans—are deployed charitably and benevolently, the reality is that workers and communities remain at the mercy of the goodwill and good faith of those with economic power. We can think of these economic relationships as exemplifying a form of *dyadic domination*: a binary relationship between two visible and identifiable parties (workers and managers; producers and financiers) characterized by a severe power imbalance. This is precisely the kind of unfreedom that animates movements for worker justice and labor organizing. It also lies behind how historically progressive reformers have viewed concentrated corporate power as a threat to liberty and economic citizenship going back to what Louis Brandeis called the "curse of bigness."

There is a second kind of domination, which we might call *systemic domination*. It refers to conditions where the dominator is not a discrete actor. Rather, systemic domination arises from the cumulative effects of systemic practices and background rules—from systems of white supremacy, patterns of racial and gender discrimination and structural economic inequities, to the concentration of environmental and health harms on communities of color that constrain the lived reality of membership and inclusion. For example, systemic domination is one way to understand how the combination of historical disinvestment and redlining, predatory lending, and gentrification can combine to produce racially disproportionate harms on communities of color. Even if landlords, lenders, and policymakers may not always intentionally discriminate, the aggregate result of historical and current policy choices means that there will be a major racial disparity in wealth and opportunity.

The political realm is marked by the same background structural disparity of power and the problem of *political domination*. As a growing body of social science research has documented, this concentration of political power is often in direct relation to efforts to further concentrate economic wealth, and vice versa.[7] As political power is concentrated in more unaccountable ways, the result is precisely the threat of domination that animates attempts to fragment, distribute, and hold accountable political power—whether through classic republican constitutional forms like the separation of powers, or democratic systems like elections, or other forms of democratic institutional design. Indeed, democracies don't just "die," they are dismantled, as interest groups seek to gain greater advantage, increasingly altering the background rules of politics—through voter suppression, gerrymandering, changes in campaign finance laws, and the like—to accumulate greater and greater political power.

In each of these three variations of dyadic, structural, and political domination, the common challenge is not just about economic shares of who gets how much; rather, it is about agency and power. From the manager and monopolist to the background rules of economic and racial subordination to the hoarding of political power, each of these types of domination is driven by a kind of unequal, functional sovereignty where one set of actors—private firms, unchecked political elites, policymakers—exercise power over individuals and communities, restraining their freedom and life opportunities without sufficient contestation, accountability, or responsiveness. Absent checks and balances on—and outright ownership of—these forms of power, those individuals and communities affected by these actors are not truly free to flourish, thrive, and live lives of value. Furthermore, these different modes of domination often interact and intersect; as Tommie Shelby describes in his chapter in this book, for example, the toxicity of the prison system stems from the way in which mass incarceration fuses the economic domination of privatization and the profit-motive with systemic racism and the domination of an unaccountable state that exercises carceral power, particularly over communities of color.

Unlike "inequality," domination as a conceptual framework points to a very different approach to remedies. The goal is not merely to redistribute income or wealth but rather to build a political economy in which we limit those coercive powers and systems that are not subject to checks and balances. It also requires the affirmative investment in domination's inverse: political agency, the capacities of communities to contest and check concentrated power and to participate in the (re)shaping of political, economic, sand social conditions. As Danielle Allen, Deva Woodly, and Julie Rose suggest in their respective chapters, the pursuit of justice is really the pursuit of an affirmative conception of human flourishing, of a world in which we can imagine emancipation from systems of injustice, and celebrating difference without domination.

Structural justice, then, requires checks and balances on these various forms of domination. The degree to which democratic equality is realized in practice depends on the degree to which these public, private, and systemic forms of domination are checked. This in turn suggests that the realization of inclusive and equitable democratic freedom requires a form of state power—and in particular, administrative regimes that are capable of, and responsive to, those threats of domination. Furthermore, this construction of state power itself needs to be democratically accountable, otherwise we risk replicating relationships of political domination.

The construction of state capacity—and the degree to which that capacity is democratically constituted—is thus a key battleground where visions of justice are made real or are frustrated. Indeed, the task of building such institutions for accountability, agency, and democracy against different forms of domination faces a critical barrier in the set of ideas, interests, and institutions that have dominated our political economy over the last 50 years: neoliberalism.

NEOLIBERALISM AND THE BATTLE OVER PUBLIC POWER

A central challenge to this vision of democratic freedom—and a key driver of domination—is neoliberalism. While the term is often used widely, neoliberalism is not just a synonym for capitalism, nor is it simply about a policy agenda of unfettered markets and hostility to government regulation, though these are related concepts. Rather, neoliberalism is better understood as a *worldview*: an individualized, marketized notion of freedom and social structure that emphasizes the supremacy of market transactions and a hostility to collective social goods. And neoliberalism is also best understood as a *political agenda*, where specific interests have strategically and opportunistically driven institutional changes animated by and validated under this worldview. While a full exposition of neoliberalism and its elements is beyond the scope of this chapter, it is important to understand these two components of neoliberal political economy in order to ground our understanding of what kinds of political institutions need to be (re)built to overcome domination and realize a more liberatory and inclusive twenty-first-century political economy.

As a worldview, neoliberalism seeks apolitical, economistic forms of social ordering. This vision of political economy evokes values of agency, freedom, and neutrality, but in ways that operate to evade or contain democratic politics. Consider, for example, Friedrich Hayek's canonical account of market order. For Hayek, the freedom of market ordering stems from the abilities of the market to create spontaneous, welfare-maximizing order, free of the inevitable failures and corruptibility of political "central planning." The outcomes of such a system are necessarily fair and not subject to claims of "social justice" since markets are by their nature (for Hayek anyway) impersonal systems without moral will or discriminatory intent.[8] Crucially, this worldview is not just about economics; rather, it has a central political dimension as well. As a result, the political institutions needed to sustain social welfare, on this view, are simply those basic rules of property, contract, and physical security that enable markets to function.

Conceptually, this neoliberal worldview levels a dual attack on ideals of democracy and inclusion. First, by valorizing markets as self-correcting and welfare-enhancing, this framework erases from view the kinds of dyadic and structural domination that afflict economic realities for so many. Second, this worldview is skeptical if not outright hostile to various forms of governmental economic policy. Baked into this account is a vision of politics as inherently corruptible, inefficient, and ineffective. Insofar as there is an affirmative vision of legitimate state action in this account, it is a narrow technocratic notion of public power tethered to expertise, focused on the minimalist task of mitigating market failures rather than on more robust and transformative visions of equity, inclusion, and democracy-enhancing public policy. The effect of this critique is to cut off at the knees many well-intentioned policies for social justice: however admirable the goals of mitigating inequality or promoting opportunity, if government is more likely than not to be captured or to fail, then economic regulation and public policies are self-defeating.[9] At the same time, the neoliberal worldview is not truly anti-statist but instead deploys state power to realize this illusion of stateless "free markets." Think of, for example, state regimes of financial (de)regulation; the enforcement of rules of property, tort, and contract law; the deploying of state power to fracture other forms of solidarities and collective action such as organized labor or public ownership. These are affirmative exercises of state power through which a neoliberal order is built and realized.

However, neoliberalism has a political dimension in another sense: not in its worldview as articulated by intellectuals, theorists, and academics, but in the way in which this worldview has fueled and justified a specifically political project of organized interests and policymakers, as an exercise of political power and political-institutional change. Indeed, the idea of neoliberalism has helped animate and legitimize the efforts of particular constituencies to remake economic and political institutions in ways deeply inimical to democracy and conducive to domination. As recent scholarship in history has documented, key constituencies seized on neoliberal concepts to advance their policy agendas. The business community organized more effective lobbying and advocacy vehicles through the Chamber of Commerce, the Business Roundtable, and other coordinating systems, backed in part by the parallel formation of a validating ideas infrastructure as funders like the Olin Foundation helped produce a generation of lawyers and economists who could develop and validate these policy changes.[10] A similar story has been traced in context of civil rights and racial inequality. Indeed, many of these same funders and interest groups backing the rise of big business under the rubric of free market/anti-government ideas also deployed these tropes to push back against federal commitments to civil rights following the 1954 landmark school desegregation ruling of *Brown v. Board of Education* and the passage of the Civil Rights and Voting Rights Acts in 1964 and 1965.[11] This is not to say that all of these thinkers, interest groups, and elected officials moved in lockstep. Rather, neoliberal concepts of markets, individual free choice, and skepticism of government formed a common conceptual resource and glue across these different interests—business interests, social conservatives seeking to restore "traditional" roles and orderings after the upheavals of movements seeking to advance racial and gender justice, and those more openly hostile to desegregation.[12]

This combination of interests and ideas produced a set of neoliberal institutions, remaking economic and social policy. These efforts were successful in undoing much of the New Deal social contract, moving economic policy away from its prior focus on Keynesian macroeconomic management and a robust safety net. The result was a significant shift in public policy toward deregulation of finance and corporate power, the undermining of organized labor, and the undoing of the social safety net. These shifts originated in the 1970s but accelerated through the administrations of Ronald Reagan and George H. W. Bush—often gaining adherence among centrist liberal policymakers like during the Clinton administration.[13] This in turn exacerbated the lived realities of economic domination for many communities. Similarly, these efforts at neoliberal policy change yielded a gradual erosion of civil rights protections and a recreation of patterns of racial segregation and inequality everywhere from urban planning to predatory lending to the exclusions of women and communities of color from much of the modern safety net.[14] Consider, for example, how neoliberal concepts of freedom of choice are deployed to justify white flight or the resistance to desegregation or legal claims by corporations to resist economic regulations and protections for reproductive rights under the guise of freedom of association.

Yet despite this deregulatory push, the politics of this neoliberal era have also amplified the excesses of governmental coercion that serve to preserve inequality and the hoarding of wealth and opportunity: the rise of mass incarceration, crackdowns on labor, and the like. Neoliberalism, then, is not really an abandonment of the state but rather a strategic use of public policy to encase existing economic, racial, and gender inequities, immunizing them from contestation.[15] The notion that neoliberalism is the rejection of state power is itself, then, an illusion.

The net result is a systematic exercise of state power that has opportunistically dismantled key democracy- and equity-enhancing institutions, concentrating control and hoarding wealth and opportunity for the few, all validated by an appeal to free markets and ineffective government as cover. Indeed, it is easy to cast contemporary battles over "big government" and "free markets" as a continuation of long-running philosophical debates between laissez-faire and libertarian political economy and more egalitarian conceptions. But these contemporary fights take place in context of an *already-existing* democratic institutional context where institutions—like labor law, economic regulation, civil rights enforcement regimes, and more— are already in place, thanks to the state-building efforts of prior waves of social reform. As a result, the threat to *dismantle* or *repurpose* these institutions has a very direct implication for the perpetuation of structural injustice by altering a set of instrumentalities and tools whose existence makes possible the contestation and mitigation of structural forms of injustice.

Highlighting the political-institutional dimensions of neoliberalism as a worldview and as a policy agenda is critical for informing our approaches to structural justice. If the problem of inequality and injustice is a structural one rooted in domination—the concentration of unaccountable economic and political power—then it follows that freedom and inclusion require democracy—the institutionalization of accountability and agency of communities over these forms of power. But neoliberal thought and policies operate to both erase the *idea* of domination (through appeals to frictionless markets) and the institutions built to *counteract* domination (through economic and social policies for regulating corporate power, providing public goods and a safety net, and enforcing civil fights and inclusion). The challenge, then, lies in constructing new democratic institutions capable of realizing inclusion—and undoing the legal-institutional changes brought about in the neoliberal era.

The Political-Institutional Imagination under Neoliberalism

Structural injustice, I suggest above, manifests through different types of domination: the dyadic domination of individuals and communities under arbitrary private power (of managers, firms, financiers, or monopolists); the structural domination whereby background rules of economic and social ordering create relations of power and subordination such as systemic racialized or gendered discrimination; and the public domination by unaccountable state actors. Freedom requires the dismantling of these forms of domination and the fair and equal access to those basic goods that are essential for human flourishing. But that goal in turn requires that we remake our background economic and social order—and that we create new forms of public power capable of effectively and accountably advancing policies in pursuit of these aspirations.

None of this is novel; indeed, the history of American political economy and state-building can be told in part as a story of successive waves of structural reform aimed at creating new modes of democratic self-governance suited to this challenge. The Industrial Revolution, for example, spurred the organization of the labor movement, the Progressive and Populist movements, and the creation of the modern administrative state dedicated to protecting labor and consumer rights and reining in corporate power. The movements for freedom from slavery and its legacy—whether the First Reconstruction of the post–Civil War era or the Second Reconstruction of the 1960s—similarly transformed not only the moral imagination of our democracy to propose a racially inclusive democracy, but also attempted a legal-institutional transformation: creating new constitutional requirements and administrative bodies to protect civil and voting rights.

It is precisely because of these advances that the political-institutional effects of neoliberalism are so pernicious. A growing literature has documented how socioeconomic inequity is perpetuated by a failing democratic system, as wealthier and whiter communities are more able to vote, to influence politics through donations, or to be represented among candidates and policymakers.[16] No doubt, ensuring a well-functioning and representative electoral democracy is critical to making government respond more readily to the needs of the whole public. But what is often overlooked is how the day-to-day operations of governance have also been skewed to perpetuate rather than dismantle domination.

As a political agenda, neoliberalism has involved a systematic reconfiguration of state power through its attack on both the idea and the reality of public power, with the effect of dismantling these tools, in ways that help restore and institutionalize prior relationships of economic, racialized, gendered inequity and subordination. These long-term effects of neoliberal thought and policy can often be overlooked in the day-to-day battles over individual economic policies or political headlines. But when viewing the cumulative result of the ideas, interest group pressures, and policy changes of the last 40 years, we can see a clear impact on remaking state power to serve, rather than dismantle, the perpetuation of domination and inequity in our political economy. Across different policy domains, three clear shifts stand out: (1) the privatization of governance; (2) the constricting of democratic public power; and (3) the weaponization of administration. These strategies serve to frustrate the aspirations for emancipation, flourishing, and structural justice; they also represent modes of hoarding and shifting power, along the lines that Yochai Benkler also describes in his chapter in this volume.

THE PRIVATIZATION OF GOVERNANCE

An obvious effect of neoliberal thought and policy is the deregulation of the market. Consider, for example, how the administration of Donald Trump focused on dismantling the Consumer Financial Protection Bureau (CFPB) while loosening labor, environmental, financial, and health insurance regulations. Nor is this a recent phenomenon: policy fights over deregulation have been a mainstay of both conservative and liberal policymakers especially since the Reagan era of the 1980s.

But these policies are about more than just undoing economic regulations. They represent rather a shift in power and governance *away* from public institutions *toward* private actors. Consider the CFPB's "forced arbitration rule." One of the central features of the modern economy is how companies increasingly deploy mandatory arbitration clauses in consumer and labor contracts, requiring consumers and workers alike to take any disputes to private arbitration rather than to formal legal proceedings in court or in administrative agencies. But arbitration is both costly and involves procedures that are highly limited, skewed to favor the interests of the business itself. In late 2016 through 2017, the CFPB issued a regulation barring these clauses from consumer contracts.[17] After taking the White House in 2017, the Trump administration with support from Congress overturned this rule—and in the following months, sought to defund and weaken the CFPB itself.[18] This represents more than a policy a shift; it is rather a major change in who gets to govern and decide matters of economic unfairness, moving that power away from public institutions like the courts and the CFPB to the private halls of arbitration.

Or consider how economic deregulation shifts the balance of power for workers and firms. The undoing of labor regulations and workplace protections has been a recurring pattern in both the Bush and Trump administrations. Without workplace protections for safety, dispute resolution, and pay equity issues, workers are essentially left subject to what Elizabeth Anderson has called the "private government" of managers, firms, and profit-maximizing boards. Similarly, the reduction of enforcement of antitrust laws starting with the Reagan administration in the 1980s and the undoing of financial regulations from 1980 through the 2009 financial crisis, and then again under the Trump administration, reflect a similar shift in power, a change in who is actually governing the economy. As Brandeis and other antitrust reformers of the early 1900s noted, the modern financial giants like J. P. Morgan and monopolists like the railroad, telecom, and oil titans of the era were effectively the decision-makers of the modern economy: through their control of these essential goods and services, they could decide which communities could bring their goods to market, what businesses would rise or fall, and what prices could be extracted in return.[19] The same is true of today's financialized economy, as private equity and investor interests—and new forms of corporate concentration—increasingly govern the market to fuel their returns, rather than to serve overall public welfare.[20]

Thus, while deregulation in a neoliberal era is often justified as a return to more efficient market allocation and a celebration of market freedom, untrammeled by government interference, this is misleading. Markets are not intrinsically free; rather, they are simply different institutional forms of allocating power and coming to collective decisions. And crucially, they represent a mode of governing and decision-making where property owners and wealthier interests are by definition more influential. The move to privatize, then, is not about freedom versus government; rather, it is about transferring decision-making from *public* government to *private* government. This is not to say that public government is intrinsically good or virtuous; indeed, governments and public agencies can often themselves fail or become captured or corrupt under pressure from the same kinds of wealthy interests that dominate the economy. But the move to privatization and financialization *do* represent a clear attempt to allocate economic decision-making to spaces that are *not* subject to the checks and balances of the Constitution or to the public forms of accountability in democratic electoral politics.[21]

CONSTRICTING EMANCIPATORY PUBLIC POWER

Running in parallel to the push to privatize government is a second pattern in neoliberal statecraft: the *constricting* of what remains of public governmental power in the first place. This pattern is a product of legal and policy decisions that work to narrow the range of permissible activities that government can undertake in the first place—and to impose greater barriers and hurdles on the exercise of governmental authority. A century ago in the Progressive era, as reformers sought to build the modern social contract and labor movements, they faced a powerful counterreaction from business interests and a conservative judiciary, which in cases like the 1905 *Lochner v. New York* struck down such reforms under laissez-faire conceptions of state and market.[22] *Lochner* came to stand in the popular and political imagination of the era for both a narrow vision of market freedom that ignored the domination of workers and communities at the hands of new industrial corporations—and for the ways in which the law was being deployed through judicial decisions to kneecap attempts by democratic movements and legislatures to mitigate these excesses of industrial capitalism. In the modern era, this threat of "Lochnerism," of the constricting of governmental power to preserve imbalances of economic power, has revived in a variety of forms.

First, a central project of the neoliberal and conservative legal imagination since the 1970s has involved a gradual narrowing the constitutional powers of Congress to enforce its most transformative egalitarian provisions in the Fourteenth Amendment.

In the aftermath of the Civil War, the radical Republicans of the Reconstruction era passed the Thirteenth, Fourteenth, and Fifteenth Amendments, which, though not without faults, radically remade the Constitution, for the first time establishing a constitutional democracy in the United States no longer formally rooted in slavery. While the Thirteenth Amendment formally abolished slavery, it was the Fourteenth Amendment which sought to ensure equal protection, due process, and the privileges and immunities of citizenship—and which allocated to Congress for the first time the power to legislatively enforce these goals. Yet right away, the more radically emancipatory potential of the Fourteenth Amendment was undercut. As Black Americans exercised political power and gained elected office at record levels in the 1870 and 1872 elections, a wave of white supremacist paramilitary violence violently attacked Black voters and leaders. The Supreme Court then intervened in a series of cases in the 1870s to gut the enforcement powers of Congress, render newly passed civil rights legislation moot, and throw out the murder convictions for perpetrators of political violence against Black voters.[23] It was not until a century later that *Brown v. Board* (1954), the Civil Rights Act (1964), and the Voting Rights Act (1965) renewed the promise of the Fourteenth Amendment's protections for equality.

Though less blatant, the backlash to the civil rights movement operated in a similar fashion: the combination of a conservative Supreme Court and a Congress under pressure from neoliberal and anti-civil-rights pressures gradually eroded the Constitutional and legislative provisions aimed at enforcing social and economic equality. This shift is particularly pronounced since the 1970s and the Supreme Court's lurch from the liberal Warren court to a more conservative majority following Richard Nixon's aberrational four Supreme Court appointments. For example, the Fourteenth Amendment equal protection doctrine moved to a more restrictive intent requirement for proving constitutionally invalid racial discrimination—effectively immunizing various forms of structural economic and racial injustice, such as racialized criminal justice enforcement and zoning practices, from constitutional challenge.[24] Under the Rehnquist and Roberts courts of the 1990s and 2000s, the Supreme Court similarly moved to a more neutral, color-blind view of equal protection that effectively removed requirements for school desegregation.[25] Similarly, the Fourteenth Amendment's provisions of equal protection and due process are preemptively narrowed by a series of decisions spanning the Redemption era and the Rehnquist court that imposed strict "state action" requirements, further immunizing various forms of private discrimination from constitutional challenge.[26] The Supreme Court also restricted Congress's powers under the Fourteenth Amendment to enforce inclusion, most infamously in John Roberts's 2013 ruling gutting the Voting Rights Act—leading directly to the modern wave of voter suppression tactics across the country.[27]

A second line of attack has involved the weaponization of the First Amendment to similar effect: the narrowing of the permissible scope of equality-enhancing governmental action. Consider, for example, how in recent years free speech and free association claims have been deployed by businesses seeking to excuse themselves from antidiscrimination protections for LGBTQ individuals or from federal requirements to ensure access to contraceptive care and reproductive health.[28] Similarly, corporate free speech claims have been employed to dismantle restrictions on corporations and wealthy individuals flooding elections with private campaign expenditures that radically shift political influence upward.[29] At the same time, First Amendment claims for free speech and free association have ironically been deployed by the Supreme Court to weigh *against* the abilities of workers to organize and associate.[30] This "First Amendment Lochnerism"—where economic regulations and labor organizing are both limited in the name of the free speech rights of corporations and individuals—serves a similar purpose: the neutering of public power especially as it is deployed to balance economic power and inequalities.[31]

These lines of attack—encompassing different Constitutional provisions—have a suffocating quality to them. Congressional power to enforce ideals of equality and inclusion has been constrained. Where Congress and courts have responded by grounding civil rights and economic inclusion measures under different provisions—such as moving from Fourteenth Amendment to Commerce Clause justifications for antidiscrimination and social welfare laws like the Civil Rights Act and the Affordable Care Act—those moves have also subsequently been narrowed by further court rulings.[32] Even where there are well-established regimes for inclusion and ensuring the balance of democratic power, like the Voting Rights Act, recent holdings have undercut those as well. The combined result is a constricting of public power—specifically those uses of public power that are designed to combat economic, social, or political domination.

WEAPONIZING ADMINISTRATION

The first two themes of privatized government and constricted public power both operate in the same fashion: reducing democratic public political power and shifting more control to (unchecked) private actors. But there is a third pattern to neoliberal statecraft that involves not the dismantling of state power but rather its weaponization in the service of more exclusionary ends.

Take, for example, the pattern, especially since the 1980s, of increasingly punitive and aggressive requirements for enrolling in safety net programs. Applicants are subjected to invasive inspections, mountains of paperwork,

and often demeaning and arbitrary interviews before accessing social programs like food stamps, unemployment protections, or welfare. Scholars of
the safety net have long noted how these policies, which accelerated during the Reagan, Bush, and Clinton years, have been designed to limit access
to these benefits,[33] and further, how the welfare bureaucracy has often been
weaponized to dehumanize individuals seeking to gain access to benefits—
and how these barriers to entry are themselves often a product of a combination of racialized and anti-government sentiment.

This weaponization of administrative regimes is also present even in the
context of those emancipatory protections nominally protected by the Constitution itself. Formally recognized Constitutional rights depend on a vast
infrastructure of implementation in order to be realized. As Cary Franklin
has argued in context of reproductive rights, attacks on the "infrastructure
of provision"—the geographical dispersion of clinics, the kinds of hoops
that doctors and clinics have to jump through to gain state licenses and
approvals—can functionally reduce a constitutionally recognized right in
dramatic ways, even absent a frontal attack on the right itself.[34] These types
of attacks on the (public and private) bureaucracy of administration of reproductive rights led to corrective attempts like the expanded "undue burden" standard codified in *Whole Women's Health v. Hellerstedt*. A similar fight
is now underway in regard to voter suppression. Voting rights advocates
have long raised concerns about how the very administration of electoral
infrastructure—processes for voter registration, voter ID, and the very placement and quality of voting machines—can have dramatic impact on who
actually votes. These administrative apparatuses have been increasingly weaponized to deliberately undermine the access to the ballot, particularly for
communities of color, particularly after the gutting of the VRA preclearance
regime in *Shelby County v. Holder*. Stacey Abrams's lawsuit, *Fair Fight Action v.
Crittenden,* identifies a wide range of such abuses arising from the 2018 Georgia gubernatorial race, which she narrowly lost to the then secretary of state,
Brian Kemp. Like *Whole Women's Health*, this suit paints a broad picture of the
administrative apparatus needed to make good on the constitutional right to
vote—and the ways in which that apparatus can be weaponized to systematically and strategically undermine that right for particular communities.

There is another context where administrative institutions are essential
to equal citizenship—and where they can be deployed systematically to instead create unequal forms of citizenship. This scenario involves the *unshack-
ling* of administrative authority into unchecked, arbitrary state power that
strips target communities of the protections and securities of citizenship.
Consider, for example, contemporary concerns over the weaponization of

immigration enforcement in recent years, from the inhumane family separation crisis at the border to the increased use of Immigration and Customs Enforcement (ICE) raids on immigrant communities, often falsely targeting legal immigrants in communities of color. These tactics represent administrative authority stripped of the checks and balances that nominally arise from administrative law—and deployed systematically to reassert a racialized conception of citizenship and membership, of who belongs and who doesn't.

What these fights highlight is the dynamic interaction between formal Constitutional rights and administrative infrastructures of provision. The experience of membership and inclusion depends greatly on how governance regimes, administrative institutions, and enforcement systems operate. But administrative agencies, once created, do not automatically or necessarily operate in egalitarian ways. The control and management of those infrastructures are critical to ensuring nominal rights are in fact realized. Absent that degree of control and accountability, these administrative systems are likely to be used to undermine rights for particular communities, resulting in a de facto form of tiered, hierarchical membership. The result is that even where the moral content of citizenship leads to commitments to redress political, economic, and social forms of subordination or domination, the very control and implementation of administrative systems can lead to a lived reality of tiered membership, where some communities fully experience the benefits of citizenship and others do not. This third challenge of weaponized administration is crucial to note, because it underscores that the role of administrative authority in realizing citizenship is not just a matter of *more* government; rather, it is a matter of *responsive and accountable* government.

Freedom, Democracy, and the Rebuilding of Public Power

As the previous examples underscore, the patterns of neoliberal statecraft have operated to systematically undo institutions built to prevent domination and advance a more emancipatory, inclusive, empowering vision of democratic equality. The key lesson here is that political-institutional development is central to the realization of democracy and freedom and to overcoming domination. This in turn suggests that the building of new institutions is a critical area of focus for reformers, thinkers, and advocates in this New Gilded Age of twenty-first-century inequities. The aspirations for democratic, equal citizenship require administrative bodies, enforcement regimes, and infrastructures of provision to ensure fair and equal access to basic public goods. Economic freedom and democratic equality thus require a concerted effort to (re)build public institutions designed to enforce equality and advance structural justice.

In the modern context, this means that the project of structural justice requires building and expanding public power in ways that secure the authority, capacity, and accountability to address the kinds of structural inequities that animate twenty-first-century capitalism. Administrative institutions are central to redressing private and systemic forms of domination. Through administrative institutions (whether federal, state, or local), we have innovated institutional structures to redress forms of concentrated and unchecked private power—from antitrust to labor law to corporate law and more. Even as battles for formal socioeconomic rights have fallen short in Constitutional jurisprudence, arguably those moral claims have driven the creation of a modern administrative apparatus charged with securing broad protections for social and economic citizenship, through administrative regimes governing concerns like consumer protection, environmental justice, labor rights, antidiscrimination law, disparate impact, and more. These administrative systems enforce ideals of equality outside of the courts, through (legislatively authorized) administrative processes.[35]

Consider the Flint water crisis noted at the outset of this chapter. A vision of structural justice and democracy points toward a number of implications for how to approach that crisis. First, it suggests that governance needs to be wrested back from private actors—for example, investor interests and private companies that come to control privatized utilities—back into the public sector. But second, it also demands a more democratically accountable public governance regime for the water utility itself, that empowers Black and brown communities and grassroots communities most affected by the operations of the utility. And it requires a utility committed to human flourishing, with requirements for fair pricing, nondiscriminatory access, and the like.[36]

This linkage between administrative institutions and moral citizenship suggests a theory of social change that centers the need to construct and defend equality-enhancing governance regimes. Advancing justice requires building public institutions that are democratically accountable and responsive, and that have the authorities and capacities to ensure equity and justice, dismantling systems of domination and inequality. These public institutions are a necessary foundation for advancing an expansive vision of social and economic citizenship. As the recent revival of interest in "constitutional political economy" and "administrative constitutionalism"[37] suggests, the moral appeals to membership, inclusion, equality—and against forms of economic and social domination—require more than formal, textual Constitutional change to be realized. And indeed, the central battles for this fight for inclusion may not even involve the courts or the constitutional text so much as it requires popular movements, public debates over values, and then legislative and regulatory implementation of those values. This view of social change moves the terrain of contest away from formal Constitutional law to the broader domain of small-c constitutional public law infrastructures, encompassing legislation, regulation, state and local administration, and more. As Marc Stears notes in his chapter in this book, this view of social change requires a balancing of the transformative and aspirational vision for the future, with a pragmatic and realistic commitment to building specific policy levers and institutional designs. While legislation, regulation, and public policy are often viewed in technical, technocratic terms of optimizing policy efficiency, this approach suggests a much broader moral and political orientation toward policy. As Danielle Allen has suggested in her reformulation of the concept of "planning," the stakes of policy design, on this view, are not well captured in concepts of economic efficiency or cost-benefit analysis, but rather in terms of the moral implications for citizenship—and the very real questions of political power and accountability as they play out in the often-overlooked domain of administration.

As noted earlier, past historical moments of expanding the reach and substantive meaning of membership have been accompanied by significant moments of state- and institution-building. The upheavals of industrialization helped drive the development of the modern safety net and administrative state in the late nineteenth century. The civil rights movement not only helped secure major legislation like the Voting Rights Act and Civil Rights Act, but it also led to the formation of new institutions of public power imbued with the authority and capacity to enforce these new moral commitments: a Department of Justice enforcing preclearance requirements and overseeing voting rights, a federal bureaucracy monitoring issues of discrimination, and the like.

What, then, must today's reformers look to do in this regard? There are some key institutional design lessons that can be gleaned from the history of progressive, inclusionary, emancipatory statecraft.

First, consider three brief historical touchstones for this question.

Industrialization and the rise of public utility. In the late nineteenth century, the upheavals of industrialization created new forms of economic precarity, exploitation, and immiseration—a kind of systemic domination in the form of the new rules of the unequal industrial economy. This experience fueled new social movements for worker power and for economic freedom from this new form of economic dislocation. But this was also a period of dramatic *institutional* innovation. Reformers for the first time created new administrative bodies and oversight bodies, enforcing requirements for nondiscrimination, fair pricing, and consumer protection. The linchpin of these efforts was the idea of public utility regulation: that essential goods and services could not be left in the hands of unchecked private actors; that these goods and services needed to be publicly provided and subject to public accountability; and that the mechanism for ensuring access and accountability would be administrative entities that combined democratic responsiveness with new forms of expert public administration. These public utility and administrative bodies were first pioneered at the municipal and state level, encompassing everything from milk to transport to telecommunications, and formed the foundation for the emergence of the federal New Deal regulatory state in the 1930s.[38] These efforts also involved the formation of the first social insurance programs that would become the foundation for the New Deal safety net and the rise of economic citizenship protections like Social Security and the protections of the New Deal era.[39]

Corporate power and the role of structural limits. Also in the late nineteenth and early twentieth century, the rise of megacorporations, financiers like J. P. Morgan, and corporate monopolists like the Vanderbilts, the Goulds, and the Rockefellers drove another key administrative and regulatory innovation: progressive taxation and anti-monopoly, financial, and corporate governance regulations. As Rebecca Henderson, Malcolm Salter, and Chris Eaglin note in their chapters, the structure of the corporate form is a key issue for contesting domination. The response to these forms of dyadic domination at the hands of private power led to reforms that sought to deploy the powers of the state to prophylactically and structurally limit private power. The concern here was less with stopping specifically blameworthy conduct on the part of these monopolists and corporations; instead, the goal was to preemptively limit the size, power, and reach of these firms, so as to preclude the kinds of economic exploitation and undue political influence that accompanied the rise of such tremendous concentrations of wealth and power.

Systemic discrimination and civil rights enforcement. Another historical administrative innovation can be found in the attempts to address systemic forms of racialized and gendered bias and discrimination. Rather than relying just on individualized enforcement against specific malefactors—although that remains a mainstay of civil rights and tort law—the administrative dimensions of civil rights involved attempts to create more systemic protections against racial and gender inequality. Think, for example, of the Voting Rights Act system of "preclearance" designed to mitigate attempts at voter suppression. Similarly, the Obama administration experimented with new regulatory approaches to reduced economic segregation through its "Affirmatively Furthering Fair Housing" program, which set out goals of equality to be achieved through regional urban planning procedures that took desegregation as a key objective and stakeholder consultation as a primary requirement.[40] Or consider how the Environmental Protection Agency (EPA) Office of Environmental Justice designed to address the racially disparate concentration of environmental harms arising from pollution and racially inequitable urban planning.[41]

While a systematic accounting of these experiments and their lessons are beyond the scope of this essay, these brief examples do point to some design lessons and principles for today's reformers seeking to institutionalize a political economy of justice.

First, any administrative and institutional regime for protecting against domination and advancing a more equitable and inclusive vision of democracy will need to establish and enforce structural limits on concentrated economic power through bright-line rules and prophylactic limits. Think, for example, about how antitrust law imposes restrictions on the size and concentration of megafirms, or how following the 2008–2009 financial crisis, policymakers considered but failed to enact policies to "break up" financial conglomerates and severely restrict the types of financial transactions that modern firms could engage in. In place of such structural and prophylactic rules, contemporary economic regulation over the last few decades has tended to favor a more "managerial" approach: leaving market concentration and actors in place but using regulation to encourage better firm conduct or to mitigate market failures. By contrast, a structuralist approach to regulation would instead consider preemptive restrictions on firm size, powers, and behaviors as a way to preclude problematic conduct and to limit in advance the undue concentration of economic—or, for that matter, political—influence on the part of megafirms. Structural limits represent a much more robust and effective protection against domination in the economic arena. Such a structuralist approach to regulation would in many ways harken back to the aspirations of Progressive era anti-monopoly reforms and the kind of more transformative and egalitarian reform visions arising from the most recent financial crisis.[42]

Second, an inclusionary administrative institutional regime will have to restore and reinvent mechanisms for enforcing the values of equality and inclusion—particularly in context of systemic economic, racial, and gender forms of exclusion and exploitation. Just as the Civil Rights Act and Voting Rights Act created new enforcement tools for the federal government, today's reformers will have to devise similarly novel and powerful enforcement systems. In particular, such systems will require sufficient and expanded authority to monitor and regulate abuses. Consider, for example, how the creation of the Consumer Financial Protection Bureau generated a more centralized and empowered enforcement apparatus, whereas before its creation, many issues of consumer exploitation where left unchecked, as regulatory authorities for different types of products and behaviors were scattered across several different competing and uncoordinated agencies. The environmental justice movement's effort to create a centralized Office of Environmental Justice in the EPA represents another (albeit more modest) example of this principle of consolidating authorities. Similarly, authority will have to be expanded through statutory measures that give regulators the powers to redress systemic disparities without having to show specific intent. The Civil Rights Act's disparate impact provisions offer one example of broad mandates. Finally, these institutions will need novel ways to monitor for abuses and enforce remedies. Toward the latter days of the Obama administration, regulators began to experiment with more high-yield enforcement regimes that targeted the root causes of systemic inequities—for example, using labor law to impose fines on parent companies rather than subsidiaries or using regulators to prod metropolitan regions to coordinate on plans to promote economic desegregation.[43]

Third, these new administrative institutions and remedies need to also be reconstituted in more specifically democratic, participatory modes. As Charles Sabel and Dani Rodrik and Leah Downey argue in their chapters, responsive and accountable and recursive modes of organization are essential to tackling complex problems of justice; the administrative state should be constructed in this spirit. Recently, grassroots movements for economic and racial justice have experimented with policy shifts that directly empower stakeholders in administrative governance—for example, appointing workers to wage boards setting state-level labor policies, or including tenants and residents on community oversight boards charged with monitoring the outcomes of local economic development projects. These experiments build on a rich and global tradition of participatory governance that can be adapted for a more democratically responsive and accountable administrative regime. Indeed, a democratic political economy ought to institutionalize greater power and voice for the most directly impacted communities to share in the designing and implementing of public policy—in contrast to either market-oriented or technocratic modes of governing.[44] This also means bringing greater inclusive governance to the economic arena directly, as more and more firms and industries can consider models of codetermination, worker and stakeholder participation on corporate boards, and worker-led corporate governance.

Conclusion

We are living in a moment of radical rupture and transformation, where economic, social, political, and ecological crises are opening our societies up to terrifying dangers. But it is also a moment of possibly transformative change advancing ideals of democracy, inclusion, and freedom.

The inequities of our twenty-first-century political economy are at their core problems of domination, of the concentration of unaccountable power, and the systemic reinscription of relationships of subordination and unfreedom. The response to this moral challenge requires not just new policies for economic inclusion but a more thorough remaking of our economic and social order to dismantle systemic economic, racial, and gender inequities. Furthermore, achieving this end requires the construction of effective and powerful forms of *public power*, which must itself be democratically responsive and accountable. Neoliberalism, however, poses a further challenge to this aspiration, as a worldview, a political agenda, and a mode of statecraft that has focused particularly on erasing domination from view and dismantling those institutions built in prior generations to contest domination. A central challenge, then, for a more inclusive and emancipatory political economy is to rebuild (or build anew) institutions of governance capable of counteracting and undoing systems of domination.

This is partly a matter of policy and institutional design. We need a new generation of administrative bodies, civil rights enforcement regimes, and regulatory restraints on private corporate power and on financialized and monopolistic interests. It is also a matter of mobilization, organization, and advocacy: today's social movements are demanding transformative change to address questions of inequality, worker justice, racial justice, gender justice, environmental justice, and much more. Like the transformative movements of the Reconstruction era, the Progressive era, or the Civil Rights era, we are in a movement moment where the boundaries of the possible are being renegotiated.

But this challenge of building new institutional mechanisms for advancing an inclusive political economy also represents an ideational and conceptual challenge. This vision of inclusionary administration and state power represents a direct challenge to decades of neoliberal presumptions. It means reconceptualizing freedom not as a narrow property of individuals and "free markets" but rather as a result of deep commitments to equity, human flourishing, and dignity—and a rebalancing of economic and political power. It means reconceptualizing equality not as the surface equality to transact on the market but the deep equity to stand in relations of equal moral worth and standing in the polity. And it means reconceptualizing politics not just as the domain of power or the realm of capture and corruption, but rather as a democratic space of collective participation and shared self-governance.

These shifts represent a challenge to conservative and neoliberal politics. But it also represents a challenge to some long-held presumptions within liberal thought. Focusing on power and domination is a more radical orientation than liberal thought emphasizing values of consensus, of good governance, of equality, of opportunity narrowly construed.[45] This emphasis on both robust and participatory democratic governance means stepping outside of familiar "good governance" models of reform—which tend to emphasize transparency, rationality, and civility as ideals—to instead thinking about institutional design as a project of power: first, of empowering those most affected and most marginalized, and second of exercising state power to dismantle systemic forms of domination and inequity.[46] This also means rethinking the familiar legal liberal fascination with courts, judges, and technocratic expertise and imagining more transformative, bottom-up, democratic forms of governance and social change. These shifts will not always be easy or even universally acclaimed. But if we are to overcome the inequities of the current moment, we must imagine new forms of administration, governance, and public power that can rise to the task. Anything less will be not enough to fulfill the aspirations for an inclusive, equitable, multiracial twenty-first-century democracy.

Notes

1.   See Lee DeVito, "The Number of Flint's Students with Special Needs Has Increased by 56% since the Water Crisis, according to Reports," *Detroit Metro Times*, August 28, 2019, https://www.metrotimes.com/news-hits/archives/2019/08/28/the-number-of-flints-special-needs-students-has-increased-by-56-since-the-water-crisis-according-to-report.

2.   See Sarah Frostenson, "America Has a Water Crisis No One Is Talking About," *Vox*, May 9, 2017, https://www.vox.com/science-and-health/2017/5/9/15183330/america-water-crisis-affordability-millions; Jacey Fortin, "In Flint, Overdue Bills for Unsafe Water Could Lead to Foreclosures," *New York Times*, May 4, 2017, https://www.nytimes.com/2017/05/04/us/flint-water-home-foreclosure.html?_r=0.

3.   See K. Sabeel Rahman, "Infrastructural Exclusion and the Fight for the City: Power, Democracy, and the Case of America's Water Crisis," *Harvard Civil Rights-Civil Liberties Law Review* 53 (2018): 801–29.

4.   See, for example, Iris Marion Young, *Responsibility for Justice* (Oxford University Press, 2011); K. Sabeel Rahman, "Constructing and Contesting Struc-

tural Inequality," *Critical Analysis of Law* 5, no. 1 (2018): 99–126; Amna Akbar, "Toward a Radical Imagination of Law," *NYU Law Review* 93, no. 3 (June 2018): 405–479.

5. See Young, *Responsibility for Justice*, 52–59.

6. See, for example, Elizabeth Anderson, *Private Government* (Princeton University Press, 2017).

7. See, for example, Martin Gilens, *Affluence and Influence* (Princeton University Press, 2014); Larry Bartels, *Unequal Democracy* (Princeton University Press, 2017).

8. See, for example, Friedrich Hayek, "'Social' or Distributive Justice," in *The Essence of Hayek*, ed. Chiaki Nishiyama and Kurt R. Leube (Hoover Institution Press, 1984).

9. This skepticism can be seen in the political science expounders of neoliberal thought—for example, the rise of "capture theory" and public choice economics advanced by thinkers like George Stigler, James Buchanan, and Gordon Tullock. See S. M. Amadae, *Rationalizing Capitalist Democracy (University of Chicago Press, 2003)*. For an account of how this skepticism of government animated many political narratives against social reform, see Albert Hirschman's classic book, *Rhetoric of Reaction (Harvard University Press, 1991)*.

10. See Kim Phillips-Fein, *Invisible Hands (W.W. Norton, 2010)*; Angus Burgin, *The Great Persuasion (Harvard University Press, 2015)*; Jacob Hacker and Paul Pierson, *American Amnesia (Simon & Schuster, 2017)*; Lawrence Glickman, *Free Enterprise (Yale University Press, 2019)*.

11. See Nancy Maclean, *Democracy in Chains (Penguin Random House, 2017)*.

12. See Felicia Wong, "Building Post-Neoliberal Institutions," *Democracy: A Journal of Ideas* (Summer 2019).

13. See Jacob Hacker and Paul Pierson, *Winner-Take-All Politics* (Simon & Schuster, 2010); Katharina Pistor, *The Code of Capital* (Princeton University Press, 2019).

14. See, for example, Richard Rothstein, *Color of Law* (Liveright Publishing, 2017); Mehrsa Baradaran, *Other People's Money* (Belknap Press of Harvard University Press, 2017).

15. See Quinn Slobodian, *The Globalists* (Harvard University Press, 2018).

16. See, for example, Gilens, *Affluence and Influence*; Nicholas Carnes, *White-Collar Government* (University of Chicago Press, 2013); Hacker and Pierson, *Winner-Take-All Politics*; Bartels, *Unequal Democracy*; Kay Lehman Schlozman, Sidney Verba, and Henry Brady, *Unheavenly Chorus* (Princeton University Press, 2012).

17. See, for example, Consumer Financial Protection Bureau, "New Protections against Mandatory Arbitrations," 2017, https://www.consumerfinance.gov/arbitration-rule/.

18. See, for example, Eric Goldberg, "Correcting the Record on the CFPB's Arbitration Rule," Consumer Financial Protection Bureau, October 16, 2017, https://www.consumerfinance.gov/about-us/blog/correcting-record-cfpbs

-arbitration-rule/; see also Sylvan Lane, "Trump Repeals Consumer Arbitration Rule, Wins Banker Praise," *The Hill*, November 1, 2017, https://thehill .com/policy/finance/358297-trump-repeals-consumer-bureau-arbitration -rule-joined-by-heads-of-banking.

19. See, for example, Daniel Rodgers, *Atlantic Crossings* (Harvard University Press, 2000); K. Sabeel Rahman, *Democracy against Domination* (Oxford University Press, 2017), chap. 3.

20. For a documentation of today's corporate concentration crisis and the role of modern finance in reshaping market dynamics, see, for example, Rana Foroohar, *Makers and Takers* (Crown Business, 2016); Matt Stoller, *Goliath* (Simon & Schuster, 2019); Tim Wu, *The Curse of Bigness* (Columbia Global Reports, 2018).

21. For a broader version of this critique of privatization, see Jon Michaels, *Constitutional Coup* (Harvard University Press, 2017).

22. *Lochner v. New York* (1905).

23. See, for example, *US v. Cruikshank* (1876); *Civil Rights Cases* (1883). See also Jim Pope, "Snubbed Landmark: Why *United States v. Cruikshank* Belongs at the Heart of the American Constitutional Canon," *Harvard Civil Rights-Civil Liberties Review* 49 (2014).

24. See *Washington v. Davis* (1976).

25. *Parents Involved in Community Schools v. Seattle School District No. 1* (2007).

26. See, for example, *Civil Rights Cases (1883); Jackson v. Metropolitan Edison Co.* (1974); *Deshaney v. Winnebago County* (1989).

27. *Shelby County v. Holder* (2013).

28. *Masterpiece Cakeshop v. Colorado Civil Rights Commission* (2018); *Burwell v. Hobby Lobby* (2014).

29. *Citizens' United v. FEC* (2010).

30. See, for example, *Janus v. AFSCME* (2018).

31. See Jed Purdy, "Beyond the Bosses' Constitution," *Columbia Law Review* 118, no. 7 (November 2018): 2161–86.

32. See, for example, *US v. Morrison* (2000) and *NFIB v. Sibelius* (2012).

33. See, for example, Kathryn J. Edin and H. Luke Shaefer, *$2.00 a Day: Living on Almost Nothing in America* (Mariner Books, 2016); Michael Katz, *The Undeserving Poor* (Oxford University Press, 2013).

34. Cary Franklin, "Infrastructures of Provision," unpublished manuscript, 2017, draft on file.

35. For a longer version of this argument, see K. Sabeel Rahman, "Constructing Citizenship," *Columbia Law Review* 118, no. 8 (December 2018): 2447–503.

36. See, for example, K. Sabeel Rahman, "Infrastructural Exclusion and the Fight for the City," *Harvard Civil Rights–Civil Liberties Law Review* 53 (2018): 533–62.

37. See, for example, Gillian Metzger, "Administrative Constitutionalism," *Texas Law Review* 91 (2013).

38. See William Novak, "Law and the Social Control of American Capitalism," *Emory Law Journal* 60, no. 2 (2010).

39. See, for example, David Moss, *When All Else Fails* (Harvard University Press, 2002).

40. See Olatunde Johnson, "Beyond the Private Attorney General: Equality Directives in American Law," *NYU Law Review* 87 (2012).

41. For a longer version of this argument, see K. Sabeel Rahman, "Reconstructing the Administrative State," *Harvard Law Review* 131 (2018).

42. For a discussion of structuralist regulation in context of finance, see, for example, Rahman, *Democracy against Domination*, chap. 7. In context of information platforms, see K. Sabeel Rahman, "Regulating Informational Infrastructure," *Georgetown Law and Technology Journal* 2, no. 2 (2018).

43. See, for example, David Weil, "Creating a Strategic Enforcement Approach to Address Wage Theft," *Journal of Industrial Relations* 60, no. 3 (2018): 437–60; Johnson, "Beyond the Private Attorney General: Equality Directives in American Law."

44. See, for example, K. Sabeel Rahman and Hollie Russon Gilman, *Civic Power* (Cambridge University Press, 2019), 169–203.

45. See, for example, Elizabeth Anderson, "What Is the Point of Equality?" *Ethics* 109, no. 2 (January 1999); Rahman, *Democracy against Domination*, 105–11.

46. See Rahman and Russon Gilman, *Civic Power*, 18–27.

13 *Governing Money Democratically: Rechartering the Federal Reserve*

LEAH DOWNEY

Money connects all members of a polity.[1] It is central to the project of collective life; we all use it, desire it, and rely on it. Money is the instantiation of our social and economic interdependence. If democracy is, at base, collective governance of our collective life, then it would seem that governance of the money supply should be central to the project of democracy. I argue here for regularly rechartering the Federal Reserve System in an effort to establish monetary policy, governance of the money supply, as a fundamental part of the democratic endeavor.[2]

Delegation has been part of democratic governance for centuries. Life in the modern world is a series of delegations: we delegate our political power to elected representatives, we delegate our parental duties to teachers and nannies, we delegate the responsibility for our health to medical professionals, we delegate the task of fixing our pipes to plumbers, and the list goes on. Unsurprisingly, then, much of democratic political theory in the modern period has been focused on the relationship between the people and their delegates, most especially, their elected representatives. Democracy itself, conceived of as rule by the people, depends on the nature and strength of this relationship. If the strength of this relationship should wither away, the health and sustainability of the democracy would be in danger.

The basic democratic commitment is that citizens should make self-constituting choices themselves or should elect people to make those choices on their behalf.[3] The ossification of the administrative state is a threat to this promise. In this chapter, I focus on the form that threat takes vis-à-vis monetary policy, defending the claim that democratic power over the macroeconomy has atrophied and suggesting a remedy. While my focus is monetary policy, the thrust of the argument offered here applies broadly to the administrative state.

The chapter proceeds in four parts. First, I outline the political environment at the founding of the Federal Reserve (the Fed). The Fed's design is the result of political compromises made in 1913 that are no longer salient to the democratic governance of the money supply of 2020. The second part goes on to ask, if that is true, why has so little changed? I explore both the general benefits of temporary legislation as well as the specific use of temporary charters to establish central banks in US history. Third, I employ the work of Jean-Jacques Rousseau to argue that there are fundamental, democratic reasons for regular rechartering. The final section offers a provocative suggestion for restructuring one aspect of the Fed to illustrate the wide range of possibilities for that process. The conclusion considers how the threat of climate change, and current central bank responses to it, intersect with my argument.

It's Not 1913 Anymore

The Federal Reserve Act of 1913 established the Federal Reserve System (the Fed). The culmination of a long and messy political battle, the Federal Reserve was a compromise constructed along two primary axes: How centralized or decentralized should the central bank be? Should it be public or private?

Commercial bankers were the most prominent advocates of establishing a central bank at the time. The Panic of 1907 lingered in the air. The crisis had been quelled largely by J. P. Morgan wielding his personal and political prowess to coordinate a private bank bailout. Going forward, however, bankers did not want to rely on such informal means for securing the financial system. Instead, they preferred the idea of establishing a central bank, a formal institution that could act as a lender of last resort—a backstop against bank runs.[4]

Beyond concerns of financial security, American bankers felt they were falling behind their European counterparts. European finance was buoyed by Europe's central banks. Centralized reserves meant more profitable lending as well as more security in banking. If bankers do not have to hoard reserves for fear of a bank run, they are able to lend more and thus earn more. As Paul Warburg, the most prominent advocate of this approach, said: "Our banking system must mobilize its reserves." He drew a comparison between America's financial system before the Fed to a military system that prevented generals from putting troops where they are most necessary and effective.[5]

Bankers wanted the new bank to be privately controlled. In their view, the country's political class simply did not have the proper training to responsibly govern centralized reserves efficiently. This view continues to motivate support for the independence of the modern Federal Reserve.[6] Senator Robert Owen, one of the founding fathers of the Federal Reserve System, wrote:

In developing the Federal Reserve bill there was a fierce controversy as to whether bankers or private individuals should govern the credit system or whether the United States should do so through a Board of Governors who should take an oath of office of loyalty to the public and become officially responsible to the public under their oath of office. The big bankers and certain representatives demanded bank control.[7]

Bankers preferred a central bank that was both centralized and private. Achieving this aim proved politically impossible.

A second group had different ambitions for the Fed. As well as striking fear into the heart of bankers, the Panic of 1907 ignited a surge of popular distaste for concentrated private interests. The public was not pleased with the economic wrath of the Panic of 1907, nor with what they took it to reveal: that a very small group of men more or less ran the entire financial system. This group came to be known as the "Money Trust."

A congressional subcommittee, led by Arsène Pujo of Louisiana, was established to investigate the Money Trust." The Pujo hearings were well publicized and highly influential, taking place at the very same moment the Federal Reserve Act was being debated. These twin reactions to the Panic of 1907, while largely separate processes, were not entirely independent: in the shadow of the Pujo hearings, legislators could not be convinced to give more centralized power to private bankers. In this spirit, a group of congresspeople, sometimes called the antitrust Democrats, advocated for a central bank that would divert credit to small banks and businesses. They hoped the reintroduction of healthy competition in the banking sector would break up the Money Trust.[8] They wanted a central bank that centralized reserves under *public* control.

The agricultural community had yet another set of plans for a central bank. Their primary concern was credit allocation. Farmers tethered to the cycle of the harvest found it very difficult to get credit when they needed it.[9] Agricultural advocates in the discussions surrounding the founding of the Fed proposed a central bank that could directly allocate credit to certain sectors.[10] They were worried the central bank would be used exclusively to bail out bankers, leaving farmers high and dry. The agricultural community, like the antitrust Democrats, favored a centralized, public Federal Reserve System.[11]

Many rejected the project of centralizing power over the money supply wholesale. General aversion to the idea of a central bank was known as "the ghost of Andrew Jackson." This opposition, spanning the political spectrum, has been largely attributed to a commitment to federalism, a sort of American allergy to centralized power. Warburg expressed it well:

> It was generally held that the centralization of banking would inevitably result in one of two alternatives: either complete government control, which meant politics in banking or control by "Wall Street", which meant banking in politics. Abhorrence of both extremes had led to an almost fanatic conviction that the only hope of keeping the country's credit system independent was to be sought in complete decentralization of banking.[12]

Some were not entirely opposed to establishing a central bank but rejected the centralization of power. The most prominent figure who held this position was Congress member Carter Glass. Glass was vehemently against centralization simply because he opposed any augmentation of federal power. As a brutal segregationist, Glass fought any increase in federal "interference" on the grounds that it posed a risk to segregation. He also embodied the old Democratic fear that allowing centralization in finance would cede power to northeastern elites at the expense of the rural, southern, and western parts of the country.

To achieve his desired aim, establishing a central bank, President Woodrow Wilson had to navigate the political morass between those who wanted a centralized private bank, those who wanted a centralized public bank, and those who could not countenance a centralized bank at all. He compromised on all fronts. Ultimately, he attempted to establish a form of financial federalism to mirror the nation's political federalism.[13] The result was a Federal Reserve System made up of 12 regional reserve banks, decentralized and privately owned, and one public capstone body located in Washington, DC.

Today's Federal Reserve System is a legislative Frankenstein: the jerry-rigged structure of private, public, centralized, and decentralized elements cobbled together over a century ago largely remains.[14] Twelve regional Federal Reserve Banks (FRBs) make up a decentralized web of private corporations located today exactly where they were placed just after the founding of the Federal Reserve. The reserve banks were largely placed where the commercial banks wanted them to go—including cities that today seem faintly absurd. Why do we need an FRB in both Kansas City and St. Louis?[15]

As a private corporation, each reserve bank has a president and CEO as well as a board of directors. Each board has nine people, split into three categories: Class A, B, and C. Class A are bankers appointed by the stockholder banks, Class B are nonbankers appointed by the stockholder banks, and

Class C are nonbankers appointed by the Federal Reserve Board of Governors.[16] In short, the board of each reserve bank is two-thirds stockholding bankers or stockholding banker appointees. The president and CEO of each Reserve Bank board attends and participates in all meetings of the Federal Open Market Committee (FOMC), the US monetary authority.[17] The Reserve Bank presidents rotate into voting positions on the FOMC, except the New York Reserve Bank president, who always votes. The FOMC meets in Washington, DC, and has 12 voting members. The seven members of the Board of Governors sit on the FOMC. Governors are appointed by the president of the United States and confirmed by the Senate for staggered 14-year terms.[18] Together, the Governors and the CEOs of the regional Federal Reserve Banks make national monetary policy.

While the regional banks are private and decentralized and the monetary policymaking authority (the FOMC) is a centralized blend of private and public powers, the execution of monetary policy is centralized and private. Anytime the Federal Reserve System directly engages with the market, with the exception of crisis facilities, it does so through "primary dealers."[19] Primary dealers are securities brokers that trade directly with the Fed. They are required to bid when the Fed conducts open market operations and to provide information to the Fed's open market trading desk. These 20 or so financial institutions buy Treasury bills sold at action and resell them to other major financial institutions, including large commercial banks.[20] As Senator Royal Copeland once put it, "When it became necessary to create a Federal Reserve system of banking, it was recognized that such a system could best be put into effect *through* the banking industry."[21]

In sum, the Fed's original design was the product of a compromise between those who wanted a centralized central bank and those who did not, those who advocated for private control and those who wanted public control. The Fed still has many of the characteristics driven by this, now obsolete, compromise. In today's economic and political context, what is the point of having privately owned reserve banks? What is the justification for having the CEOs of those banks create national monetary policy? Why pay dividends to member banks? Why aren't all banks, and bank-like entities, member banks? Why conduct monetary policy exclusively through primary dealers and member banks? Answers to these questions can be traced back to historical and political contingencies, but can any of them be traced to contemporary democratic commitments, or described as the outcome of contemporary democratic debate?

Then again, all institutions are a product of history. To point out this simple fact in the case of the Fed might be of academic interest, but should it change anything about how we govern monetary policymaking? Every generation inherits its institutions from the generations previous. I have outlined the political roots of the Fed's contemporary institutional structure not merely to show the contours of the compromise that birthed it, but to demonstrate how remote that compromise is, both temporally and politically.

Jeremy Bentham derided the rule of the dead over the living.[22] His warning was not a call to burn down all existing institutions at the start of every generation. Instead, he wanted each generation to *see itself* as a source of democratic power, as possessing the capacity to rule its collective life together. Exhibiting such power does not require each generation to create new institutions from scratch. It does mean, however, that when existing institutions become *mere* relics of history rather than historical institutions that continue to serve the contemporary democratic will, the living must be willing and able to change them.[23] In 1927, a few senators extended the Fed's charter in perpetuity, making future alternations to the institution much more difficult to achieve. This is the decision we need to revisit.

Why Recharter? The Historical Case

Rechartering is one form of temporary legislation. Legislation designed to have a limited duration has been used for generations for two primary purposes. First, it can garner more political support than permanent legislation. When a bill is temporary, legislators are more likely to see it as a democratic experiment, one that will necessarily be reassessed, and could be reversed in the future. Second, temporary legislation has been used to allow democratic legislatures to maintain power over the administrative state. Temporary legislation establishes regularly occurring moments for the exertion of democratic power, for the exercise of the legislatures' democratic muscle. Importantly, rechartering provides a valuable form of legislative iteration. In this book, Dani Rodrik and Charles Sabel outline "an iterative model of strategic collaboration between private actors and the state" to develop "good jobs" in the context of pervasive uncertainty. The pervasive uncertainty they identify in the labor market derivative of "differentiated local conditions, and the evolving nature of the goals" can also be found in monetary policy. Rechartering is an iterative approach to delegation that injects democratic flexibility into monetary policymaking.

Perhaps the most well-known form of temporary legislation is the sunset clause. A recent example from American history is the Patriot Act. The Bush administration passed the law in the wake of the September 11, 2001, terrorist attacks, temporarily expanding criminal and intelligence search and surveillance authority. Some of these expansions were set to expire a few years after the bill passed. The moment of potential sunset, December 2005, sparked significant congressional and public debate about the programs set to expire.[24]

In eighteenth-century England, "the use of sunset clauses was associated with Parliament's effort to control the growth of the administration."[25] As Parliament sought to govern an increasingly complex society and economy, sunset clauses recognized the need for expertise and for democratic control of that expertise. Delegation might be inevitable, but it would also be temporary.[26] Sunset clauses continued to play an important role well into the twentieth century.[27] The idea was that Parliament should have a "role in monitoring, scrutinizing, and affirming the continued effectiveness of legislation."[28] Parliament iteratively monitored "the subordinated bodies and reaffirm[ed] their actions" to ensure debate about their powers and purposes was kept firmly within the sphere of democratic politics.[29] Sunset clauses also became popular in the US in the 1970s, "depicted as a cure-all to the ills of inefficient government."[30]

Rechartering forces elected representatives to confront the politics of an agency's decision-making publicly and to either endorse the approach actively and publicly or to reject it, also actively and publicly. There have been three central banks in US history. All three were originally established with temporary charters. The first two were not rechartered. In 1811, Congress voted not to renew the charter of the First Bank of the United States by only one vote. In 1832, Congress voted to recharter the Second Bank of the United States only to have the bill vetoed by President Jackson.

The Federal Reserve Act of 1913 chartered the central bank for 20 years. The temporary charter aided the passage of the legislation by presenting the central bank as an experiment, one that would inevitably be reassessed and reevaluated and would not be allowed to continue on the basis of inertia or private interest alone. Legislators at the time came to the collective conclusion that the matter was too important, too contentious, and too uncertain to warrant indefinite support.

And yet, in 1927 Congress made the Federal Reserve's charter permanent. Between the founding of the Fed in 1913 and 1927, the US economy experienced rapid growth, stable interest rates, few crises, rising gold reserves, and increased international economic prominence.[31] As H. H. Preston wrote in June 1927 in *The American Economic Review*, the Federal Reserve System "was held to have abundantly justified its continuance by its successful support of the American financial situation during the war and in the post-war period of economic readjustment."[32] Advocates in the Senate took advantage of the favorable economic and political conditions to add an amendment extending the Federal Reserve System's charter in perpetuity to a bill that had already passed the House, the McFadden Act.

The explicit aim of the amendment's advocates—led by Carter Glass—was to solidify the Federal Reserve's place in the administrative state in its current form.[33] While the banking and business communities supported the extension of the Fed's charter, Representative Louis Thomas McFadden was not pleased with the amendment. He did not oppose the Federal Reserve, nor an extension of its charter, but he was worried that adding what he took to be a highly consequential amendment to his bill might endanger its chances of passing.

There were others who objected to Glass's last-minute addition. Senator Burton Wheeler from Montana filibustered the bill unsuccessfully. Wheeler took issue with Glass's opportunism. He questioned the ad hoc nature of the amendment, arguing that an extension of the Fed's charter deserved more attention from both congressional chambers.[34] Furthermore, in concert with many others, he challenged the need to recharter the Fed years before its charter expired.[35] He suggested that "the reason that the life of the Federal Reserve Board is being continued here now in this fashion is so that it won't be discussed on the floor of the next session of Congress."[36] Contemporary media came to the same conclusion:

> The conservative element intends, therefore, to write the charter of the Federal Reserve board into the law of the land where it will take an affirmative act of repeal to remove it, confident that it will take a much longer time to bring about such a step than a substitution of one economic theory for another, if the Federal Reserve charter should be allowed to lapse or approach an end.[37]

Those in opposition to the amendment were fighting for flexibility; "the tie that binds all of these various elements in opposition to the Federal reserve system is the thought that by preventing long life for the existing scheme of things greater opportunity will exist for the substitution of some other plan when the sentiment can be crystallized in favor of it."[38] Glass and his supporters took advantage of the moment to cement their preferred version of the Fed in permanent legislation. "None of those who believed in the soundness of the present system of monetary control was willing to gamble that future Congresses—not even the Seventieth—would grant the authority now contemplated."[39] Glass was successful.[40] The amended bill passed in the Senate with less controversy than expected.[41]

Notably, the McFadden Act did not merely extend the Fed's charter for another 10 or 20 years in light of what some saw at the time as the Fed's track record of success. It extended the Fed's charter *in perpetuity*. The democratic experiment, as such, was over. The implication was that advocates believed any future changes to the Fed need only be marginal. They had locked the Fed out of reach of conventional democratic opposition. Just a few months after the bill was passed, H. H. Preston again wrote, "If re-charter had been too long delayed, the question might have become a partisan issue. While the strength of the opposition does not now [June 1927] appear to likely have developed to a point where re-charter would have been defeated, it could have become a very disturbing influence."[42] The McFadden Act should not be seen as evidence of a deep and lasting social consensus behind the structure and aims of the Federal Reserve System. The charter was a late addition to an existing bill and received little attention or debate. If Congress had waited for the rechartering deadline in 1934, the debate would have taken place in the midst of the Great Depression, and one can only suppose that the debate, if not the decision, would have looked very different in that context.[43]

Amendments to the Federal Reserve Act have passed since the charter was extended. None, however, have led to wholesale debate about the aims, tools, and failures of the Federal Reserve System, let alone wholesale change.[44] In contrast, monetary policy itself has changed dramatically since 1927: compare the activist policies of the postwar period, the anti-inflation battles of the 1970s and 1980s, and the "unconventional" monetary policies invoked in the wake of the Global Financial Crisis of 2007/2008. Central bankers themselves recognize the dynamic character of monetary policy and the need for regular reassessments. Every five years the Canadian central bank takes a good look at itself, reassesses its performance, and discusses possible reforms with the Canadian parliament.[45] The Norwegian central bank conducts regular reviews in which it engages external auditors to make an unbiased assessment.[46] In the summer of 2019, the Fed conducted an examination of its approach to monetary policymaking, and Chair Jerome Powell suggested that this will likely become a regular occurrence.[47]

Internal reassessments are reasonable by all accounts. Central bankers have a hard job, and they have to conduct it in a changing world. Internal reassessments, however, are by no means comprehensive and they are hardly democratic. They take place within the confines of the central bank's congressional mandate and the existing institutional structures. The same is true of the Fed Chair's regular reports to Congress. Since 1978, the Fed Chair has delivered a semiannual report to Congress on the state of the economy and the progress of monetary policy. These reports should be seen for what they are, however: largely pro forma events. The Fed Chair comes to Congress to deliver a highly stylized report and take questions. In the question portion of the testimony, members of Congress are permitted to challenge the Fed Chair. But it is just that: Congress members challenging the Fed Chair, making their case for change or asking for clarification. The Fed Chair controls the room, explaining to Congress how the central bank seeks to maintain price stability and full employment.[48] In other words, the semiannual testimony of the Fed Chair is more of an expression of the Fed's power over monetary policy than it is an expression of congressional power over the Fed.

Contrast this with what history's most powerful theorists of democracy have considered necessary for a successful democratic society. Jean-Jacques Rousseau wrote, "The depositories of the executive power [the government] are not the masters of the people, but its officers; that the people can appoint them and dismiss them at pleasure; that for them it is not a question of contracting, but of obeying."[49] Democracy is, at its very root, about empowering the people.[50] In a democracy, then, the people should hold ultimate decision-making power and experts should act as stewards or advisers. In Plato's *Protagoras* (319c), Socrates explains that in technical subjects such as shipbuilding, the Athenians would call on those with expert knowledge:

> If anyone else tries to give advice whom they do not consider an expert, however handsome or wealthy or nobly born he may be, it makes no difference. The members reject him nosily and with contempt, until either he is shouted down or desists, or else he is dragged off or ejected by the police at the orders of the presiding magistrate. (*Protagoras* 319c).

The Athenians needed technical experts and scientific reasoning to identify points of choice and stakes in policymaking and yet insisted that control over these choices remained with the people. The role of technical experts in classical democracy was consultative, not determinative.[51]

The opposite seems to have developed in the case of contemporary central bank review processes. The Bank of Canada sets the questions, does the research, and then makes suggestions to the Canadian parliament. The Canadian central bank has never proposed major changes.[52] Even more insular, the Fed's recent review was conducted by the Fed for the Fed. The agenda was set by the Fed and the research was conducted and presented by academics at the invitation of the Fed.[53] Furthermore, any changes to future monetary policymaking processes will take place only if the Fed adopts them unilaterally. In other words, even when it comes to the review process, ultimate, effective decision-making power over monetary policy rests with central bankers rather than the democratic legislature.

All three American central banks were originally given temporary charters. This allowed advocates to fashion a broad coalition for what was, at base, a democratic experiment. In 1927, with the McFadden Act, Carter Glass and his supporters extended the Federal Reserve's charter in perpetuity. In so doing, they achieved their explicit aim in making it more difficult for democratic politicians, for future Congresses, to make changes to US monetary policy.[54] The next section goes beyond the substantive reasons for reassessing the structure of the Federal Reserve System here and now, over a century after it was founded, to argue that *regularly* rechartering the Fed is itself a matter of democratic sustainability.

Why Recharter? Democratic Sustainability

To see the importance of rechartering the Fed, we have to take a deep dive into democratic theory. Jean-Jacques Rousseau distinguished between government and sovereign. The democratic sovereign—the true possessor of political power—is the citizenry. The government is not "the masters" of the people but its "officers," the set of officials who conduct society's day-to-day business within the remit set for them by the sovereign. Making this distinction is what enabled Rousseau to uphold "democratic sovereignty" while opposing "democratic government."[55]

Rousseau envisioned a polity in which the democratic sovereign delegated political power to the government.[56] Subsequently, the government would be provisionally empowered to make political decisions, exercise political judgment, and adjudicate political trade-offs. The sovereign's delegation of policymaking power to the government was democratically legitimate, in Rousseau's view, because the sovereign retained ultimate power, able to change or overrule the government at any time. Rousseau's theory can also be extended to a second moment of delegation: first, the democratic sovereign delegates power to a government, and then that government (specifically the legislature) delegates policymaking power to the administrative state, including the central bank. On Rousseau's theory of democratic legitimacy, the central bank, too, should be an officer of the democratic sovereign, not its master.

The democratic legitimacy of the sovereign's delegation is not related to how the sovereign delegated power, nor to whom it is delegated, nor to the nature of the delegated decisions. According to Rousseau, the democratic sovereign could legitimately delegate power to a single dictator-oracle—for instance, someone who makes all policy by appeal to their mystical whims. This would be democratically legitimate by virtue of the fact that the sovereign could choose to revoke the delegated powers at any time.

Applying the same logic to the second moment of delegation, we can argue that the legislature can legitimately delegate policymaking power to the central bank on any terms, provided the legislature maintains the power to revoke or change the terms of delegation at any time. In other words, it does not matter if the central bankers are experts or if their work is merely technical. All that is required to maintain the continued democratic power of the legislature over the central bank is regular legislative engagement in the matter. We might ask, then, can the legislature maintain its power if it has delegated the responsibility for monetary policymaking to the central bank *in perpetuity*?

Rousseau worried about the government usurping the sovereign's political power.[57] He suggested a way to ward off usurpation: frequent citizen assemblies in which the citizens, as sovereign, ask and answer two questions:

- Whether it pleases the sovereign to maintain the present form of government?
- Whether it pleases the people to leave its administration to those at present entrusted with it?[58]

Regular democratic engagement in the policymaking process was required, according to Rousseau, to reassert the political power of the sovereign over the government, thereby preserving the democratic character of the state.[59]

Rechartering the Fed would make institutional change more regular and more democratic. Rousseau recognized the democratic benefits of *regularity* in reassessments. He worried that the government would actively prevent the sovereign from assembling periodically to reassert its fundamental political power. For this reason, he thought that citizen assemblies would be more successful in warding off governmental usurpation of political power if they did not have to be formally convened because then the government "cannot interfere with them, without openly proclaiming [itself] a violator of the laws and an enemy of the state."[60] In other words, regularity in democratic interventions makes them more likely to occur and thus supports democratic capacity by fighting atrophy. Regular exercise of the democratic muscle makes it stronger. Similarly, I suggest, regularity in rechartering would strengthen democratic power of the legislature over the Fed.[61]

Rousseau was not the only theorist or observer of democracy to think that exercising democratic power through regular reassessment mattered. This was a familiar idea in ancient democracies. An individual to whom power had been delegated would return to the assembly to be judged by the citizenry.[62] This backward-looking assessment of delegated power necessitated a certain kind of risk, for there were no specified criteria against which to judge the success of the delegation. This allowed the delegate to adopt a certain level of creativity, flexibility, and discretion. Modern forms of delegation are almost always forward-looking, resting on statutes or mandates defined by Congress. The Federal Reserve System is no different, mandated to promote price stability and maximum sustainable employment. Within these guardrails, decision-making is left to the discretion of agencies.[63] There is no moment in which Congress is forced to look back and ask whether the delegation is serving the public good. Rechartering would reinstate a form of intentional, backward-looking assessment.

Economists today vehemently defend the delegation of monetary policymaking power to independent central banks and argue that political involvement in monetary policymaking is inevitably detrimental. Setting aside the merits of their arguments, I simply observe that delegating monetary policy does not require doing so on one set of terms in perpetuity.[64] Political involvement in regularly rechartering the Fed is not the same as political involvement in making monetary policy.

Advocates of central bank independence like to invoke Ulysses tying himself to the mast to motivate the claim that Congress might have good reason to restrict its own power over monetary policy through delegation to an independent central bank. Recalling Rousseau, however, if Congress does not revisit the conditions of delegation by untying itself from the mast on occasion to exercise its democratic muscles, then they will atrophy. As atrophy sets in, untying oneself becomes increasingly difficult. In other words, delegating monetary policy may not in and of itself constitute a democratic ill; however, failing to regularly revisit the matter democratically does.

What Could Rechartering Bring?

So what could rechartering bring? First, it would create an opportunity to change those aspects of the Federal Reserve System that the Fed cannot change on its own, even if it wanted to: the structure of the regional reserve banks, the 6 percent dividend, the makeup of the boards, and so on. The only body who can make these changes is Congress. It would similarly create the opportunity to change those aspects of the Federal Reserve System that it would be ludicrous for the Fed to be responsible for addressing: How does the Fed, as it currently operates, meet the democratic needs, desires, and fundamental values of the nation? Again, the only body that should address this is Congress.

It is, of course, possible that regularly rechartering the Fed could become a procedural rubber stamp. If the Fed's history and the "Audit the Fed" movement are anything to go by, however, that seems unlikely. Regularly rechartering the Fed could lead to major changes. It could help reinforce democracy by creating an institution through which "the people engage in collective action to govern ourselves and our larger political economy."[65] In other words, it could become a tool for the construction of structural justice, as outlined by Sabeel Rahman in another chapter this book. In the remainder of this section I sketch one proposal for restructuring part of the Fed pursuant to these aims. This sketch is a provocation intended to push readers to consider the truly wide range of alternatives that might be considered in the course of regular rechartering.

Why not have Congress recharter the Federal Reserve System in such a way as to affect a transition of the privately held regional Federal Reserve Banks into regional state investment banks? These investment banks could be capitalized using the same funds that the commercial member banks currently put into buying the stock of the regional banks. State investment banks are not a new idea.[66] They were particularly popular in the postwar era and some continue to flourish today.[67] Converting regional Federal Reserve Banks into state investment banks is a proposal worth considering for two reasons: first, because of the documented success of state investment banks and the opportunities they offer for promoting wide-reaching economic health in society, and second, because of an amenable shift in monetary policymaking implemented in the wake of the Great Financial Crisis. I will consider these two reasons in reverse order.

Before 2008, monetary policy was largely executed through open market operations (OMOs): the FOMC would decide on a target for the federal funds rate—the interest rate at which banks lend to one another overnight, usually to meet reserve requirements. That rate was communicated in a directive to the Federal Reserve Bank of New York, which bought and sold Treasuries to and from primary dealers in order to hit the target rate. Things have changed.[68] Since 2008, the Fed has paid banks interest on the reserves they keep at the Fed. Monetary policy is now largely executed by the FOMC changing the interest on excess reserves (IOER). In altering IOER, the Fed is able to (dis)incentivize private money creation, thereby influencing the price of credit on the market and, as such, inflation. In short, with the introduction of an IOER regime, the Fed is able to pursue its price stability aim without having to conduct any OMOs.[69]

This has changed the landscape of monetary policy. As former hedge fund manager Ángel Ubide writes, "With these changes, central banks severed the link between monetary policy and inflation. Inflation is no longer a monetary phenomenon in the strict sense—different levels of money growth can deliver the same level of inflation."[70] As a consequence, monetary policymakers can hit their inflation target independent of the size of the balance sheet. The supposition in conventional monetary policy circles is that this frees up balance sheet operations for addressing liquidity shortages. But note that, by this same sentiment, the IOER regime also frees up balance sheet operations for funding other projects, like a collection of regional state investment banks.

Now let us turn to how a network of state investment banks could create opportunities for promoting wide-reaching economic health in society. Credit provision in the United States today is biased. The poor, racial minorities, and women are all less likely to have access to good credit.[71] Creditworthiness is a slippery concept, and its amorphous nature sustains this bias. Currently the Federal Reserve's approach to governing the money supply depends on how commercial banks define creditworthiness.[72] The Fed incentivizes banks to lend, and banks lend on the basis of their own creditworthiness assessments. If state investment banks were free to allocate credit to individuals, businesses, or projects directly, this would change.[73] State investment banks could define creditworthiness on their own terms, a chance for democratic engagement in the monetary policymaking process. As Julie Rose suggests in a chapter in this book, the collective aims for macroeconomic policies, including credit policies such as these, may be much broader than promoting aggregate economic growth. Congress could establish transparent, democratically specified standards for credit aimed, for example, at avoiding social, political, and economic domination.[74] Or regional investment banks might focus their investments on tranches of assets that appeal to a wide variety state interests, perhaps related to a concept of flourishing, as outlined in another chapter in this book by Deva Woodly.

A web of regional state investment banks could also fight local dislocations resulting from federal policies. Recent research has reinvigorated the worry that globalization has led to local dislocations in the labor market. People are unemployed and unless they can easily retrain or are willing to move great distances they suffer. In view of this issue, politicians and economists alike have advocated revisiting the idea of regional investment.[75] Regional state investment banks would be an ideal way to deliver the capital necessary for regional investment. They would be local entities with local knowledge and an expertise in assessing creditworthiness.[76] Finally, regional state investment banks would also provide an easy alternative mechanism for the FOMC to increase aggregate demand when necessary. Instead of conducting open market operations only through a narrow and concentrated set of primary dealers, the FOMC could use the regional investment banks, scattered across the country, as decentralized, public conduits for demand management.

This is just one suggestion. My aim here is not to offer a comprehensive defense of this alternative to the status quo. Rather, my goal is to demonstrate that the Federal Reserve, as currently constituted, is out of date. It was the result of a contingent political compromise in 1913. Over 100 years later, and many economies since, we still have yet to reevaluate our approach to governing the money supply comprehensively. This is inexcusable. Money is the stuff of our collective life. If democracy entails citizens collectively governing their collective lives, then surely it requires democratic governance of the money supply. As I have argued here, by regularly rechartering the Fed, we can both move beyond the obsolete institution we currently use to govern our money supply and prevent democratic atrophy by exercising the democratic power of the legislature over the central bank.

Climate Conclusion

Jens van 't Klooster wrote recently, "The question of how to design a central bank and its mandate cannot be decided in isolation from the broader economic policy goals of a government."[77] He continued, "Even if the monetary policy goals agreed before the crisis were relatively uncontroversial then, this is no longer the case now."[78] In other words, the aims, effects, context, and tools of monetary policy change over time. It seems ludicrous to suppose that despite these dynamics, the political stance on governing and conducting monetary policy should remain unchanged. Climate change is case in point.

To conclude the chapter, I would like to draw attention to the recent efforts central banks around the world have made to address the threats of climate change. There is now an organization called the Network for Greening the Financial System (NGFS) that includes 36 central banks—including most major central banks with, until very recently, the notable exception of the US Federal Reserve System.[79] The NGFS has set out to "introduce a series of practical actions aimed at ensuring climate risks are fully factored into future financial decision-making."[80] Thus far, actions have included the development of a handbook on assessing and managing environment-related risks, integrating sustainability into central bank portfolio management, and data collection from financial firms on environmental aspects of finance. Some central banks have also started to promote the idea of climate stress tests, in which central banks test the macroeconomy's capacity to respond to climate shocks.

The efforts of central bankers to address climate change underline the oddity of the contemporary approach to governing the macroeconomy. The Network for Greening the Financial System has been careful to point out that they are on solid footing in addressing climate change: "Climate risks ultimately have a material bearing on financial stability. Therefore, supervising climate risks is a legitimate interest for central banks with a financial stability mandate."[81] This is, on one hand, a good sign. It means central bankers are attentive to their democratic legislative mandate.

On the other hand, the ease with which climate change is defended as within the jurisdiction of the independent central bank is revealing. Benoît Cœuré, former board member at the European Central Bank and former deputy governor of the Reserve Bank of Australia, said climate was likely to affect food and migration patterns (which affect macroeconomic variables), making them a monetary policy concern. If everything that influences food and migration patterns is within the proper remit of the central bank, however, one wonders what sits outside the set? After all, this would seem to include health policy, refugee policy, education policy, and much more.

Beyond this, consider the effects of having an independent central bank addressing the effects of climate change independently of the rest of the government. Taking the Fed as our example, the central bank would address the effects of climate change *on price stability and maximum sustainable employment*, as that is its congressional remit. First, it is not clear how the "effects of climate change" on price stability should be understood. This would of course depend on how one defines the effects of climate change, and what time horizon one considers. If the actions taken thus far are any indicator, central banks seem to be most concerned with the risk climate disasters pose to the financial stability.

The state as a whole, in contrast, may wish to address broader climate concerns: the security of coastal communities, impending refugee crises, the threat posed by increasingly dangerous and erratic weather events on infrastructure and state security, and so on. These goals may come into conflict with the central bank's aim of price stability in two ways. First, focusing on price stability may lead central bankers to be increasingly concerned with systemic financial risk. The central bank might decide that banks should be less leveraged to protect the system against financial crises that may come downstream of climate disasters. This goal could conflict with the state's aim of increasing innovation and investment in safer infrastructure.

Second, the contemporary approach to conducting monetary policy precludes the use of monetary policy tools in pursuit of anything but price stability. Thus, they cannot be employed to prepare the nation for impending climate disasters or in support efforts to prevent them. Embracing a system of regularly rechartering the Fed could change this. If the Fed were regularly rechartered it would be easier for Congress to regularly adjust the aims and priorities of the central bank. As Julie Rose and Deva Woodly both argue elsewhere in this book, there are worthwhile social goals other than stable output growth. Regularly rechartering the Federal Reserve would allow Congress to explore this possibility. More specifically, Congress might ask itself: Does it make sense to prioritize price stability in light of the impending threats of climate change? Might we, perhaps, accept near-term price instability in exchange for a future in which the nation was better adapted to and prepared for climate threats?

Money is a reflection of what we value as a society. How we govern it reflects our collective aims: what we wish to build, to promote, to protect, and to accomplish. As such, I have argued that money should be governed democratically. What the climate change case underlines is that democratic priorities, needs, and desires all change over time.[82] For money to be governed democratically, for monetary policy to be responsive to these changes, Congress must, from time to time, revisit the matter.

Notes

1. More precisely, it connects all members of a currency zone, or even more broadly, the web of all people with access to the particular currency. But as this chapter is about monetary policy, which is taken to be the practice of governing the currency from the perspective of a national currency, as such, I will stick to political boundaries.

2. I make no commitments about a timeline for rechartering. The original charter was for 20 years; given the dynamism of the contemporary economy, I have something shorter in mind.

3. Benoist (2011), 53.

4. James Livingston's history of the Fed argues that the Federal Reserve Act was a corporate effort to protect capital market from monetary instability. See Livingston (2006).

5. Prior to the centralization of reserves in the US system, there was a precarious three-tiered system of reserves. This system, or so Warburg and his compatriots argued, led to an overabundance of reserves being held in vaults to hedge against the possibility of a bank run. As a result, reserves that could be "working" in the system (i.e., supporting more credit) were standing idle. For more on this, see Lowenstein (2015).

6. In his textbook on macroeconomics, Gregory Mankiw defends the independence of monetary policy as follows: "If politicians are incompetent or opportunistic, then, we may not want to give them the discretion to use the

powerful tools of monetary and fiscal policy." He continues, "Macroeconomics is complicated, and politicians often do not have sufficient knowledge of
it to make informed judgments . . . the political process often cannot weed
out the advice of charlatans from that of competent economists." (Mankiw
2014, 389)

7. Owen himself fought against complete banker control. He argued for keeping "control of the credit system of America [in] the United States Government." See "Owen Upholds Act of Reserve Board" (1927).

8. Brandeis is emblematic of this view. For more on this, see Peer (2019), 7.

9. For this reason, the populists of the day—with William Jennings Bryant
as their figurehead—advocated bimetallism. They wanted a more elastic
money supply.

10. This was a debate fundamentally about what should count as money in
society. Nadav Orian Peer nicely explicates this using Christine Desan's
work on money as a legal phenomenon. Desan emphasizes the importance
of collective, democratic power in defining a unit of account and the major
implications of how we choose to do this. When the central bank agrees to
lend against particular types of collateral, it essentially converts that collateral into legal tender, thereby advantaging the members of society with
such collateral. The Federal Reserve Act allowed member banks to transform
illiquid collateral into newly issued Federal Reserve notes. Agricultural advocates wanted farmland and equipment to count as permissible collateral. For
more on this, see both Peer (2019) and Desan (2015).

11. The two groups differed on their preferences for the powers, aims, and tools
given to a centralized public bank. For more on this, see Peer (2019).

12. Garrett 1968, 8.

13. For more on the development of the Fed along the two axes, and the political game Wilson engaged in to pass it, see Conti-Brown (2016).

14. There are two primary moments of change in the structure of the Fed worth
mentioning here: the Banking Act of 1935 and the Fed-Treasury Accord of
1951. The Banking Act of 1935, largely written and promoted by Mariner
Eccles, increased the centralization of monetary policymaking power and
located it in the federal government. It created the modern Board of Governors and Federal Open Market Committee (FOMC), which is the American
monetary policy authority. Eccles wanted to abolish the regional reserve
banks to achieve complete centralization of the system, but Senator Carter
Glass, still holding sway in Congress, fought to keep the regional reserve
banks alive. In 1951, the Treasury and the Fed were locked in a battle over
macroeconomic jurisdiction. The two institutions ultimately settled their
differences with the (in)famous "Fed-Treasury Accord" in which the Federal
Reserve and the Treasury agreed to a détente and, de facto, to central bank
independence. For more on the accord, specifically the political nature of the
battle that led to it, see Epstein and Schor (2011).

15. The following are the 12 cities that have Reserve Banks: Boston, New York,

Philadelphia, Cleveland, Richmond, Atlanta, Chicago, St. Louis, Minneapolis, Kansas City, Dallas, and San Francisco.

16. This last category is usually determined with heavy input from the Reserve Bank board (bankers and banker appointees).

17. The Dodd-Frank bill, passed in the wake of the Great Financial Crisis, altered the mechanism by which Reserve Bank boards elect a president. Those members of the board who occupy Class A are no longer allowed a vote in the election for the Reserve Bank president and CEO. All board members may still participate in removing a bank president and CEO.

18. Terms are almost never completed. These positions are often taken by former and future bankers themselves. The FOMC is an active site of capture. For more on this, see Adolph (2013).

19. Open market operations (OMOs) used to be the primary means of monetary policy. Now, monetary policy is conducted by manipulating interest on excess reserves (IOER). But insofar as the Fed does still engage directly with economy through the market, it is done through primary dealers.

20. The list changes fairly regularly. Currently, primary dealers include BNP Paribas, Barclays, Bank of Nova Scotia New York Agency, BofA Securities, Citigroup Global Markets, Goldman Sachs, Credit Suisse, Deutsche Bank Securities Inc., HSBC Securities (USA) Inc., JPMorgan Securities LLC, Morgan Stanley & Co LLC, and Wells Fargo Securities LLC.

21. Senator Copeland, speaking on S. 2122, Congressional Record (January 10, 1926). CR-1926-0115, 69th Congress, 1st sess., Emphasis my own. There is not much written about *why* this is the case. My own view is that it is a historical artifact. Central banks, all over but definitely in the US, began as private entities, owned by private banks. It therefore made sense in those times to disseminate liquidity through the member banks. When central banks were made public (or mostly public), the mechanisms of transmission were left unchanged.

22. He made this comment in discussing the worth of constitutions (Bentham 2002, 237).

23. Even conventional economists and practitioners like Lawrence Summers are beginning to outline the pitfalls, or "the suboptimality of our current monetary policy framework" (Summers 2018, 7).

24. See the report commissioned by Senator Diane Feinstein to assess the provisions set to expire: "USA Patriot Act: Sunsets Report" (2005).

25. Kouroutakis 2016, 62. Sunset clauses were also sometimes used to express opposition to a bill, when a dissenting minority could not stop passage but could insert a sunset clause.

26. Kouroutakis 2016, 66.

27. In the twentieth century, parliamentarians began to worry about the extent of delegation. In response, they set up a committee "tasked with investigating the issue and exploring solutions on implementing safeguards against the abuse of the delegated powers." The result was a report which stated

that "delegating power to modify provisions of statute, should never be used except for the sole purpose of bringing an Act into operation and should be subject to a time limit of lone year for the period of its operation." See Kouroutakis (2016), 69. There the author is quoting the Donoughmore Report, a report to Parliament on *Minister's Powers* in 1932 aimed at examining administrative law.

28. Greenberg 2018.

29. Kouroutakis 2016, 69.

30. Ranchordás 2014, 59. In 1969, Theodore Lowi proposed a "'Tenure of Statues Act' with sunset of five to ten years on the duration of agencies and their regulatory programmes in order to ensure their reassessment after a period of time" (Ranchordás 2014, 20).

31. It should be noted that this period was an economic boon from one particular class perspective. It was also a time of immense strife in labor relations, including many violently suppressed strike actions.

32. Preston 1927, 216.

33. Glass may have also had personal reasons for so vehemently promoting the Bank's charter extension. He saw himself as one of the Fed's founders; extending its charter in perpetuity secured his legislative legacy. See Wasson (1927).

34. "In my judgement, 20 per cent of the senators in this body do not know what is in this bill and have not read it. There is no need to jam through this legislation in the closing hours of this session when it is not understood by the people, the nation, and even the members of the senate, not even the members of the committee which reported it out" (Baxter 1927).

35. "Reserve Bank Extension Opposed in Committee" (1926). The *Wall Street Journal* headline further noted that "House Group Would Eliminate Proposal to Extend Charters from McFadden Measure—Would Postpone Action."

36. Baxter 1927.

37. Baxter 1927.

38. Baxter 1927.

39. Baxter 1927.

40. The agricultural advocates lost again. Senator Smith Brookhart of Iowa advocated fiercely on the Senate floor for a Federal Reserve System that was not so embedded in the banker community. Specifically, he advocated for a cooperative banking system designed to promote farmers' interests: "I concede to the commercial interests the right to have their own competitive banking system with reserve bank and all under their own control; but I demand in behalf of the farmers and the people who labor with hand or brain the same right under the law to organize a cooperative system with cooperative reserve and all under their own control." Senator Brookhart, speaking on S. 2120, Congressional Record (January 10, 1926). CR-1926-0115, 69th Congress, 1st sess. This argument belies how obvious it was at the time that the Fed was created by commercial bankers for commercial bankers.

41. "National Bank Branch Bill Passes Senate" (1926).

42. Preston 1927, 217.

43. In fact, we know it did, as the Banking Act of 1935 altered the structure of the Fed.

44. The most radical alterations were the Banking Act of 1935 and the Reform Act of 1977, frequently associated with the Humphrey-Hawkins Act of 1978. The most recent is the Dodd-Frank Act passed after the Great Financial Crisis. Dodd-Frank focused primarily on regulatory matters, with minimal adjustments to monetary policymaking with the exception of curtailing emergency lending eligibility (eligibility must be determined generally not specifically, and approved by the Treasury) and limiting who can access the discount window.

45. Fuhrer et al. 2018.

46. This is particularly odd if you think monetary policy should be democratic matter. See Norges Bank (2015).

47. "Fed Likely to 'Institutionalise' Policy Framework Review, Powell Says" (2019).

48. For an example, see Powell (2019) for Chair Jerome Powell's testimony before Congress on February 26, 2019.

49. Rousseau et al. 2002, bk. 3, chap. 18.

50. Ancient democracy was first and foremost a form of power (-cracy): the power of the people (demos). In the eighteenth century, this shifted with the development of representation.

51. Ober and Hedrick 1996.

52. Murray 2018.

53. It should be noted that the review included a set of nationwide events by the name Fed Listens, with the intention of reaching out to the community. These events were organized, executed, and analyzed by the Fed.

54. Glass and his supporters acted as handmaidens of the central bank, aiding in what Rousseau might have described as the central bank's usurpation of the legislature's political power. It is a concept that I will turn to in the next section.

55. Tuck (2015), 124–42.

56. To be precise, Rousseau rejected the possibility of "delegating" or "representing" sovereign power altogether. Strictly speaking, I have anachronistically employed these terms here. However, it is my interpretation that Rousseau's theory is compatible with the concepts of delegation and representation *as I employ them*. To defend this claim, I rely on Melissa Schwartzberg in her interpretation of Rousseau, seeing fundamental laws not as binding the sovereign but as enabling it—a model she adopts from Stephen Holmes. Schwartzberg (2003), 388.

57. Rousseau et al. 2002, chap. 18.

58. Rousseau et al. 2002, bk. 3, chap. 18.

59. "Assemblies of the people," Rousseau writes, "are the shield of the body politic and the curb of the government" (Rousseau et al. 2002, chap. 14).

60. Rousseau et al. 2002, chap. 18.
61. Why do we need formal rechartering rather than simply letting the legislature act to change the conditions of delegation when it feels it needs to?
It takes more to get Congress to act to overturn actions than to pass basic
legislation, for one. Second, Congress has reason to shirk its duty (Elgie and
Thompson 1998). Furthermore, spontaneous legislative action is less likely
to happen organically in a depoliticized environment like monetary policy.
For more on this, see Hay (2007); Roberts (2010); Braun (2014).
62. This process is called *euthuna*, or "public audit": "the examination of a public
official's record and financial accounts at the end of his year in office." See
the glossary of Buckley (2006).
63. Under the prevailing Chevron doctrine, as long as the agency's interpretation of the congressional mandate or law is "reasonable," it cannot be legally
challenged. This gives a *huge* amount of interpretive discretion to administrative agencies. See McConnell (2018); "Chevron U.S.A. Inc. v. Natural
Resources Defense Council, Inc., et al." (1983).
64. In fact, to continue to reap the benefits of delegating monetary policymaking power to experts, rechartering, or at least reevaluation will likely be
required. For example, the contemporary approach to monetary policymaking was designed largely to fight inflation. Today, inflation is by no means
central bankers' primary concern. Thus, the system needs to be revisited.
We are seeing this in the myriad of internal reevaluations starting to take
place recently in central banks all over the world, including but not limited
to the Federal Reserve, the European Central Bank and the Bank of England.
Important to note here is that these are *internal* reevaluations aimed at
evaluating the technical approaches to seeking unchanged political aims. I
am arguing for *political* reevaluation of both aims and practices.
65. See K. Sabeel Rahman's chapter in this book.
66. There are modern proposals not for state investment banks (SIBs) but rather
for the Fed to allow citizens to hold accounts there, which is similarly radical and could have some similar effects. See Ricks, Crawford, and Menand
(forthcoming).
67. The existing German state investment bank was formed as part of the Marshall plan. In 2018, it was Germany's third largest bank by balance sheet. For
more on state investment banks, see Ryan-Collins (2015).
68. To be precise, the bill that authorized IOER passed in 2006 and was not supposed to be implemented until 2011. In wake of the Great Financial Crisis,
implementation was moved up to 2008.
69. This is true in theory. In practice, the Fed has a "leaky floor." This means the
IOER regime is not as effective as it might be because it does not apply to all
depositors at the Fed; specifically, it does not apply to Government Sponsored Entities (GSEs), which opens up an arbitrage opportunity and makes
IOER policy less effective. This is largely understood in the literature as the
result of an inefficient policy choice, one that could easily be rectified.

70.　Ubide 2017, 72.

71.　Sarah Quinn writes, "There has been no time period or region [in American history] in which credit distribution has not been distorted by racism." For more on these biases, see Quinn (2019); Jacobs and King (2016). Under the current regime, the poor are much less likely to have permissible collateral. What defines permissible is central to the question of credit allocation. For the history of this debate see supra note 11.

72.　The agricultural populists fought hard at the founding of the Fed to create a central bank that recognized farmland and farm equipment as permissible collateral.

73.　Fannie Mae and Freddie Mac are good evidence of the US successfully doing this. Prior to the 2007/20008 financial crisis, they held high minimum standards for loan quality and were still able to support many in getting mortgages who would otherwise have been denied (Tooze 2018, 47).

74.　In the same spirit as the defense of state investment banks outlined here, see Mazzucato and Penna (2016).

75.　Cory Booker has promoted this idea by developing the concept of "opportunity zones." See also Banerjee and Duflo 2019.

76.　Again, creditworthiness would be defined politically, not by the profit mechanism.

77.　Van 't Klooster 2020, 592.

78.　Van 't Klooster 2020, 596.

79.　It is worth noting that this is a voluntary body and that four-fifths of central bankers surveyed by *Central Banking* do not believe climate change poses a major risk to financial stability. See Jeffery (2019).

80.　Jeffery 2019.

81.　Jeffery 2019.

82.　This point is further emphasized by the fact that central bank independence has been suspended in times of war and monetary policy employed as a state tool. This was particularly and explicitly true of monetary policy in the US during World War II. For more on the political battle to instate independence in the wake of WWII, see Epstein and Juliet Schor (2011).

References

Adolph, Christopher. 2013. *Bankers, Bureaucrats, and Central Bank Politics: The Myth of Neutrality*. Cambridge University Press.

Banerjee, Abhijit V., and Esther Duflo. 2019. *Good Economics for Hard Times*. PublicAffairs.

Baxter, Norman W. 1927. "Political Clevage in Senate Indicated by Bank Bill Vote: Replacement of Parties Held Possible Result in Cloture Action Today. Wheeler Conducts One-Man Filibuster Asks Why Reserve Charter Be Renewed 8 Years before It Expires." *Washington Post (1923–1954); Washington, D.C.* February 15.

Benoist, Alain de. 2011. *The Problem of Democracy*. London: Arktos.

Bentham, Jeremy. 2002. "Projet of a Constitutional Code for France." In *The Collected Works of Jeremy Bentham: Rights, Representation, and Reform: Nonsense upon Stilts and Other Writings on the French Revolution*, edited by Philip Schofield, Catherine Pease-Watkin, and Cyprian Blamires. Oxford Scholarly Editions Online.

Braun, Benjamin. 2014. "Why Models Matter: The Making and Unmaking of Governability in Macroeconomic Discourse." *Journal of Critical Globalisation Studies*, no. 7, 48–79.

Buckley, Terry. 2006. *Aspects of Greek History: A Source-Based Approach*. Routledge.

"Chevron U.S.A. Inc. v. Natural Resources Defense Council, Inc., et al." 1983. *U.S.* 467:837–66.

Conti-Brown, Peter. 2016. *The Power and Independence of the Federal Reserve*. Princeton University Press.

Desan, Christine. 2015. *Making Money: Coin, Currency, and the Coming of Capitalism*. Reprint ed. Oxford University Press.

Elgie, Robert, and Helen Thompson. 1998. *The Politics of Central Banks*. Routledge Advances in International Relations and Politics, 7. Routledge.

Epstein, Gerald, and Juliet Schor. 2011. "The Federal Reserve-Treasury Accord and the Construction of the Post-War Monetary Regime in the United States." University of Massachusetts Amherst Political Economy Research Institute. Working Paper No. 273, November 8.

"Fed Likely to 'Institutionalise' Policy Framework Review, Powell Says." 2019. *Central Banking*, October 31.

Federal Reserve History. 2013. "McFadden Act of 1927," November 22.

Fuhrer, Jeffrey C., Giovanni P. Olivei, Eric S. Rosengren, and Geoffrey M. B. Tootell. 2018. "Should the Fed Regularly Evaluate Its Monetary Policy Framework?" IDEAS Working Paper Series from RePEc, St. Louis.

Garrett, Franklin Miller. 1968. *A History of the Federal Reserve Bank of Atlanta, Sixth District*.

Greenberg, Daniel. 2018. "The Constitutional Value of Sunset Clauses: An Historical and Normative Analysis." *Statute Law Review* 39, no. 3 (October): 350–51.

Hay, Colin. 2007. *Why We Hate Politics*. 1st ed. Polity.

Jacobs, Lawrence, and Desmond King. 2016. *Fed Power: How Finance Wins*. Oxford University Press.

Jeffery, Christopher. 2019. "A Climate of Change." *Central Banking*, May 31.

Kouroutakis, Antonios. 2016. *The Constitutional Value of Sunset Clauses: An Historical and Normative Analysis*. Routledge.

Livingston, James. 2006. *Origins of the Federal Reserve System: Money, Class, and Corporate Capitalism, 1890–1913*. Cornell University Press.

Lowenstein, Roger. 2015. *America's Bank: The Epic Struggle to Create the Federal Reserve*. Penguin Press.

Mankiw, N. Gregory. 2014. *Principles of Macroeconomics*. Cengage Learning.

Mazzucato, Mariana, and Caetano C. R. Penna. 2016. "Beyond Market Failures: The

Market Creating and Shaping Roles of State Investment Banks." *Journal of Economic Policy Reform* 19, no. 4 (October): 305–26.

McConnell, Michael. 2018. "Kavanaugh and the 'Chevron Doctrine.'" *Hoover Institution*, July 30.

Morgan, Ricks, John Crawford, and Lev Menand. 2020. "FedAccounts: Digital Dollars." George Washington Law Review.

Murray, John David. 2018. "Why the Bank of Canada Sticks with 2 Percent Inflation Target." *Brookings*, June.

"National Bank Branch Bill Passes Senate." 1926. "Measure Already Approved by House and Differences Expected to be Eliminated in Quick Order. Few Changes Are Made. Indeterminate Charters for Banks of Federal Reserve System Is One Provision." *New York Herald, New York Tribune (1924–1926); New York, N.Y.* May 14.

Norges Bank. 2015. "External Evaluations," August 12.

Ober, Josiah, and Charles W. Hedrick. 1996. *D mokratia: A Conversation on Democracies, Ancient and Modern.* Princeton University Press.

Orian Peer, Nadav. 2019. "Negotiating the Lender of Last Resort: The 1913 Federal Reserve Act as a Debate over Credit Distribution." *NYU Journal of Law & Business* 15, no. 2 (Spring): 452.

"Owen Upholds Act of Reserve Board." 1927. "Senator Says Congress Meant Federal Body to Fix Banks' Rediscount Rates. PLAN FOUGHT BY BANKERS Measure Passed, He Asserts, to Bar Private Persons From Causing Panics. BILL SUPPORTED BY WILSON Senator Relates History of Bill to Put Control of Currency in Government's Hands." *New York Times*, sec. business opportunities.

Powell, Jerome H. 2019. "Semiannual Monetary Policy Report to the Congress." Before the Committee on Banking, Housing, and Urban Affairs, US Senate, Washington, DC. February 26.

Preston, H. H. 1927. "The McFadden Banking Act." *American Economic Review* 17, no. 2 (June): 201–18.

Quinn, Sarah. 2019. *American Bonds: How Credit Markets Shaped a Nation.* Princeton University Press.

Ranchordás, Sofia. 2014. *Constitutional Sunsets and Experimental Legislation.* Edward Elgar Publishing.

"Reserve Bank Extension Opposed in Committee." 1926. *Wall Street Journal (1923–Current File); New York, N.Y.,* March 18.

Roberts, Alasdair. 2010. *The Logic of Discipline: Global Capitalism and the Architecture of Government.* Oxford University Press.

Rousseau, Jean-Jacques, Gita May, Robert N. Bellah, David Bromwich, and Conor Cruise O'Brien. 2002. *The Social Contract and The First and Second Discourses.* Edited by Susan Dunn. Yale University Press.

Ryan-Collins, Josh. 2015. "Is Monetary Financing Inflationary? A Case Study of the Canadian Economy, 1935–75." Levy Institute Working Paper No. 848, October.

Schwartzberg, Melissa. 2003. "Rousseau on Fundamental Law." *Political Studies* 51, no. 2 (June): 387–403.

Summers, Lawrence H. 2018. "Why the Fed Needs a New Monetary Policy Framework." *Brookings*, June.

Tooze, J. Adam. 2018. *Crashed: How a Decade of Financial Crises Changed the World.* Viking.

Tuck, Richard. 2015. *The Sleeping Sovereign: The Invention of Modern Democracy.* Cambridge University Press.

Ubide, Ángel. 2017. *The Paradox of Risk: Leaving the Monetary Policy Comfort Zone.* Peterson Institute for International Economics.

"USA Patriot Act: Sunsets Report." 2005. Department of Justice.

Van 't Klooster, Jens. 2020. "The Ethics of Delegating Monetary Policy." *Journal of Politics* 82, no. 2 (April): 587–99.

Wasson, R. Gordon. 1927. "Carter Glass Fathers the Federal Reserve Act." *New York Herald Tribune (1926–1962); New York, N.Y.* March 20.

14 *Polypolitanism*
An Approach to Immigration Policy to Support a Just Political Economy

DANIELLE ALLEN

Introduction: Justice by Means of Democracy

In my book *Justice by Means of Democracy*, I argue that a rightly constructed theory of justice will start from the premise that political equality is non-sacrificeable. The route to justice, I argue, is through and only through democracy.[1] I make the case that human flourishing depends on individual empowerment in the form of both negative liberties or private autonomy—which secures the ability to chart one's life course and craft a way of life—and positive liberties or public autonomy—which provides people, as political agents, with the opportunity to be cocreators of the norms and laws that establish the constraints on private autonomy. Public autonomy also goes by the name of "political equality," and the negative liberties are a necessary component of viable political equality. In other words, pursuit of political equality requires securing both negative and positive liberties. In contrast, pursuit of negative liberties merely has often been seen as compatible with the sacrifice of positive liberties.[2] Only the former path—the pursuit of political equality that necessarily incorporates pursuit of negative liberties—provides a sound foundation for human flourishing, I argue. Within the polity, a theory of justice that treats political equality as non-sacrificeable recognizes human moral equality in full and seeks to build political institutions, structure social policy, cultivate economies, and enable inclusive cultural work so as to protect egalitarian access to political power.

If human flourishing rests on political equality, then it also depends on an ideal of non-domination. Political equality is achieved when no individual or group can dominate any other individual or group within the polity, where domination is defined as having arbitrary reserve control over others.[3] The ideal political institutions of a liberal, rights-protective democracy are designed so as to hedge against any given member of the polity dominating any other, or any group another group, but political institutions themselves are insufficient to ward off the emergence of domination. The protection of basic liberties—including the liberty of association—will ensure that social difference emerges within the polity. The challenge for a theory of justice anchored in the non-sacrificeability of political equality is also to offer frameworks for the organization of both social and economic life that ward off the likelihood that difference, which emerges from freedom, comes to articulate with domination. Doing this requires both protecting basic rights and adopting the principle of "difference without domination," in addition to the Rawlsian difference principle.[4] Since the protection of freedom will ensure that difference emerges, the pursuit of justice requires continually analyzing the forms of difference that do emerge—whether in the social or economic realm—to ascertain whether they have come to articulate with the domination of some by others and to work to break up those emergent power monopolies.[5] To eschew domination is not to renounce hierarchy; legitimate hierarchies avoid the arbitrary exercise of power and any rights-violating exercise of power. It is instead to counter incipient monopolies—political, social, or economic.

To pursue the application of a principle of difference without domination in the social realm, I have commended the ideal of a connected society as a guide to social policy.[6] A connected society supports cosmopolitan bonding relationships—forms of in-group relationship that also cultivate openness to connections across lines of social division. A connected society also designs institutions—both private and public—to maximize the formation of bridging social ties. Support of this kind for the emergence of bridging social networks, on top of healthy bonding networks, leads to forms of social policy that, I posit, are most likely to succeed in advancing the principle of difference without domination.

What sort of political economy embodies the principle of difference without domination? What sort of political economy might be built on a theory of justice that treats political equality as non-sacrificeable? The goal of political economy, on this account of justice, is to build empowering economies— economies that empower the citizenry broadly to succeed as civic agents. This is not a new idea. Both Aristotle and the founders of the United States thought that a "middling" or "middle-class" economy was the necessary foundation for a polity of free and equal citizens. Similarly, nineteenth-century American president Abraham Lincoln believed that the economy of a republic had to rest on "free labor" in order for the citizenry to remain free from domination and fully empowered. In contrast to Aristotle and the first generation of American founders, however, Lincoln also connected the idea of an empowering economy to that of a nonexploitative economy. "As

I would not be a slave," he wrote, "so I would not be a master. This expresses my idea of democracy. Whatever differs from this, to the extent of the difference, is not democracy."[7] Ultimately, for him, the need to rest the republic on an empowering economy required the eradication of enslavement so that the empowerment of some would not rest on expropriation from others. The effort to end enslavement—for all the twists and turns of the tactics and strategies with which Lincoln pursued it and for all the unevenness of the effort's results—attempted a fundamental reorientation of American political economy.[8] Lincoln sought to make a commitment to labor relations without domination and exploitation a precompetitive matter.

With regard to the economic realm, I similarly argue that the goal is to ascertain how to build nonexploitative and empowering economies. Exploitation is that act of profiting from vulnerabilities that characterize those in the weaker position in a relationship of domination. An economy will be nonexploitative, in other words, when it is also free from relations of domination. The largest problem of exploitation that comes into view when one considers the contemporary economy of the US is the large dependence of the economy on undocumented workers who have little access to civil and political rights. In other words, the social phenomenon that most urgently requires our attention as part of an effort to build a just political economy is immigration. This is not a merely contingent feature of the contemporary situation. Rather, the question of who gets to be a citizen, and in which polity, is, I will argue, the first economic question. It establishes the foundation of all labor policy and conditions for labor mobility. As such, immigration and polity membership policies are among the constitutive building blocks of the global economy.

Ascertaining how to build nonexploitative and empowering economies for a citizenry of political equals turns out to require, as a foundational matter, a just immigration policy.[9] My goal in this chapter is to outline an approach to immigration policy that is compatible with the principle of difference without domination. I will make the case that we need a new conceptualization of political membership.

To pursue such a fresh conceptualization of political membership, I will begin by looking at the relationship between the ideal of an empowering economy in a domestic nation-state context and questions of membership. This will be followed by a look at the relationship between the structure of the global economy and the world's rules for political membership. After we have considered the history of these relationships and what we can learn from them about the puzzles to be solved in building an empowering and nonexploitative economies, I will consider one recent proposal for adjusting global immigration and membership rules, the Visas between Individuals Program

(VIP). Proffered by economist Glen Weyl and legal theorist Eric Posner in their book *Radical Markets,* this idea for adjusting membership rules has as its goal not the cultivation of empowering economies but the achievement of global distributive justice. While they have since moved beyond this policy, the VIP proposal usefully clarifies the logical conclusions of some quite common utilitarian and distributive justice views and therefore continues to be relevant for clarifying the conceptual choices in front of us. I will criticize the VIP policy and offer an alternative conceptual framework, which I call "polypolitanism," and some examples of policies that might instantiate it. By polypolitanism, I have in mind the idea that any one of us might have affiliations with multiple political communities and many political roles. Whether we have access to political equality is not a unitary question but rather a question of how our memberships accumulate and interact. This idea should help us reconceptualize political membership generally, in ways that open up resources for a revised and empowering approach to political economy.

Empowering Economies, Difference without Domination, and Immigration

Immigration policy is fundamentally about questions of membership. Who gets to belong to a particular society? Most importantly, who gets to be a citizen? Who gets access to this vaunted political equality that, I am arguing, is the foundation of full justice? Issues of migration, immigration, and naturalization are clearly political questions. Beyond that, they might seem at first glance to be social, not economic, questions. But this is incorrect.

Above I argued that a framework for social policy that accords with the principle of difference without domination will focus on building a connected society, one that supports cosmopolitan bonding relationships (to repeat: in-group relationships that also cultivate openness to connections across lines of social division) and where private and public institutions are designed to maximize the formation of bridging social ties. These principles pertain regardless of what the democracy's membership policies are. In fact, in an essay, "Toward a Connected Society," I outlined the features of a connected society without once considering the question of who can be a member and how membership is determined in that kind of society. Regardless of who the members are—to what degree they are native-born or immigrants, speakers of a dominant or minority language—the principles of a connected society are the same. Their implementation will change with the demographic facts on the ground but the principles themselves will not. The nature of the social differences with the potential to fragment a society and that need to be overcome will vary, but even relatively homogenous societies have fallen into civil war. Similarly, one or another migration or membership policy will put varying kinds of pressure on the institutions of a connected society, but in each case, the connected society ideal establishes a goal to support cosmopolitan bonding relationships and to maximize bridging relationships. There may be interesting empirical questions to consider about the rate of social dynamism that can be sustained, given particular institutional configurations of bonding and bridging relationships.[10] But those are empirical questions. Variations in membership policy do not change the theoretical fundamentals of the connected society ideal.

The same cannot be said of the economic realm. Here the question of who gets to be a member of which polity and on which terms is, perhaps, the first economic fact. Since property rights, for instance, are anchored by the legal regimes of particular political communities, membership in a specific political community (or lack thereof) even precedes property. Relatedly, the mobility of labor, a constitutive element of the global economy, is fully dependent on immigration and membership policies. The question of what sorts of immigration and membership policies we build will constrain the possible set of political economies. As we turn from the application of the principle of difference without domination in the social realm to the economic realm, the question of membership in the polity—of who has visiting, residential, and/ or national political rights—becomes distinctively salient. The allocation of membership within particular national polities is one of the building blocks of the global economy and therefore of the economy of any particular polity. Questions of just approaches to migration, immigration, and membership are a necessary way station on the path to envisioning a just political economy.

The effort to envision forms of political economy that align with the principle of difference without domination intersects with the question of membership in political communities in three ways. First, there is the fact that previous efforts to build empowering and egalitarian economies have often not only failed to align with the principle of difference without domination but have actually proactively used domination as a tool to support the construction of an empowering economy for a privileged group of people classed as citizens. Second, in our current world, the opportunity to migrate presents would-be migrants with a meaningful chance to improve their own economic and social prospects, but the asymmetry between the human right to freedom of movement, as articulated in the Universal Declaration of Human Rights, and the absence of a right to be received in any particular place (except in the case of refugees) sets up potential conditions for exploitation. Third, the world's membership and migration policies structure the world's labor market and therefore structure the potential of both global and national economies for growth, efficient operation, and equitable distribution of the gains of productivity. Not only migrants themselves but also receiving societies stand to benefit materially from labor mobility (even if some specific members of the receiving societies might lose out). In other words, the material bases of an empowering economy are affected by the world's membership and migration policies. If we are to maximize the power of the global economy to deliver to the world's peoples the material bases for civic agency, we need approaches to membership that make it possible for the workers of the world to move. Yet the coupling of the material benefits of migration to both migrants and receiving societies with the asymmetry between rights to move and rights to be received further entrenches the vulnerability of would-be migrants to exploitation. By organizing the world's labor market, the world's membership policies structure the potential of both global and national economies for growth, efficient operation, and equitable distribution of the gains of productivity and simultaneously establish patterns of power and vulnerability for the world's populations.

How historically has the goal of an economy that empowers a body of citizen-equals been linked through membership policies to the problem of exploitation? How do frameworks of membership structure the economy and patterns of power and vulnerability? Understanding these two things will help us develop parameters for an empowering economy that accords with the principle of difference without domination.

Empowering Economies and the Historical Problem of Exploitation

As I said above, political economies directed toward the empowerment of the citizenry are not new. Both Aristotle and the founders of the United States thought that a "middling" or "middle-class" economy was the necessary foundation for a polity of free and equal citizens. In ultimately seeking an end to enslavement, Lincoln pursued an empowering economy that also ruled out the most extreme forms of domination in labor relations and made a commitment to "free labor" a precompetitive feature of market societies. Importantly, in deciding to fight enslavement, Lincoln sought to replace the founding generation's model for a political economy of empowerment. The founders of the early American republic did indeed seek to ground political equality on economic egalitarianism. For instance, the Georgia land lottery gave land out to white men, widows, and orphans in equally sized plots via a random process.[11] Yet the land lottery was, of course, not open to the enslaved population. Even more fundamental, the land that was being given away had been expropriated from Native Americans. In other words, an empowering economic egalitarianism was created by virtue of designating a subset of people as existing outside the circle of political inclusion.[12] Indigenous Americans had access to none of the tools economist Albert Hirschman considered necessary for both freedom and a well-functioning economy: exit, voice, or influence through loyalty.[13]

Historical versions of the commitment to a theory of justice grounded in the non-sacrificeability of political equality have typically relied, for their conceptual and practical success, on exploitation of those outside the penumbra of protection. This is a philosophical error that requires correction. The correction we need is the one Lincoln offered—namely, the recognition that democracy should be defined by the following moral orientation: "As I would not be a slave, so I would not be a master." The example of the Georgia land lottery brings into view that a twenty-first-century effort to ground a theory of justice on the non-sacrificeability of political equality within a polity also has the burden of explaining how an economic order can be constructed that supports a domestic project of political equality without making the exclusion of others from access to political equality a necessary condition of its own success. This is the twenty-first-century equivalent to the nineteenth-century injunction to imagine an economy without enslavement.

Why should we care whether a domestic project of protecting political equality and of securing an empowering economy exploits the lack of access of others to political equality? The ground for our own pursuit of political equality is a recognition of its value to human flourishing generally. This general applicability of the value of political equality is the reason we should respect its importance for those outside our own domestic project as well as for those protected by the penumbra of our domestic commitments. Such respect need not come in the form of bringing about political equality for others. We cannot wave a magic wand and transform every person on the globe into a citizen in a well-functioning democracy. Indeed, not only can we not do so; we should not do so. Political equality is not something that some can create for others; democratic agency must be made by its own agents for themselves. It would be a violation of the principles defining this account of how to achieve justice through democracy to force others to be free, for instance at the tip of a spear.[14] The questions of how to structure membership in national polities to support the project of justice is more complicated than the democratizing invasions of various imperial armies (including those of the US) have seemed to suggest. *Instead, respect for the value of political equality to human beings generally entails refusing to take advantage of the vulnerabilities that accrue to those who do not have access to political voice and influence.*

The membership policies of the world's countries create vulnerabilities by differentially distributing political equality. Some countries offer political equality to some residents but not others; some countries offer political equality to only a very few residents. Some people have access to voice and influence because of the membership status into which they were born; millions are stateless and have no access to voice and influence at all. Of course, economic inequalities within any given country also affect who has genuine access to voice and influence, but membership policies are prior even to this. The question of how the globe arranges its membership policies will affect the degree of vulnerability we are morally obliged to avoid taking advantage of. As those of us in the protected space of democracies seek to build empowering economies, our work is less likely to slip into injustice to the degree that vulnerabilities of others stemming from the lack of access to political equality are minimized. We ought therefore to seek this minimization in order to protect ourselves from slipping into acts of injustice. Our moral question is this: How can we avoid treating other parts of the globe as the founders treated Indigenous Americans?

Before we can explore how to build empowering and nonexploitative economies, then, we need to ascertain how to build membership policies for the globe's states that simultaneously, and in relation to each other, maximize the potential of labor to move, for the migrants' own sake as well as for the sake of the economies of receiving societies, while minimizing the vulnerability of the world's populations to exclusion from political equality. Here, then, are the first rudiments of a just system of membership for the world's states and for a just political economy focused on the development of economies that are simultaneously empowering and nonexploitative:

1. *the global membership system should maximize the freedom of labor to move;*
2. *while minimizing the vulnerability of the world's populations to exclusion from political equality.*

How do frameworks of membership structure the economy and patterns of power and vulnerability? We need a full understanding of this question if we are to develop a political economy that accords with the above criteria.

How Frameworks of Membership Structure the Economy

The world has never seen an economy dis-embedded from social relations, nor is such a thing imaginable.[15] The world's global economy is embedded not only in the political systems of particular nation-states but also in a global system structured above all by rules about membership, migration, and im-migration. Those rules of membership typically flow from underlying para-digms for belonging—the two dominant ones have been nationalism and cosmopolitanism.

In *Radical Markets*, Weyl and Posner offer a very helpful review of the inter-twining history of capitalism and migration from the eighteenth century to the present; through their review we can also see the intertwining histories of nationalist and cosmopolitan concepts.

In the late eighteenth century the protectionist mercantilism of the early modern European sovereigns gave way to policies of free international trade advocated by thinkers like Jeremy Bentham, Adam Smith, and David Hume. These political philosophers argued that free exchange across borders—of goods, capital, and credit—would maximize the total welfare delivered by an economy to the citizens of any given nation.

Importantly, migration was not a focus of the work of the eighteenth-century free marketeers, largely because migration just did not matter that much at this point in time. Despite the age of exploration and the significant movements of people effected by the transatlantic enslavement trade, "per-sistent differences in mass living standards across countries were unknown until the late nineteenth century" (Weyl and Eric Posner 2018, 133). As Weyl and Posner put it, in the late eighteenth and early nineteenth century, the most extreme gaps in prosperity, as between China and the United Kingdom, "were only a factor of 3," while by the 1950s the gap had reached a factor of 10. They combine several historical datasets on global inequality and show a remarkable transformation in the period between 1820 and 2011. Most impor-tantly, income inequality across countries "increased from about 7% in 1820 to about 70% in 1980"; since 1980, the degree of inequality has shrunk some-what, thanks to growth in China and India, but is still at about 50 percent. At the same time, average within-country income inequality has held relatively steady and even shown a slight decline. That decline reflects both increases of inequality in wealthy countries and decreases of inequality in developing countries. The combination of the dramatic increases in between country inequality and the modest decrease of within-country inequality means that on the whole global inequality is far greater now than it was in the early nine-teenth century. In other words, people's standard of living varies significantly with the accident of where they were born. The consequence of these eco-nomic facts is, as Weyl and Posner argue, that the world of Bentham, Smith, and Hume was one "in which migration did most people little good" while "ours is one in which migration can be a primary route to well-being and prosperity for most people in the world" (Weyl and Eric Posner 2018, 135).

Whereas the early theorists of capital argued for the free movement of goods and capital, they made no equivalent case for the free movement of people. This was not because they were against such free movement but simply because migration was not relevant to maximizing the efficiency of the globe's economy in the late eighteenth century. That has changed in the intervening centuries. And as it has changed, the globe's countries have also become more controlling of migration. Migration was relatively unrestricted until the early twentieth century. Then the wealthy countries of the world began to close their doors to migrants, doing so just when migration had begun to matter from the point of view of maximizing the capacity of the global economy to deliver welfare to all the world's peoples (Weyl and Posner, 137). Over the course of the twentieth century and into the early twenty-first century, as the globe marched forward breaking down residual forms of trade protectionism and mercantilist economic policy, capital was set free to flow across the globe in the direction of its maximally efficient allocation. For the most part, labor was not similarly enabled to travel. Those with higher levels of education have been able to move freely, but less well-educated workers have not shared that same mobility.

Where experiments were made, as in the European Union, which permitted free movement of the citizens of member states within the boundaries of the EU, the asymmetrical flows of people from poorer countries, such as Poland, to wealthier ones, such as the United Kingdom, generated forms of backlash to the necessarily ensuing cultural hybridization. In other words, the EU experiment discovered that different kinds of friction attach to the movement of peoples than to the movement of capital. The frictions are not a matter of interest rates or the availability of viable investment vehicles. Instead, they consist of matters of language, culture, and religion—the bases for collaboration. The well-functioning of human beings depends not merely on each individual's competencies and resources but also on the capacity of communities to build healthy patterns of interaction. Cultural connection and integration are necessary for the successful movement of people; the frictions attached to the movement of labor need to be addressed as part of thinking about how to maximize the productive potential of the world's labor markets. Yet the resistance to the free movement of ordinary workers means that the gains from freely moving capital go largely to the owners of capital, and the growth of a globalizing world has been captured by wealth elites rather than being "widely shared" (Weyl and Posner,140).

In addition to pointing out that methods of globalization have freed goods and capital to flow to where they can best be put to use without having similarly freed labor and that these methods have consequently resulted in unequal gains in the global economy, Weyl and Posner also underscore the consensus among economists that nearly all of the benefit to be had from liberalizing trade and capital flows has already accrued. At this point, the single component of the global economy with the biggest potential for positive impact on the distribution of wealth and the material bases for welfare around the world is migration policy. In short, membership policies—in the form of restrictive immigration policies in the early part of the twentieth century; European experimentation with liberalization of membership in the late twentieth century; and European retrenchment in the twenty-first century—are currently the most important constitutive element for adjustments to the functioning of the world's economy. Since no national economy can now operate without attention to its place within a global economy, the question of what just and empowering economic policy might be at home depends on each country's approach to migration and membership and the world's resulting aggregate framework. This story of restrictive immigration policies, experimentation with openness, and retrenchment reflects an underlying dialectical argument between nationalist and cosmopolitan concepts for thinking about membership. The former dominates the current structure of the global economy, but both are relevant to understanding its operations.

Thanks to the Treaty of Versailles and its articulation of principles of national self-determination, later reinforced through the United Nations, a concept of a culturally unified people that determines a life-form for itself undergirds common contemporary expectations for how membership in a polity will operate. The nationalist concept of membership is therefore frequently "ethnonationalist." Immigration poses a challenge by definition because it very often entails the arrival within national borders of people without a historic or cultural connection to "the people" who define and "determine" the polity at issue. The settler societies—the United States, Australia, and Canada—have always been the exception to this model, as countries where immigrants overran Indigenous populations and therewith obliterated any stable concept of a cultural basis for membership. While these countries have themselves seen episodic efforts to establish a cultural basis for membership—and the US is living through such an effort now—the thoroughgoing hybridity of the population makes this an impossible task. Nonetheless, these countries, too, have sought significant immigration restrictions, reinforcing by practice, if not by ideology, the dominant pattern in the globe of nationalist, and even ethnonationalist, models of membership. Importantly, these nationalist models of membership restrict the capacity of the globe's political economy to maximize material welfare for all the peoples of the earth. The protection of the nationalist ideal depends on relegating some populations around the globe to deeper forms of poverty than is, strictly speaking, economically necessary. With restrictive membership policies, the effort to pursue an empowering economy in any developed country means that the benefits of internal egalitarianism rest on exploitation of peoples outside the borders of the country, much as was the case when the economic egalitarianism of the early American republic rested on the exploitation of native peoples.

This picture of the relationship between membership policies and political economy has, of course, also generated an extreme position at the other end of the ideological spectrum: a cosmopolitan ideal of membership. On this ideal, the gains to distributive justice to be had from allowing the free movement of peoples mean that all the countries of the world should have open borders. With labor able to move freely, the globe's economy would generate maximally fertile conditions for material welfare, and the wealth produced would be distributed in a maximally egalitarian fashion. This is a utopian picture of the relationship between membership policies and economic policy. It treats the phenomenon of human movement as on the same footing as the movement of capital, as if people and capital can move with equivalent degrees of frictionlessness. But the cosmopolitan vision for how to maximize distributive justice founders on the unwillingness of populations in any given society to admit any and every one to membership in their society accordingly as arriving migrants see fit. Nor is this unwillingness altogether reprehensible. Social cohesion reduces the transaction costs within an economy and so is also a contributor to productivity. If we increase the movement of labor for the sake of economic growth, we should avoid doing so in ways that simultaneously undermine growth by increasing the friction of within-economy transactions. The cosmopolitan ideal founders because it fails to address the frictions that necessarily attend the movement of peoples and that introduce additional transaction costs to the functioning of an economy.

The nationalist model of membership entails members' of wealthy countries securing their material good by exploitation and at the expense of those in other countries. The cosmopolitan model of membership entails members of less well-off countries improving their material well-being at the expense of the viability of the political and social institutions of receiving countries. The flaws of the nationalist model lead us to ask how to build membership policies that do not build a domestic egalitarian empowering economy on the exposure to domination and exploitation of those not included within the penumbra of political membership. The flaws of the cosmopolitan model lead us to ask how to minimize the specific kinds of friction that attend the movement of people and the harms that may be done by those frictions to those who have "high functioning" political and social institutions.[16] The former correction requires finding a path to free movement of labor coupled with access to political voice; the latter correction requires finding methods for reducing the frictions attendant on movement. We can modestly adapt our framework for a just political economy that cultivates economies that are simultaneously empowering and nonexploitative:

> *The global membership system should maximize the freedom of labor to move by means of a framework that:*
>   *a. Minimizes the vulnerability of the world's populations to exclusion from political equality.*
>   *b. Reduces the frictions attendant on migration.*

The first prong proposes a correction to nationalist and ethnonationalist approaches to immigration and membership; the second, a corrective to cosmopolitanism.

A Modest Proposal: The Visas between Individuals Program

Before I turn to my own proposal for an approach to immigration that aligns with the criteria sketched above, I want to review one recent policy idea that attempted to free labor to move (counter to the nationalist paradigm) while also reducing the frictions of movement (counter to the cosmopolitan paradigm) and that sought to do so in the interest of securing global distributive justice. I have in mind a proposal mooted by Weyl and Posner called the Visas between Individuals Program (VIP). Although their arguments have now evolved beyond this formulation, the proposal is useful for bringing to the surface the consequences of attending only to the material benefits of immigration, via a focus on distributive justice, without also attending to protections for political equality.

The VIP policy proposes a market-based policy designed to minimize the frictions of migration by aligning the incentives of migrants and native-born citizens through market transactions.[17] The objective of this proposal is to unlock global economic growth in a fashion that will bring more equitable distribution of the material benefits of growth across the world's populations. The VIP proposal is that citizens of wealthy countries ought to be permitted to sponsor workers of their choice from elsewhere in the world, much as companies are currently often able to sponsor highly skilled workers. Any individual citizen would be able to sponsor one worker at a time and either a "rotating cast of temporary guest workers" or "one permanent migrant over a lifetime."[18] Sponsorship would include securing housing, health care, and employment for the migrant and a commitment to pay the migrant some specific amount, set at a level that sponsors could expect to earn money either by having the migrant work for them in some fashion or by finding the migrant employment at a higher wage rate and pocketing the difference. For this to work, on the VIP proposal, migrants are permitted to work for less than the country's minimum wage, though all other worker protection laws and regulations would cover migrants. Sponsors would themselves be civilly liable should the migrant they are sponsoring commit a crime of any kind or abscond from their designated residence. Nor would migrants automatically receive any commitment to permanent residence in the receiving country. The VIP proposal optimistically conjures up a scene in which, after a period of enhanced earnings in the receiving country, migrants will want to go home and help reboot the economies of their home countries.[19]

The goal of the VIP program is to turn migration into something that benefits a receiving country's native citizens. Native-born, low-skilled workers in a wealthy country might find themselves displaced by a migrant willing to work for less, but they could sponsor that same migrant by being a manager of the workers who take their place. By turning migration into something that could economically benefit non-elites in the native population, the VIP program is designed to take the sting out of the cultural impact of the arrival of those who speak different languages, eat different foods, worship different gods, and sing different songs. Nationalism and cosmopolitanism are reconciled, or such is the aspiration, in the cause of global distributive justice.

In originally presenting the VIP policy idea, Weyl and Posner acknowledged that their program might seem objectionable, at first blush, on the grounds that it is rather like a program of indentured servitude. They sought to ward off this objection by asserting that "migrants would be free to leave at any time" and that the program is analogous both to the programs by which companies bring in high-skilled workers and programs by which families bring in au pairs. But in fact, neither assertion helps the case. Someone earning below minimum wage is unlikely to be in a position to travel back to their home country and will in most cases be at the mercy of their sponsor if they wish to secure exit.[20] In addition, an important requirement of the programs in the US in which corporations sponsor highly skilled workers is that these workers be paid at the prevailing wage. The VIP policy explicitly depends on abandoning such a requirement. And programs for au pairs have recently come under great scrutiny because they are rife with exploitation.[21]

Indeed, another analogous practice of migrant sponsorship—namely, sex trafficking—crystallizes the inadequacies of the proposal. The VIP policy does not include sponsorship of migrants into illegal work and therefore explicitly rules out such forms of "migrant sponsorship" as are represented by sex trafficking. Nonetheless, features of the program bear important similarities to sex trafficking. The migrants will be dependent on their sponsor for any access to their rights; and their economic power within the receiving country will be limited in ways that undermine any meaningful access to exit or voice. The VIP policy rests on an account of how the economy of the world will be better off, using this model, with increased productivity and gains shared between citizens in wealthy and poorer countries. But the migrant workers would be vulnerable to exploitation to such a degree that we should expect that gains projected to accrue to them are likely to be captured by sponsors and others in the receiving country. Since their gains would be at the mercy of the good faith behavior of their sponsor, they would be exposed to the arbitrary power of their sponsor day in and day out, and so would be subjected to domination. In addition to the likely capture of their material gains by those in a position to dominate them, we would have to add into the balance of an assessment of such a program the psychological and social costs to them of an ongoing experience of domination. The productivity expected from this mode of free movement of labor would be undercut by the hindrances to productivity introduced by domination.

This is not to say that indentured servants have never flourished. Surely, some did or currently do in those parts of the world where indentured servitude still operates. But it is to say that any broad economic gains that arose in the seventeenth and eighteenth century from indentured servitude are unlikely to have been distributed equally or equitably.[22] Moreover, the monetary gains achieved through this approach to productivity growth are offset by the psychological and social costs of domination. These are real and measurable as demonstrated by measurement of the reverse by Richard Wilkinson and Kate Pickett in *The Spirit Level*. The VIP policy is not a solution to the question of how to organize membership in the world's polities with a view to promoting empowering economies in accord with the principle of difference without domination and a standard of justice. It does, however, help bring into focus how market mechanisms can help reduce the relevant kinds of frictions and transaction costs associated with the free movement of labor.

Weyl and Posner called their program the VIP plan. We might call it, more loosely, a free market approach to membership. In their model, the boundaries of membership would adjust wherever a free market transaction leads to a stable relationship between a sponsor and a migrant. The boundaries of polities—and of who is inside each one of them, whether as a citizen or not—would continually shift as market forces move labor around the world. Yet just as the nationalist and cosmopolitan views were each compromised by a form of exploitation, the VIP model, too, was so compromised, in this case by the exposure of migrants to domination by sponsors.[23] The value of their model was to identify the dynamics of a global labor market and free market transactions as elements of a system of membership that might help us toward nonexploitative economies, but they failed to adjust their model to protect against the domination of migrants.

Taking what is positive and seeking to avoid what is negative in the VIP program, we can make another adjustment to our criteria for a policy that might build empowering economies in accord with the principle of difference without domination:

1. *The global membership system should maximize the freedom of labor to move by means of a framework that:*

    a. *Creates incentives for host citizens to welcome migrants and migrant integration, and thereby avoids an increase to transaction costs in the receiving economy.*

    b. *Ensures that migrants have access to political equality within receiving countries.*

An Alternative: Polypolitanism

A viable membership policy, I suggest, will be one that provides migrants access to the protections of political equality while simultaneously maximizing the value of the liberalization of labor markets. That is, any liberalization of labor markets must be constrained by the requirements that migrating laborers have access to political equality and that the receiving country be able to integrate immigrants. How might that be done?

I have been arguing that the set of just polities that can sustain human well-being across all of its dimensions include only those forms of political arrangement that provide access to political empowerment in relation to polity-level decision-making. This might seem to lead to the requirement that every resident in a polity have access to citizenship rights to provide that access to political empowerment. Indeed, historian of political thought, Richard Tuck, argues for just this position, and he connects it to a defense of restrictive immigration policies. Yet against this position, I will argue that the range of political arrangements that can provide protection of political empowerment is broader than is typically recognized. While provision of citizenship to residents in a polity is the fundamental means of providing access to political empowerment, it is not the only means. Here is where we run into, and must adjust, the rigidity of our expectations with regard to membership policies. Our cultural horizons have been trained for so long on a nationalist framework that we can scarcely imagine political equality outside the context of national political institutions. The invocation of access to political equality leads us immediately to think that what must be meant is that those to whom that equality will be provided will be voting in national elections. My goal in what follows will be to sketch some of the other routes available to protections for political equality.

With but the smallest step back from the nationalist view and a shift of focus, we can readily see that each of us who lives in a developed democracy possesses multiple political memberships. We are political members of our towns, of our states or federal subunits, as well as of the national polity. If we are a member of a labor union, we also have access to political equality through that solidaristic structure. If we are an employee at a corporation, under current US law, that corporation can function as a "person" in political discourse and presumably does so on our behalf. If we are a member of a political party, we have access to political equality through that organization. We might remind ourselves that at an earlier point in American politics, it was commonly the case that some people could vote in city elections, say, but not in state or national elections. Takoma Park, Maryland, currently gives municipal voting rights to noncitizens who do not have the right to vote in national elections. If we could recover an orientation to the multiplicity of kinds of membership that provide access to political voice and influence, and so to political equality, we would have more tools available for building fresh paradigms for immigration. Those of us who are members of developed democratic nation-states have no necessary requirement to think of ourselves as either nationalists or cosmopolitans. We might instead thing of ourselves as "polypolitans"—people who are members of several polities simultaneously. As polypolitans, we have multiple avenues for accessing political power and protecting our interests. The odds are that most polypolitans use many fewer of the resources of political power than are available to them. Polypolitanism also provides resources for giving migrants access to political voice.

Polypolitanism is not a new phenomenon; it has perdured alongside democracy since its inception. Ancient Athens found polypolitanism a great challenge as it periodically had to tamp down the emergence of power channeled through tribal affiliations rather than through the political institutions of the city. Indeed, the fact of polypolitanism can bring instability when political affiliations at different levels come into conflict with one another. The

US Civil War is a good example here of the consequences when national and regional affiliations and forms of membership came into conflict with each other. Moments of crisis have often made visible the degree to which people function in the world in "polypolitan" ways; the crisis emerges when they have to choose between their loyalties to different political institutions and therefore to different avenues for voice. Yet, despite the dangers of reminding people that they have access to a multiplicity of political memberships, that multiplicity of those possible membership roles may provide an important institutional opportunity as we try to reenvision just politics and economies in the twenty-first century.

Here, then, are the rudiments of a just system of membership for the world's states, now modestly revised for a final time to incorporate the idea of polypolitanism:

1. *The global membership system should maximize the freedom of labor to move by means of a framework that*
    a. *Creates incentives for host citizens to welcome migrants and migrant integration, and thereby avoids an increase to transaction costs in the receiving economy;*
    b. *Draws on the resources of polypolitanism to ensure that migrants have access to political equality within receiving countries.*

One possible approach to membership policies that would meet these criteria would adopt the sponsorship model proposed in the VIP framework but would align it more closely to the policy design in which corporations sponsor highly skilled migrants. The key difference would be that the program would not place the power of sponsorship in the hands of individuals. Instead, it would place it in the hands of corporate bodies that can provide voice and influence, and therefore political equality, to those who are their members. By "corporate bodies," I do not simply mean for-profit or commercial corporations; I mean, rather, all the organizations of civil society. In particular, cities, states (understood as subunits of the national polity), labor unions, faith organizations, and other civil society organizations could serve as sponsors for migrants into roles for which migrants would be paid a prevailing wage and in exchange for a fee they would pay to their sponsor. Indeed, Canada has successfully operated precisely such a program for refugee admissions for four decades. The proposal here is to expand that model to migration generally. The number of available sponsorships could be calibrated annually in relation to the size of the population, with the goal perhaps of hitting a target of admissions of 1 percent of the existing population annually.[24] Sponsored slots could be divided between permanent resident slots and temporary worker slots, as long as there is also a policy in place for opening the possibility of permanent residency to qualifying temporary workers after a set time period. Sponsors would benefit financially from their sponsorship.[25] The fees paid to sponsors could support a market in sponsorship just as fees paid to the providers of study abroad programs support a market in study abroad programs. Sponsorships of this kind would accelerate migrant integration—by making the sponsoring organization responsible for that integration. Sponsoring organizations would be held accountable through routine auditing by an Office of Civil and Political Rights, which would also approve organizations to be sponsors in the first place. They would be held to account specifically for their role in protecting the rights of migrants and giving them voice.[26] Sponsorship approaches to migration would permit greater intentionality around migration policy, including greater responsiveness to specific labor market needs and attention to regional economic variation as regional sponsors take responsibility for clarifying and presenting their specific needs.

The proposal is in effect an updated and formalized variant of an informal nineteenth century approach to supporting labor migration: the use of transnational workers' mutual aid associations. In the nineteenth century, as laborers were migrating from agricultural to urban areas, and also from one part of the globe to another, they commonly formed mutual aid associations.[27] I am thinking of organizations like the Independent Order of Odd Fellows, Masonic lodges of various varieties, the Knights Templar and Knights of Columbus, and many other organizations. Civil society associations of these kinds formed—in advance of the development of the liberal welfare state—to secure health care, unemployment insurance, and retirement resources for the unprotected workers of the nineteenth century. Because these organizations were cross-regional and even transnational, they could support the movement of laborers to markets where opportunity was greater as well as facilitate their integration on arrival. In addition, they often provided voice for the politically voiceless. As an example, consider the Prince Hall Masons, formed in the late eighteenth century in Boston, to provide political power to disfranchised African Americans. The Prince Hall Masons achieved their formal organizational status through affiliation with a network of Scottish Masonic lodges—securing voice for themselves that was not available within US political institutions. With solidaristic efforts through the Prince Hall Masonic lodge, these African American laborers were able to pursue the abolition of enslavement in Massachusetts (achieved in 1783), to contemplate removing themselves to Africa (a question of late-eighteenth-century labor mobility), and to develop resources to deliver education to the children of their community. The emergence of the welfare state and the institutional-ized provision of social rights led to the waning of associations of this kind. But we might now encourage their regrowth in support of a sponsorship model for immigration, and the provision of voice and influence to migrants, the components of political equality.

Indeed, the Canadian model has inspired the growth of new associations of this kind. Where once they formed primarily to secure something like social rights for workers, now they might instead operate to deliver voice, to protect civil rights, and to provide representation in political processes, in that sense delivering political rights. With the opportunity for migrants to secure protection through political voice in solidaristic societies of this kind, developed economies could set a pace for the rate of admission of mi-grants into full national citizenship that avoids cultural backlash while also avoiding falling into the injustice of maintaining a caste system where some members of the polity are permanently disfranchised. Just as native-born citizens pass through stages of membership and participation, so too might migrants. Rather than being simply without political voice, they might—as polypolitans—begin their lives as civic agents in their receiving societies by means of access to political voice through avenues other than national po-litical institutions. They might begin with participation in solidaristic civil society organizations. Nor should we forget, of course, that some migrants will have access to political voice through the political institutions of their sending country. Receiving countries ought also to ensure that the embassies and consulates of sending countries are appropriately empowered to provide voice to migrants from their countries.

The Canadian model for the private sponsorship of refugees is widely rec-ognized as a success; the question, then, is whether we can indeed extend such a model to migration generally and, as we do, offer migrants a "polypoli-tan" path to political equality that includes participation in and representa-tion through solidaristic civil society organizations.

Conclusion

Because the functioning of an economy interacts with the political system in which it operates, it can be tempting to think that particular economic goals ought to be achieved by means of adjustments to the underlying political regime. In some cases, this instinct may be correct. The end of the commu-nist structures of the former Soviet bloc, for instance, was very much in the interest of the economic well-being of the populations living under Soviet jurisdiction but could be achieved only by means of adjustment to the undergirding political structures. Yet the economic benefit was not the reason for seeking an adjustment in the direction of democratic politics. The choice of a polity form rests not on economic foundations but on broader conceptions of human well-being. Consequently, the question of which polity forms can sustain human well-being should be answered prior to the effort to answer questions about which economic systems to adopt. That is, the complete set of polity forms that can sustain human well-being, across all of its dimensions, establishes limits on possible structures for a just political economy.

Connected societies live up to the principle of supporting difference without domination and in so doing lay the groundwork for empowering economies. Connected societies can be pursued on a nationalist model, or a cosmopolitan model; to achieve not only a social universe but also a political economy that lives up to the principle of difference without domination, however, we need to transition to a polypolitan model. For market economies, the requirements of a just polity establish what sorts of commitments should be precompetitive—for instance, a commitment to the protection of positive and negative liberties and a commitment to free, nonexploitative labor. These precompetitive commitments will be most flexibly fulfilled through a polypolitan approach to membership.

This concept of polypolitanism brings into salience the fact that it is possible for any individual to have simultaneous political memberships in more than one political community; this idea in itself introduces new flexibility into how we think about borders, membership, and immigration. In other words, I argue for an approach to analyzing access to political empowerment that recognizes the possibility that individuals may hold multiple and diverse kinds of memberships in a diversity of polities. The aggregate of the memberships they possess should result in their political empowerment in relation to the polity-level decision-making that affects them. This look at how any given person aggregates membership and pathways of access to political empowerment provides a route to versatility with regard to how we think about immigration, migration, borders, and the global movement of labor. The value of this versatility is that it embeds protection for political empowerment or political equality in the foundations of any just political economy while also maximizing the set of polity forms available to support empowering economic well-being across the globe.

Some economists have been tempted into advocating for caste systems in their effort to achieve a maximally egalitarian distribution of the fruits of productivity. In so doing, they have sought to answer the questions put on the table for them by political philosophy. The reigning paradigm raised the question: How can we distribute the fruits of the world's productivity in the way that benefits the least well off? Though Weyl and Posner may already have moved beyond their arguments in *Radical Markets*, in that book in effect they simply answered the question that had been posed to them by philosophers. They responded that we could achieve global justice by giving up on political equality. In this answer, they were in good company. John Rawls, too, sometimes argued that political equality should be sacrificed in response to limiting material conditions. In other words, Weyl and Posner gave the right answer to the question that has been put to economists by philosophers for the last three decades. It is a question about distributive justice that had implicitly taken political equality out of the equation, and economists answered the question by taking it out explicitly. We get this kind of answer—proposing intentional establishment of a caste system—*because* we philosophers had already taken political equality out of the equation that we are asking economists to solve. We stopped conveying its importance to them. Can we, then, develop a different political economy if we put a different question on the table? If we ask for a political economy structured by a commitment to political equality, will we get one?

With the principle of difference without domination, the ideal of a connected society, and the flexible possibilities of membership policies and opportunities for political voice defined by polypolitanism, I believe that we have at least the first conceptual tools for building empowering economies.

Notes

1. On my argument, benevolent autocracies may be able to achieve material well-being for their population, but by definition they will never achieve the basis for full human flourishing and so will never achieve full justice (Sen 1999a, 1999b). This normative fact, however, does not itself in any way determine what the foreign policy stance should be of democracies toward nondemocracies, and that is not an issue I address in the book. Rawls (1993) does a good job of distinguishing the differing foreign policy stances that democracies might take toward other democracies, toward autocracies that are well ordered in being in effect benevolent and delivering basic rights protections, and toward autocracies that are not well ordered. I largely concur with his discussion there.

2. *Justice by Means of Democracy* (University of Chicago Press, forthcoming). In addition to making this case in the book, I make it in an essay, "Difference without Domination: Toward a Revised Theory of Justice," in *Difference without Domination: Pursuing Justice in Diverse Democracy*, ed. D. Allen and R. Somanathan (University of Chicago Press, 2020).

3. Pettit 1999, 2014; Rogers 2020.

4. The challenge for a theory of justice anchored in the non-sacrificeability of political equality is also to offer frameworks for the organization of both social and economic life that ward off the likelihood that difference, which emerges from freedom, comes to articulate with domination. Doing this requires both protecting basic rights and adopting the principle of "difference without domination," in addition to the Rawlsian difference principle. The difference principle is defined by Rawls in such a way as that it could easily incorporate the principle of difference without domination, insofar as any decision that results in domination of those who are least well off would also violate the difference principle. (In some sense, Rawls moves in this direction when in section 36 of *Theory of Justice*, he lays out the forms of compensation that are necessary to preserve the fair value for all of equal political liberties in the face of wealth inequality.

   However, in practice, most people have interpreted the difference principle in a purely distributive fashion, where the relevant object of distribution is material resources, not control rights. Consequently, it is important to articulate the principle of difference without domination as a second and separate additional principle, which focuses on the allocation of control rights that flow from particular decisions and social arrangements. There is a subsequent question, which I have not yet addressed, as to whether the principle of difference without domination could in fact replace the difference principle. This would require that the standard articulated here for the allocation of control rights of necessity also result in just distributive outcomes, and that just distributive outcomes be defined in terms of access to control rights. If this were to be the case, then difference without domination could supplant the difference principle. I have not, however, pursued either the empirical or analytical elements of this question at this point and so for the time being assume that "difference with domination" is an additive principle, not a substitute for the difference principle.

5. Allen and Somanathan 2020.

6. Allen 2016a.

7. Lincoln and Basler 1953.

8. Foner 2010; Witt 2012.

9. Compare Carens 2010, 2013; Miller 2016; Meissner 2019; Salam 2018; Shachar 2009, 2020; and Song 2018.

10. For an innovative approach to understanding the operations of social dynamism, see Farrell, Shalizi, Allen, forthcoming.

11. Allen 2016b.

12. I note that exclusion is a form of domination when those who are "included" and those who are "excluded" are both incorporated in a single social system—for instance, a global economy driven by those in the category of the "included." Relationships of domination have often been misrepresented as simpler relationships of inclusion and exclusion. This tends to result in a misdiagnosis of what is required to rectify the position of those in the

"excluded" category. Typically, the necessary rectification will not be inclusion merely but a more significant restructuring of relationships between those in each group in order to achieve non-domination. See Allen 2005.

13. Hirschman 1970. See also Shelby (2015) for an interesting use of these ideas for contemporary discussions of relative empowerment and disempowerment within the citizenry.

14. Despite my best arguments on behalf of justice as I understand it, there will be those who choose another path and eschew democracy. I recognize this as an inevitable fact of the world. My orientation toward those leaders and citizens who make this choice is like that articulated by Michael Walzer (2008) in an essay "On Promoting Democracy": in general, I would hope to offer aid and comfort by peaceful means to those within their polity who seek to build democracy by peaceful means.

15. Polanyi (1944) 2002.

16. By "high functioning," I mean societies characterized by high degrees of social capital working in support of rule of law institutions free of corruption. Of course, some would also argue that it might be worth reintroducing frictions to the movement of capital.

17. The Global Compact on Migration, passed by the United Nations in December 2018, also focuses on achieving alignment between the interests of the different stakeholders in migration policy in order to reduce friction. It seeks to achieve this alignment not through market transactions but through inclusive and participatory decision-making processes. See General Assembly, United Nations (2018).

18. López-Guerra (2020) offers a provocative argument that every citizen ought to be able to sponsor as many migrants from abroad as they might otherwise bring into the polity by way of childbirth. That is, every citizen would have a right to "make new citizens," and they could exercise this right either through birth or through sponsorship.

19. Weyl and Posner 2018 start each chapter or their book with a utopian fiction imagining the world that would obtain if their policies were in place. Some of these narrative elements introduce ideas that go beyond what would actually necessarily follow from their policies. In this sense, they conjure up romanticizing fantasies.

20. The Canadian refugee sponsorship program has had problems of this kind when it was individual sponsorship; a newer Dutch model avoids similar financial relationships because of the problems that arise from financial entanglement of the two parties with each other.

21. See Kopplin 2017 on recent investigations into au pair programs in the US.

22. See Galenson (1984) for an analysis of what indentured servants gained and lost via indenture.

23. See Kopplin (2017).

24. Canada has established this goal of admitting migrants each year at a rate of 1 percent of its existing population. To provide a sense of scale here, a 1 per-

cent admission rate in the US would mean about 3 million people a year. Currently, the US admits 1 million legal immigrants a year. International students are currently admitted on what is effectively a sponsorship model; the country currently manages the admission of approximately 1 million foreign students annually. A target of 1 percent of population would, therefore, be a significant upward movement of effort. The goal would not be to get there overnight, but to begin to build from the existing figure of 1 million (or 2 million if we wish to count the students) toward 3 million over a period of five to 10 years as a society becomes better equipped to manage migration through a sponsorship program and with the intentionality exhibited in the Canadian program.

25. This is also the existing structure of foster care programs, which give evidence both of the benefits of this approach and also the dangers of abuse.

26. In July 2020, when the Trump administration sought to withdraw visas from all international students who would be enrolling only in online courses in the wake of universities shift to online learning during the Covid-19 pandemic, universities leaped into action, suing the administration and forcing the withdrawal of the rule. This was a powerful example of how sponsoring organizations can function to protect the rights of migrants.

27. For a good review of the role of mutual aid societies within the US, see Beito (2000), Kaufman (2002, 286), and Skocpol (2003). Many of the associations they discuss were transnational; for instance, the Odd Fellows and the histories outlined here also have their European counterparts. Beito (2000) in particular focuses on the provision of social benefits.

References

Allen, Danielle. 2005. "Invisible Citizens: On Exclusion and Domination in Ralph Ellison and Hannah Arendt." In *Nomos XLVI: Political Exclusion and Domination*, edited by M. Williams and S. Macedo. New York: NYU Press, 29–51.

———. 2016a. "Toward a Connected Society." In *Our Compelling Interests: The Value of Diversity for Democracy and a Prosperous Society*, edited by Earl Lewis and Nancy Kantor, 71–195. Princeton, NJ: Princeton University Press.

———. 2016b. "Recovering Equality in America." *Foreign Affairs*.

———. 2020. "Difference without Domination." In *Difference without Domination: Pursuing Justice in Diverse Democracies*, edited by D. Allen and R. Somanathan. Chicago: University of Chicago Press, 27–58.

Allen, Danielle, and Rohini Somanathan. 2020. *Difference without Domination: Pursuing Justice in Diverse Democracies*. Chicago: University of Chicago Press.

Beito, David T. 2000. *From Mutual Aid to the Welfare State: Fraternal Societies and Social Services, 1890–1967*. Chapel Hill: University of North Carolina Press.

Carens, Joseph. 2010. *Immigrants and the Right to Stay*. Cambridge, MA: MIT Press.

———. 2013. *The Ethics of Immigration*. New York: Oxford University Press.

Farrell, Henry, Cosma Shalizi, and Danielle Allen. Forthcoming. "Evolutionary Theory and Endogenous Institutional Change." On file with authors.

Foner, Eric. 2010. *The Fiery Trial: Abraham Lincoln and American Slavery*. New York: W. W. Norton.

Galenson, David. 1984. "The Rise and Fall of Indentured Servitude in the Americas: An Economic Analysis." *Journal of Economic History* 44, no. 1 (March): 1–26.

General Assembly, United Nations. 2018. *Report of the United Nations High Commissioner on Refugees, Part II, Global Compact on Refugees*, 73rd session, supp. no. 12.

Hirschman, Albert O. 1970. *Exit, Voice, and Loyalty: Responses to Decline in Firms, Organizations, and States*. Cambridge, MA: Harvard University Press.

Kaufman, J. 2002. *For the Common Good? American Civic Life and the Golden Age of Fraternity*. New York: Oxford University Press.

Kopplin, Zack. 2017. "'They Think We Are Slaves': The U.S. Au Pair Program Is Riddled with Problems—and New Documents Show That the State Department Might Know More than It's Letting On," March 27. *Politico*.

Lincoln, Abraham, and Roy P. Basler. 1953. *The Collected Works of Abraham Lincoln, 1809–1865*. Abraham Lincoln Association (Springfield, IL) and New Brunswick, NJ: Rutgers University Press.

López-Guerra, Claudio. 2020. "Immigration, Membership, and Justice: On the Right to Bring Others in the Polity." In *Difference without Domination: Pursuing Justice in Diverse Democracies*, edited by D. Allen and R. Somanathan. Chicago: University of Chicago Press, 311–38.

Meissner, Doris. 2019. "Rethinking US Immigration Policy New Realities Call for New Answers: Concept Note." Migration Policy Institute.

Miller, David. 2016. *Strangers in Our Midst: The Political Philosophy of Immigration*. Cambridge, MA: Harvard University Press.

Pettit, Philip. 1999. *Republicanism: A Theory of Freedom and Government*. New York: Oxford University Press.

———. 2014. *On the People's Terms: A Republican Theory and Model of Democracy*. Cambridge: Cambridge University Press.

Pickett, Kate, and Richard Wilkinson. 2011. *The Spirit Level: Why Greater Equality Makes Societies Stronger*. New York: Bloomsbury Press.

Polanyi, Karl. (1944) 2001. *The Great Transformation: The Political and Economic Origins of Our Time*. 2nd ed. Foreword by Joseph E. Stiglitz; introduction by Fred Block. Boston: Beacon Press.

Rawls, John. 1971. *Theory of Justice*. Cambridge, MA: Harvard University Press.

———. 1993 (2011). *Political Liberalism*. Expanded ed. Columbia Classics in Philosophy. New York: Columbia University Press.

Rogers, Melvin. 2020. "Race, Domination, and Republicanism." In *Difference without Domination: Pursuing Justice in Diverse Democracies*, edited by D. Allen and R. Somanathan. Chicago: University of Chicago Press, 59–92.

Salam, Reihan. 2018. *Melting Pot or Civil War? A Son of Immigrants Makes the Case against Open Borders*. New York: Sentinel.

Shachar, Ayelet. 2009. *The Birthright Lottery: Citizenship and Global Inequality*. Cambridge, MA: Harvard University Press.

———. 2020. *The Shifting Border: Legal Cartographies of Migration and Mobility*. Critical Power Series. Manchester: Manchester University Press.

Sen, Amartya. 1999a. *Development as Freedom*. New York: Knopf.

———. 1999b. "Democracy as a Universal Value," *Journal of Democracy* 10:3–17.

Shelby, Tommie. 2015. "Impure Dissent: Hip Hop and the Political Ethics of Marginalized Black Urban Youth." In *From Voice to Influence*, edited by Danielle Allen and Jennifer S. Light, 59–79. Chicago: University of Chicago Press.

Skocpol, T. 2003. *Diminished Democracy: From Membership to Management in American Civic Life*. Norman: University of Oklahoma Press.

Song, Sarah. 2018. *Immigration and Democracy*. New York: Oxford University Press.

Walzer, Michael. 2008. "On Promoting Democracy." *Ethics and International Affairs* 22, no. 4 (Winter): 351–55.

Weyl, Glen and Eric Posner. 2014. "A Radical Solution to Global Income Inequality: Make the US More Like Qatar," *New Republic*.

———. 2018. *Radical Markets: Uprooting Capitalism and Democracy for a Just Society*. Princeton, NJ: Princeton University Press.

Witt, John Fabian. 2012. *Lincoln's Code: The Laws of War in American History*. New York: Free Press.

Acknowledgments

We thank the Hewlett Foundation for support of this project; the extraordinary staff at Harvard's Edmond J. Safra Center for Ethics who helped bring this project to fruition; and colleagues around the world who are working on bringing a new and just paradigm for political economy into being.

Contributors

Danielle Allen is James Bryant Conant University Professor at Harvard University and the author and editor of many books of political theory, including *Education and Equality, Difference without Domination: Pursuing Justice in Diverse Democracies* and *Democracy in a Time of Coronavirus.*

Yochai Benkler is the Berkman Professor of Entrepreneurial Legal Studies at Harvard Law School. His work focuses on how institutions, particularly of law, technology, and ideology, shape power in economy and society. His books include *Network Propaganda: Manipulation, Disinformation, and Radicalization in American Politics* and *The Wealth of Networks: How Social Production Transforms Markets and Freedom.* His work can be freely accessed at benkler.org.

Leah Downey is a PhD candidate in government at Harvard University and a visiting academic at the Sheffield University Political Economy Research Institute (SPERI). Her research develops a political theory of economic policymaking, specifically a democratic theory of macroeconomic policy. Her work has been published in the *Journal of Political Philosophy, Foreign Policy*, and *The Guardian.*

F. Christopher Eaglin is a PhD candidate in strategy at the Harvard Business School and a visiting scholar in the Strategy Department the Fuqua School of Business at Duke. His research explores how to build inclusive and productive economies, focusing on the roles of entrepreneurship, corporate power, and public policy in both emerging and developed markets.

Samantha Eddy earned her doctorate in sociology from Boston College. She is currently teaching at the College of the Holy Cross.

Rebecca Henderson is the John & Natty University Professor at Harvard University. Her research explores the degree to which the private sector can play a major role in building a more sustainable economy. Her most recent publication is *Reimagining Capitalism in a World on Fire*, which was shortlisted for the FT/McKinsey 2020 Business Book of the Year.

K. Sabeel Rahman is an associate professor of law at Brooklyn Law School, currently on leave serving as senior counselor in the Office of Information and Regulatory Affairs in the Biden-Harris Administration. He was previously the president of Demos. His research focuses on issues of economic power, democracy, and structural reform. He is the author of *Democracy against Domination* and *Civic Power* (co-authored with Hollie Russon Gilman).

Dani Rodrik is the Ford Foundation Professor of International Political Economy at Harvard University. His current work focuses on how to create more inclusive economies in developed and developing societies. His newest books are *Combating Inequality: Rethinking Government's Role* (2021, edited with Olivier Blanchard) and *Straight Talk on Trade: Ideas for a Sane World Economy* (2017).

Julie L. Rose is an associate professor in the Department of Government at Dartmouth College. Her research examines questions of economic justice, particularly related to work and leisure, economic growth, gender and caregiving, and inequality. She is the author of *Free Time*.

Charles Sabel is a professor of law and social science at Columbia Law School. Previously he was Ford International Professor of Social Science at MIT. Recent work develops pragmatist ideas into a general conception of democratic experimentalism, with particular attention to regulation, provision of social services, and climate change.

Malcolm S. Salter is the James J. Hill Professor, Emeritus at the Harvard Business School. Since 1967, his work has centered on matters of corporate strategy, organization, and governance. He is the author of *Innovation Corrupted: The Origins and Legacy of Enron's Collapse*; co-author of *Changing Alliances*, a study of industrial governance in the world auto industry; and *Diversification through Acquisition*, a study of how to create real economic value through corporate diversification.

Juliet B. Schor is a professor of sociology at Boston College. Previously she taught in the Department of Economics at Harvard University. She works on the platform economy, time use, and climate change. She is the author, most recently, of *After the Gig: How the Sharing Economy Got Hijacked and How to Win It Back*.

Tommie Shelby is the Caldwell Titcomb Professor of African and African American Studies and of Philosophy. His research focuses on how to understand racial, economic, and criminal justice. He is the author of *Dark Ghettos: Injustice, Dissent, and Reform* and *We Who Are Dark: The Philosophical Foundations of Black Solidarity*.

Josh Simons is a postdoctoral fellow in technology and democracy at the Carr Centre for Human Rights and the Edmond J. Safra Centre for Ethics, Harvard University. His research explores the relationship between democracy and technology, and his first book, *Democracy against Prediction: Citizen Rule in the Age of Machine Learning*, will be published later this year.

Marc Stears is author, most recently, of *Out of the Ordinary: How Everyday Life Inspired a Nation and How It Can Again*. He was a senior advisor and chief speechwriter to Ed Miliband, the former leader of the British Labour Party, and now directs the Sydney Policy Lab at the University of Sydney.

E. Glen Weyl is Microsoft's Office of the Chief Technology Officer Political Economist and Social Technologist (OCTOPEST), the founder of the RadicalxChange Foundation, and co-author, with Eric Posner, of *Radical Markets: Uprooting Capitalism and Democracy for a Just Society*.

Deva Woodly is associate professor of politics at The New School. She is the author of *The Politics of Common Sense: How Social Movements Change Public Discourse and Win Acceptance* and *Reckoning: Black Lives Matter and the Democratic Necessity of Social Movements*.

Index

Made in the USA
Las Vegas, NV
29 June 2022

50898800R00233